THE BIRTH OF BRITISH AIRPOWER

Titles in the Series

Airpower Reborn: The Strategic Concepts of John Warden and John Boyd
The Bridge to Airpower: Logistics Support for Royal Flying Corps Operations on the Western Front, 1914–18
Airpower Applied: U.S., NATO, and Israeli Combat Experience
The Origins of American Strategic Bombing Theory
Beyond the Beach: The Allied Air War against France
"The Man Who Took the Rap": Sir Robert Brooke-Popham and the Fall of Singapore
Flight Risk: The Coalition's Air Advisory Mission in Afghanistan, 2005–2015
Winning Armageddon: Curtis LeMay and Strategic Air Command, 1948–1957
Rear Admiral Herbert V. Wiley: A Career in Airships and Battleships
From Kites to Cold War: The Evolution of Manned Airborne Reconnaissance
Airpower over Gallipoli, 1915–1916
Selling Schweinfurt: Targeting, Assessment, and Marketing in the Air Campaign against German Industry
Airpower in the War against ISIS
To Rule the Skies: General Thomas S. Power and the Rise of Strategic Air Command in the Cold War
Rise of the War Machines: The Birth of Precision Bombing in World War II
At the Dawn of Airpower: The U.S. Army, Navy, and Marine Corps' Approach to the Military Airplane, 1907–1917

The History of Military Aviation
Paul J. Springer, editor

This series is designed to explore previously ignored facets of the history of airpower. It includes a wide variety of disciplinary approaches, scholarly perspectives, and argumentative styles. Its fundamental goal is to analyze the past, present, and potential future utility of airpower and to enhance our understanding of the changing roles played by aerial assets in the formulation and execution of national military strategies. It encompasses the incredibly diverse roles played by airpower, which include but are not limited to efforts to achieve air superiority; strategic attack; intelligence, surveillance, and reconnaissance missions; airlift operations; close-air support; and more. Of course, airpower does not exist in a vacuum. There are myriad terrestrial support operations required to make airpower functional, and examinations of these missions is also a goal of this series.

In less than a century, airpower developed from flights measured in minutes to the ability to circumnavigate the globe without landing. Airpower has become the military tool of choice for rapid responses to enemy activity, the primary deterrent to aggression by peer competitors, and a key enabler to military missions on the land and sea. This series provides an opportunity to examine many of the key issues associated with its usage in the past and present, and to influence its development for the future.

THE BIRTH OF BRITISH AIRPOWER

Hugh Trenchard, World War I, and the Royal Air Force

PETER DYE

Naval Institute Press
Annapolis, MD

Naval Institute Press
291 Wood Road
Annapolis, MD 21402

© 2024 by Peter J. Dye
All rights reserved. No part of this book may be reproduced or utilized in any form or by any means, electronic or mechanical, including photocopying and recording, or by any information storage and retrieval system, without permission in writing from the publisher.

Library of Congress Cataloging-in-Publication Data

Names: Dye, Peter, author.
Title: The birth of British airpower : Hugh Trenchard, World War I, and the Royal Air Force / Peter Dye.
Other titles: Hugh Trenchard, World War I, and the Royal Air Force
Description: Annapolis, MD : Naval Institute Press, [2024] | Series: History of military aviation | Includes bibliographical references and Index
Identifiers: LCCN 2024013815 (print) | LCCN 2024013816 (ebook) | ISBN 9781682471821 (hardcover) | ISBN 9781682478639 (ebook)
Subjects: LCSH: Trenchard, Hugh Montague, 1873-1956—Military leadership. | Trenchard, Hugh Montague, 1873-1956 — Friends and associates. | Baring, Maurice, 1874–1945. | Great Britain. Royal Flying Corps — Officers—Biography. | Great Britain. Royal Flying Corps — History. | Great Britain. Royal Air Force — Officers—Biography. | Great Britain. Royal Air Force—History. | World War, 1914-1918—Aerial operations, British. | Air power—Great Britain—History—20th century. | Marshals—Great Britain—Biography. | BISAC: HISTORY / Wars & Conflicts / World War I | HISTORY / Europe / Great Britain / 20th Century
Classification: LCC DA89.6.T7 D94 2024 (print) | LCC DA89.6.T7 (ebook) | DDC 940.4/4941—dc23/eng/20240819
LC record available at https://lccn.loc.gov/2024013815
LC ebook record available at https://lccn.loc.gov/2024013816

♾ Print editions meet the requirements of ANSI/NISO z39.48-1992 (Permanence of Paper).
Printed in the United States of America.

32 31 30 29 28 27 26 25 24   9 8 7 6 5 4 3 2 1

First printing

For the town of Saint-Omer
Who welcomed the Royal Flying Corps
Witnessed the birth of the Royal Air Force
And proudly celebrated its centenary

Pour la ville de Saint-Omer
Qui a accueilli le Royal Flying Corps
A été témoin de la naissance de la Royal Air Force
Et dont, ensemble, nous avons fièrement célébré le centenaire

Contents

Acknowledgments   *xi*
List of Acronyms and Abbreviations   *xiii*

Introduction   1
CHAPTER 1. An Unlikely Soldier—An Unlikely Partnership   11
CHAPTER 2. Leadership and Friendship   25
CHAPTER 3. Ambition, Jealousy, and Division   39
CHAPTER 4. Building a Leadership Team   51
CHAPTER 5. Functioning as a Team   63
CHAPTER 6. An Airpower Visionary   73
CHAPTER 7. An Inspirational Leader   85
CHAPTER 8. Followers as Leaders   96
CHAPTER 9. Delivering Airpower   107
CHAPTER 10. Transforming Warfare   122
CHAPTER 11. Servant of the Statesman   136
CHAPTER 12. Resignation   152
CHAPTER 13. Regeneration   165
CHAPTER 14. Reinstatement   177
CHAPTER 15. Reconstruction   189
CHAPTER 16. Conclusions   198

Appendix A. Maurice Baring's War Diary and Notebooks   205
Appendix B. Operational Tempo   207
Appendix C. Artillery Cooperation: Air Combat Losses, 1917–1918   210
Appendix D. Operational Wastage   213

Notes   219
Selected Bibliography   269
Index   287

Acknowledgments

MY THANKS GO TO ANDREW CORMACK, who suggested that Maurice Baring's service as a staff officer was worthy of study, and to David Walker, who encouraged me to broaden the story to address contemporary leadership challenges. I am deeply grateful to the present Lord Trenchard for the loan of Maurice Baring's wartime notebooks—a gesture that proved to be the catalyst for this book. I am also grateful to Sandy Hunter and Paul Springer for their personal encouragement (on respective sides of the Atlantic). Emma Davidson, at the New York Public Library, provided access to the Baring material held in their special collections. Hartlyn Haynes, at the Harry Ransom Archive, University of Texas, was equally helpful in enabling access to their Baring Collection. Trevor Henshaw, as ever, willingly gave his time and expertise in analyzing air operations on the Western Front. His book, *The Sky Their Battlefield*, offers a magisterial overview of the British air war during World War I but never loses sight of the human cost. My thanks are owed to Mike Meech, another indefatigable researcher, who has continually unearthed important documents. I must also thank the Smithsonian Institution's National Air and Space Museum for awarding me the Verville Fellowship, which provided the time and space to complete my research. Special thanks are owed to Heather Venable and Seb Cox for their guidance in helping structure the final manuscript. Finally, I extend my appreciation to the wider Baring "family," notably Nicholas Baring, Hugo Brunner, the late Matthew Festing, Louis Jebb, John Jolliffe, Emma Letley, Richard Marson, Timothy Palmer, and David Wake-Walker. They have all assisted me in shedding light on an extraordinary man, a remarkable staff officer, and a friendship that altered the course of history.

Acronyms and Abbreviations

ACM	Air Chief Marshal
ADC	Aide-de-Camp
AFBSC	Air Force Board Standing Committee
ANH	Albums of Nan Herbert
AVM	Air Vice-Marshal
BEF	British Expeditionary Force
CAS	Chief of the Air Staff
CFS	Central Flying School
CIGS	Chief of the Imperial General Staff
CinC	Commander-in-Chief
COS	Chief of Staff
CUL	Cambridge University Library
DGMA	Director General of Military Aeronautics
DMA	Directorate of Military Aeronautics
FA(A)	Fliegerabteilung Artillerie
GHQ	General Headquarters
GOC	General Officer Commanding
GQG	Grand Quartier Général
GSO	General Staff Officer
HC	House of Commons
HQ RAF	Headquarters Royal Air Force
HQ RFC	Headquarters Royal Flying Corps
IAAC	Inter-Allied Aircraft Committee
IABF	Inter-Allied Bombing Force
IWM	Imperial War Museum
MP	Member of Parliament
MRAF	Marshal of the Royal Air Force
NAL	National Aerospace Library

ACRONYMS AND ABBREVIATIONS

OHL	Oberste Heeresleitung
PSO	Personal Staff Officer
RAF	Royal Air Force
RAF IF	Royal Air Force Independent Force
RAFM	RAF Museum
RFC	Royal Flying Corps
RNAS	Royal Naval Air Service
SLT	Senior Leadership Team
SO	Staff Officer
TFP	Trenchard Family Papers

Introduction

THIS WORK IS ABOUT A REMARKABLE FRIENDSHIP: a friendship forged in World War I that facilitated the creation of the world's first independent air service; an unlikely, barely credible partnership between a professional soldier and a scholar-poet-playwright-novelist. It is part history, part biography, part treatise, and part reflection. Hopefully, the reader will forgive the anecdotes that draw on personal experience to examine the nature of leadership and demonstrate why the challenges faced by senior commanders in World War I are of continuing relevance.

It may appear (at least to external eyes) that military organizations are characterized by uniformity in thought, word, and deed. The reality could not be more different. This is especially true of senior officers, who, while exhibiting a veneer of similarity, retain a high degree of individuality. Careful recruitment, early indoctrination, intensive training, adherence to well-defined social norms, shared etiquette, and common standards of dress (in and out of uniform) cannot eradicate personality or offer any guarantee about behavior. In fact, the need to employ such proactive and intrusive methods speaks to a constant battle between individuality and institutional norms. Senior officers, apparently immersed in the rituals and ethos that define military service, are just as likely to rebel as their juniors. Moreover, success, in the form of rapid advancement, imbues a self-confidence that resists conformity and encourages eccentricity.[1]

In describing the tensions and disagreements in the highest ranks of the British air services, the Royal Flying Corps (RFC), the Royal Naval Air Service (RNAS), and their successor organization, the Royal Air Force (RAF), I am not arguing that aviation leaders are somehow different from other military leaders. An alternative narrative, focusing on the senior leadership of the British Army and Royal Navy, would likely paint a similar picture. Indeed, since the first direct entrants to the RAF did not achieve the very highest ranks until after 1945, the individuals central to this story were all recruited and trained by the other services, spending their formative years either soldiering or at sea.[2] Nevertheless, the process of creating and sustaining an effective air weapon placed huge demands on senior officers and created an unprecedented dynamic that tested loyalties and fractured relationships. Given the obstacles to success, it is surprising that the attrition was not higher. Innovation is never easy in any sphere, and there is never a shortage of casualties.

Air leadership should not be separated from other forms of military leadership. It may once have been fashionable to suggest otherwise, when military aviation was still in its infancy, but inspiring human beings in wartime requires the same qualities and skills in every fighting environment. Robert Wright, in his biography of Air Chief Marshal (ACM) Sir Hugh Dowding, commander-in-chief (CinC) of Fighter Command during the Battle of Britain, claimed, "These air marshals of the Royal Air Force had become a race apart from the usual run of Service chiefs. While in some respects there was a blending of their Army and Navy backgrounds, the air had given them something more than just a Service background. The outstanding quality in that was that it made them men who were nearly all pronounced individualists."[3]

Wright confuses the outcome with the man. Fighter Command's success in the summer of 1940 was owed to many factors, but inspirational leadership on the part of CinC Fighter Command was not one of them. Dowding's failure to resolve the destructive arguments and barely disguised antagonism between his immediate subordinates was no aberration; rather, it was (as we will see) a pattern dating back nearly a quarter of a century, to the earliest days of World War I. The characteristics of a good leader—self-awareness, integrity, vision, humility, moral courage, honesty, drive, consistency, and loyalty—are universal and timeless. They are not confined to air leaders, as distinct from other types of military leadership.[4]

Numerous books have been produced on the history of British military aviation, alongside biographies and autobiographies, but none have analyzed the role of senior leadership in creating the "Third" Service.[5] My focus on the RAF can be readily explained; it is the organization I know best. Moreover, personal experience has afforded some understanding of the challenges of high command and the role of senior officers. A further factor was my involvement, at the turn of the century, in developing the RAF Senior Leadership Team (SLT)—comprising all one-star officers and above (at that time, some thirty-five individuals). This initiative emerged from separate papers on ethos and leadership that I took to the Air Force Board Standing Committee (AFBSC) in 2002 and 2003, respectively.[6] The SLT concept, based on a Royal Australian Air Force initiative, was intended to provide a coherent and dynamic leadership group during a period of considerable organizational turbulence and fractured command arrangements. This experience revealed stark differences in temperament and personality between individual senior officers with an appetite for change that ranged from the reactionary to the radical.

The variation in character, motivation, and style (the last is more important than one might think) in a select group of high-achieving individuals sharing the same ethos, who had trained and worked together for over thirty years, was unexpected. The RAF has never been hewn from a single block, but the picture that emerged showed much less homogeneity in thinking and behavioral preferences than might be expected. In the absence of any intermediate entry to the highest ranks, the only route to the top has been from the bottom; however, there is no evidence that this process has produced a succession of clones. While it may be popular to regard the likes of Major General J. F. C. "Boney" Fuller and Air Commodore Lionel Charlton as military "outsiders"—rare voices willing to challenge the establishment—it is possible that there was greater diversity among their contemporaries than is usually acknowledged.[7] If so, the arguments and tensions found within the senior leadership of the RFC during its formative years may have been as much about personality as about professional differences.[8]

Personal experience with several major transformational programs has demonstrated that the senior leadership team must share, and be seen to share, the same vision.[9] Organizational change exacerbates internal divisions and can rapidly lead to a breakdown in behavior unless leaders are visible and aligned. The potential for failure is magnified if people feel marginalized, neither looking to their neighbor for support nor offering support. Addressing this issue is more difficult in large organizations because the ties that bind individuals are that much looser. Inspirational leadership is fundamental in meeting these challenges, but the impact of senior commanders can be tenuous. Contact with their subordinates, even in a small headquarters, is rare and fleeting. Most staff will have a general awareness about a particular senior leader, but this will likely be based on reputation rather than direct experience. The shared stories that determine how a commander is perceived are often driven by rumor rather than by firsthand knowledge. In constructing such narratives, the influence of personal style looms large. I have observed a headquarters wary of telling their commander-in-chief anything of substance—in case they were criticized or subjected to detailed follow-up questions—only to see the position reverse in a matter of weeks when their successor demonstrated (in a casual and spontaneous manner) that he was happy to trust his staff. The result was greater openness and a willingness to raise "difficult" issues. Both commanders spent much the same amount of time in their offices as they did on external visits, but the contrast in how they handled themselves had far-reaching consequences for their reputations and the way business was conducted.

The RAF is a meritocracy that rewards potential as well as performance. It has no hesitation in commissioning officers from the ranks, although none (so far) have emulated Sir William Robertson and become the professional head of their service.[10] Because the RAF relies on technology and actively encourages the professional development of its noncommissioned ranks, there has always been a close relationship between officers and other ranks—closer than that routinely found in the other services. Rigid distinctions simply do not work in an environment that concedes respect based on knowledge as much as on status.[11] This manifests itself in many ways: for example, there has always been a reactionary element in the RAF, particularly where drill is concerned. I recall one defense minister gravely proclaiming that the RAF couldn't march, as if this criticism (if correct) undermined any pretense to be a military organization. We bristled at such prejudice, while likely agreeing with T. E. Lawrence (or "Lawrence of Arabia") that "our job is the conquest of the air, our element. That's more than large enough effort to comprehend all our intelligence. We grudge every routine duty, such as are invented for soldiers to keep them out of mischief, and perform our parades deliberately ill, lest we lose our edges."[12] The same minister (but probably not the Treasury) would likely have been appalled by Lawrence's conclusion that "whenever the public see a detachment of airmen on a ceremonial (bull-shit) parade, they should realise that these, their very expensive, servants are being temporarily misemployed—as though cabinet ministers should hump coal in office hours."[13]

This is not to suggest that the RAF is some sort of egalitarian enterprise, free of the divisions that otherwise characterize society. In its early years, much of the RAF's social thinking was distinctly Edwardian. Even then, however, class and background were not a bar to advancement. A private income was not essential to pursue an Air Force career. Allegiance to a squadron was important, but it never represented the emotional and professional home that the regiment (or corps) offered army officers. Social cohesion between senior RAF officers can be looser than that found in the other services. The focus on individual skills and the implicit acknowledgment that, at least in the technical sphere, other ranks are the equal of officers, has created a less rigid and more malleable culture. Pilots have traditionally filled the bulk of the RAF's senior ranks but, since the end of the World War II, an increasing number of officers from other branches, and genders, have been promoted to air rank and served on the AFBSC. Advancement is highly competitive, and because retirement is fixed by age (albeit that service beyond fifty-five is possible), there are a finite number of individuals to fill key appointments. Rivalry within year groups can be fierce and sometimes less than friendly—precisely because the individuals have known each other for a considerable time. No senior officer has ever lacked ambition, but failure to gain advancement while others succeed can be the most corrosive of emotions. It blights friendships, creates enmity, and can lead to difficult relationships when an officer who believes they have been unfairly passed over is required to work for someone previously more junior. It is a rare individual who congratulates themselves on how far they have come rather than fretting about how much more they could have achieved.

It might be thought that all of this would detract from the smooth running of any organization. The high degree of individuality among senior officers can certainly result in variable performance and unpredictable behavior. I have known air marshals unwilling to make decisions other than to recruit deputies of the same disposition, endlessly calculating the relative advantage between action and inaction. Others have proved bold and decisive, demonstrating energy and clarity of vision. I have worked for, and alongside, air marshals acutely conscious of their own good fortune. Indeed, it has often seemed that those who had never striven for advancement (but achieved it all the same) somehow avoided the need to sacrifice humility on the altar of ambition. Self-awareness is not unusual among air marshals, although it should be said that self-absorption is a more common condition. While the chief of the Air Staff (CAS), as the professional head of the RAF, has a large (but not exclusive) hand in selecting their successor, this has never prevented changes in style (and often substance) between incumbents. A similar picture applies across all senior RAF ranks. The replacement of air officers every two to three years, whether in command or staff appointments, creates a dynamic that encourages fresh ideas and new approaches while limiting radical change. This continuous process of renewal and realignment depends as much on differences as on similarities within the leadership team. From an organizational perspective, differentiation can enhance decision-making in an uncertain and rapidly changing environment. The ability of a single individual to process information and weigh options based solely on their personal experience is increasingly difficult, if not impossible. Command decisions cannot be subordinated to a committee, but deferential acquiescence is equally dangerous. Without diversity of experience, character and personality within their senior leadership team, commanders are denied access to alternative perspectives.

A further aspect that should be borne in mind is that the influence of senior officers does not end with retirement. Not every CAS is elevated to the House of Lords or serves for as long as Marshal of the RAF (MRAF) Sir Hugh Trenchard, but he was not unique in his willingness to provide advice to his successors.[14] The ex-chiefs are not so much a power behind the throne as an informal standards committee, protective of their service and its reputation. This role has likely diminished, with the recent trend for many of them to enter the world of defense procurement, lobbying, or politics. Whether or not their subsequent contributions are always welcome—it can sometimes verge on pious hand-wringing—it would be naive to ignore the impact. A more significant and enduring role for the ex-chiefs is the opportunity to mentor younger officers. Similar examples of patronage occur in all large organizations, but it is not unknown for future chiefs to be identified, and their subsequent careers carefully managed, more than a decade ahead (while still leaving sufficient candidates to cope with attrition through accident or misadventure). The potential for scandal, accident, or sudden illness is never far from the mind of the air secretary in building a succession plan for the RAF's senior leadership. Experience has demonstrated that air marshals are no more immune to the "human condition" than flight lieutenants.[15]

None of this makes the RAF dysfunctional—quite the opposite. Without individuality, there are no tensions, no argument, and, to be honest, no progress. Rarely does a new commander fail to initiate a change in direction—occasionally backward, but always different. Working toward a shared purpose does not require individuals to abandon their personal interests, ambitions, and prejudices. These differences are largely lost in organizational noise, but not at the highest ranks. It might be thought that enmity between senior officers (both personal and professional) is of the past, a product of the extraordinary circumstances facing the RAF in its earliest years. This is an overly optimistic view; indeed, there is no reason why we should expect harmony between senior officers, but antagonism between individual air marshals has an immediate and damaging impact on their staffs, who are drawn into a proxy war. This is as true today as it was a hundred years ago, although before we rush to condemn those who successfully led the RAF in two world wars, we should consider whether any organization comprising large numbers of sentient human beings can separate emotion, prejudice, and personal belief from day-to-day business. Without individuality, there is no imagination, no innovation, and no way to confront new threats and new opportunities. A dynamic and diverse senior leadership team is the foundation of military success and, in war, the price of victory. As ever, however, it is a matter of finding the right balance.

When Sir Hugh Trenchard retired in 1929, after ten years as CAS, he was presented with a farewell gift from his senior Air Force colleagues. Trenchard's note of thanks, although characteristically restrained, expressed his gratitude to the "Bow and Arrow Brigade"—those officers who had served with him at Headquarters RFC (HQ RFC), the army's aviation headquarters on the

Western Front, responsible for directing air operations in support of the British Expeditionary Force (BEF) during World War I. The role of this small group of individuals has never been explored in detail, yet they were critical, not only in developing an effective air weapon but also in creating the preconditions for the formation of the RAF, an event traditionally ascribed to a combination of political expediency, strategic opportunity, economic necessity, and logistic efficiency.[16] These factors were undoubtedly important, but they do not adequately explain why such a momentous decision was taken during the largest and most testing war undertaken by Great Britain (up to that date) and why such a radical and unprecedented idea was so strongly supported. The extensive historiography on the establishment of the RAF says little about these aspects or the pivotal role played by HQ RFC, yet it was the professionalism and reputation of the headquarters staffs that provided the foundation for the decision to create a separate air arm. As Jeremy Black has observed, great events need not have great causes.[17] The RAF came into being as much through administrative efficiency and management competence as operational brilliance.

The development of airpower during World War I was a complex, instinctive, and sometimes erratic process. The focus of the fighting was the Western Front, where the strongest adversaries—France, Germany, and Great Britain—confronted each other in a positional battle that lasted for just over four years. Military aviation made huge strides during this time, as aviators, engineers, and designers experimented with new techniques and rapidly improving technologies. Innovation and imitation went hand in hand as the respective air commanders strove to gain a decisive advantage. There were no boundaries to what aviation might achieve on the battlefield, other than imagination, and there was no shortage of imagination. Tactical advance was met by tactical response. Innovative technology generated more innovation. New roles generated counter-roles. It is hardly surprising that the evidence for how military doctrine evolved to incorporate aviation is diverse and sometimes contradictory. In attempting to make sense of this maelstrom of ideas, innovation, and progress there is the danger of imposing a pattern—an "airpower learning curve," if you will—that makes more sense than is truthful. This is particularly the case when we consider the influence of World War I on the employment of airpower in World War II. The shadow of the Combined Bomber Offensive lies uneasily over the Western Front and its historians.[18]

At the start of World War I there was no indication that airpower would become a decisive factor on the battlefield. The possibility of air combat, of bombing the enemy's homeland and sinking warships from the air, had all been discussed, but developing these capabilities and establishing their utility fell far behind the rhetoric. Little was certain about the types of aircraft that would be needed, how they would be organized, and how they were to be employed. There was, for example, no agreement on the respective advantages of airplanes and airships. There was no clarity on whether flying squadrons should comprise a single type or multiple types.[19] We take it for granted that modern warfare is three-dimensional, but this was not the view prior to 1914. Over the next four years the air arms of all the major powers expanded hugely. By the Armistice, the British, French, and Germans could each deploy thousands of machines across the battlefront in a wide range of roles, including strategic bombing. The utility of airplanes emerged slowly but rapidly gained momentum as the importance of artillery cooperation and aerial photography was recognized. This was a period of rapid change and violent debate about the potential of airpower and how it should be employed. As aviation capabilities improved, tactics evolved and new strategies emerged. This was not a linear process and was marked by failure as much as by success, and by excessive optimism as much as by blind resistance. This study will show how personality and character influenced the direction and speed of airpower development and how differing organizational decisions (in essence, who controlled what and who reported to whom) were responsible for the divergent strategies adopted by the British, French, and Germans.

The importance of individuals is underscored by the status of the respective leadership teams. Senior aviators in the British air services were invariably younger and enjoyed a higher rank than their French and German counterparts, even though British military aviation was the smallest of the three when war broke out. Central to any discussion of the British air services during World War I is Hugh Trenchard, the dominant figure in British military aviation for fifteen years and, behind the scenes, for over thirty. Leadership in wartime is a difficult balancing act. Commanders need to offer certainty while managing the uncertainty that war brings. Neither side plans to lose;

neither side expects to lose. Confidence that the enemy can be beaten, confidence in one's colleagues, and confidence in one's weapons and tactics provide the bedrock for all military organizations, yet these very certainties are most at risk when the fighting begins. A major general before he was forty-two, Trenchard had to face these realities while coping with the extraordinary and evolving nature of air warfare, in which small groups of men flew in machines, operating from bases far to the rear, and fought each other above and often well beyond the front line—a war that was so different that journalists and politicians resorted to the language of medieval warfare, describing pilots as knights of the sky and lauding their chivalric combat. The contrast with the stalemate in the trenches could not have been starker.[20] Trenchard met these challenges through single-mindedness and force of character, even though his personality was deeply flawed, and even though he lacked many of the skills required for high command. These weaknesses should have resulted in failure, but Trenchard succeeded because he recognized his deficiencies and found colleagues and friends who could substitute for what he lacked. Or, to be more precise, he found colleagues and one exceptional friend—Maurice Baring. This study explores how two individuals with divergent personalities, contrasting qualities, and very different social backgrounds built a friendship that helped transform the British air effort on the Western Front. It was as unlikely, and as fragile, as any relationship forged in wartime, yet it lasted for more than thirty years.

CHAPTER 1

An Unlikely Soldier—
An Unlikely Partnership

MAURICE BARING WAS ONE OF THE MORE UNLIKELY soldiers to join the British Expeditionary Force (BEF) sent to France following the German invasion of Belgium, and Britain's declaration of war against Germany on 4 August 1914.[1] Conscription, introduced in January 1916, saw significant numbers of men enter the army who were neither physically nor temperamentally suited to military life.[2] However, at the start of the conflict, the War Office could pick and choose whom they accepted. Against all the odds, the forty-year-old Baring, journalist, author, poet, and playwright, without military experience or martial skills, arrived by steamer at Boulogne on the evening of Tuesday, 11 August 1914—as an intelligence officer attached to HQ RFC—three days before the BEF's commander-in-chief, Sir John French, set foot in France.

Baring's friend and colleague, the writer Hilaire Belloc, who had completed French military service, also volunteered for the BEF but was summarily rejected by the War Office. Admittedly, Baring was four years younger, but how did he find himself in uniform when even younger soldiers, both part-time and professional, were denied the same opportunity? It was a question that perplexed his friends Conrad Russell and Auberon "Bron" Herbert, both

11

of whom were in the Yeomanry.[3] Incidentally, the word "uniform" should be employed with caution, in view of Baring's chronic inability to dress the part. Nan Herbert (Bron's sister) recorded how Baring was quite unable to tie up his puttees without the assistance of others.[4] Following Baring's death, on 14 December 1945, MRAF Sir Hugh Trenchard, known throughout the RFC as "Boom" because of his deep, gruff voice and brusque manner, wrote to *The Times* adding his personal recollections to the obituary published the previous day:[5]

> Major Maurice Baring was on the staff of Headquarters RFC. He had met me when I first landed in France. I had always intended not to keep him as I did not know him, but the very first day he showed me his complete lack of self-interest, his complete honesty and his wonderful loyalty to Sir David Henderson and others. He was a genius at knowing the young pilots and airmen. He knew more about what mattered in war and how to deal with human nature, how to stir up those who wanted stirring up, how to damp down those who were too excitable, how to encourage those who were new to it, and in telling me when I was unfair more than any other man I know. He was a man I could always trust. He was my mentor and guide and, if I may say so, almost my second sight in all the difficult tasks that came in future years. In the words of a great Frenchman, there never was a staff officer in any country, in any nation, in any century like Major Maurice Baring. He was the most unselfish man I have ever met or am likely to meet. The Flying Corps owed this man much more than they know or think. His *R.F.C. H.Q.* should be read and re-read even partially to understand this great man. He never once failed me, though I must have tried him highly. All the juniors had confidence in him, and all the seniors loved him. It was he who brought the tone of "service" into the RFC and brought into it altogether a feeling of doing service to help other men and save lives in the Army on the land and in the Navy at sea. I can pay no higher tribute; words fail me in describing this man.[6]

There are two aspects of Trenchard's eulogy that merit explanation—the identity of the "great Frenchman," and the significance of *R.F.C. H.Q.* The "great Frenchman" is generally assumed to have been Marshal Ferdinand Foch, the Allied Supreme Commander in 1918. Foch's name was first suggested by Laura Lovat in her memoir, describing Baring's final years as her house guest in Scotland, incapacitated by Parkinson's disease.[7] The "great Frenchman" was not Foch but General Edouard de Castelnau, an officer of considerable ability and charm who commanded the French Second Army on the outbreak of war (when Foch was one of his subordinates).[8] De Castelnau's reputation suffered when his 1914 offensive into Lorraine failed, but he played a critical role in the Battle of the Marne, holding Nancy in the face of heavy German attacks. He was also instrumental in saving Verdun but lost his post after Nivelle replaced Joffre as commander-in-chief of the French armies.[9] When Nivelle was sacked and replaced by Pétain, with Foch as chief of the General Staff, de Castelnau was appointed to command the French Eastern Army Group. Notwithstanding his evident abilities and sympathetic personality, de Castelnau was a polarizing figure who excited as much criticism as praise.[10]

It was de Castelnau who made it possible for the RAF Independent Force (RAF IF) to mount a bombing campaign against Germany during the summer and autumn of 1918. Trenchard (as commander of the RAF IF) paid tribute to the "very valuable assistance which he [de Castelnau] and his staff gave me, and for advice which helped me over the many difficulties inseparable from an organization of such a kind."[11] Trenchard (with Baring as his interpreter) had numerous meetings with de Castelnau during the summer and autumn of 1918. Baring provides an emotionally charged picture of de Castelnau. "To hear him talk was like reading, was to breathe the atmosphere in which classic French was born, racy, natural, idiomatic and utterly free from anything shoddy, artificial or pretentious."[12]

The two men unquestionably got on well together. They had much in common. Both came from aristocratic families, and both were staunch Catholics. While Baring's praise for de Castelnau may well have been influenced by their shared faith, he was not alone in his admiration. An American liaison officer at de Castelnau's headquarters described de Castelnau as "the most dignified, charming and courteous man I have met and common knowledge in France that his very great ability and services to his country in defending Nancy and Verdun have never been duly recognized because of his well-known loyalty to the Catholic Church." British prime ministers Herbert Asquith and Lloyd George both rated de Castelnau as one of the war's ablest military leaders.[13]

For his part, de Castelnau became a great admirer of Trenchard and Baring. Speaking in London, in June 1922, he referred to conferences attended at Trenchard's headquarters and remarked that "the austerity of these conversations was tempered by the humour and wonderfully cultivated alertness of his friend Maurice Baring."[14]

R.F.C. H.Q. 1914–1918 (to give it its full title), Baring's account of his experiences as a staff officer on the Western Front, was published to critical success in May 1920. The book and its enthusiastic reception marked his transformation from journalist and part-time army officer to man of letters. It was an unlikely outcome, even though it had always been Baring's ambition to become a full-time writer. As late as December 1918, he had been enthusiastic about continuing to serve Trenchard, wherever his career might take him. Yet, three months later, when Trenchard was appointed CAS, Baring declined the opportunity to become his private secretary: "I think you want a younger man and not a bald-headed, ½ blind crock with ½ his inside cut out and an inflamed bladder and an inflated prostate gland and in perpetual danger of having colitis."[15] Four years' service on the Western Front, and the loss of friends and colleagues, had taken their toll. His brother's offer of an increased allowance, and a substantial legacy, provided the opportunity to choose a new path. Between 1920 and 1938 Baring would write thirty books—almost all novels, unlike his pre-war output, which largely comprised plays, poems, travel books, and essays.[16] Trenchard never blamed Baring for his change of heart, and the pair remained close for the remainder of their lives; indeed, Baring was Trenchard's best man when he married Katharine (Kitty) Boyle in July 1920.[17]

The publication of *R.F.C. H.Q.* can be regarded therefore as both a private apology and an artistic turning-point. Baring's account of his time in a wartime headquarters is not unique, but it is exceptional in the quality of its writing, vivid imagery, and emotional power.[18] *R.F.C. H.Q.* offers an evocative and entertaining narrative that showcases Trenchard as a brilliant, determined yet sympathetic commander. It does not shy away from describing the heavy losses endured by the RFC, but it has a lightness of touch that provides an underlying optimism tinged with humor. The book was described by Charles Grey, the editor of *The Aeroplane* and infamous for his "pungent pen," as one of the best about World War I. Other reviews were equally positive, albeit less effusive.[19] Trenchard was delighted—the book emerged amid strenuous efforts on the part of the army and navy to regain control of military aviation. In his eyes, *R.F.C. H.Q.* enhanced the RAF's reputation and helped cement its separate identity. At a reunion dinner in June 1920, Trenchard spoke to the assembled officers about how Baring had shown the RAF at its best, with that touch of human nature for which it was famous in the war and which had made it great: "Everything in his book brought back most vividly to them those wonderful days when they risked and won so much."[20]

How—and, just as importantly, why—does a middle-aged journalist, poet, humorist, and university dropout join the RFC, and how does such an unpromising candidate become Trenchard's mentor and earn de Castelnau's warm approval? Baring provided a partial autobiography, *The Puppet Show of Memory*, and has been the subject of at least three separate biographies.[21] All have explored his life in varying detail, yet the critic T. J. Binyon claimed that he was still "no wiser about why 'Foch' [de Castelnau] and Trenchard should have spoken as they did."[22] Baring's friends and contemporaries also struggled to reconcile the man they knew with the staff officer described by Trenchard. Conrad Russell wrote that "no man ever got such praise as Maurice got from Trenchard. I was very glad. It's strange to think that Maurice's real claim to greatness may be as a staff officer—not as a man of letters." According to Grey, never uncertain in his views or his many prejudices, Baring was "a poet by nature," a man who combined "the soul of a junior subaltern with the erudition of an Oxford Don." A fellow author admitted that Baring's charm almost eluded analysis, contrasting the compassionate, contemplative, priest-like artist with the most delightful and accomplished jester.[23]

Much of this collective bewilderment stems from the contradictions in Baring's life. Flippant, carefree, and a practical joker, he produced heartfelt poetry on the death of friends and family. An outstanding journalist and humorist, he longed to be a serious writer. Charismatic, with many deep friendships, he found no life companion. An inveterate traveler who admired and enjoyed German culture, he ardently supported the war. He was a man with many women friends, yet never (it is believed) had an affair; a man of deep faith, who was the life and soul of every party; self-conscious, yet self-deprecating; a man who comforted others but sought constant reassurance; a writer who chose words and phrases with exquisite care yet struggled with a typewriter's keyboard. The search for an explanation as to why Baring made such a good staff officer recalls Winston Churchill's comment about the Soviet Union, which he described as "a riddle wrapped in a mystery inside an enigma."[24] The key to understanding the riddle that was Maurice Baring lies in the mystery of his motives and the enigma that was his personality. As we will discover, it is also the key to understanding Trenchard's character.

Maurice Baring was born into a life of privilege. His father, the first Lord Revelstoke, was a hugely successful financier—a senior partner at Barings Bank, a director of the Bank of England, and chairman of Lloyds. The eighth of ten children, and the third of four brothers, Baring enjoyed a raucous, happy childhood on the family estate at Membland, South Devon. The Barings, and their cousins the Ponsonbys, were great players of word games. He would use the Baring-Ponsonby private language, "The Expressions," to amuse and confound for the next forty years.[25] It is said that he inherited his parents' charm and their love of music and the theater. However, there was also an anarchic streak that hardly suggested banking as a future career. An imaginative and lively child, he enjoyed his time at Eton, although (in his own words) "he was no good at games and no good at work." He found exams challenging, particularly if they involved arithmetic or geography. On the other hand, he had an ear for languages and excelled at French, both written and spoken.[26] In 1890 (when he was just sixteen) Baring's world came close to collapse from a sudden financial crisis that threatened to wipe out the family fortune. His eldest brother John took over the running of the bank, but the repercussions would follow Baring for most of his life. Unsuited to banking, and without financial security, his future was uncertain. His letters and subsequent writing suggest someone who felt adrift in the world, uncertain of either his place or direction. The early death of his mother in 1892 (aged fifty-three), and of his father just five years later, can only have added to this unease.

Before Baring left Eton, it was decided that the Diplomatic Service offered him the best chance of a career. Accordingly, in the autumn of 1892, he left for Hildesheim to learn German, the first of many visits he would make to Germany. During these long stays he came to appreciate German literature and music.[27] For the next six years, Baring's life would center on his efforts to enter the diplomatic service. He passed into Trinity College, Cambridge, in 1893, but disliked the curriculum and left the next year without taking any exams. A period at a crammer followed, but even so, he twice failed the civil service entrance exam. This was followed by two terms spent at Oxford (although he was technically not part of the University) until he finally joined the diplomatic service in 1898.[28] Baring was initially employed as an attaché in Paris, followed by similar posts in Copenhagen and Rome (including a long leave spent in Russia), but he soon decided that diplomacy was not for him.

During these years abroad, Baring's literary efforts attracted increasing interest. His first work, a parody of contemporary French authors, had been produced while he was still at Hildesheim, although it was not published until three years later. This was followed by a small volume of poems. Baring hoped that he might now be able to build a literary career. He traveled to Moscow shortly before the outbreak of the Russo-Japanese War, intending to learn more about the country and its literature. Three months after arriving, he abandoned these plans and headed to Manchuria as a news correspondent, attached to the Russian army, for the *Morning Post*. Baring's dispatches from the fighting were well received.[29] On his return to London, he continued to work for the *Morning Post* as both drama critic and special correspondent in Russia (1905–8) and Constantinople (1909). By 1912, he was working for *The Times*, covering the war in the Balkans, but when he reached Belgrade, he discovered that he could not get to the front, so he returned via Constantinople, where he volunteered in a cholera hospital, reporting on the dreadful conditions faced by the sick and wounded.

Baring felt that the essence of journalism was "sensation captured on the wing."[30] In this task he was as skilled as he was successful. He couldn't ignore his ability as a war correspondent—after all, journalism paid his way for a decade—but he was self-deprecating about his talents. Baring's underconfidence and lack of personal ambition were as much part of his character as his premature baldness (which he typically mocked). His notes on Manchuria were "merely the jottings of the fleeting impressions of an ignorant and bewildered civilian," while his role was "to give a faint shadow of the pictures that have imprinted themselves on my memory, glimpses and sidelights into the war, such as one obtains at a railway station by putting a penny in the slot of a small machine." That may be so, but it is impossible not to be moved by Baring's account of the wounded at Sha-Ho, or the cholera hospital at San Stefano.[31]

Baring's life up to World War I was a quest for meaning. He found part of what he was looking for in the Catholic Church, which he joined in 1909 (a decision he said he never regretted), but he also sought a temporal anchor, evidence that he had something to contribute to the world. His successive careers as diplomat, journalist, army officer, and novelist were part of this journey. Along the way he gathered numerous friends, who offered the encouragement and support he needed. Friendship was central to Baring's life. He formed his deepest attachments either at college or university. He met Edmund Gosse and Ethel Smyth through his Eton connections.[32] Edward (Eddy) Marsh was one of Baring's greatest admirers. They were introduced at Cambridge in 1893 and would remain close for the next fifty years.[33] Through Marsh, Baring met several other close friends, including Conrad Russell and George Grahame, later ambassador to Belgium. All three attended the same crammer for civil service candidates. While at Oxford he formed equally close friendships with Hilaire Belloc, Bron Herbert, Raymond Asquith, John Buchan, and (through Belloc) Gilbert (G. K.) Chesterton. There were also family friends, including Evan Charteris, Juliet Lowther (Lady Duff), and Ettie Grenfell (Lady Desborough), through whom he met Herbert (H. G.) Wells.[34]

Ettie Grenfell, who lost two sons in World War I, wrote to *The Times* on Baring's death highlighting not only his literary accomplishments but also his generosity, adding that "he believed in the best in human nature and succeeded in producing it from his friends."[35] Marsh concurred, writing, "I cannot but believe that at the General Resurrection, Maurice Baring, of all men now living, will be the most warmly greeted by the greatest number of his fellow-creatures from every country and continent, and from every walk of life."[36] Baring made friends easily, while his character and personality ensured that these relationships rarely faded. His unselfishness, good humor, and natural empathy meant that those closest to him never felt used or obligated. He was a faithful companion, an entertaining correspondent, and a sympathetic listener. After Raymond Asquith was killed, he wrote to Marsh that "all our friends of every generation appear to be doomed," and to other close friends that "he felt as if the scaffolding of life was crashing about me daily." The structural reference is no coincidence, Baring had built his life on friendship, and the death of so many whom he loved and admired threatened his very being.[37]

Hugh Montague Trenchard was born barely a year earlier than Baring but was brought up under very different circumstances.[38] He had none of the benefits of wealth, class, or position. Trenchard was the third (and second son) of six children, and his father, Henry Trenchard, was a solicitor (as had been his father and his father's father) practicing in Taunton, Somerset. Trenchard's education was more than problematic. His writing and communication skills were poor, although he excelled at arithmetic. He was a good shot and excellent horseman but had little obvious interest in learning. It has been suggested that Trenchard suffered from dyslexia (which would account for his eccentric spelling and disjointed English), but he possessed few compensating abilities (beyond countryside sports) and had little interest in the arts. We now know that he possessed an exceptional intellect and powerful intuition—which were hidden by a profound inability to express himself clearly. A career in the military was an obvious choice for a second son with few accomplishments, but Trenchard's efforts to join the Royal Navy foundered when he failed the entrance exam. As there was little prospect that he would be any more successful in passing the exams for the military academies at Sandhurst or Woolwich, it was decided that he should join the militia, which offered an alternative and less academically demanding route to a commission in the regular army.[39]

With his future still uncertain, Trenchard's life took a dramatic turn for the worse when his father filed for bankruptcy. The family's fall was rapid and very public, as was the loss of their social standing. The events were covered in detail by all the local and county newspapers. The first reports emerged in May 1889 when their house and grounds were put up for sale. Two months later, under the headline "Failure of a Local Solicitor," the *Western Gazette* announced that a receiving order had been made against Henry Montague Trenchard, who had debts of £11,251 and an expected deficiency of over £5,000. There were more than thirty-seven individual creditors who were likely to lose much of the monies owed. The *Chard and Ilminster News* reported that the £9,000 trust fund settled on Henry's wife at marriage (which would have gone to the couple's children on her death) had been entirely exhausted. Such was the local feeling that the family was shunned by neighbors and ignored in the street.[40]

It is difficult to exaggerate the impact of these events on an impressionable, inarticulate sixteen-year-old, who was struggling at school and uncertain about his future. The only home that Trenchard had ever known was sold, together with all its contents (including some of his personal possessions). His father never worked again, and his parents would subsequently live in a series of boardinghouses until their respective deaths in 1914. Both suffered badly from ill health in their later years, his mother becoming addicted to pain-killing drugs (which he tried unsuccessfully to stop). Only the generosity of family friends allowed Trenchard to complete his education. The hope that he might make something of himself must have looked increasingly unlikely when he failed the army entrance exam on his first and second attempts. Family humiliation appeared to have been compounded by personal failure. Unexpectedly, on his third effort, and after two years' service as a probationary subaltern with the militia, he finally (but only just) passed the exam for a regular commission.

Trenchard had few natural or inherited advantages, yet his official biography dwells (over several pages) on the family's antecedents and the stories of famous (though distant) ancestors, explaining how these had enthralled the boy as he was growing up.[41] Trenchard would not be the first self-made man to claim noble lineage or to resurrect a long-dead title when raised to the peerage, but everything in his future life suggests that he was immune to self-importance or vanity. For Trenchard, his family's history was a story of honor and status twice lost—once by accident of history and once by his father. It may seem strange to suggest that tales of medieval chivalry and knightly deeds motivated a man so closely associated with the rise of airpower, but for Trenchard they represented immutable values—principles that should govern a man's life. This ingrained belief explains his violent reaction to what he saw as disloyal or disrespectful acts and his willingness to throw everything away in the process. Even those who admired and appreciated his many qualities found that Trenchard was prone to finding insults where there were none. Such destructive outbursts stemmed from a combination of emotional immaturity and a visceral commitment to a code that he could neither ignore nor likely explain. Adversity in childhood can have negative consequences, but it can also create a burning desire to succeed. How individuals compensate for their experiences will vary, but character and personality play a part. Some become self-reliant, trusting their own instincts. Some create origin stories to escape their predicament. Others have difficulty with emotional relationships and find happiness elusive. These outcomes are unpredictable, and the mechanisms complex, but Trenchard's emotional detachment, lack of close friends, preoccupation with ancestral values, single-mindedness, and relentless determination are characteristic strategies for coping with childhood trauma.[42]

On 8 September 1893, the twenty-year-old Trenchard was gazetted as a second lieutenant in the Royal Scots Fusiliers, based in India on garrison duties. The army provided him with a fresh start in life and offered the purpose and sense of belonging that he desperately needed. The same might be said to a varying degree of all subalterns joining their first regiment, but Trenchard was a particularly vulnerable and isolated young man. The wider family had helped him in the immediate aftermath of his father's bankruptcy, but they could not restore his self-respect. Trenchard was not by nature a demonstrative person, but his family's humiliation drove him to bury his feelings even deeper and avoid situations where this emotional barrier might be compromised. He exploited his natural terseness to say very little and to reveal even less. Tall and sinewy, with wayward hair and a head too small for his body, Trenchard employed his height and deep voice to distance himself from his colleagues. Age, inexperience, and shared circumstances might otherwise have warranted a close friendship with his fellow subalterns. As his future wife, Kitty Boyle, explained, "For the first time it was borne on me how lonely and friendless he was. There was a definite sense of shame about him which put a chip on his shoulder and made him almost aggressively determined not to accept anyone as a real friend, however hard they tried."[43]

Trenchard had little to do with his siblings after leaving Taunton. A rare meeting with his elder brother is described by Trenchard's biographer as "opening a door on a world he had disowned."[44] Wounded by his family's downfall, wary of friendship and struggling with self-confidence, the young Trenchard was determined to show that he could amount to something. This determination was made more obdurate and unyielding by the resentment he felt at being unable to communicate his thoughts and ideas. The army offered him a secure home, a place to heal his emotional turmoil, and, just as importantly, an opportunity to demonstrate his abilities in a visible, practical way. These themes—shame, failure, and frustration—would mark Trenchard's character and shape his personal and public behavior for over sixty years.

Trenchard adapted rapidly to India. He became an enthusiastic and successful polo player and took advantage of the generous leave allowance to hunt and shoot upcountry. A good organizer, an expert marksman, all-round sportsman, and accomplished rider, he proved a reliable and conscientious junior officer. A stern figure, Trenchard nevertheless showed a genuine concern for the welfare of his men. Trenchard's aloofness and his unwillingness to engage in social activities may have appeared to be the behavior of a prig, but they were driven by his lack of money (he would later use part of the £10,000 voted by Parliament for his wartime service to pay off his father's remaining debts) and the self-restraint that he believed an officer should demonstrate both on and off duty. Trenchard was not religious, but he believed in redemption through discipline and hard work—qualities that had evaded his father, with tragic results.[45] He was also an angry and impatient young man who disdained those he judged unworthy of respect and resented orders that he either disliked or felt to be misguided. This was more than youthful intolerance; it was driven by his insatiable insecurity and bitter experience. His time in India taught him that those with power were not necessarily deserving of power and that authority had to be earned rather than taken.

Desperate to see action, Trenchard managed to be transferred to South Africa in the early stages of the Boer War but was hit by a rifle bullet to the chest after just four months. The wound almost proved fatal. He survived, but with permanent damage to one lung and his right arm. While the near-death experience may have softened his anger, it did not weaken his determination. It also made him vulnerable to debilitating migraines at times of stress. After a brief convalescence, Trenchard returned to South Africa, where he became something of a troubleshooter, working directly for Lord Herbert Kitchener to restore fighting efficiency in poorly performing units. As a result, he was appointed a brevet major in 1902, at the relatively young age of twenty-nine. Placed in charge of a mixed mounted unit, he proved an inspirational and vigorous leader, on one occasion almost capturing the entire Boer government. Trenchard's three years in South Africa gave him a taste for adventure but also an appreciation for irregular forces. More importantly, it strengthened his leadership skills and helped shape his views on how wars should be fought and organized, particularly the value of offensive action against a skilled and elusive enemy.

At the war's end Trenchard looked for opportunities elsewhere, since returning to his regiment would have meant reverting to employment as a captain. Service with the West African Field Force offered a way to retain his rank and see more active service. He arrived in Nigeria in 1903 and over the next seven years proved to be a highly effective field commander. As in South Africa, his military success was built on taking the offensive rather than waiting on events. Trenchard's achievements in leading a succession of expeditions to pacify the region saw him take over the Field Force in 1907, with the temporary rank of lieutenant colonel. West Africa was not a healthy posting for a man with one lung, and three years later, after a serious illness, he had to return to England to recuperate. Awarded the Distinguished Service Order, he took some time to recover before rejoining his regiment (then based in Ireland), but soon grew frustrated with his duties and the limited opportunities for advancement, a situation not helped by twice failing the entrance exam for Staff College. When Eustace Lorraine, with whom he had served in Nigeria, wrote encouraging him to learn to fly and join the RFC, he seized the opportunity and gained his pilot's certificate in 1912, shortly before his fortieth birthday and the cut-off date for applicants.[46]

The RFC was largely the preserve of young men. It was desperately short of senior officers—most of Trenchard's contemporaries regarded aviation as dangerous and, even if one survived, tantamount to career suicide. A senior major, he was appointed an instructor at the Central Flying School (CFS) in Upavon, responsible for training army and navy aviators. Within a year, he was promoted to deputy commandant CFS (in the rank of temporary lieutenant colonel) and brought his formidable organizational skills to putting the RFC's flying training on a sound footing. His orderly at Upavon recalled that Trenchard never said anything that was unnecessary and demanded instant compliance with his instructions, adding that although he "gave the impression of a little bit of an ogre," he also had a reputation for being efficient and just. Trenchard was as strict with young officers as he was with other ranks. "We were all a little bit scared of him. He was very, very severe and his manner was quite frightening."[47]

Trenchard's efforts at Upavon were formally recognized in January 1914 when he was made a Companion of the Order of Bath. *The Aeroplane* trumpeted that the award was thoroughly deserved, describing the recipient as an organizer of the first class, with a splendid service record, on whom had fallen "the onerous duties of staff officer with the attendant worries of inculcating a proper spirit of discipline into what might, owing to the irregular nature of the work, have been a far less orderly establishment."[48]

At this point, a disinterested observer might have predicted that Trenchard was destined for a successful but unspectacular career as a professional soldier, possibly culminating in a return to his regiment. A more senior command was unlikely in the absence of Staff College training. The same observer would have found it more difficult to predict Baring's future, given the latter's varied and somewhat erratic career choices, but it would probably have involved a mixture of journalism, literary criticism, and humorous writing. The possibility that Trenchard and Baring's paths might cross would have seemed improbable, and the suggestion that the pair would become firm friends so far-fetched as to be impossible.

CHAPTER 2

Leadership and Friendship

LEADERSHIP AND FRIENDSHIP ARE RARELY PAIRED. Despite the considerable volume of literature analyzing every aspect of modern leadership, friendship is seldom discussed, yet Xenophon of Athens, the Greek philosopher, soldier, and historian, wrote some 2,500 years ago that friendship was central to military leadership.[1] All too often, however, leadership is presented as a singular activity that allows little time for self and even less time for friendship. A recent study commented that the subject of loneliness was strangely absent from leadership literature, adding that "leaders are *not* immune from the need to have at least one person in their everyday social environment with whom they can confide their personal worries, thoughts and feelings."[2]

The importance of followership and the role of senior leadership teams have been increasingly stressed as military organizations, and the means of waging war, have become more complex, yet leadership training remains focused on the qualities needed by individuals—even though common sense says that no one person can possess every leadership attribute, let alone all the right attributes in the right balance. Decisiveness must be tempered by reflection, detachment by empathy, analysis by instinct, logic by emotion, and explanation by inspiration. However, the belief persists that leadership qualities can be identified, taught, and learned, as if leaders functioned in isolation.[3] This error is compounded by the tendency to confuse leadership with command—a transactional process that avoids the need for social interaction. Yet we know that success in leading a large enterprise is as much about negotiation as about control and that influence is as important as direction. The more senior the position, the less direct power it attracts. The senior leaders in a large organization, a chief executive or a commander-in-chief, must operate through others, relying on mutual respect and goodwill to achieve their goals—a process described by Samuel Huntington as "vertical bargaining."[4] Senior leaders can attempt to avoid negotiation by going over the head of their subordinates or bypassing entire management levels, but such attempts cannot deliver sustained effect within a hierarchical organization. Unless the line of command is separated from the reporting chain, the friction of self-interest will impede and ultimately defeat direct control. It is tempting to argue that there are alternative organizational models, for example a start-up company, built on disruptive technology, with few norms or an established hierarchy. However, the opposite appears to be true: it is the shared values, teamwork and friendship binding the founding leadership group that give these organizations the agility and energy needed to prosper in a dynamic environment.

There are few jobs more stressful and more isolated than wartime command. Even in peacetime, chief executives can experience significant isolation, compromising decision-making and reducing their effectiveness, a problem made worse by their status and the perception that relationships should be personally detached and objective.[5] General Erich Ludendorff, First Quartermaster General of the German armies on the Western Front, was supported by one of the most proficient general staffs of the twentieth century, yet he behaved increasingly erratically during the summer of 1918. Driven by ambition and an aggressive self-confidence, Ludendorff was unburdened by self-doubt.[6] However, his emotional isolation left him vulnerable and increasingly debilitated as the military situation deteriorated.[7] Ludendorff's doctor reported that he had "only worked, worried, body and mind tensed, no relaxation, no fun, hastily eaten meals, he had not breathed correctly, had not laughed, had seen nothing of nature or art, heard nothing of the rustle of the forest and the ripple of brooks, and thereby had all the longer, all the more hurt his force of energy and creative power and this himself."[8] Norman

Dixon recognized the enormous strain involved in wartime decision-making. Indeed, he speculated that it might be thought surprising that anyone could do the job at all.[9] Dixon went on to suggest that good generals might be distinguished from bad in their ability to resist stress and to continue, even when things went wrong.[10]

Numerous studies have indicated that friends are a critical source of social support and can help combat loneliness, depression, and anxiety.[11] Friendship is a relationship with broad and ambiguous boundaries, but it is characterized by companionship, intimacy, affection, and mutual assistance. All too often, however, workplace friendship is viewed as incompatible with leadership—a condition that either threatens the professional detachment needed by a leader or, at best, represents a distraction that interferes with objective decision-making and gives rise to the suspicion of favoritism. Friendship in adults is generally based on similarities in attitudes, values, and beliefs, but as we have seen, senior officers are characterized more by their diversity than by their conformity.[12] A shared profession does not mean that a commander will have colleagues with the same attitudes and beliefs, or colleagues who enjoy the same interests and activities. Senior leaders need friends they can turn to for support as much as they need subordinates to implement their decisions. There is no such thing as a "Leader for All Seasons"; every successful leader needs someone who can help them adapt to circumstances and events.

Military organizations are by necessity hierarchical, leaving limited opportunities for senior leaders to confide in others, to share their ideas, concerns, and fears, or simply to relax. This is not necessarily a problem. Social isolation can have benefits. It allows operational decisions to be taken without the burden of extraneous detail and provides an emotional barrier between the commander and those who must do their bidding. However, this can also mean that leaders become self-focused and less willing to see other points of view (the bunker mentality). The loss of empathy can also lead to a decreased concern for others. Thus, while isolation may help with the mental resilience required to cope with the pressures of wartime command, it can also mean that advice is ignored and alternative strategies are overlooked.

The British military, like all other militaries, provides senior officers of two-star rank (major general) and above with personal staff. The more senior the officer, the greater the number and rank of their entourage. Their primary role is to meet the commander's personal and functional needs. To do so, they need to control access to the commander if timely decisions are to be made. The most effective personal staffs give their commander time and space while still making them available to others. There is a fine line, however, between protection and confinement. Responsibility for managing the commander's time is a power that can be abused. Moreover, the "umbrella" offered by the commander's rank and prestige, and the intense loyalty created by great soldiers, can encourage personal staffs to act in ways that disrupt a headquarters: in protecting their principal they can create division rather than harmony.[13] Trenchard's colleague, de Castelnau, was a remarkable soldier with many qualities, but the behavior of his personal staff impeded effective decision-making. Jean de Pierrefeu, responsible for the daily military communiques of the French operational headquarters (GQG) during World War I, contrasts the general affection in which de Castelnau was held with the deep suspicions harbored about his entourage. When de Castelnau was appointed Joffre's deputy (and chief of staff) in 1915, a silent struggle emerged between the officers who arrived with him (including de Castelnau's nephew) and the existing headquarters. De Castelnau's staff took it upon themselves to oppose the hostility that they felt was unfairly directed at their chief. De Pierrefeu commented that while it was "a kind of ambition for a subordinate to do his best to secure credit for his chief," their loud criticism of the other staffs and regular complaints to the politicians in Paris meant that it was initially impossible for de Castelnau to see Joffre alone. Douglas Haig, who encountered de Castelnau's staff on several occasions, was moved to describe his senior staff officer, Major François Camus, as a rather poisonous creature.[14] The British were no less prone to such behavior than their Allies. Philip Gibbs wrote of the BEF's General Headquarters (GHQ) staff that "within their close corporation there were rivalries, intrigues, perjuries, and treacheries like those of a medieval court. Each general and staff-officer had his followers and his sycophants, who jostled for one another's jobs, fawned on the great man, flattered his vanity, and made him believe in his omniscience."[15] Even if Gibbs was exaggerating to make a point, it is evident that a commander's personal staff cannot be guaranteed to provide the emotional support and honest advice needed in wartime. No man is an island, and neither is a military commander. Every great general has found a deputy, an aide, a close colleague, or a chief of staff to guide, confide, and sometimes chide them.[16] The brief histories that follow illustrate how four wartime commanders, denied the opportunity to create social connections by their rank and status, found ways to build relationships that offered the support and encouragement they needed.

Ulysses S. Grant led the Union army to victory in the American Civil War and would later serve two terms as president of the United States.[17] Raised in Ohio, Grant attended West Point but resigned his commission in 1854 to join his family in Illinois, where he found work in his father's leather goods store. It was at a public meeting that Grant first met John Rawlins, a local lawyer with a gift for public speaking.[18] Grant envied the younger man's strong convictions and powerful rhetoric, while Rawlins was impressed by the ex-soldier's tales of military campaigns. When the Civil War broke out later that year, Grant rejoined the army and asked Rawlins to become his assistant adjutant general. It was an unexpected decision, given their brief friendship and Rawlins' lack of military experience, but Grant was a good judge of character. Rawlins would remain continuously at his side over the next four years as Grant rose from captain to lieutenant general in command of the Union army. "Within a few months an association was to be formed between these two remarkable but dissimilar men which was destined to be not only unique in American history but of incalculable benefit to the country."[19]

Rawlins was outgoing, a lifelong teetotaler, and a self-made man from an impoverished family. His father, an alcoholic, was absent for long periods, leaving Rawlins to act as head of the family. By contrast, Grant was a modest, if not shy, and self-effacing man, who disliked public speaking and was not given to boasting. He also had a problem with alcohol; indeed, his resignation from the army was the result of heavy drinking. Their contrasting personalities made them an odd couple, yet they developed a deep and productive relationship. Rawlins was rarely absent from Grant's side. Self-confident, courageous, articulate, and fiercely loyal, Rawlins would write, "The more I know him, the more I respect and love him."[20] Grant was erratic and ill-disciplined in his paperwork and needed Rawlins to allow his office to function effectively. Beyond managing Grant's mail and writing his orders, Rawlins adopted the role of protector, defending Grant's reputation and safeguarding his health (Grant regularly suffered from stress-related migraines).[21] It was said that Rawlins could speak with Grant more candidly than anyone else in the army: "His friendship for his chief was of so sacredly intimate a character that he alone could break through the taciturnity into which Grant settled when he found himself in any way out of accord with the thoughts and opinions of those around him. Rawlins could argue, could expostulate, could condemn, could even upbraid, without interrupting for an hour the fraternal confidence and goodwill of Grant."[22] Despite a mercurial temperament, Rawlins was essentially kind and could be approached quite freely by junior members of staff. Grant respected Rawlins for his selfless behavior, writing to Lincoln in 1862, "I would be pleased if you would give Colonel Rawlins an interview and I know that in asking this you will feel relieved when I tell you he has not a favour to ask for himself or any other living being."[23]

Rawlins was the opposite of Grant in more ways than just their relationship with alcohol. He was a master of profanity with an aggressive temper, while Grant was never known to swear (he once jested that he kept Rawlins on his staff "to do his swearing for him") and was slow to rile, although he could exhibit stubbornness verging on intransigence. A complex character, Grant was reticent, with a quiet sense of humor, but when he wanted, he could be a skilled and animated conversationist. His failure to make any significant reference to Rawlins in his autobiography (written at the end of his life) disappointed those who were aware of their closeness. Grant mentioned that Rawlins had been very useful but said little else—even though during the war he had written that Rawlins "comes the nearest to being indispensable to me of any officer in the service." Various explanations have been offered, ranging from Grant's determination to rebut his political opponents (who suggested that Rawlins rather than Grant was the military strategist) to Grant's discomfort at Rawlins' role in his conquest of alcoholism.[24]

Rawlins was certainly not averse to offering Grant military advice, but, as in the case of Sherman's 1864 "March to the Sea" (which he strenuously opposed), this could be of questionable value. He was, however, undoubtedly influential in Grant's handling of administrative and political affairs. When Grant banned all Jews (against Rawlins' advice) from his military district because of their perceived malpractices, Lincoln rapidly rescinded the order.[25] Rawlins nagged (and on occasion berated) his friend about his drinking, but vigorously defended the latter's reputation when the same concerns were raised by others. Rawlins proved particularly effective in developing positive coverage in the newspapers and advancing Grant's political reputation with the Lincoln administration. Grant's rise to high command was meteoric, but he had his share of military failures and suffered heavy casualties in a succession of battles. The widespread criticism of Grant's performance caused him to consider resigning several times. Rawlins provided the loyalty, friendship, support, and understanding that Grant needed to succeed in a long and difficult war. The view in Washington was that Grant would remain successful "as long as Rawlins stood by him as guide, philosopher and friend."[26] After the war, Grant turned to politics. He was elected president in 1868 and persuaded Rawlins to join his cabinet as secretary of war. Less than a year later, Rawlins died suddenly from tuberculosis, aged just thirty-eight.

Rawlins was loyal to his commander, honest in his opinions, and selfless in his actions. While it may be going too far to claim that Rawlins "merged his individuality in that of Grant," he provided many of the qualities and attributes that Grant lacked as a leader and military commander. Those who saw their relationship felt that Rawlins' main accomplishment was to "round out, into complete symmetry, the character and military genius of U.S. Grant." Recent scholarship supports this conclusion, adding that "by providing an agreeable and supportive atmosphere for the general, without which Grant would have succumbed to depression and loneliness, Rawlins made an essential contribution to his victorious career."[27]

When Haig was appointed the BEF's new commander-in-chief in December 1915, he selected Lieutenant Sir Philip Sassoon to be his private secretary.[28] Sassoon, an army reservist and serving MP, had been attached to Sir John French's staff at the start of the war before being appointed ADC to Henry Rawlinson (IV Corps), where he proved reliable, efficient, and hard working.[29] Baring and Sassoon knew each other well; they shared many of the same acquaintances. Sassoon, a first-generation Anglo-French Baghdadi Jew, was a popular figure in pre-war society. He was handsome and cultured, with a good intellect; he was also wealthy, and, just as importantly, welcome at court.[30] As Haig's private secretary, Sassoon was responsible for personal or sensitive correspondence, managing his diary, accompanying him on visits, dealing with the press, managing VIP visitors, and organizing conferences. Sassoon's political and society contacts proved extremely useful, although his growing responsibilities excited the jealousy of some on Haig's staff, including the chief of intelligence, Brigadier General John Charteris.[31] Sassoon spoke French fluently and had family in France, but it was his links to the British establishment that proved most important. He managed Haig's relations with the press, corresponding regularly with Lord Northcliffe (Alfred Harmsworth) and Geoffrey Robinson (the editor of *The Times*).[32] Sassoon was particularly influential in encouraging Haig to engage more productively with reporters. If Haig had had the choice, he would have avoided all newspapermen. Courteous, self-assured, and totally confident that the Germans would be defeated, Haig had his own connections with the establishment, including the king (Haig's wife was a long-standing member of the royal household). Haig was a shy, reserved figure who was not comfortable with public speaking or displays of emotion. He had difficulty in finding words, whether small talk or matters of urgency.[33] Sassoon may have appealed to him because of their very differences, much as he tolerated Charteris' boisterous humor. "Haig did not talk much himself, but he enjoyed gaiety and wit in others, and he appreciated conversational brilliance. This partly explains his paradoxical choice of Sir Philip Sassoon as his private secretary. Aesthete, politician, millionaire, that semi-oriental figure flitted like some exotic bird of paradise against the sober background of GHQ."[34] It was certainly an odd pairing, the elegant twenty-seven-year-old socialite politician and the dour middle-aged professional soldier, but they formed a productive working relationship that lasted the war.

Haig and Sassoon were close, but it was not a deep friendship. Sassoon worked at the heart of GHQ, but he was "primarily an arranger and an observer, an 'attendant lord.'"[35] This sense of detachment characterized his interactions with Haig. There was respect and admiration, but no personal or social intimacy. While Sassoon was loyal to his "Chief," he was no sycophant, and it is wrong to claim that he was one of a circle of "simpering, awestruck admirers." In letters to his wife Haig could be critical about Sassoon, who, in turn, was not above criticizing Haig in private or disparaging the décor in the Haig's family home.[36] Haig appreciated Sassoon's efforts, but there was no possibility that he would look to him for support or encouragement. It is generally assumed that Sassoon was a homosexual, although there is no direct evidence. The question would have been of little concern to Haig (or indeed Trenchard) but may explain why Sassoon, despite his wide circle of friends, remained something of a solitary figure, lacking any known close relationships.[37] He found the loss of so many of his contemporaries difficult to bear. While Sassoon occupied an important position, resentment about his comfortable life at GHQ (and the awards that he received) caused him to question his role. Geoffrey Robinson offered reassurance: "I trust you're not going to worry because you're not living in a rabbit-hole. Sir D. could never find anyone to do for him quite what you're doing, and I feel that it's one of the chief evidences of his wisdom that he picked you out for a place *in which you must stay.*"[38]

After the war, Sassoon fought energetically for proper recognition of Haig's achievements.[39] His dealings on the subject and evident abilities led to his appointment as Lloyd George's Parliamentary Private Secretary, Haig's avowed enemy. Reflecting on his return to politics, Sassoon wrote, "I think I am right to go, although the severing of ties, especially such pleasant happy ones as these have been, is always heart sickening. I shall never be sufficiently grateful to Douglas Haig for all his kindness to me." The two men would continue to correspond in the following years, but there was no great warmth.[40] Sassoon went on to have a successful political career, serving twice as undersecretary of state for air (1924–29 and 1931–37), working closely with Trenchard at the Air Ministry. He famously made his Park Lane apartment available to the Air Staff during the 1926 General Strike, when Trenchard reassembled his original leadership team to run the RAF's emergency cell. Sassoon died suddenly in 1939 after a short illness.

Bernard Montgomery led the British Army to victory in North Africa and northwestern Europe during World War II. At his side was Brigadier Francis "Freddie" de Guingand, who was appointed Montgomery's chief of staff in August 1942 and served in this capacity until the end of the war.[41] The two men had been friends since serving together in the 1920s, but their personalities were very different. In selecting de Guingand, Montgomery acknowledged that they "were complete opposites; he lived on his nerves and was highly strung; in ordinary life he liked wine, gambling, and good food. Did the differences matter? I quickly decided that they did not; indeed, differences were assets."[42] Montgomery was aloof and restrained and had no time for anything other than the task at hand. De Guingand was boisterous, outgoing, and good-humored, and he liked to party. As he explained, "You cannot spend all your time working and thinking about the war even when you are living through great events or planning tremendous operations. Life at a big headquarters has its amusing human side; it has to have, or everyone would go round the bend."[43] Notwithstanding their differences, or perhaps because of them, they made a highly effective pairing.

Montgomery was a polarizing figure, with as many supporters as detractors. A charismatic commander, he inspired great loyalty, but he was also an egotist and self-publicist who regularly upset his peers and superiors; at one point his abrasive behavior put the Anglo-American alliance in jeopardy. Unlike Trenchard, Montgomery was not burdened by self-awareness. He had little patience with others and genuinely believed that what they might call conceit was merely self-confidence. He would have been surprised to learn that his advice was regarded as condescending, his explanatory comments as tactless, and his isolation in a forward headquarters as aloofness.[44] Nevertheless, the choice of de Guingand suggests that he realized (perhaps unconsciously) the impact he had on others. Indeed, Montgomery developed a habit of sending de Guingand to meetings on his behalf. Although this could cause resentment, there were fewer altercations.[45] Montgomery routinely expressed contempt toward, or at least indifference about, most of his seniors, yet he was considerate to subordinates and encouraged junior officers. De Guingand's diplomatic skills were regularly called on to smooth over problems caused by his notoriously difficult commander. The most serious occasion occurred in January 1945 when Montgomery's tactless and poorly phrased remarks at a press conference threatened to drive a wedge between the Allies. It was only de Guingand's swift reaction, and his close relationship with Lieutenant General Walter Bedell "Beetle" Smith, Eisenhower's chief of staff, that saved Montgomery's career. Montgomery had not been wrong in matters of fact, simply in the way that he explained them. Once again, however, he was blind to the impact of his words.[46]

Montgomery gave de Guingand exceptional authority, instructing his staff that every order issued by de Guingand was to be accepted as coming direct from him and had to be obeyed without demur. It was a decision he never regretted.[47] De Guingand's appointment derived from Montgomery's search for clarity and simplicity. He believed, in effect, that every problem had a heart and that if you could find it, resolution would present no difficulty.[48] With de Guingand running the headquarters and working on the detailed planning, Montgomery had more time to concentrate on such questions. It also meant that he could operate a small tactical headquarters, well forward of his main headquarters—he was determined to avoid the example of World War I generals, who rarely saw their soldiers. This meant that an enormous burden was thrown on de Guingand, whose health broke down more than once under the strain.[49] Montgomery was not slow to acknowledge the debt that he owed to de Guingand:

> His fertile brain was full of ideas, and he was never defeated by the difficulties of any problem. He could take from me an outline conception of a plan, work out the staff details, and let me know quickly if it was possible from a staff point of view: and if not, what changes in substance were desirable. . . . I trusted him completely; he seemed to know instinctively what I would do in any given situation, and he was always right.[50]

As different as they were, "the marriage between these two personalities, so diametrically opposed in most other respects stood firm to the end of the war."[51] Some of Montgomery's behavior may be attributed to an unhappy, austere childhood. At least one historian has blamed Montgomery's mother as the source of his dysfunctional personality, suggesting that the young, able officers whom Montgomery surrounded himself with represented the family he never had. There is no doubt that Montgomery was unhappy as a child and that he had negative personality traits. On the other hand, it is difficult to separate these traits from the qualities that made him so successful—drive, energy, optimism, self-confidence, and a single-minded focus.[52] Montgomery was able to ameliorate his destructive behavior by finding an able deputy who shared his work ethic but not his personality. De Guingand counterbalanced his commander's negative qualities while not interfering with those that made him a great general.

Omar Bradley led the largest force ever assembled under a single American commander (forty-five divisions and 1.3 million men). He was the last, of only five officers, awarded the rank of General of the Army. When Bradley was promoted major general in March 1942 and appointed commander of the 82nd Infantry Division, he asked for a junior officer to act as his aide. Second Lieutenant Chester "Chet" Hansen, a recently commissioned officer with a degree in journalism, joined Bradley and would remain with him for the next nine years. During this time, Bradley rose from corps to army commander and finally to commander of the 12th Army Group.[53] Bradley possessed an innate shyness and reticence, but his mild-mannered exterior disguised a volcanic temper. He could also be narrow-minded, resentful, jealous, and even ruthless.[54] Hansen was able to modify Bradley's behavior and provide skills that his commander lacked. As might be expected, Hansen had a more positive view of the role of the press than his commander did. It was Hansen who persuaded Bradley, an intensely private person, to agree to be interviewed by the journalist Ernie Pyle. The subsequent article did much to substantiate the image of Bradley as "The GI's General." Hansen's writing abilities were also put to good use, as Bradley readily acknowledged. "Among many other fine qualities, Hansen proved to be an artist at putting words together, thus filling a much-needed gap in the 'old man's skills.'"[55] Bradley believed that "a confident leader should invite constructive criticism and it is a grave error for any leader to surround himself with a 'Yes' staff."[56] As one observer noted, Bradley chose as his aides highly competent, bright young men with gregarious and outgoing personalities, just the opposite of his own, adding, "I sometimes wonder if he tended to dote on the sons he never had."[57]

General George S. Patton would describe Bradley (in his private diary) as mediocre, timid, and conservative, but these views were undoubtedly colored by jealousy.[58] Unlike Patton's, Bradley's personality and leadership style were understated. An outstanding general and a great leader, he nevertheless had his weaknesses and made his share of mistakes. It has been said that Bradley showed himself more ruthless than Montgomery in sacking corps and divisional commanders, reflecting his conviction that leadership mattered at every level.[59] Bradley was neither the perfect soldier nor the perfect man. He could be lethargic in his generalship and sometimes failed to respond effectively to legitimate concerns. In his private life, he had at least one affair, and possibly more (which Hansen may or may not have known about). It was also not in Bradley's nature to forgive. "Beneath that placid exterior was an intense, even touchy nature, capable at times of violent bursts of temper."[60] He could exhibit personal pique and be preoccupied with his status and rank. De Guingand's frantic efforts to undo the damage caused by his commander's disastrous press conference managed to paper over the cracks but could not salvage the relationship with Bradley, who never forgave Montgomery.[61]

Hansen kept a personal record of the war that was more comprehensive and detailed than Baring's war diary, offering a unique view of Bradley's methods, his decision-making, and the working of the headquarters. One historian has applauded Hansen's "sure eye for the telling detail and the ironic voice of a thoroughly modern observer."[62] The diary provided the basis for Bradley's highly successful World War II memoir, *A Soldier's Story*, which Hansen ghost-wrote.[63] After the war, Hansen moved with Bradley to the Veterans Administration in Washington. When Bradley became the U.S. Army's chief of staff in 1948, Hansen went with him to the Pentagon, and when Bradley was appointed the first chairman of the Joint Chiefs of Staff in 1949, Hansen became his special assistant. In 1951, Hansen transferred to the U.S. Air Force and was assigned to the Central Intelligence Agency (CIA), where he worked for "Beetle" Smith. Bradley, who retired from active duty two years later, described Hansen as not just an aide but "an associate and friend" who provided "devoted and invaluable assistance."[64]

Although Rawlins, Sassoon, De Guingand, and Hansen occupied different positions (adjutant general, private secretary, chief of staff, and military aide), there are some common threads:

- **Loyalty.** All exhibited deep loyalty to their commander, but not so overwhelming that they were driven to damaging behavior in response to perceived rivals or threats.
- **Status.** Three of the four were not professional soldiers. They had no expectations of a military career and were in uniform only while the war lasted. As such, they were without ambition (in their own eyes and in the eyes of others). Some did gain significant advancement, but this was not their primary motivation.
- **Age.** All were younger than their commander—the youngest, Hansen, was seventeen years junior to Bradley—but most were born within the same decade as their commander.
- **Independence.** All freely subordinated themselves to their role, while retaining independence of thought. It takes a rare individual to remain true to themselves in the presence of a strong personality or near power.

- **Communication skills.** All had exceptional communication skills. This was less about being able to write (although two of them became published authors) than about having the ability to listen to conversations, observe events, sense emotions, and weave these disparate threads into an accurate and credible narrative.
- **Contrasting personalities.** All exhibited a markedly different personality from their commander, offering contrasting qualities that balanced and enhanced the commander's public behavior and decision-making.
- **Different perspectives.** All offered differing perspectives, by virtue of their background and experience, that helped to counter complacency and arrest the tendency to a rigid mindset or "groupthink."
- **Sense of humor.** All possessed a gregarious nature. They were outgoing and demonstrative, whether it was their sense of humor or (as in Rawlins' case) the ability to swear. They were neither courtier nor court jester, although there were elements of both in their behavior.
- **Social intelligence.** All had strong interpersonal skills and could engage with a wide audience, building bridges and sensing issues before they were too late to be resolved. By helping maintain group coherence they demonstrated the importance of social intelligence in sustaining military organizations, where empathy, adaptability, and timing are important contributors to operational effectiveness.[65]

For Grant, Haig, Montgomery, and Bradley, friendship played an important role in reducing the burden of command. Although the level of emotional support and degree of social interaction varied, members of their personal staff were encouraged to offer constructive advice and feedback. Contrasting personalities and different perspectives helped create a more well-rounded commander, better able to cope with the immense pressures and demands of wartime leadership. It was a process facilitated by loyalty and honesty, but most importantly, it was anchored in friendship.

CHAPTER 3

Ambition, Jealousy, and Division

AT THE START OF WORLD WAR I, THE RFC HAD BEEN in existence for a little over two years. Brigadier General Sir David Henderson, director general of military aeronautics (DGMA) and the army's senior aviator, was a passionate supporter of military aviation, but Britain lagged both Germany and France in the number of aircraft. When the RFC gathered for a training camp at Netheravon in the early summer of 1914, it was unclear how the air arm would be employed in the event of a European war. Detailed mobilization planning had started in 1912, but not until 1913 was it agreed that the bulk of the BEF would be deployed to France on the outbreak of war.[1] When the War Office notified units to prepare for war on 29 July 1914, seven RFC squadrons had been formed, although only five were fully equipped with airplanes. It was David Henderson's close relationship with Sir John French (CinC BEF) that ensured the RFC would not only join the BEF but also report directly to the CinC through Henderson, as General Officer Commanding (GOC) of RFC.[2] This decision would have significant implications for the future of British airpower. By establishing his personal control of the RFC, Henderson introduced a different organizational model from that of the French and Germans, where aviation units were subordinated directly to individual armies and only a few residual elements (such as airships) were retained under the general headquarters. Henderson believed that until his fellow generals had a better understanding of aviation, the best use of the RFC's relatively few aircraft was in conducting strategic reconnaissance on behalf of GHQ, rather than being employed piecemeal by the corps commanders. He did this mainly because "he knew the senior army officers were completely ignorant of the uses and limitations of aircraft and that he believed they would dissipate them to no purpose."[3] These temporary arrangements would soon offer a career path for professional airmen to advance to the highest ranks and pave the way for Trenchard's meteoric career.[4]

Shortly after Britain declared war on Germany, Baring met with Henderson at the War Office. The two men had been social acquaintances since 1897, but their relationship had undoubtedly benefited from Baring's long-standing association with Bron Herbert.[5] Herbert (who became Lord Lucas in 1905) had served as private secretary to Richard Haldane (secretary of state for war) from 1907 to 1908 before being appointed undersecretary of state for war (with a place on the Army Council). Henderson knew Herbert both professionally and socially; indeed, Baring and Henderson had dined together at a supper party hosted by the Herberts less than three weeks earlier.[6] Baring omits to mention this in *R.F.C. H.Q.*, or, indeed, that he lunched twice with the prime minister (Herbert Asquith) in the week that war was declared.[7] Henderson made no promises, but two days later, he wrote saying that he had found Baring a place in France, as a lieutenant in the Intelligence Corps, attached to the RFC. Since there was no similar organization within the BEF, Henderson had something of a free hand in determining the exact composition of his headquarters, finding room for another three attached officers.[8] The decision to offer Baring a temporary commission was not unusual, even without a medical examination or induction training. Evan Charteris and Philip Sassoon, who both served with the BEF, came from similar backgrounds and would prove successful in staff appointments.[9] Baring may not have been the most promising of military material, but he was young enough to join up, and his fluent French and German were important skills. There remains a suspicion, however, that without Henderson's sponsorship (and, quite possibly, the prime minister's tacit encouragement) Baring would likely have been rejected by the War Office.

By the end of November 1914, over 1 million men had volunteered for the British Army. Each had their reasons for joining up, but honor, duty, and a desire to serve the country in its time of need were sufficient for most. Baring's motives were perhaps more complex. He was unquestionably a patriot and, while in France and Germany, had vigorously defended his country against criticism of its conduct in the Boer War. There also were family influences: two brothers were in the process of rejoining the army and would soon serve in France. However, unlike most of those flocking to the recruiting offices, Baring had witnessed what quick-firing artillery and machine guns could do to the human body. Although he believed that "wars and armies were necessary evils and inevitable, if painful, results of human nature," he also knew that modern war would bring "unalterable horror, misery, pain, and suffering." When asked by Henderson whether he wanted to go to war to serve his country or go to war for the fun of going to war, he replied that it was "for the fun," although he later wrote that this was disingenuous, as he felt he would be of more use as an interpreter in France than sitting in an office.[10] Baring's explanation is itself disingenuous. While it is true that he was allergic to office work, he had come to believe that war was "like the palace of truth," acting as a touchstone on men's characters, revealing vices, follies, and failures, weaknesses as well as unexpected surprises, "the self-sacrifice of the indifferent, the unworldliness of the worldly, the unselfishness of the selfish." In Conrad Russell's opinion, Baring could not resist the call of the drum. Baring's years as a war correspondent and his service on the Western Front would appear to support Russell's view, but it is also possible that Baring believed that joining the BEF offered an opportunity to find his own, private touchstone.[11]

When the RFC was deployed to France in August 1914, Henderson was supported by a small headquarters organized into three departments: Operations; Personnel; and Logistics.[12] Lieutenant Colonel Frederick Sykes, who had been promised command of the RFC in the event of war, agreed to work under Henderson as his chief of staff (COS).[13] The decision was sensible, as it gave the RFC a strong and influential leader at GHQ, but it left a legacy of resentment between Henderson and Sykes. The situation was not helped by the bitter rivalry between Sykes and Trenchard, the next two most senior RFC officers. Although Sykes was an acting lieutenant colonel, Trenchard (also an acting lieutenant colonel) was by far the senior major. To complicate matters, Sykes was a substantive major in his regiment, the 15th King's Hussars, while Trenchard was only a substantive captain in the Royal Scots Fusiliers. All might have been well if there had been mutual respect between the two men. It was not uncommon in the British Army for a junior (with acting rank) to exercise command over a senior. Sykes was urbane, articulate, ambitious, and Staff College trained—everything that Trenchard was not. A man of considerable ability, he was nevertheless widely disliked. It is claimed that his regiment ensured that he spent much of his time seconded to other units. An excellent staff officer, Sykes seems to have inspired little confidence among those serving under him. "He had a first-class brain and a personality that strangely engendered mistrust in everyone who dealt with him. An able man, socially a pleasant man, but always gave the impression of being a self-seeking schemer." When Sykes left for France, Trenchard was given command of the Military Wing at Farnborough. The transition was confused and undignified. Trenchard resented being left in England to manage the RFC's remnants, but blamed Sykes rather than Henderson for his predicament.[14]

The RFC's first weeks in France were chaotic as the BEF advanced, retreated, and advanced again. In addition to conducting strategic reconnaissance, there were early efforts with artillery cooperation, initially using light signals, and then more successfully with wireless, as well as experiments in bomb dropping and photography. The RFC's squadrons, working closely with GHQ, established a good reputation that was enhanced by their role in helping to discover the change of direction by Alexander von Kluck's First Army that precipitated the First Battle of the Marne and halted the German advance. This led to the "rush for the sea," as both sides moved north to outflank the other. Edward Spears has stressed the importance of the information provided by the RFC's aviators, who often personally briefed the BEF's commanders. This included the reconnaissance report on the German attempt to outflank the BEF at Mons on 22 August 1914, described by Spears as "probably the most fruitful of the war." There have been suggestions that the RFC's role was exaggerated, but Joffre had no doubt. Speaking immediately before the Battle of the Marne, Joffre described the vital role played by the RFC in watching and following the change in direction of the German First Army. Thanks to the RFC, "he had been kept accurately and constantly informed of von Kluck's movements. To them he owed the certainty which had enabled him to make his plans in good time."[15]

Throughout these weeks Henderson's leadership and good humor lifted the RFC's spirits and made the uncertainties more bearable. According to Baring, Henderson never showed the slightest sign of anxiety: he was "never hasty, though he must have been anxious and often very tired; never downcast, though he must have known the situation accurately all the time."[16] During these initial months, Baring spent much of his time either purchasing sundries for the officers' mess or sorting out billeting problems. There is no reference to intelligence work. Indeed, with the arrival of a French liaison officer Michel (Prince Joachim Napoleon) Murat, there was also no immediate need for him as an interpreter. Henderson, as a brigadier general, did not qualify for an aide-de-camp (ADC). Basil Barrington-Kennett, the RFC's adjutant, discharged some of these duties, but Baring took over the routine aspects, such as procuring items for the mess. It was not the war that Baring had envisaged; he confided to Nan Herbert that he "spent the whole morning arranging about forage, buying disinfectants and three planks."[17]

During the second week of October 1914, GHQ arrived at St-Omer, where it would remain for the next eighteen months. HQ RFC took up residence in a small chateau outside the town, near the pre-war racecourse that provided a large landing ground and space for the RFC's four squadrons.[18] The "chateau" was really a large villa, and the RFC filled it to overflowing. The working conditions were not ideal—the rooms were cold and cramped and lacked toilets or electricity. Bedrooms doubled as offices, and there was little attempt to create any permanent arrangements, in the expectation that the front might suddenly move again.[19] After two months of fighting, it was obvious that Britain faced a long war against a larger, stronger, and better-equipped enemy. As a first step, French proposed to double the size of the BEF, increasing the number of infantry divisions from six to twelve—grouped into two armies, each of three corps—and tripling the number of RFC squadrons in France to twelve. The War Office was supportive, although Kitchener could see that a considerably larger force would soon be needed.[20] The immediate challenge was how to organize the larger RFC. This was primarily a matter for Henderson and his CinC, who had repeatedly expressed his satisfaction with the RFC's performance.[21] Henderson acknowledged that under the existing arrangements "the RFC as a whole is now too large, and the squadron is now too small a unit for efficiency." To decide on the best way forward, he sought the views of Sefton Brancker (assistant director of military aeronautics) and Trenchard, who argued that an expanded RFC would be too big for a single commander and that control of the squadrons should be given to the individual corps commanders, relegating GOC RFC to a support role responsible for administration and logistics but not for operations, much as the French air service was organized.[22] It was said that now the front had stabilized there would be less need for strategic reconnaissance and that in future the bulk of the RFC's employment would be tactical. Indeed, Joffre had already recognized this possibility and instructed his army commanders in late August to allocate more aviation support to corps and divisional artillery.[23] Henderson, supported by Sykes, held the opposite view and insisted that command of the RFC should not be transferred to the corps commanders. Kitchener agreed and directed that the RFC's squadrons should be grouped into two wings, each headed by a wing commander, answerable to GOC RFC. Trenchard was brought out from England to command the First Wing (attached to Haig's 1st Corps).[24] Sykes later claimed that had Trenchard's proposals been accepted, "the RFC as a separate service would virtually have ceased to exist." Even allowing for Sykes' desire to score points, there is some truth to his criticism. However, Trenchard's views had more to do with a lack of operational experience than a failure of imagination. Henderson and Sykes had seen firsthand how little the BEF's generals understood military aviation. They both believed that only professional airmen could be trusted with control of the RFC's squadrons, and Trenchard would soon share this view.[25]

Just as these issues were being settled, Major General Samuel Lomax (1st Division), was badly wounded by German shellfire. Temporary command fell to Herman Landon, who was commanding 3rd Brigade. In a matter of days, however, Landon needed to be invalided home, and Henderson was selected to replace him, on promotion to major general. This was undoubtedly Sir John French's decision, but it would have had to have been endorsed by the War Office, which appears not to have informed Kitchener. Henderson's imminent departure raised several questions, including who was to be appointed GOC RFC and who was to serve as DGMA at the War Office. This was resolved by appointing Sykes GOC RFC (as a full colonel) and promoting Brancker to deputy DGMA (as a lieutenant colonel). When Kitchener learned of Henderson's move, he promptly reversed the decision, although he allowed Brancker and Henderson's promotions to stand. It has been implied that Trenchard had a hand in all of this, but there is no direct evidence, although he certainly complained vociferously to GHQ about having to work for Sykes.[26] It is more likely that Kitchener had his own reasons for retaining Henderson as DGMA and GOC RFC. Diminishing the authority of DGMA (by down-ranking the post) would have dangerously slowed the expansion of the RFC—at a time when Brancker was already finding it a struggle to secure the resources for additional squadrons, even with Henderson's direct help. Losing the most senior RFC officer, and the BEF's most experienced aviation leader, to fill a post that many other officers could have occupied had little to commend it other than expediency.[27] In any event, Henderson did not return to HQ RFC until late December, while a new commander was found for the 1st Division and while Trenchard and Sykes did their best to avoid each other.[28] As this was playing out, the 1st Corps staffs discovered that Henderson had brought Baring with him as his personal interpreter, a post not recognized in the authorized war establishment. This was no minor argument, since Haig, the commander of the 1st Corps, was keen to avoid the staffs being burdened by "hangers-on." Henderson's return to HQ RFC ended the controversy, but the situation as a whole highlighted the considerable flexibility afforded to the RFC in staffing matters—a flexibility otherwise denied to the BEF.[29]

More troubling, from the perspective of their future relationship, was that Trenchard (who was desperate to serve in France) had accepted command of the RFC's First Wing on the understanding that he would work directly under Henderson rather than Sykes. Henderson must have known that Trenchard would react badly to the news of Sykes' appointment, yet he had not warned him of the possibility, even though it had emerged as early as 13 November when Henderson had a private conversation with Baring. The decision was not generally known until 19 November, the day after Trenchard reached St-Omer from Farnborough. Baring appears to have changed the entries in his war diary to suggest that Henderson had no forewarning (at least, not before Trenchard's arrival). He may have been motivated to avoid a potential rupture between two men—the account in *R.F.C. H.Q.* is masterfully vague about the timing of events. Trenchard was none the wiser about Henderson's role, and the two had an amicable meeting on 22 November, Henderson's last day at HQ RFC. Afterward, Henderson commented to Baring that Trenchard "ought to be given a division at once."[30]

No one involved in this saga emerges with much credit. A great deal of time, energy, and emotion was expended in a debate that had little bearing on the conduct of the war. One might think that officers should focus on fighting the enemy rather each other. Unfortunately, arguments and personal disagreements between senior commanders are not uncommon in wartime. Private animosities can become serious obstacles because the stakes are so much higher. Personal antagonism can overwhelm professional relationships and corrode the trust between leaders, and between leaders and their subordinates. Working in an operational headquarters is challenging at the best of times, but war brings a whole new level of problems. While there is greater clarity of purpose, there is also relentless pressure to deliver. Individuals and teams are tested as they never are in peacetime. Small disagreements can become fatal. Baring's decision to edit his diary suggests that he understood this paradigm only too well.

The New Year opened with Henderson back in charge of the RFC, but as a two-star reporting directly to CinC BEF. Henderson's status and rank meant that HQ RFC was always in vicinity of, but physically separate from, GHQ. Just as importantly, it also meant that he could exercise much greater influence over the development of military aviation than his opposite numbers in the French and German air services.[31] At that time, the senior German aviation field commander was Lieutenant Colonel Hermann von der Leith-Thomsen. His equivalent in the French air service was Lieutenant Colonel Joseph Bares.[32] Neither officer had operational control of his respective aviation section, unlike Henderson, who had full command and was able to engage at an equal rank with the BEF's divisional commanders. The paradox is that the British Army had significantly fewer frontline machines than either the French or the Germans. By March 1915, the RFC had just under 100 aircraft on the Western Front, compared to 390 aircraft with the French air service and approximately 450 aircraft with the Luftstreitkräfte (German air service). The RFC staffs (ten officers and fifty men) were close enough to the army and corps headquarters for daily contact, but far enough away to underscore the RFC's operational independence. By contrast, Leith-Thomsen and his thirty-nine staff were based with the German high command, the Oberste Heeresleitung (OHL), while Bares (with a similarly small staff) was based with the French high command, the Grand Quartier Général (GQG).[33]

There were also demographic differences between the three air services, reflecting the recruitment and employment policies of their respective armies.[34] Strict seniority governed eligibility for promotion in the French and German armies, where there was a large pool of regular officers to support the growth in military aviation. The small size of the pre-war British Army meant that there were not enough regular officers to fill the additional command appointments needed by a rapidly expanding BEF, let alone the RFC. The position was exacerbated by the War Office's decision to employ only commissioned pilots and observers, unlike the French and Germans, and only allow pilots to fill command appointments. The immediate solution was to appoint promising but relatively junior officers to flight and squadron commander positions and to give them acting rank to match their responsibilities. The shortage of experienced aviation officers led to Henderson's decision in early 1915 that squadron commanders should not fly. The immediate cause was the death in a flying accident of Major George Raleigh, commanding Number (No.) 4 Squadron. Charles Longcroft, who had only recently left France to form a new squadron in the United Kingdom, had to be rushed back to take his place.[35] The lack of experienced officers also had an impact on the War Office. Brancker complained to Henderson, "We must wake up in the senior officer line or get left." There was no easy answer when there were simply not enough individuals with the requisite skills and experience to fill the RFC's leadership roles.[36]

Over the next few months, Baring gradually assumed the position of personal staff officer (PSO), since Henderson, now a major general, had the support of an ADC.[37] As the title implies, a PSO works directly with the commander (who is usually at least four ranks senior) without any intervening staff. It is a personal appointment (in that the commander selects the appointee), although this does not necessarily guarantee a successful relationship. The commander and PSO are rarely separated. When the commander is in the office, so is the PSO. The PSO accompanies the commander on visits, sits in on meetings (to record actions and decisions), and monitors telephone calls, as well as managing incoming and outgoing correspondence. When there is no ADC, the PSO may also be required to undertake ceremonial, social, and housekeeping tasks. Even when there is an ADC, the PSO may still be responsible for managing the commander's personal staff. The PSO must tread a fine line between deference and intimacy. There are few junior officers who can say that they know a senior officer so well. Even fewer can say that they know their likes and dislikes, abilities and weaknesses, ambitions and fears. A PSO is therefore in a privileged position and is afforded the respect that this demands. The PSO acts separately to the COS, who is responsible for executing the commander's decisions. The COS is usually one or two ranks junior to the commander, but always senior to the PSO. In a busy headquarters, or a large command, the COS may only see the commander once or twice a week. As a result, it often falls to the PSO to communicate the commander's views and decisions to the COS and, by extension, to the other department heads. In this sense, the PSO acts as the staff's eyes and ears—a vital role when the commander is away from the headquarters. Of course, this is not a one-way process: a good commander will also use the PSO as their eyes and ears.

A commander's time is precious. There are more documents to read, more meetings to chair, more units to visit, and more people to talk with than can be handled in a normal working day (even if the commander never sleeps). The PSO must manage what the commander sees and does—without impeding the efficiency of the headquarters. This requires tact, competence, and, sometimes, guile. There is a constant struggle between accessibility and chaos. If the commander is to have space to make timely and informed decisions, the PSO must regulate visitors and manage the flow of information, filtering incoming correspondence (discarding some and diverting others for action elsewhere), drafting letters, and commissioning advice. To do this successfully, the PSO must know the commander's mind and be the commander's voice, even when the commander hasn't spoken. The role of a PSO is therefore a delicate balancing act. It needs to combine modesty with assertiveness, closeness with distance, and familiarity with respect. An effective PSO is a mixture of confidante, amanuensis, dogsbody, go-between, spy, conscience, and éminence grise, but above all, there must be mutual respect and trust between the PSO and their commander.

Once in France, Baring's relationship with Henderson became increasingly intimate. By March 1915, Baring started to refer in his war diary to "David" rather than "The General," as he had previously done. The pair had known each other for nearly twenty years and shared the same circle of friends, but the war drew them even closer. Even with Baring's support, however, Henderson was under increasing strain. Throughout his time in France, indeed until the decision to create the RAF, Henderson retained his post as DGMA. This was possible only because day-to-day management of the department was undertaken by Brancker. While Brancker had Henderson's authority, he did not have his rank, which disadvantaged the RFC in its fight for resources with other army departments and the RNAS.[38] This placed an unwelcome burden on Henderson, just as the role of GOC RFC was growing in importance. To exacerbate matters, Henderson was not well. He was incapacitated for a week in March 1915 and had to recuperate in the South of France.[39] Although he came back refreshed a month later, he would continue to suffer from ill health for the rest of the war.[40]

During Henderson's absences Sykes took temporary command of the RFC, but there was widespread suspicion that he was maneuvering to take Henderson's position full time, although, as Sykes was still only an acting lieutenant colonel and Trenchard was now a brevet lieutenant colonel (reportedly at Kitchener's direction), Trenchard was now unquestionably the senior. In May 1915, it was decided that Sykes should be sent (on promotion) to the Dardanelles to review the employment of aviation and make recommendations on future requirements. Sykes' departure removed a divisive influence, even if it meant the loss of an efficient staff officer. It was rumored that the move was no coincidence and that Henderson, on returning from sick leave, had discovered an "awful intrigue." There is no direct evidence, but Sykes was certainly not liked within the headquarters.[41] Whatever the cause, Henderson's bad relationship with Sykes had become widely known. When a commander admits to a "very unfavourable" opinion of his immediate deputy, there can be only one outcome.[42] Sykes' successor was Robert Brooke-Popham, who had been responsible for the headquarters' administration and logistic activities since the start of the war, until taking command of the newly formed Third Wing in March 1915. Henderson had initially offered the COS role to Trenchard, but the latter declined, as he wanted to retain his field command.

By the summer of 1915, a year after its arrival in France, the RFC had tripled in size, from some 800 personnel and four squadrons to over 2,800 personnel and twelve squadrons. Plans were in hand to at least double these numbers in the next twelve months. Henderson realized that the existing command arrangements would need to evolve further and persuaded Sir John French and the War Office that there should be an intermediate (brigade) level between HQ RFC and the wings. Each RFC brigade would control two wings (one dedicated to army cooperation and the other to corps cooperation) comprising up to four but ultimately up to nine squadrons. It was now patently obvious that one man, however experienced and energetic, could no longer perform the duties of DGMA and GOC RFC while also commanding the RFC in the field. When Henderson returned to London in August 1915 to resume full-time control of his department, Baring was filled with consternation: "Having been with him [Henderson] since the beginning of the war, I looked upon his presence as a matter of course, apart from all such questions as old acquaintance, friendship and my appreciation of what he had been and done, and of his indescribable kindness to me personally, and all of the qualities which everyone who came into close contact with him felt and knew." For his part, Henderson had come to appreciate Baring's many qualities, telling his wife that he was a "treasure" and "an angel to all the men in the Flying Corps."[43]

CHAPTER 4

Building a Leadership Team

WITH SYKES IN THE MEDITERRANEAN, TRENCHARD was the obvious (if not the only) candidate to succeed Henderson in France. Baring and Trenchard had met for the first time the previous winter. Sent to collect Trenchard from Boulogne, Baring had asked how he could identify the colonel only to be told that he would recognize the "soft, gentle voice." It didn't take him very long to realize that this was intended as a sarcastic comment. The appointment of a new commander—Henderson technically remained GOC RFC until October 1917—threatened to upset the small world that was HQ RFC. Baring wrote later that there can rarely have been a closer intimacy than those who formed the headquarters during the first few months in France.[1] Trenchard felt no obligation to any of them. He was wary of Brooke-Popham, regarding him as a potential rival, and was skeptical about Baring's abilities, although he was willing to wait to see if he could be of any use. Baring was understandably perturbed.

Trenchard's arrival marked the point at which the RFC moved from being a small band of enthusiasts who all knew each other and improvised daily to a professional, properly resourced organization, embracing men with a wide range of skills from all walks of life.[2] Over the next six months, Trenchard assembled a group of highly capable staff officers who were not only effective in their individual roles but also functioned smoothly as a team. Not everyone survived the process. Baring's qualities soon become apparent, and within a matter of weeks Trenchard regarded him as indispensable. A relieved Baring reported to Nan Herbert that the whole situation had changed—not just because he was a quick interpreter but also because he could write letters.[3] By contrast, Major Richard Pope-Hennessy, a Staff College graduate, who would retire as a major general, failed to meet Trenchard's requirements. Pope-Hennessy was physically brave but nervous in front of a strong personality and preferred to trust, rather than to challenge, anyone who appeared to know more about a subject than he did. He might have prospered under Henderson, but he failed under Trenchard and was sent to a wing headquarters before returning to regimental duties.[4] Brooke-Popham was moved sideways to focus on personnel and logistic duties, where he proved highly effective, and Philip Game took over as COS.[5] Game, who knew nothing of military aviation, was not happy at being removed from the staff of 46th Division, but Trenchard was determined to bring in some "fresh blood." Game's arrival caused resentment among the existing staff, who objected to an interloper entering the precincts of HQ RFC, but this quickly disappeared when Trenchard demonstrated his confidence in their collective decision-making. When Brooke-Popham's wide responsibilities proved too much for a single man, his deputy, Francis Festing, was promoted and appointed to handle all the RFC's personnel issues and manage the headquarters.[6] Festing's immediate predecessor, Major Herbert "Alf" Reynolds, had been sent home in disgrace for repeatedly disobeying Trenchard's order that he cease employing a private car as his personal transport. Baring recorded that the GOC's mood was not helped when Reynolds broke a glass cupboard in the mess anteroom while doing conjuring tricks.[7] Game took some time to find his feet, but Trenchard was certain that he had the right man:

> The General talked to me about it yesterday and said quite decidedly that, unless I particularly asked to get away, he meant me to stop here. I told him my view was that I could not do the work as it ought to be done and knew it and lacked self-confidence and felt that I was not pulling my weight. I am quite convinced this is so, but he stuck to his point. . . . He is

a splendid man himself and has done wonders with the RFC and if I can help him, even a little, I suppose I ought to stick it out.[8]

Baring, Brooke-Popham, Festing, and Game proved to be a formidable combination.[9] Brooke-Popham, quiet, reflective, and immensely hard-working, had an unrivaled grasp of the RFC's supply and engineering needs. He developed a comprehensive and innovative logistic system that sustained the front line in the face of heavy attrition. "Brookham" sometimes overthought decisions, but he was a loyal subordinate who became a lifelong friend. According to Game, Brooke-Popham's efforts "were always so utterly unselfish and always made with cheerfulness."[10] Game himself was an outstanding staff officer, charming and highly efficient; he brought energy and rigor to the RFC's operational processes, "the ideal definer and executor of Trenchard's planning." His quiet precision and deep command of staff work made a great impression on visitors.[11] Festing, who had an attractive, sympathetic personality and a great capacity for friendship, was extraordinarily accessible, but single-minded in his devotion to his job. He understood the mentality of flying men and had a detailed understanding of personnel issues and a genius for remembering people and all about them, their capacities, and where best to place them.[12] Shortly after the Somme offensive had ended, Brancker proposed that Game (and later Brooke-Popham) be moved, but Trenchard strongly resisted the idea—he had found his senior leadership team and was not about to see it disbanded.[13]

Having selected his senior subordinates, Trenchard was relaxed about how they divided their responsibilities. This flexibility meant, for example, that some functional areas, such as signals and photography, moved from Brooke-Popham to Game as technology evolved and as the operational situation demanded. Unlike Henderson and Sykes, Trenchard was not staff trained, but he provided Brooke-Popham and Game (both of whom were Staff College graduates) with clear and unambiguous directions while leaving them the freedom to determine their execution. "It is for me to say what I want. It is for you to see that I get it. How you see you get it is your affair, not mine."[14] Paradoxically, this freed Trenchard to focus on the front line. Baring has left us a comprehensive description of Trenchard's methods. It is worth recounting in detail because it demonstrates not only Trenchard's relentless drive but also the problems it could create for the staff.[15]

The first thing he wanted me to do was to make notes for him [see appendix A]. The General's system of note-making was like this. He visited squadrons or depots or aircraft parks as the case might be and took someone with him who made notes (for the next four years the someone was me) of anything they wanted. In the evening, the notes used to be put on his table typed, and then he would send for the various staff officers, who dealt with the matters referred to in the notes and discuss them. The first thing he would ascertain was if the matter mentioned in the note had a real foundation; for instance, whether a squadron which complained they were short of propellers had not in fact received a double dose the day before. If the need or the complaint was found to be justified and reasonable, he would proceed to hasten its execution and see that the necessary steps were taken. If the requests were found to be idle or baseless, the squadron or the petitioner in question would be informed at once. But where the general differed from many capable men was in this: He was never satisfied in investigating a request or a grievance or a need or a suggestion. After having dealt with it he never let the matter rest but, in a day, or two's time, he would insist on hearing the sequel. He would find out whether Squadron B had received its split pin or what Mr A had answered from England when asked for it. This did not conduce our repose, but it did further the efficiency of the RFC.

There are serious dangers when a senior commander shows this level of interest in day-to-day business. The staffs can resent being challenged about problems they were previously unaware of and can become exasperated when issues are raised that they believed had already been resolved. At the same time, the intermediate command chain can feel marginalized, if not undermined, when units go behind their backs with a complaint (even if it is with the commander's encouragement). In improving the RFC's efficiency, it would have been only too easy to alienate headquarters staffs and embitter subordinate commanders. Brooke-Popham admitted that Trenchard's regular unit visits were unprecedented, but argued that they were driven by keenness rather than a lack of trust in the headquarters staffs.

Did Trenchard's frontline visits really improve efficiency, as Baring suggested? Sergeant Alfred Nicod of No. 60 Squadron certainly thought so. The geared Hispano engines fitted to their SE5A single-seat fighters had suffered significant reliability problems when first introduced in August 1917, but after Trenchard visited the squadron at St-Marie-Cappel (with Baring taking copious notes), matters soon improved.[16] What is more certain is that Trenchard's visits boosted morale. Captain Norman Macmillan recalled how Trenchard gathered the pilots and observers of No. 45 Squadron on their airfield in June 1917 and, without any formality, spoke words of encouragement that would "ring clearly down the years."[17] Trenchard's interest in the front line was not confined to the RFC. As Geoffrey Bromet, commanding No. 8 Squadron RNAS, recalled, "Boom Trenchard gave us the best of everything, gave us a good airfield, gave us a good squadron alongside us, he made it the duty of his staff to see that we got everything we wanted for our comfort and efficiency, and he visited the squadron regularly." Such visits to the front line, albeit successful, were highly unusual. Neither Haig, nor his army commanders, would have considered visiting so many units so frequently, nor would they have done so in the absence of their respective brigade or divisional commanders.[18]

Henderson's relationship with Sir John French would provide the foundation for the equally close relationship between Trenchard and Haig, who replaced French in December 1915. According to Sam Hoare, "Trenchard worked well with Haig and Haig worked well with Trenchard."[19] Trenchard, as commander of the First Wing attached to Haig's 1st Corps, had already impressed the new CinC. There are contradictory views about Haig's attitude toward military aviation. According to Sykes, Haig believed that flying would never be any use to the army and that the only way for a commander to get intelligence was using cavalry. Even if he had once expressed such views, Haig had seen firsthand the utility of aircraft in securing timely and accurate intelligence during the 1912 army maneuvers. As CinC BEF, Haig proved to be a strong supporter of the RFC and Trenchard. Although he had little knowledge of flying, Haig had an instinctive understanding of what airpower might contribute to the battlefield and was content to defer to Trenchard's advice on all aviation-related matters.[20] For his part, Trenchard had immense admiration for Haig, whom he regarded as one of the greatest men of the century. After the war, Trenchard would vigorously defend Haig's reputation, believing that it was only his fortitude and determination that had delivered victory. Trenchard wrote that he was nervous before his first meeting with Haig, but

John Moore-Brabazon, who had a firsthand view of their relationship, claimed that Trenchard was always anxious in front of Haig. Their encounters were so frequent that Haig gave Baring the nickname "Nicodemus," although the latter thought that Haig had probably confused "Nicodemus" with "Silenus."[21]

Trenchard had two unique, but related, characteristics that set him apart from others. One was the speed with which he made decisions, and the other was his inability to explain how he came to these decisions. He rarely changed his mind once a decision had been made. Brooke-Popham, sharing his recollections with Trenchard about their time in the headquarters, remembered that "you often used to say in France that the best is the enemy of the good and I'm sure it was the strongest of all your good points that you always made up your mind to a definite course of action and stuck to it."[22] This philosophy underpinned his management style and ensured that subordinate formations rarely had to wait for an answer from HQ RFC. Philip Gribble, an army officer who transferred to the RFC in 1915, believed that sitting on the fence helped no one and that even if 50 percent of Trenchard's decisions were wrong, he nonetheless achieved striking success: "He took action and every other time he was right."[23] According to Brooke-Popham, Trenchard was

> one of those people who have the faculty of seeing the essence of a problem at once and of realising the things that really matter. . . . Some people would say that Trenchard had an instinct for knowing what was right, I'd say that it was more passing over the intermediate stage of thought so rapidly that he didn't have to register them in his brain and, more or less jumped at once to the right decision. This had the disadvantage that Trenchard often found it difficult to explain to others why he acted or thought as he did.[24]

It was not just Trenchard's thought processes that were difficult to discern. The words he employed frequently failed to match what he was trying to say. The headquarters staff had to interpret or deduce what their commander had said or, rather, what he had meant to say.[25] For the duration of World War I, the task of sorting out what Trenchard meant fell to Baring. He found it an immense strain (at least initially), but discovering that he could meet entirely unreasonable expectations was also strangely satisfying:

I am having such fun doing Staff Officer's work. Trenchard dictates letters quicker than the shorthand writer and I sweat to get it down. Luckily, I have vast experience in dictation and with shorthand. He also explains things very quickly, and incoherently and wants one to make them plain for him. It's alright when one knows what it is beforehand, but if one doesn't, *it's awful*. I haven't failed yet, but I feel I shall. Last night, he talked about a string of quite incoherent subjects after dinner, and said, now I want that made plain. This is the only occasion in my life [in] which I've been able to force *my brain* to work. I went downstairs and condensed what I thought he meant into two sentences, and had it typed. Then I showed it to him, sweating with funk that it was *all wrong*. He said, "that is exactly what I meant." Oh! Y dear, the relief.[26]

Responsibility for taking dictation would pass to Corporal (later Flight Sergeant) Tom Bates, who fitted in admirably with Trenchard's ways. As soon as Bates entered the GOC's office, in response to the bell summoning him, Trenchard would start dictating, often striding up and down the room, but Bates never missed any essential fact and would make clear the most disjointed remarks.[27] Trenchard was even in the habit of dictating a letter while simultaneously conducting an interview, much to the surprise of junior officers such as Lieutenant Hubert Charles, an engine specialist summoned to brief the GOC.[28] It has been suggested that Baring did Trenchard's writing, but the surviving documents, and contemporary accounts, indicate that the ideas all originated with Trenchard—however imperfectly expressed. Even after Baring's "polishing" touches, there was no escaping Trenchard's characteristic style.[29] While Baring may not have been the originator of Trenchard's correspondence, he was undoubtedly the facilitator. Part of Baring's genius was his power of seeing the trend of thought and its expression in others, even more quickly than they did themselves. As a result, he was the perfect interlocutor for a commander who found it difficult to communicate his intent.

A PSO can ask questions that their commander cannot (or would be unwise to) ask. By the same principle, the PSO can answer questions that their commander cannot properly ask of other subordinates. Well before the campaign of "air agitation" gained significant political support, Baring was writing to his friends regarding the destructive criticism of the air service that was appearing in the newspapers and specialist publications, such as *The Aeroplane*. Being on active service, he was not allowed to write to the press, but he made no bones about exhorting Lady Desborough, "Ettie," to "talk about this to all the influential people you know."[30] As her friends included Lord Kitchener, Arthur Balfour, and Lord George Curzon (all government ministers), this was no small request. Baring had his own contacts among the establishment. This became critical when the government set up two committees in early 1916, under Mr. Justice Bailhache, to investigate the administration of the RFC. Hilaire Belloc could be relied on for support, but Baring also wrote to Marsh (deputy private secretary to the prime minister) seeking his help, and to Professor Spenser Wilkinson (Chichele Professor of Military History at Oxford).[31] Wilkinson, a well-connected military commentator, had expressed concerns about the air situation, accusing ministers of bungling by ignorance. Baring's lengthy letter rebutting Wilkinson's arguments could not have been more different from the light-hearted fare routinely offered to his regular correspondents. Forceful, focused, and assured, Baring revealed a deep understanding of technical, supply, and operational matters.[32] None of this can have occurred without Trenchard's tacit agreement or even without his active encouragement. For their part, the recipients of these letters would have assumed that Baring was speaking for Trenchard.

Trenchard told his biographer that men in command must not be flooded with detail, adding that Baring was brilliant at this task. He certainly proved an adept "gatekeeper," managing visitors and correspondence, while avoiding the temptation to isolate his commander. All too often, a headquarters can become too protective. Staffs, bound by patronage, ambition, and self-interest, tend to "form a group around the commander, to surround him jealously, to filter the very air he breathed."[33] Despite the closeness of his senior team, there was little prospect that Trenchard would become isolated—not while he continued to visit up to a dozen units a week. However, the opposite problem, a commander isolated from his staff, was never a realistic prospect—not while he depended on them for the skills he lacked.[34] Baring, without personal ambition or self-regard, was driven by what he thought was best for Trenchard and for the wider RFC. Unlike the public (and even some in the army), he believed in the importance of staff work. He acknowledged that being on a staff didn't change someone into superman or an angel, but he challenged the perception about "idle brass hats" and "pompous red tabs." The public had no knowledge of the "incessant hard work of the most harassing and responsible nature." Baring's spirited defense may have owed something to the fact that his younger brother, Hugo Baring, had recently joined the general staff, having been wounded at Ypres.[35]

As a professional journalist, Baring might be expected to have excellent contacts in the press, but his friendship with Hilaire Belloc proved particularly helpful. Under Belloc's editorship, the wartime journal *Land and Water* had gained a large and influential readership, selling as many as 100,000 copies a week. *Land and Water* was an early supporter of the RFC, stressing its vital contribution in the successful retreat from Mons and its increasingly important role on the Western Front. Belloc largely confined his writing to the higher direction of the war, employing other contributors to comment on specialist aspects, but he fully understood the potential of military aviation.[36] When air agitation gathered pace in early 1916, Belloc wrote in an editorial,

> The British Air Service has been the most conspicuous success of the whole war. It has led the Allies in almost every new departure. It showed its supremacy at the very outbreak of hostilities. It has brilliantly maintained that supremacy through all these months. It has exhibited in every part of it a unity of direction and a rapidity of development which are nothing short of a triumph for the British Service amongst all the belligerent powers. To interfere with and change an arrangement of that kind at this moment could not possibly be anything other than a blunder.[37]

At Baring's suggestion, Henderson and subsequently Trenchard invited Belloc to France to tour the squadrons and undertake a program of lectures. *Land and Water* would continue to voice strong support for the RFC and its senior leadership for the remainder of the war.[38]

Henderson, who had many society friends and was close to both French and Kitchener, didn't need to rely on Baring's private connections. Trenchard, on the other hand, had few influential friends and even fewer society friends.[39] As an established member of the Edwardian upper class, Baring knew everyone of importance or, if he didn't, knew someone who did. His eldest brother, John Baring (2nd Baron Revelstoke) was one of King George V's most trusted friends. Other brothers were active in banking, the army, and industry. Their family confidante, Ettie Grenfell (Lady Desborough), had been a member of the Royal Household since 1911, while Lady Juliet Duff was a close friend of Queen Mary. Baring had himself spent two weeks at Hildesheim learning German with the Duke of York (the future King George VI). He was on familiar terms with numerous politicians (Herbert Asquith, Lloyd George, and Winston Churchill) as well as diplomats, civil servants, journalists, and writers such as G. K. Chesterton, John Buchan, and H. G. Wells. When Asquith visited Trenchard's advanced headquarters at Fienvillers, in September 1916, he found a familiar face in Baring—a close friend of his son, Raymond Asquith, and a first cousin of his principal private secretary, Maurice Bonham-Carter. For his part, Asquith had a high opinion of Baring. When asked whom he considered a man of genius in his generation, he reportedly answered: "For genius, in the sense of spontaneous, dynamic intelligence, I have no doubt that I would say Maurice Baring."[40]

Although Trenchard presented a severe, undemonstrative face to the world, there was a softer, more emotional side to his character. He had a fondness for the quirky, for adventurers, for people who knew their own mind. His energetic sponsorship of irregular forces in South Africa and his sudden decision to learn to fly were part of this pattern of behavior, as was his later friendship with T. E. Lawrence. Trenchard's appetite for the unusual extended to the headquarters, which became a busy, cosmopolitan establishment with a constant flow of visitors and an ever-changing population of attached officers. The widespread desire "to do their bit" had encouraged many over-age volunteers, generally lacking in relevant skills or experience, to offer themselves for military service. Although there was an increasing number of sedentary and administrative posts to fill—as Britain's military economy rapidly expanded—individuals with social connections and a determination to see the "real war" were less easily fobbed off. Baring was not the only example of someone who prevailed on friends and acquaintances to help find employment with the BEF. The RFC's shortage of staff-trained officers, and its willingness to recruit from a wide background, meant that it became a haven for those who might have been difficult to place elsewhere. Even so, HQ RFC seems to have attracted more than its fair share of the cultured and well connected.

The process started under Henderson, with the arrival of the fifty-year-old barrister Evan Charteris. Charteris, a close family friend of Baring's, would serve as a staff officer for much of 1915, before joining Brancker at the War Office. It is unclear how much Charteris, who was well over the age for volunteering, contributed to the RFC's war effort. Charteris was "somewhat of a sybarite, an eclectic and an epicurean," which made his regular shopping trips with Baring a lively affair. He had a tart, keen sense of humor, hated pomposity, and was "a welcome figure in the more intellectual sections of London society."[41]

The next to join, in September 1915, was another of Baring's friends, Lord Hugh Cecil. Known as "Linky" (his family claimed that his shambling gait resembled that of "the missing link"), Cecil was an unusual, if not eccentric, character.[42] A serving MP, he had been awarded his pilot's certificate in April 1915, allegedly on the grounds that he promised never to fly again. Cecil, who was completely unmechanical and regarded the bicycle as a dangerous mode of travel, was initially employed selecting candidates for pilot training. His technique comprised a series of questions about school, academic achievements, and sporting interests. The process was more gentle conversation than stressful interrogation—one successful candidate recalled that his interviewer was "bald, mild, with good hands and a most charming manner."[43] How, or why, Cecil came to be attached to HQ RFC is uncertain, although it can only have been with Trenchard's approval. Captain Archie James encountered Cecil on several occasions and found him a brilliant and charming man, even if he wasn't sure of his function on the staff.[44]

The last of these extracurricular arrivals was Sir John Simon, another serving MP, who had joined the Asquith government as solicitor general in 1910, aged just thirty-seven, and three years later was elevated to attorney general, with a seat in the cabinet. Simon, who had a formidable reputation as a defense barrister, was on the pacifist wing of the Liberal Party. He was expected to resign on the outbreak of war, but remained in the cabinet and, when the coalition government was formed, accepted the position of home secretary. Simon was strongly opposed to conscription and resigned when it was introduced in January 1916. He returned to his legal work, while continuing to serve as an MP. By the summer of 1917, he had decided to follow the example of many others in Parliament and serve in France. This may have saved him from the potential embarrassment of being conscripted or (equally embarrassing) of being offered an exemption when conscription was extended to all men between the ages of eighteen and fifty.[45]

Simon's arrival was not without controversy. Shortly before joining the BEF, he had participated in perhaps his most famous case, the prosecution of Lieutenant Douglas Malcolm for the murder of his wife's lover. Simon appeared for the defense and, in a case lasting just two days, persuaded the jury to acquit his client—even though English law made no provision for a "crime of passion." Trenchard appears to have had reservations about his latest recruit, particularly as Simon had written to his constituents explaining that, although there was little that a man of his age and training could contribute by joining the army, he had concluded that it was his duty.[46] Simon, who would stand accused of being Britain's worst foreign secretary since Ethelred the Unready (one historian has challenged this statement, arguing that Ethelred was not all that bad), found it difficult to find his feet in the headquarters. Game regarded him as a "perfectly useless" person and "a stock illustration that talents in one sphere are not necessarily transferable to another."[47]

Against the odds, Trenchard found productive employment for both Cecil and Simon. Their presence reflected his tolerance of the unusual, if not the eccentric, but also represented an investment in the future. Both men were highly intelligent, well educated, and, just as importantly, well connected—it was even suggested that Simon could be a future prime minister. Trenchard claimed that Simon was forced on him by Haig, but if so, Trenchard was the beneficiary.[48] After a period of familiarization, Simon was assigned to Paris to review the RFC's contracts with French manufacturers. According to Simon's biographer, this was a task "of considerable detail and difficulty which required tact, a good knowledge of French and a very clear head."[49] Trenchard was extremely happy with the outcome, and Simon was soon given a series of other projects. For his part, Simon quickly fell under Trenchard's spell: "To be with him when he was visiting a squadron on the eve of battle, which would call for the highest endurance of pilots and observers, was an experience which explained the devotion with which he was universally regarded. He could be hard and unyielding—and 'Boom' was sometimes not too precise in language—but he everywhere inspired a sense of confidence and attachment."[50]

CHAPTER 5
Functioning as a Team

AS THE SCALE AND SCOPE OF THE AIR WAR GREW, so did the number of staff needed to manage these activities. When Trenchard took command, HQ RFC comprised around sixty personnel. By the summer of 1917, it had grown to more than seven hundred (including forty officers). Their responsibilities included

- exercising operational control of the RFC's squadrons, consistent with GHQ's strategic direction;
- providing the link between GHQ and the RFC, and between Directorate of Military Aeronautics (DMA) and the RFC;
- liaising with the Allied air services (the RNAS, the French army's air service, and the U.S. Army Air Service);
- organizing the supply, transportation, storage, and issue of all aeronautical stores, including aircraft and aeroengines;
- managing the repair and maintenance of all RFC equipment;
- liaising with the BEF for the supply of nonaeronautical stores, including food, clothing, fuel, and munitions;
- the administration, discipline, training, and welfare of all RFC personnel in France and Belgium (totaling over 50,000 personnel by the Armistice);
- preparing, operating, and maintaining (several hundred) aerodromes.[1]

The RFC's continuing expansion demanded close cooperation between Henderson (responsible for training, equipment and personnel) and Trenchard (responsible for operations). Routine matters were handled by Brancker, who maintained a regular correspondence with Trenchard. These demi-official, largely typewritten letters were not copied beyond their respective offices. Trenchard consistently shows a patience and pragmatism that belies his reputation as a difficult or divisive figure. They also lack the deference one might expect between a major general and a colonel. Trenchard is honest where he is at fault and constructive where problems have been created by others. When Brancker complained that Trenchard had been communicating directly with the Training Brigade without informing the War Office, Trenchard apologized, saying that he had spoken informally to a visiting officer from one of the training schools and had not intended that they should make changes without Brancker's approval.[2] HQ RFC's staff officers came from all walks of life. Appointments were filled by a mixture of young aviators, otherwise unfit for frontline duties, and (generally) older nonaviators with specialist skills. At the start of the war the "aviators" were junior in rank with limited responsibilities, but over time they became suitable for wider employment.

Captain (later Wing Commander) Edward "Teddy" Corballis, a twenty-six-year-old pre-war pilot, had been injured in 1915. Unable to continue flying, he spent six months with Brancker in Whitehall before joining the headquarters where he worked for Game, rising in rank and responsibilities before returning home as a lieutenant colonel to join the new Air Ministry. Among the "nonaviators" was Captain Collingwood Ingram, a thirty-seven-year-old ornithologist and infantryman, who joined the headquarters as their compass officer, working for Brooke-Popham until January 1919. Corballis, Ingram, and their fellow junior officers were the backbone of the headquarters. They relished the freedom and authority that Trenchard gave them and, in return, offered their loyalty and a determination that the RFC should play a central role in winning the war. They were far removed from the staff officers that Gibbs pilloried for their remoteness, insensitivity, and inefficiency."[3] William Joynson-Hicks (a Conservative MP), who had previously been a strong critic of the RFC, visited HQ RFC in October 1917 and came away singing Trenchard's praises: "The enthusiasm of these young men has been inspired by General Trenchard. Their bravery has been developed, and their devotion and willingness is the result of General Trenchard's teaching and training."[4]

Organization is rarely the subject of serious historical inquiry. When it is discussed, it is often in the context of failure rather than success. Military headquarters, responsible for directing and administering the myriad activities that comprise a modern army, have become synonymous with incompetence. The huge manpower losses suffered by all sides during World War I have encouraged the belief that the sacrifice of the many was due to the stupidity of the few. It has become popular to portray staff officers, living safely in their chateau, as oblivious to the awful reality of trench warfare.[5] HQ RFC largely escaped such criticism, gaining an enviable reputation, even among those pilots and observers who were sent daily into harm's way. This was partly because of the youthfulness of the RFC's senior officers (a cause for complaint by other branches of the army) and partly because of the open-mindedness and teamwork with which Trenchard's staff approached operational issues.[6] The immaturity of military aviation meant that there was little dogma, no tradition, and few vested interests to defend. As Brancker observed, there were no historical precedents to draw on, and the only guide should be practical realities: "We are at all events quite untrammeled by precedent and preconceived ideas. And if we cannot learn by the experience of others, we must try to worry out the problem on its own merits."[7]

HQ RFC adopted a collaborative approach to the development of operational techniques, recognizing that much of the relevant expertise lay with the frontline squadrons. In this context, it is worth noting that one of General Andre Voisin's major criticisms of the Division Aérienne, created in May 1918 as GQG's air arm, was that the concept was imposed from above rather than being the result of operational experience.[8] RFC doctrine was written by the practitioners, although Game coordinated the process. His staffs were active in organizing conferences (at all levels of command) to identify opportunities for improving existing policy, introducing new techniques, commissioning trials, and communicating the results. For example, the respective policies for artillery and infantry cooperation, first issued in 1916, were developed continuously through 1917 and 1918. The latter was revised in December 1917 by a small working group comprising John Chamier (Fifteenth [Corps] Wing) and two of his squadron commanders, Charles Mackay (No.

59 Squadron) and George Pirie (No. 6 Squadron). Their proposed changes were incorporated in the new edition issued in April 1918.[9] Innovative techniques introduced under Game's authority included artillery cooperation at night, detecting and attacking enemy antitank guns using dedicated low-flying aircraft and laying smoke screens to neutralize antitank guns. The latter idea emerged from a paper produced by Trafford Leigh Mallory, commanding No. 8 Squadron.[10]

Brooke-Popham and Festing took a similar approach to their logistic and administrative responsibilities. They had served on the Western Front since the first months of the war and had an instinctive appreciation for what the front line needed. Brooke-Popham met regularly with his park and depot commanders (many of whom had wide engineering experience) to address supply and technical issues, including hosting conferences where, together with the relevant squadron commanders (accompanied by their technical staffs), they would thrash out a solution. There was active encouragement for bottom-up ideas, facilitated by regular liaison visits: "A new type of aircraft would be issued to the squadrons and under service conditions the tail skids might prove weak and need frequent replacing. In the normal way, some two or three weeks might elapse before this information reached the depot in the form of increased demands. Due to our liaison system, the information was brought back within a few days, extra supplies requisitioned, and a shortage avoided."[11]

Festing oversaw an equally efficient administrative organization. A particular concern was the welfare of flying personnel. Although the causes were not fully understood, it was known that long periods of war flying were debilitating. Although squadrons were expected to fly every day when the weather was suitable, individuals were not. HQ RFC's leave policy was generous. "I had noticed that we, pilots and observers, had always been given our leave regularly and frequently—far more regularly and frequently than anyone else in France."[12] At Trenchard's insistence, HQ RFC maintained existing squadrons at full establishment, even though this delayed the creation of new squadrons, ensuring that there were always enough pilots and observers to carry out the flying task. This included increasing existing aircraft and pilot squadron establishments by up to 30 percent prior to an offensive.[13] Squadron commanders were encouraged to spot signs of exhaustion, a policy facilitated by the appointment of Major (later Lieutenant Colonel) James Birley as HQ RFC's senior medical adviser in October 1916. Birley believed that all flying was fatiguing and that there was only so much stress an individual could tolerate. Birley advised Trenchard directly, and through his efforts a specialist ward was established in 1917 at No. 24 General Hospital, Etaples, to treat airmen suffering from flying-related illnesses, including operational fatigue and what would now be labeled post-traumatic stress disorder.[14]

As in any operational headquarters, tensions could still run high—even if the staff were long-standing colleagues. Trenchard's official biographer, who admitted that his subject's character could be described as tyrannical and unconventional, claimed that the headquarters "adapted themselves without demur to Trenchard's autocratic yet flexible methods."[15] This was certainly not the case, and there were tensions between Trenchard and his senior team throughout his time in charge of the RFC. When one considers the pressure wartime brings, it is hardly surprising that arguments arose. This is not to suggest that they were at each other's throats, but Baring's ability to smooth troubled waters was not limited to managing Trenchard's behavior. Baring played a major (but less visible) role in maintaining the senior leadership dynamic.

Of course, Baring was not without his own faults or weaknesses. He was, according to those who knew him best, both nervous and fussy. His speech could be so rapid that it was hard to follow, while his laugh has been described as long and cackling, somewhere between a neigh and a crow. He could be pedantic, liable to become fixated on small details, such as the precise definition of the Royal Navy's alert bugle call.[16] For someone with no military pretensions, he was unexpectedly sensitive if correspondence didn't employ his correct rank or appointment (which his friends persisted in doing, once they knew that it would annoy him). He was never boastful, but his entry in *Who's Who* was three times the length of Trenchard's and listed all his published works and every change (ten) in rank or post.

Baring's generosity could be overwhelming: he would press rare books and gifts on his friends. Trenchard had to ask him not to waste money buying presents, but Baring continued to send him an inscribed copy of the first edition of every one of his new books.[17] For an accomplished and successful author, Baring was strangely nervous about the quality of his work, regularly seeking reassurance, although in fairness this may have been the result of the problems he encountered in finding publishers. While he could be touchingly humble and was genuinely without ego, he was by no means submissive. There was an inner resilience to his character, and while he valued the opinions of others, he tempered this with a strong streak of shrewdness.[18]

The efficient running of HQ RFC depended as much on personality, temperament, and social compatibility as on professional competence. There was literally no room for privacy or quiet routine. At the heart of the building was a "stuffy office, full of clerks and candles and a deafening noise of typewriters. A constant stream of pilots arriving in the evening in Burberrys with maps talking over reconnaissances; a perpetual stream of guests and people sleeping on the floor."[19] Studies show that small teams working under pressure in a hostile environment need not only a leader but also a "storyteller," a "clown," and a mixture of introverts and extroverts, if they are to be successful. These informal roles emerge naturally, but the most important position is that of "clown" (or court jester). The "clown" is funny and smart and knows team members well enough to defuse tensions. The "clown" is neither the leader nor a potential leader; indeed, their ability to repair relationships and modify individual and group behavior is possible only because they have no authority. It also helps if the "clown" is not a member of a well-defined group (by background, status, or employment).

A better description of Baring's position at HQ RFC would be difficult to find. For Christmas 1915, Baring sent copies of his privately printed *R.F.C. Alphabet* ("C is the Caudron that's painted all blue") to friends and the families of his fellow officers. When Festing was promoted, Baring wrote a humorous (and treasured) letter to his son (also Francis ["Frankie"] Festing, later Field Marshal Sir Francis Festing) offering advice to the fifteen-year-old schoolboy on how to deal with a general in the family. On Simon's birthday, Baring placed a personally inscribed book of poems by his knife and fork at breakfast. Such small, apparently insignificant gestures were deeply appreciated by the recipients. According to one friend, Baring had a simplicity and humility that put you at ease, while another described a rare spirit and an entrancing companion.[20] After Trenchard moved to London, Baring continued to smooth relationships in France, on one occasion telling Game that he should have pulled Trenchard's leg rather than getting involved in an argument—a remarkable instruction from a major to a brigadier general about how he should handle a major general.[21]

In a further parallel, Baring also took on the role of "storyteller." His good humor and sparkling wit at the dinner table made Trenchard guffaw with laughter, while his famous party trick, balancing a port glass on his head, encouraged his colleagues to (briefly) forget the war.[22] However, there was no escaping the mounting casualties, and Baring's literary skills were harnessed to the task of personal and collective mourning. The bulk of his creative output during the war memorialized friends killed in action, contrasting the beauty of the French countryside with the war raging above, although he found time to produce poems that were light and humorous. All were well received, perhaps none more than "In Memoriam," written on the death of Bron Herbert. It was regarded by many contemporaries as one of the best war poems. The work may have faded in popularity, but the lines "Something is broken which we cannot mend" and "High in the empty blue" still resonate.[23] Baring was acutely aware that no day passed without the RFC losing yet more men. Many of them had passed through the headquarters or been encountered on visits to the front line, and some were close friends.

Trenchard was not immune to these feelings, despite his reputation as an emotionally detached commander.[24] He cared deeply about his young officers and was troubled by their deaths. They were, he said, "young men, almost boys, boys who were poets, boys from universities, boys with great mental capacity and boys with only courage, all intent on helping the army and saving life in the army."[25] Thomas Marson recalled that Trenchard had become lean and haggard of face under the strain. Brooke-Popham acknowledged that some people thought Trenchard "hard-hearted and indifferent to heavy casualties; this was quite wrong, he had to steel himself as other commanders have had to, to drive men on to the limit of their breaking strain. I've often heard him say 'Remember that as a commander you're paid to be brutal when necessary.'" There is abundant evidence that Trenchard was not oblivious to casualty rates and adjusted both tactics and operations accordingly. In January 1916 he instructed that all reconnaissance sorties be escorted, to combat the superiority of the Fokker monoplane, and, after the heavy losses of April 1917, that the RFC stop low flying and avoid bombing raids—unless absolutely necessary—to avoid waste in pilots and machines.[26] Bernard Smythies, an experienced squadron commander, agreed that "judicious sympathy and tact can well be combined with ruthlessness when the occasion demands," but he added that "a complete disregard of casualties when a squadron has had a really bad time may be correct in theory but is not encouraging."[27] When Bron Herbert died, Baring wrote to Nan about Trenchard's wonderful understanding. Trenchard's own letter of condolence expressed deep sympathy, but it was not in his nature to show grief. Before he wrote to Nan, he had first checked with Baring that she would not be offended, as he had not wanted anyone to write when his own father had died. Archie James encountered Trenchard in 1944, when the latter had just received news that a second son had been killed in action. James realized, after the pair had paced up and down in silence, that Trenchard was unable to start the conversation and tell of his loss.[28]

Baring's good humor and sense of fun counterbalanced Trenchard's natural rectitude. To say that Baring was boisterous would be an understatement. However, like many larger-than-life characters, his exuberance disguised inner uncertainty. Lacking self-confidence, he had discovered that he had a talent for making people laugh, whether as a conjurer of words or by performing party tricks. It was part shyness, part insecurity, and part the simple pleasure he found in entertaining others. Shortly before the war, Baring delighted Lady Diana Cooper with a game of risks, rapidly slicing crusts with a sharp knife (drawing blood) and setting fire to his (remaining) hair.[29] A year later, he caused great hilarity among the wounded soldiers at Wrest Park by putting a match to the ward thermometer and persuading the matron to throw open all the windows to prevent her patients from succumbing. "He was immediately both butt and idol of the men. He became a legend and was handed on from one convoy to another as that funny chap who set the thermometer on fire."[30] Anyone else might have been labeled a show-off, but Baring's ability to entertain was matched by his ability to read the room. He knew what his audience wanted, whether it was an up-and-coming debutante, a ward full of badly wounded soldiers, or a group of hardened fighter pilots. In the autumn of 1917, William Orpen, who was working in France as a war artist, accompanied Baring on a visit to No. 56 Squadron at Estrée-Blanche:

> After lunch there would be an "official" opening of the circular saw. It was agreed that all officers and men were to attend (no flying was possible that

day) and that Maurice should make a speech, after which he was to cut the end of a cigar with the saw, then a box was made with a glass front in which the cigar was to be placed after the A.D.C. had smoked a little of it, and the box was to be hung in the mess of the squadron. It was all a great success. Maurice made a splendid speech. We all cheered, and then the cigar was cut (to bits nearly). Maurice smoked a little, and it was put safely in its box. Then Maurice was given the first log to cut. This was done, but Maurice was now worked up, so he took his cap off and cut this in halves. He was then proceeding to take off his tunic for the same purpose but was carried away from the scene of execution by a cheering crowd.[31]

Baring's success as a staff officer was not based simply, or even partly, on playing the clown. The ability to use humor to defuse criticism or lift a cloud was just one tool in an extensive armory. His skill with languages has already been mentioned, but Baring was more than an interpreter. Translating concepts from one language to another demands a deep knowledge of both culture and history.[32] With Baring at his side, Trenchard was able to converse fluently with French officers—even if they didn't speak the other's language (some might argue that Trenchard could speak neither): "Trenchard would sit on one side of Maurice Baring and the Frenchman on the other; they would talk to each other across Maurice who would interpret whilst the talk went on. I remember a French general saying one day 'How well your General [Trenchard] talks French.'"[33] Baring did more than simply smooth off Trenchard's rough edges. He helped turn a resolute, determined, yet unsympathetic commander into a respected and much-loved leader. Katharine Asquith was one of Baring's many friends to write about these transformative qualities and the impact that he had on others through his personality and behavior: "There never was anyone the least like Maurice. He had a Transforming [*sic*] effect on people quite unconsciously. He never wanted to alter them—but he made one ashamed—I did love him so."[34] This process was passive rather than active; Baring never told people what to do, but their behavior changed all the same. Veronica Maclean stressed this very point: "He never preached or rallied or *told* one anything, but one came away from a conversation with him with a new scale of values, a new insight, a vision of eternal truths. That may sound exaggerated, and precious, and thereby quite unlike him, because, in spite of the greatest sensitivity, there was something quite rugged in his character that never flinched at facing facts."[35]

Headquarters rarely receive praise, but it is difficult to take serious issue with HQ RFC, although it was by no means perfect. There was undoubtedly a failure to invest early enough in specialist medical services, although the situation improved from 1917. The employment of noncommissioned aircrew, which could have reduced some of recruitment issues associated with an all-officer aviator cadre, progressed slowly.[36] More could have been demanded of the flying training system, even though the quality of training had improved significantly by the summer of 1917. There was a lack of awareness about the potential of parachutes. It is commonly assumed that Trenchard was the obstacle, but Arthur Gould Lee, a World War I fighter pilot who retired as an air vice-marshal (AVM), rejected the rumor that it was Trenchard's responsibility and laid the blame at the War Office's door (although the Admiralty were no more progressive in this respect than the army).[37] The staffs in France were content to see parachutes employed if the practical issues involved could be resolved. Indeed, Trenchard wrote to Brancker in early 1917 urging that he not let the matter "drift away into indefinite experiments."[38] There was a persistent and exaggerated belief in the value of day bombing that resulted in high casualties for little reward. There were also times when the staffs pursued the offensive strategy without regard for the practicalities. On the other hand, they were right about the big things: the potential for airpower to make a significant contribution to winning the war; the critical importance of artillery cooperation and reconnaissance; the need for an offensive strategy to safeguard these activities; the importance of operational tempo; the benefits of flexible and responsive logistic arrangements; and the value of listening to bottom-up ideas. Above all, HQ RFC gained the wholehearted trust of its pilots and ground crew, and the confidence of CinC BEF and his subordinate commanders. Trenchard and his senior leaders were respected and seen as capable, reliable, open-minded, and forward-looking individuals who were focused on winning the war.

CHAPTER 6

An Airpower Visionary

HENDERSON, RATHER THAN TRENCHARD, was the airpower visionary. Whether through luck, pragmatism, or foresight, or possibly a combination of all three, Henderson's ideas about airpower have survived the test of time. At the outbreak of the war, the RFC in France was built around the principle of "centralised control and centralised execution." Following the changes introduced in November 1914, this became "centralised control and decentralised execution"—the founding tenet of modern airpower.[1] From this moment onward, the RFC effectively operated as a separate fighting arm, answerable only to CinC BEF. While the RFC's "separateness" was not the product of a conscious strategy, Pope-Hennessy believed that it reflected the aspirations of many aviators. Employed to revise the RFC training manual, he wrote in his diary, "Embedded in the suggestions which I have to criticise I find an idea that the RFC is to be a thing by itself. . . . This I am fighting tooth and nail."[2] Although the wing (and later brigade) commanders worked closely with their respective armies, they could be tasked only through GOC RFC. The frontline squadrons looked to HQ RFC for all operational, supply, and personnel matters, other than billeting, buildings, land, and general supplies. The efficacy of these arrangements can be judged from the fact that from the autumn of 1915 (when brigades were introduced) the RFC's organizational structure on the Western Front remained unaltered. By comparison, the French and Germans continued to make major organizational changes (while maintaining the principle that aviation units should be subordinated to their respective armies).

The RFC's "separateness" was reflected in the War Office's decision to allow HQ RFC to communicate directly with the Military Aeronautics Department on matters relating to internal administration (including the posting and promotion of personnel), rather than working through the corresponding GHQ offices.[3] Changes in establishment still needed to be approved by GHQ (because of the financial and quartering implications), but no other corps within the BEF was given the authority to manage its personnel without external scrutiny.[4] The Army Council's reasoning was that without a reserve to facilitate the creation of new units, and given the need to regularly rest pilots because of the stress of war flying, changes of personnel were much more frequent in the RFC than in other formations and were best handled by officers with specialist knowledge. While this was a sensible step, it meant that Trenchard controlled the career development of the RFC's field commanders, since promotion was largely driven by performance on operations and the Western Front was by far the largest operational theater. It is little wonder that Trenchard's relationship with the RAF's postwar leadership cadre was so close. For three years not a single squadron, wing, or brigade commander on the Western Front was appointed without Trenchard's agreement. Other than those few individuals who had served in the RNAS, all the World War II air marshals owed their careers to Trenchard's personal sponsorship.

Henderson had an instinct for how airpower could be developed and employed. An example of his farsightedness was the debate in early 1915 about the deployment of machine-gun-armed single-seat fighters. Henderson advocated the creation of dedicated fighter units, while his two wing commanders (Burke and Trenchard) argued that each squadron should be allocated a handful for close defense. As the official historian of the RAF noted, Henderson was proved right, although he acceded to his subordinates' wishes. When Trenchard took over from Henderson, he reversed the decision (against some opposition), recognizing that dedicated fighter squadrons offered a better defense for the RFC's two-seater photographic and artillery cooperation machines. In changing his mind, Trenchard demonstrated his willingness to be governed by experience rather than dogma. There are few commanders who can admit to errors and emerge the stronger for it. Henderson was also proved correct in his support for moving responsibility for aircraft production to the Ministry of Munitions. Brancker vehemently opposed the idea at the time, only to concede later that Henderson had been right. Baring's loyalty to Trenchard didn't stop him from observing that "everything to which he [Henderson] objected in the past and which was done has been proved wrong and everything which he advocated, and which was done, has been proved right."[5]

Although Henderson committed the major share of the RFC's resources to meeting army and corps needs, he retained control of the squadrons allocated to GHQ for "special strategical and patrol work." Following the RFC's arrival at St-Omer, one squadron was routinely allocated (on a rotational basis) to the air defense of GHQ and any other tasks required by CinC BEF. When the brigade organization was announced in August 1915, it included provision for "one or two wings" with HQ RFC.[6] The Ninth Headquarters Wing (formed in May 1916 under Dowding's command) had grown to seven squadrons (122 machines) by the battle of Arras. A year later it was elevated to brigade status (as IX Headquarters Brigade), with eight squadrons and 154 aircraft. By the Armistice, IX Brigade boasted seventeen squadrons and some 300 aircraft (comprising fighters, reconnaissance, and day and night bombers), equivalent to 17 percent of the RAF's frontline strength—all under the personal control of GOC RAF.[7] Trenchard and Jack Salmond (Trenchard's successor as GOC RFC) used this arrangement to create a powerful air weapon, capable of being rapidly moved to any part of the front without the prior agreement of the army and corps commanders.[8] It was the Ninth Headquarters Wing that provided the two fighter squadrons sent at twenty-four hours' notice to bolster London's air defenses in June 1917 and the two bomber squadrons sent to the Nancy area in October 1917—to open Lloyd George's strategic bombing campaign. Henderson's farsightedness provided Trenchard with the means to respond swiftly and effectively to War Cabinet directives, enhancing his personal reputation and demonstrating the RFC's operational agility. During 1918, IX Headquarters Brigade, under Brigadier Rudi Hogg, became the RAF's mobile strike force, deployed south (twice) to support the French army against the German offensives of June and July 1918, exploiting strategic opportunity (leading the vigorous but unsuccessful attacks on the Somme bridges in August 1918) and spearheading the BEF's advance during the Hundred Days campaign, where it operated successfully and repeatedly across army boundaries, while reinforcing the other RAF brigades as required.[9]

Henderson's organizational arrangements were long-lasting, but they were not perfect. It was soon realized that the existing methods of communication were incapable of providing the information needed by HQ RFC during a ground offensive.[10] At the battle of Neuve Chapelle (10–13 March 1915), Henderson established a temporary advanced headquarters at Hazebrouck to direct air operations. Henderson, Trenchard, and Salmond continued this practice for every major BEF offensive, routinely detaching a small cadre of operational staff from the main headquarters to a location closer to the battle zone. During the Somme fighting, Trenchard occupied a forward headquarters at Fienvillers. At Third Ypres, he reoccupied their old headquarters at St-Omer. These temporary headquarters illustrate an enduring problem with the RFC's organizational model—how to direct airpower in a time-sensitive environment. It was not unknown for HQ RFC to have to issue orders directly to the wings (or even the squadrons) to save time, bypassing the brigades entirely.[11] On the other hand, brigade and wing commanders found it helpful to retain personal contact with the army headquarters and encouraged them to find locations where local landing grounds were available. The unsatisfactory nature of this system was highlighted during the Battle of Amiens (August 1918) when the V Brigade commander (Charlton) was unaware that the scope of the attack had changed at the last moment, significantly restricting the RAF's contribution.[12] Thus, while both Henderson and Trenchard subscribed to the concept of centralized control and decentralized execution, communication limitations compromised this principle, particularly during major offensives.

If Henderson was the visionary, Trenchard was the executor of that vision.[13] Trenchard may not have been inspired, but he vigorously protected the organization he had inherited and introduced policies that greatly strengthened the RFC's operational effectiveness. He should be credited with two key achievements: enabling the RFC to conduct high-tempo operations; and creating an organizational culture that encouraged innovation. The first point to make is that the "relentless and incessant" offensive pursued by Trenchard was neither relentless nor incessant. The RFC operated based on maximum effort during ground offensives but flew at a reduced rate during other periods, enabling units to rest and the logistic system to recover and restock. At Messines (in May and June 1917), Trenchard concentrated his forces in time and space to match the BEF's limited objectives rather than attempting to gain air superiority over a wider area.[14] The RFC's monthly wastage in aircraft was not dissimilar to the losses experienced by the French air service (around 50 percent per month for fighter aircraft and 33 percent per month for observation aircraft), but it was able to sustain significantly better serviceability. During 1918, 80–90 percent of British frontline aircraft were serviceable (and available for flying), whereas the equivalent figure for the French air service was 63 percent, falling by as much as 40–50 percent after the first two days of heavy fighting. RFC and RAF squadrons were able to maintain high serviceability for an extended period of active operations because they were supported by a sophisticated and well-resourced logistic system. As Brooke-Popham recalled, "Trenchard with his instinct for essentials had from the early days . . . been very insistent on the need for an ample supply of spare parts for aeroplanes and engines in order to maintain a high serviceability rate."[15] An analysis of the operational effort of two artillery-cooperation units indicates that the RFC generated over 30 percent more sorties from each frontline airplane than the Luftstreitkräfte did (see appendix B).

Even contemporary observers misunderstood the nature of the RFC's offensive strategy, believing that it required the employment of a disproportionate number of fighter aircraft. An American War Department report issued in August 1918 concluded (based on erroneous data) that the British had a significantly higher ratio of fighter aircraft (55 percent) to frontline aircraft than the Germans (42 percent) and the French (34 percent). It concluded that this reflected different theories about the functions of military aviation and that "the British practice in which the air service is primarily a combatant arm whose principal duty is to seek out and destroy the enemy forces by attack from the air, contrasted with French and German applications in which the air arm's principal function was reconnaissance for the purpose of securing information on enemy positions and movements to be used in directing troop operations and artillery fire." The actual ratios were 42 percent (British) and 46 percent (German), indicating that the RFC did not place a disproportionate emphasis on fighter aircraft at the expense of reconnaissance and artillery cooperation.[16] Nevertheless, Trenchard's rhetoric about the continuous offensive was so powerful that it was easier to believe the RFC's primary interest was air fighting—even if the evidence suggested otherwise. To add to the confusion, the term "relentless" was interpreted as meaning that Trenchard didn't regard human factors as an operational constraint, even though the RFC's personnel policies were enlightened and generally in advance of contemporary practice.

By continuing with Henderson's policy of allocating the bulk of the RFC to individual armies and corps, Trenchard has also come under fire for unnecessarily limiting his ability to concentrate airpower in the same manner as the Luftstreitkräfte, who were able to rapidly redeploy their fighter squadrons as the operational situation demanded, although it should be said that this was driven as much by necessity as by doctrine. One historian has asserted that this was because the French policy of "live and let live" tied down only a small fraction of their forces.[17] Other than the Ninth Headquarters Wing (later IX Headquarters Brigade), which could be used to reinforce critical parts of the front, Trenchard had to get agreements from the relevant army commanders if he wanted to move squadrons between armies or corps. Brooke-Popham agreed that the RFC was unable to concentrate to the same degree as the Germans but claimed that this was due to the army commanders' insistence on retaining close hold of the squadrons allotted to them. Looking back, he felt that it was a pity that GHQ did not make it clear that it had the right to withdraw any or even all squadrons from an army or corps at any time.[18]

What Brooke-Popham overlooked, however, was that the RFC's record in meeting the army commanders' needs, and the latter's confidence that Trenchard could be trusted to continue to provide this support, meant that an independent air service did not represent an existential threat. The same could not be said for the French army, where there was considerable opposition to the decision by Colonel Maurice Duval (appointed by Pétain in August 1917 to replace Paul du Peuty as head of the French air service) to create an independent mobile striking force, the Division Aérienne, comprising over fifty squadrons and around seven hundred aircraft. Its mix of fighters, reconnaissance, and bombers echoed the composition of the RAF's IX Headquarters Brigade, albeit on a larger scale.[19] Under Pétain, the Division Aérienne would not only fulfill reconnaissance and observation missions but also intervene in the offensive battle.[20] It proved effective in the offensives of June and July 1918 (supported by eight squadrons of the RAF's IX Headquarters Brigade), particularly in the interdiction of the Marne River crossings. As impressive as these results were, Duval had had to strip the front line of all their day bombers. Moreover, the armies were effectively denied the ability to launch coordinated air operations in support of the ground battle; indeed, it was claimed that there were insufficient single-seat fighters left to protect the artillery cooperation squadrons.

According to Voisin, there were two contradictory policies at work: "on the one hand, the search for powerful, massive actions, with the danger of divergent efforts and lacking a precise point of application; and on the other hand, actions that are less powerful, but better coordinated with ground operations, with the fight against enemy fighter aviation as a consequence rather than as the primary aim." He quoted admiringly from the RFC's policy, issued by Trenchard in 1917 that stressed the best way for aviation to participate in the army's defensive operations was to ensure the permanent work of artillery aircraft and only afterward to attack the enemy's forces. Voisin added that the comparison was in no way intended to exalt one doctrine to the detriment of another, but simply to show that there was room for a different solution than the one favored by Pétain and Duval.[21] Although Trenchard is not specifically named, it seems that Voisin agreed that efforts in one sphere (such as bombing) should not detract from another (such as artillery cooperation).

Trenchard's grip on aviation doctrine and the RFC's status as a separate fighting arm did not go unchallenged. Prior to the Somme, the BEF's generals had been able to ignore the RFC, but once the importance of artillery cooperation and its potential for transforming the battlefield became clear, several commanders attempted to take back control of the RFC, or at least the element that most interested them. Trenchard had already pushed back against the increasing tendency for divisional and corps commanders to instruct squadrons on procedures and tactical issues. In his view, these were matters for HQ RFC in order to avoid different and potentially unsound systems being introduced.[22]

A more serious challenge emerged when Rawlinson (4th Army) wrote to Haig, followed by Henry Horne (1st Army), arguing that the RFC's artillery cooperation work should be the responsibility of the individual armies.[23]

Rawlinson proposed that the relevant squadrons should be transferred to the corps commanders, while Horne argued that improvements in artillery cooperation depended on employing trained observers, who should belong to the Royal Artillery. Trenchard pointed out that it was the pilot rather than the observer who directed artillery fire, that artillery officers would therefore need to be trained as pilots, and that additional resources would be required if artillery cooperation machines were to be permanently allocated to armies and corps. Trenchard was able to defeat the proposal (with Haig's backing), as had Henderson with a previous proposal to take control of the RFC's kite balloons, although many artillery officers believed that it was a mistake to leave such important assets with another organization.[24] Trenchard was also successful in the argument about who would provide the staff to handle the increasing volume of photographs and intelligence provided by the corps squadrons. The corps commanders had wanted to provide their own officers, only to realize that the routine rotation of corps and the frequent movement of squadrons would create considerable turnover in personnel and a loss of valuable experience.[25]

No organization is static, even if its basic building blocks don't change. Organizations need to show agility if they are to survive, particular in the dynamic and unpredictable environment that war brings. Trenchard's greatest achievement was neither his relentless energy in pursuing an offensive strategy nor his determination to safeguard the RFC's independence; it was his willingness to listen. This may appear a surprising claim, given Trenchard's reputation as someone who was intolerant of other views. Trenchard's clash with Dowding is often quoted in this context, yet Trenchard was extremely patient with a subordinate who tested him sorely. He showed similar restraint in 1923, when dealing with Charlton's concerns about the RAF's policy of air control in the Middle East and the potential for civilian casualties. Charlton, who was by then an air commodore and chief staff officer in Iraq, was replaced rather than sacked and given another appointment—much to his surprise, as he expected to be asked to resign his commission.[26] Even those who disobeyed a direct order were not necessarily treated to Trenchard's anger. Captain Louis Strange, who had been personally instructed by Trenchard in 1915 to return to England for rest after a year on active operations, failed to do so. When Trenchard later found him still in France, he sent him home immediately. Strange's subsequent career was not affected, and he ended the war as a wing commander.[27]

Organizations are more than a wiring diagram, functional blocks connected by thin black lines, printed on white paper—although this is how they are frequently represented and the image that often comes to mind when the subject is mentioned. It's always helpful to be able to visualize who does what and who reports to whom, but we can forget that organizations comprise people, hundreds if not thousands, working to a common purpose. While a wiring diagram is inanimate, organizations are anything but passive. They have a life of their own, a culture and an ethos defined by the collective behavior of their staff. Organizational culture can be difficult to identify, but leadership is the most important single factor in defining its ethos and shared values. Trenchard's regular visits to the front line, his evident interest in listening to what junior officers and airmen had to say, and his willingness to act on their suggestions created a productive and creative environment. One critic, having described Trenchard as quick-tempered and immoderate, conceded that despite these characteristics, Trenchard supported debate and encouraged young officers to develop their own ideas.[28] Trenchard may have been loud, but he was not a lout. The ability to listen to others was an important part of his character and part of the same self-awareness that led him to value Baring's abilities and to recruit staff who offered the skills that he lacked. As Trenchard explained in his personal memoir, "I then used to say, and I mean it still, and I think it is true, that I never really initiated a single change that had not come to me out of all the many criticisms and talks that young pilots had with me."[29]

As a result, HQ RFC gained a reputation for encouraging radical thinking. Squadrons were asked to experiment and to forward inventions for wider adoption. Within two months of taking over from Henderson, Trenchard had organized a competition at St-Omer between the squadrons for the best gun-mounting, awarding a prize to the winning entry. There are multiple examples of modifications undertaken by squadrons (at the instigation of both officers and other ranks) being forwarded to HQ RFC for the GOC's approval.[30] Brooke-Popham thought that HQ RFC's willingness to listen to ideas from below contrasted favorably with the Tank Corps and that much of this had to do with the GOC's example. In his view, Trenchard's unwillingness to be constrained by detail induced a flexibility of mind throughout the RFC. By "detail" Brooke-Popham meant being told that something was "impossible," a word that Trenchard claimed (in conversation with a French journalist) did not exist in either the English language or the French.[31]

The RFC was not alone in demonstrating innovation, but it was a leading exponent in introducing new roles. Neither the French nor the Germans were as productive in pushing the operational boundaries of military aviation. This was not a free-for-all. Trenchard encouraged innovation but demanded that it form part of a disciplined, coordinated effort rather than driven by the individualism that had characterized the first years of the war.[32] Much of the RFC's early practice in photography and artillery cooperation was based on techniques developed by the French air service. Key individuals in both the French air service (such as Commandant Charles de Rose) and the Luftstreitkräfte (such as Hauptmann Oswald Boelcke) were responsible for significant tactical and organizational improvements. These bottom-up initiatives transformed air warfare on the Western Front, but so did the invention of the clock code and squared maps by Captains Donald Lewis and Baron James, both RFC pilots, and the introduction of formation flying by Major Lanoe Hawker.[33]

During 1918, the British introduced a wave of new techniques, including ammunition dropping; smoke screen laying; noise masking; antitank guns suppression; and aircraft-tank cooperation. The scale and breadth of these innovations were unmatched. Experimentation and change characterized British air operations during the Hundred Days campaign, whether it was new ways to combat the infrequent but increasingly large formations of German fighters or using wireless to direct fighter bombers toward fleeting targets.[34] The RFC was a leading practitioner of signals intelligence on the Western Front. It was particularly successful in traffic analysis, for which Trenchard has received credit for his enthusiastic support. From the autumn of 1916, this was used to direct RFC fighter squadrons to the location of German spotting aircraft, disrupting their shoots or destroying the aircraft involved.[35] All of these initiatives benefited from a field commander who championed innovation, whether through invention or by copying best practice.

Perhaps the most radical development was the introduction of what would now be considered offensive counter-air (OCA) operations—aimed at suppressing enemy airpower through attacks against aerodromes and associated infrastructure. While there were individual raids by the British and French against German zeppelin bases from the start of the war as well as bombing raids by all sides against aerodromes (largely at night), there was no sustained campaign to attack the sources of enemy airpower. Aerodromes represented just one category within a broad target list for bombers, but between August and September 1918, the RAF mounted at least eleven major low-level raids, each involving around sixty aircraft (both fighters and bombers), against German aerodromes. Nothing similar had been tried previously, although the RFC had experimented with suppressing enemy air defenses (SEAD) as early as 1916.[36] Losses were few, German air defenses were surprised on every occasion, and considerable damage was inflicted on ground installations and dozens of aircraft were destroyed or damaged. Individual raids were planned in considerable detail and employed single-seat fighters to soften up the ground defenses before the bombers struck with layers of escort fighters above them. French doctrine specifically excluded the use of fighters for such missions, although the Division Aérienne was employed in mass daylight attacks against ground targets.[37] German doctrine did not exclude a ground-attack role for its single-seat fighters, but the Luftstreitkräfte never engaged in large-scale daylight raids and never used fighters to attack enemy aerodromes.

The raids petered out within two months as the speed of the Allied advance made it too difficult to identify, plan, and execute an attack before the target was evacuated. The Germans acknowledged the damage inflicted but were unable to deploy additional fighter aircraft to meet the threat and could only offer units advice on improving antiaircraft defenses while encouraging the dispersal of aircraft.[38] Although it is impossible to know whether the RAF's newfound "independence" exerted any influence in the planning of these raids, the fact that they were instigated at brigade level (rather than being a top-down initiative) seems to confirm Brooke-Popham's assertion that under Trenchard the RFC (and RAF) had become flexible in mind.

Sir John Slessor, commenting on the airpower lessons learned during World War I, wrote, "Trenchard instinctively understood the essential supremacy of the offensive in air strategic policy. . . . In this policy there was admittedly the element of 'hunch' in all strategic policymaking."[39] Slessor was right to caution that instinct may have played a part in forming Trenchard's understanding of airpower. There is always a degree of uncertainty in such matters; no decision is ever determined solely on rational, considered argument. However, in listening to his subordinates and by not being afraid to change his mind, Trenchard made it more likely that the "correct" decisions would be made. Trenchard would never have described himself as an intellectual, but he gifted the RFC something more important: the ability to harness the energy, shared insights, and individual initiatives of its people to the collective development of airpower. Trenchard's intuitive way of thinking helped establish a culture that encouraged creativity.

CHAPTER 7

An Inspirational Leader

IN THE SUMMER OF 1918, SHORTLY AFTER SALMOND had arrived in France, Philip Game wrote to his wife,

> Salmond is a good bit easier to deal with as Trenchard, with all his wonderful gifts and powers, is very childish at times and apt to look for insults. Salmond is just as good a soldier too and I have an enormous admiration for him. He has not quite Trenchard's personality of course, or his flair in some ways, but he is a real commander and is exempt from Trenchard's petty faults.

Sir Christopher Bullock, who admired Trenchard's many positive qualities, also acknowledged that he "had moods and could on occasion be intolerant and obstinate, sometimes almost childish in his obstinacy."[1] As an aviator, Trenchard had a surprising ignorance of mechanics—he might have been able to drive a car, but never did so if he could possibly help it. Nevertheless, Charles à Court Repington would describe Trenchard as "one of the few indispensable men in the Army. He has done wonders and deserves immense credit."[2]

How does someone with behavioral problems and a profound inability to express himself, become an indispensable commander and a "great man" (according to many of the most influential and important figures of his day)? These apparent contradictions stem from two factors. First, Trenchard's forceful character hid his qualities behind an unsympathetic, authoritarian exterior. Second, his exceptional self-awareness allowed him to compensate for his undoubted shortcomings. Unlike many senior commanders, Trenchard was acutely conscious of his weaknesses and willing to look to others to provide the skills he lacked. Trenchard was known to quote the family motto, "Nosce Teipsum" (Know Thyself), adding that while "nobody knew themselves, some were better at it than others."[3] According to Frederick Bartlett, an early pioneer of cognitive and cultural psychology, "everybody agrees that a good soldier must take trouble to know the character and capacity of his rank and file, and this is undoubtedly true. It is equally important that a leader should take trouble to know his own character and capacity."[4]

There is little argument about Trenchard's public face. It was described in a long editorial published in 1918 by *The Aeroplane*:

> General Trenchard made the RFC what it is. By sheer magnetic personality and strength of character he held together the moral [sic] of the Corps in 1915 and 1916.... He has made mistakes, as every other great man has made them. He has broken good men and promoted men who afterwards turned out to be failures. But such mistakes have been rare, compared with similar mistakes made by others. His enemies—who are not a few—say that General Trenchard is a Bismarck and uses Prussian methods. Those that know him best know that his kindness of heart is his greatest weakness. The fact remains that the RFC in the field worship him.[5]

A French journalist also attested to Trenchard's dominant personality: "The face, the physiognomy, the external appearance of the Commander Flying Corps on their own provide an extraordinary and deep impression of energy, vigour, balance, of beautiful bravery." While such sentiments may owe something to journalistic license, there is no doubt that French military commanders as well as journalists respected Trenchard's energy and determination.[6]

Trenchard's life and achievements are well documented, but despite two full-length biographies, his personality and character have never been fully explained. As one reviewer put it, "The real Trenchard, as opposed to the public figure, still eludes us."[7] There are numerous reports testifying to Trenchard's charisma and the affection in which he was held, yet other accounts paint him as intolerable, unfeeling, and devoid of imagination. Paradoxically, Trenchard's supporters and detractors are largely united in describing his personality. Moore-Brabazon recalls an explosive, stimulating, fierce, exasperating, lovable man subject to intense moods who preferred to beat you with a big stick in an argument rather than try to convince you—adding that those who knew Trenchard, and discounted his moods, worshipped him, although, like many other good things, he was an acquired taste.[8] One of Trenchard's more strident critics, Wing Commander "Dizzy" Allen, claims that this tall moody man, "who showed a remarkable ability and, in many ways, an even more remarkable lack of ability," was aggressive to his subordinates and quarrelsome with his seniors—in psychiatric terms, symptoms of the manic-depressive. All are agreed that his gruff demeanor and penetrating gaze could easily produce fear in juniors.[9]

Trenchard, like many men in the Victorian army, grew to adulthood during his military service. Personality is most malleable during these years, but he had no one to help manage the transition. His family's bankruptcy meant that, although he was a loving and dutiful son, he could not (or would not) rely on his father as a role model. Social interaction with peers, rather than their seniors, is the major factor in the development of young men. Trenchard's lack of a parental role model and his unwillingness to make friends and risk any form of intimacy produced an emotional immaturity that left him unable to explain his own feelings or to understand the needs of others.[10] Unwilling to form significant friendships, Trenchard regarded susceptibility to social influence as a vulnerability. Military service provided him with the self-confidence and independence to achieve success, but his leadership lacked subtlety or insight: he relied on determination and personal example to motivate his subordinates. He had little sympathy for physical weakness and was intolerant of illness, believing that good health was a question of willpower—a view reinforced by an almost miraculous recovery from his bullet wound in South Africa. Active service broadened his horizons, but it also reinforced these prejudices and did little to improve his social skills. Kitty Boyle first met her future husband shortly after his return from Nigeria. She recalled a slightly aggressive officer who had a reputation as a holy terror. She could see why young officers shrank back and had to tell him off for shouting at them too much and bullying them.[11]

When Trenchard arrived in France in December 1914, his command style had not changed greatly. He was autocratic, task-focused, and outcome-driven. Consultation and delegation were not familiar concepts. Yet within two years, the battalion commander who had bullied his junior officers, and the menacing assistant commandant who had terrified his students, had become a sympathetic and inspirational leader. Trenchard credited Baring with this transformation. As he wrote in *The Times*, "He was a genius at knowing the young pilots and airmen. He knew more about what mattered in war and how to deal with human nature, how to stir up those who wanted stirring up, how to damp down those who were too excitable, how to encourage those who were new to it, and in telling me when I was unfair more than any other man I know."[12] This was a remarkable admission by a senior military officer, but is there supporting evidence?

Assessing the impact of one individual on another is problematic. The ability to influence depends on many factors, including the strength of the relationship, personal commitment, credibility, and mutual trust. Baring certainly possessed the relevant qualities, alongside strong communication skills and an innate sense of timing. As a personal staff officer, he was uniquely positioned within the headquarters to exert influence, but he also understood the role's boundaries. He never abused Trenchard's trust or betrayed the confidence of others. In this difficult balancing act, his transparent honesty and palpable lack of ambition were essential attributes. However, influence, as opposed to persuasion, is subtle, the more so if the individuals live and work in proximity. Observation can offer some evidence, but establishing cause and effect is more speculative than deductive. Human behavior is complex, and motives are often obscure—even to the individual concerned. On the other hand, individuals do exhibit patterns of behavior, and changes rarely go unnoticed. We know that Trenchard was susceptible to influence, but did Baring really instigate a transformation?[13] Thomas Marson, who replaced Baring as Trenchard's private secretary in 1919, had an opportunity to observe the two men while he was serving as No. 56 Squadron's recording officer:

> The flying personnel were young, adventurous, gay and unorthodox and
> derisive of red tape and armchair direction. For success, the corps required
> a commander who would know and be known to all, and of whom they

could make a Caesar on one hand and a Robin Hood on the other. Trenchard's outstanding personality and tireless energy made him speedily known throughout the Corps and enabled him successfully to fill the double role, made the easier in that he was fortunate enough to have as his personal assistant throughout the war Maurice Baring, who through his own personality and abilities was an asset of untold value to the man he served and to the cause they both served. He was the link between the towering Chief [Trenchard] and the youngest and newest airman, and it is impossible to overrate his value in maintaining morale, esprit de corps and loyalty. He was above jealousies and did not tolerate personal antipathies and, being who and what he was, was welcomed on an equal footing by all and sundry whatever their rank.[14]

Marson identifies two key roles for Baring: providing personal support to Trenchard; and managing his relationship with the front line. The first thing to be said is that these activities were not part of a conscious plan—at least not at the start. The idea that Baring might have something substantial to contribute to the RFC dawned slowly.

Without knowing what I was doing I got nailed to a staff, but had it not been so I could not have come out at the beginning of the war. And at that time no one foresaw anything. As it is, I like my work and I believe I really am of some use to the General who I am working with, who is a great man with a spirit of flame. His name is General Trenchard. He says he is descended from Jack Sheppard, and I can well believe it. He has the energy in overcoming obstacles, the initiative, the swift decision, the foresight and intuition of that illustrious prison breaker. I make all his notes. And they are many, for he has the eye of an eagle. And he thinks far too quickly to write.[15]

Many of Baring's acquaintances were never persuaded that he was anything other than a square peg in a round hole. Lord Robert Cecil (Hugh Cecil's older brother) and Arthur Balfour both believed that he would be more useful in Russia, where the British ambassador had asked for Baring as part of a new propaganda mission.[16] Recalled to London in January

1916, Baring argued strongly against the appointment and feigned an illness until he could return to France. Nan Herbert informed her brother, "Grey's scheme of sending him [Baring] to Russia as interpreter of the English nation (aided by cinematograph films) having been thwarted—he returns with colours flying to his beloved 'Boom.'"[17] Trenchard was equally reluctant to be separated from Baring, not just because he needed someone with good writing skills but because he needed someone who understood him. Trenchard the senior officer might appear aloof, self-confident, and unemotional, but Trenchard the young subaltern, burdened by shame, failure, and frustration, was never far from the surface. Just how close can be judged from Trenchard's reaction when Kitty Boyle rejected his first proposal of marriage. The recently appointed CAS, soon to be made a baronet by a grateful government, instantly assumed that her refusal was due to the stigma caused by his father's bankruptcy, something he was ashamed of to his dying day.[18] Trenchard did his best to hide his true character—as much as from himself as from others. Some of this was instinctive, but it was also driven by his conscious effort to bury a traumatic past. It has been said that Baring, as a writer, was a prisoner of his childhood and early youth, a happy period that disappeared abruptly with a financial crisis. Trenchard, as a commander, was also a prisoner of his early youth.[19] Trenchard the private man was beset by uncertainties and fears; Trenchard the public figure was relentless and confident. In comprehending the former, Baring enabled the latter, allowing nature to triumph over nurture.

We know that Trenchard could be moody and unreasonable, but no commander wakes up cheerful every day. An outer office soon learns to recognize their commander's moods and make the necessary adjustments. Game learned that it was pointless trying to argue with Trenchard when he was tired. "Unfortunately, as usual, he would get to work the moment after dinner and not wait till today with the result that he was at his vaguest and *worst* as the discussion became acrimonious and helped no-one. However, he is alright today, and able to say what he means, and we have settled points a lot."[20] According to Moore-Brabazon, "Trenchard was a very difficult person, and when you wanted to see him, you had to choose the right moment, and nobody ever dared to go and see him until they had consulted the great Maurice Baring, who was always in his confidence." Moore-Brabazon believed that Trenchard's melancholy was due to the migraines he experienced at times of stress.[21] Trenchard's "moods" were infrequent, but Game became adept at finding the right moment to seek a decision, conscious of when Trenchard was unwell, not his "normal super-energetic self," or suffering from one of his "funny fits."

Not everyone in the headquarters was so adept. Game returned from leave on one occasion to find Trenchard in a state of suppressed excitement and panic. Game blamed his deputy, "Bos" Gordon, for allowing matters to get out of hand. "It will take me a day or two to get him calmed down.... Meanwhile, he is difficult as he wants everything at once and flits from one thing to another."[22] By contrast, Brooke-Popham used to send in one of his young staff officers, Captain Spenser Ellerton, for whom Trenchard had a soft spot, whenever there were difficult decisions to be made. "We had to find a presentable youngster who would never get rattled if Trenchard stormed at him and would not leave [the] office until he was perfectly clear what Trenchard wanted done."[23] Baring, as the officer closest to Trenchard, played the central role in modifying his commander's behavior within and outside the headquarters, referring to Trenchard as a torrent, a force to be directed rather than obstructed. As one beneficiary observed, "Maurice Baring . . . played a role the importance of which cannot be exaggerated. Verbally, as when visiting squadrons, or in writing from his office, he interpreted faithfully the inarticulate Trenchard's meanings. On a squadron aerodrome he would stand behind Trenchard and when some flying officer tended to be scared by Trenchard's gruff manner, Maurice would smile and wink over Trenchard's shoulder and restore confidence."[24]

Evidence for Baring's natural empathy and his desire to entertain (and occasionally educate) is found throughout his extensive correspondence. Baring wrote and received many hundreds of letters in his lifetime, only stopping in the late 1930s when he was unable to hold a pen and found it tiring to dictate. They reveal how adept he was at conveying a scene or events, deftly placing the reader in the writer's shoes. They also show his ability to modify style and content to match the recipient. Baring could be searingly honest with some (such as Eddy Marsh and Nan Herbert), while being silly and frivolous with others (such as Juliet Duff). Just as he could read an audience, he knew what his correspondents needed and expected.[25] Bron Herbert had an opportunity to see the Trenchard/Baring relationship in action:

I had lunch with Boom the other day. He has great drive but must be the most difficult man in the world to satisfy, if you're under him, because he's both things, thinking of general principles and insatiably curious about details. He fires questions of both kinds alternatively. It's a strain. When he sits down to lunch, he works off all the morning's details on each of his staff in turn and woe betide them if they can't answer. . . . Maurice has established a supreme position. When he knows a thing, no one can get it out quicker and he's got a mass of information on the details Boom loves. When he doesn't know, he becomes at once what everybody who only knows him a little think him—*the* great joke of the Flying Corps. He plays the fool everywhere and is universally adored. At the same time, they all realise that there's something behind the joke, and they're left puzzling as to what it is.[26]

Baring could not stop Trenchard behaving badly, but he could, and did, find ways to minimize the damage. The details vary with the telling, but there are multiple accounts of how Baring sanctioned Trenchard, depending on the level of transgression. "He instituted a series of punishments numbered One to Five X and varying in that order in degree of severity. Punishment Number One consisted in taking away or hiding Boom's pipe. Punishment Number Five X consisted in breaking the window of Boom's car so that he had to sit in a draught, which he abhorred." The "crimes" Baring dealt with included bullying a squadron or a junior officer, being impatient over the phone, or being rude to a new pilot. Such games may seem out of place in a military organization, particularly in wartime, but the apparent silliness masked a deeper purpose. Whether the complaint was upheld, or the punishment was ever implemented, was less important than the connection it established between Trenchard and his junior officers and, by extension, between the headquarters and the squadrons: "Maurice Baring kept the General in touch with us, and us in touch with the General. It was a truly wonderful combination. The result was good fellowship, sympathy, and unity."[27]

Trenchard lacked many of the qualities traditionally associated with successful commanders and great leaders. His public speaking abilities were poor, and he struggled to express himself, either in conversation or on paper.

Despite these major handicaps, which should have severely limited his ability to communicate, he somehow made himself understood. Bartlett argues that it is difficult for dominant personalities to lead groups defined by specialist skills unless they share the same skills.[28] Although Trenchard qualified as a pilot, he is not known to have piloted himself in France, let alone undertaken any operational sorties, yet numerous accounts refer to the high respect, if not affection, in which he was held. Gordon Taylor, an eighteen-year-old Australian pilot, recalled that "we would fly for 'Boom Trenchard,' whatever the circumstances." It was a view shared by Haig, who wrote to Lord Derby (secretary of state for war) in October 1917 that "the importance of Trenchard's personality with the flying units in the field and its direct effort in maintaining the offensive spirit in the air so vital to the success of our armies in the field is not, I think fully realized at home."[29]

Marson observed Trenchard during numerous squadron visits and concluded that what the pilots loved was the open, gruff, utterly unaffected way he would take them into his confidence. Trenchard's honesty with his subordinates, and his willingness to explain what he wanted and why—without sugarcoating—compensated for any defects in fluency or clarity. Howard-Williams was one of many who recalled being inspired by Trenchard's optimism and morale "when he visited our squadron and told us something of what was going on and what was being done for us."[30] Sholto Douglas believed that, while Trenchard's speech was nearly always disjointed or off the point, it was the spirit and humanity that counted, shining through all the awkwardness: "It gave him the unique ability of being able to raise the morale of those with whom he came in contact in a manner that was out of all proportion to the visible or audible manifestations of the spirit of the man."[31] Trenchard's uncanny ability to gain the confidence of his young officers may have owed something to his sharp recollection of what it was like to be a subaltern. Marson certainly thought so. To his mind, Trenchard was intensely human. "The youngest of his pilots was no younger than he. He had not forgotten the ideas and the sublime foolishness of youth."[32]

"Sammy" Maynard flew with one of the RNAS squadrons attached to the RFC during the Arras and Messines offensives. He thought that he was probably one of several pilots who had negligible knowledge of the connection between the air and land war. It was only when Trenchard visited, and explained to them, that he properly understood "the why and wherefore of offensive patrols."[33] Five months later, Gould Lee wrote in his diary,

> General Trenchard paid us a visit today. . . . After lunch he collected us in the anteroom, and with all of us hanging on every word, told how, when at his HQ at dawn on the 20th, he saw the low cloud and mist, he didn't expect any machines to be able to take the air. When he learned that several squadrons were already in the battle, he was very proud and pleased. . . . After this general talk, he had short private chats with half a dozen of us, including me. . . . He is a fine man, with a terrific personality, who knows how to impress and inspire us. To have a few words of praise of our work was an enormous encouragement. Trenchard is a leader after the hearts of service pilots and though we don't like some of the things we have to do, such as D.O.P.s [Distant Observation Patrols] on obsolete machines, everyone in the RFC looks up to him as a great commander.[34]

Trenchard's ability to build a close and enduring bond with the frontline squadrons says a great deal about Baring's influence and his extraordinary capacity for knowing what people were thinking about or feeling.[35] Sholto Douglas recalled,

> Whenever we heard that Trenchard was going to pay us a visit it was always our hope that Maurice Baring would be with him because Baring had a way all of his own of getting things done. He was not a soldier, and he was not an airman; but he was a man with a rare charm and such a gay humour. Essentially an individualist, which, perhaps, was the reason why he was such a success in his work in the RFC, he made friends easily, and he quickly established contact with the junior officers; and while Trenchard would be making official inspections of the squadrons, Baring used to get around and mix with and sound out the junior officers. With an intuitive sense of balance, he would then brief Trenchard on his own discoveries, and this enabled Trenchard, in turn, to produce in conversations with us odd bits of valuable information.[36]

The intimacy between Baring and the RFC's young officers is mentioned in numerous personal reminiscences. There is no doubt that he enjoyed their company and friendship. Baring was their friend and in return argued their cause. "Maurice Baring came to visit us from time to time and was adept at keeping us amused with various parlour tricks such as balancing a liqueur glass on his bald pate while reciting doggerel verse. Writer and poet, he had the knack of keeping up our spirits and advising his Master about the morale of his squadrons."[37] Marson was closer to the truth than he might have imagined when he referred to Robin Hood. Trenchard was by nature a rebel. His affection for the irregular cavalrymen he led in South Africa, and later friendship with T. E. Lawrence, stemmed from an affinity with those who would speak their mind rather than submit to Caesar. Rare individuals prepared to place principle above self-interest. It was Trenchard's fate that his physical characteristics, personality, and upbringing should mold him to the form of Caesar. Baring's achievement was not so much as to transform Caesar into Robin Hood but to allow Robin Hood to escape Caesar's shadow.

CHAPTER 8

Followers as Leaders

GIVEN THE UNIQUE NATURE OF THE AIR WAR AND the unprecedented organizational arrangements developed to support the air services, the RFC had to adopt a distinctive, if not innovative, leadership model. There was no precedent for a force based on a minority (almost exclusively officers), who operated and fought in machines, while the majority (noncommissioned officers and enlisted personnel) worked in their support, largely outside the fighting zone.[1] Air combat placed a leadership responsibility on every pilot, not just their commanders. Air-to-ground and ground-to-air communication (largely radio) was limited (radio telephony was introduced late in the war), and the only form of air-to-air communication was by visual signals. In effect, once an aircraft took off, even if part of a formation, it was on its own. Deteriorating weather, enemy fighters, and malfunctioning equipment could all provide the crew with good reason to abandon their mission and return home. As Ernest Howard-Williams, who had flown with a two-seater squadron on the Western Front, explained,

> We are thus led to conclude that good leadership, particularly in the RAF, requires something less than the qualities of the great captains; in other words, a system of leadership may well be better than despotism. Wherein it is perhaps fortunate that leadership in the air is not the prerogative of a

select few. Perhaps the best leaders are those who obey at the same time, unknown.²

This devolved form of leadership (or "followership," as it might now be termed) was central to what RFC and RAF veterans called the "air force spirit": the personal commitment and self-discipline of individual pilots, observers, and air gunners working to a common purpose. It was this shared ethos that enabled squadrons to continue fighting despite technical inferiority or heavy losses. These numerous but solitary leaders were "cast in a frail mould, of average moral courage, with ordinary powers of concern."³ The number involved was not particularly large, less than two thousand (largely officers) by the autumn of 1917, although this total was constantly being refreshed—to replace combat casualties, the sick, or those returning to home establishment.⁴

Trenchard subscribed to a paternalistic view of leadership—as practiced by the pre-war British Army—but establishing a personal relationship with his airmen (equivalent to the strength of two battalions), scattered across more than sixty locations along one hundred miles of front, was not straightforward.⁵ Each squadron comprised an average of thirty to forty officers, generally aged between eighteen and twenty-five, drawn from a wide background. A significant proportion were volunteers from the "old commonwealth" (Australia, Canada, New Zealand, and South Africa) and, while willing to fight for Britain's cause, were not known for their deferential behavior. Compared to the BEF, the RFC was a cosmopolitan organization of individuality and variety. Herbert Griffith, an infantry officer, sent from a corps headquarters in April 1917 to take up the job of branch intelligence officer with No. 15 Squadron, found some forty officers drawn from across the empire, promoted from the ranks and mixed with "the average types of young English public-school boy (who were on the whole in a minority)." To his mind, this was variety and innovation with a vengeance, particularly as there was "nothing quite so uniform in the world as the average officers' mess of an average English regiment. Most of the officers have probably been to the same half-dozen schools, and, owing to the territorial base of most regiments, may even have come from the same county." According to Griffith, the RFC's ethos was very simple: "Carry out your flying to the utmost limit of your endurance.

Apart from that, get all the fun you can."⁶ An army padre who joined the RFC in 1917 wrote home that he was warmly welcomed but that "they are nearly all kids, the average age is about twenty."⁷

Willy Coppens, the leading Belgian fighter ace, operated from the same airfield as an RFC squadron for several months in 1917. He was impressed by the RFC's evident efficiency and technical competence, seeing its organization and attitude as very different from that of his own service:

> Whereas legend had it that the British pilots flew just when and how they liked, we discovered that, on the contrary, they worked strictly according to detailed instructions coordinated with the orders issued to neighboring squadrons, and that their work was highly intensive. Their discipline was strict, without being of the Prussian variety, and showed itself in a genuine respect for their superior officers and an unquestioning obedience to all orders received, even where these led to certain death. But how else could it have been? They were all officers whose chiefs set the example and were promoted not by seniority but by selection.⁸

Not everyone was impressed by the RFC. Game, who would become a key figure in Trenchard's headquarters, was shocked when he first arrived (under protest): "I don't like the RFC crowd and all their habits and customs annoy me."⁹ However, the postwar depiction of the RFC as a bastion of callow, hard-drinking, young public-school types, intolerant of colleagues from the lower social classes, are wide of the mark. Marson was one of many ex-RFC officers who vigorously rejected the image of heavy drinking and piano burning:

> We were neither a wild nor a drinking squadron—not the officers, nor the N.C.O.s, nor the men. I do not intend by this statement to cast reflections or to suggest that we were unusual in this respect. Since the war some published accounts of life in Air Force messes have conveyed the impression that our main job in the war was the consumption of champagne and oysters. Actually, no fighting squadron could have retained its efficiency except on terms of sobriety.¹⁰

Trenchard could have chosen to exercise "distant" leadership, as did many of the BEF's senior commanders, but his subordinate commanders, almost as young and inexperienced as their junior officers, also needed encouragement and support. During April 1917, the RFC lost 422 aircrew, roughly 25 percent of those employed on the Western Front. Over the next six months the casualty rate fell, but it still averaged over 250 pilots and observers each month, or some 13 percent of those employed. The actual wastage was higher when sickness, unsuitability, and accidental injury are considered. It was also not spread evenly: some units suffered as much as 40 percent casualties in a single month. Inspiring a squadron to continue fighting under such circumstances demands exceptional and sustained leadership—at all levels of command. Smythies felt that this was one of the RFC's greatest leadership challenges, adding that those wing and brigade commanders who occasionally flew not only gained a better appreciation of frontline duties but also engendered respect as well as raising morale among junior pilots—a problem made all the more difficult by the rule that squadron commanders should not fly.[11] Even when this was relaxed in 1917, squadron commanders were still not allowed to cross the lines.[12] There were exceptions, of course, notably on fighter squadrons, but it was still unusual for a squadron commander to join an offensive patrol, and if they did so, it was a flight commander who led the formation. Command in the air was a tenuous concept anyway, especially with corps and night bombing squadrons, where most of flying was undertaken by single aircraft, and with day bomber squadrons, where they rarely if ever flew as a single unit. Trenchard's personality, openness, and willingness to listen to his junior officers were undoubtedly inspiring, but he could not be everywhere at once. Moreover, what he did achieve came at personal cost. After one tour of the front line Baring wrote in his diary,

> Yesterday and the day before we visited nine squadrons and three kite balloons. And the General spoke to all the pilots and saw everything. He rides the whirlwind and directs the storm and kindles in everyone he sees an undying spark. But he was white with fatigue afterwards. I can't tell you how tiring it must be for him since I myself, who only look on, am worn to a shred.[13]

It was not the role of the brigade or wing commanders to supervise the squadrons—if their work was completed satisfactorily and in accordance with HQ RFC policy. It had been the practice, as early as 1915, to limit intervention by higher authority: "If initiative is to be encouraged, allowance must be made for individual characteristics and the wing commander must often be content to see his subordinates deal with matters in a somewhat different manner from that which he himself would adopt if he were a squadron commander."[14] Brigade and wing commanders were active in liaising with their "parent" corps and armies, preparing battle orders, coordinating the work of their squadrons, and identifying ways to progress the air war more effectively, such as Edgar Ludlow-Hewitt's efforts, as commander of Third Wing, to improve the cooperation between aircraft and infantry. Observing from the air the efforts of his squadrons during the first week of the Somme offensive, he drafted a paper on contact patrols aimed at improving the existing techniques.[15] Neither brigade nor wing headquarters were particularly large, comprising a handful of officers and support staff, perhaps a dozen all told. This limited the extent of their activities, which were largely administrative. Charlton felt that his executive duties as commander of V Brigade were less exacting than those he had encountered at home working for the training division. By contrast, Hogg, the commander of IX Headquarters Brigade, was kept particularly busy during the spring and summer of 1918, managing the short-notice redeployment of his force as the military situation rapidly evolved.[16] Overall, however, it is difficult not to sympathize with James' view that the RFC (and RAF) had one too many levels of command on the Western Front.[17]

All of this placed a considerable burden on the individual squadron commanders, who were required to be part manager, part headmaster, and part welfare officer. Their immediate responsibility was to allocate tasks to flights, in accordance with the wing's operational orders, and to ensure that these duties were successfully completed. They also oversaw all technical work and more general activities including administration, lectures, instruction, and (infrequently) drill. Their main concern, however, was maintaining morale.[18] As one experienced squadron commander observed, "The spirit of a squadron is the chief factor upon which success and good results depend." He added that in order to be successful, "it is absolutely essential that a spirit of keenness and cheeriness should pervade the squadron and grumbling and cantankerous officers should be quickly removed."[19] Discipline was the foundation for operational success, but individuals who proved unsuitable, either through temperament, competence, or physical inability, were returned to England rather than being punished or otherwise sanctioned. Squadron commanders personally interviewed every new arrival to explain the work they would be involved with and the difficulties they would likely encounter. Not every pilot or observer who arrived on the Western Front proved able or willing to make this commitment. A significant proportion were returned to England after only a brief stay. On No. 9 Squadron, a two-seat unit employed on artillery cooperation, infantry support, and photographic reconnaissance, just under a third of all aircrew served for less than a month.[20] The reasons included unsuitable temperament, accidental injury, sickness, physical disability, and poor flying. For these reasons, HQ RFC assumed (for planning purpose) that the average tour length for a corps pilot or observer was four months and that of a fighter pilot was two and a half months.[21]

The debilitating impact of war flying was readily acknowledged, particularly on those flying at high altitude (over 16,000 feet) without oxygen.[22] One squadron commander believed that two high patrols a day rendered officers inefficient at the end of five summer months. Managing the issue was not as simple as setting a limit. Keith Park thought this was a disruptive policy, as some pilots believed that they were entitled to be sent home to England when they achieved a recognized number of flying hours and their work fell off thereafter.[23] To provide some relief from stress, and to vary their routine, squadron commanders arranged social events, inviting dinner guests from local army formations and organizing concert parties, and laid on transport for trips to the nearest town. Denis Winter has claimed that fighter pilots were sustained by the regular routine of their life and by fear of letting down their colleagues. However, he goes on to say that the squadron commander's style was a form of democratic dictatorship, "a formulation of majority opinion, a leadership of equals."[24] This is too much of a generalization. Some squadron commanders were greatly respected, if not loved, but others were barely tolerated. Sholto Douglas (No. 84 Squadron) fell into the latter category, evidenced by the assault he was subjected to one dark evening involving a group of his pilots.[25] A punctilious and strict commander, Sholto Douglas had annoyed them by his inflexible policy on formation flying and the ridicule they had faced when failing to follow his orders. The culprits were never identified, and no punishment was forthcoming.

Sholto Douglas' pragmatism in not escalating the incident echoes Trenchard's own approach to such issues, notwithstanding his reputation as a strict disciplinarian. It is true that Trenchard insisted on observing the formalities and conventions that underpinned a military organization. Garrison duty in India, and active operations in South and West Africa, had confirmed his view that discipline was the foundation of military efficiency—in peace and war. He was not a martinet, however, obsessed with rules and regulations, unable to consider the intent as well as the letter of the law. He also knew that war demanded implicit trust between officers and those they led—built on respect, loyalty, and shared danger. This explains why the same man who was punctilious on the parade ground could lead a ragged group of colonial horsemen, including a staff officer who weighed over three hundred pounds, and turn it into a formidable fighting force. In France, Trenchard showed a degree of discretion and sympathy that belied his reputation as a stickler for the rules. It is tempting to see Baring's influence at work, although if this was the case, the door was already half-open.

Brooke-Popham recalled at least one incident where Trenchard would have been within his rights to demand that a RNAS squadron commander be court-martialed but instead quietly transferred the entire unit out of the line.[26] The incident highlights a wider problem: the lack of motivation in some of the naval aviation units operating along the Dunkirk coast. The losses incurred by the RNAS squadrons allocated to the RFC and the length of time that many pilots had spent in France had created a morale problem in some units. Their commander, Captain Charles Lambe, was sympathetic, but he also believed that "a large proportion of the officers prefer the comfortable surroundings of an aerodrome situated near London to the glamour and glory of the battlefield."[27] It appears that the relentless pressures of the Western Front were too much for many individuals. Rather than tackle the problem head-on, Lambe dangled the prospect of a posting home for three months and suggested that operations could be curtailed once the offensive (Third Ypres) was underway. This appears to have done little to improve operational effectiveness and was in stark contrast to Trenchard's uncompromising message about the importance of offensive action. Indeed, the RNAS were aware that the disaffection of a few could affect the many. "A pilot who shows signs of war strain or fatigue should be sent home for a rest immediately the symptoms appear. His retention, more particularly if he is a flight commander, will tend to affect others and foster the spread of disease throughout the squadron."[28] The Canadian official air services history suggests that RFC morale remained high because Trenchard's policy "winnowed out" the weaker or less capable pilots. Although it is true that the RFC was vigorous in removing individuals who proved ineffective, the key difference between the two organizations was that Trenchard never tried to hide the reality of what he was asking his squadrons to do.[29] Trenchard knew that he was asking a lot of his squadron commanders and that he was not well placed to judge their performance. He would later write,

> It must be remembered that commanding an air force from the ground is much harder to command fairly and justly than commanding armies on the ground. A good general realises the difficulties and tries to picture what is in the mind of the man who does the work whenever they make their criticism, and to keep a calm and balanced head and fair judgement, but it is much harder for the air marshal to realise all the difficulties and to be fair and keep a balanced judgement.[30]

There were several instances where newly appointed squadron commanders had to be returned home or sent back to their original regiment or corps because they couldn't provide the required leadership. Major George Todd was appointed to No. 4 Squadron in September 1916 but was posted to the Home Establishment four months later, after being judged "slow to command a squadron in the field efficiently." Major Percy Atkinson (commanding No. 11 Squadron) was sacked in March 1917 after an extended trial. He was reported to have been a hard worker, but temperamentally unsuited to the role. Atkinson rejoined the Royal Field Artillery and won the Military Cross for gallantry in September 1918. Major Henry Walker was removed from command of No. 15 Squadron in January 1918, after an extended review period, based on his poor organizing abilities and an inability to get the best from his subordinates. It was said that he would frequently undertake the more dangerous missions himself rather than ordering one of his officers.

Walker was awarded the Croix de Guerre in April 1918.[31] None of these individuals were incompetent or lacked bravery (as their subsequent careers confirmed); they were simply unable to meet Trenchard's expectations. It may be significant that almost every letter between Trenchard and Brancker during the period 1916–17 touches personnel matters, particularly the problems of finding suitable candidates for command appointments. As Smythies concluded, "From observation of numerous squadrons, the importance of the personality of the commander is deeply impressed on my mind. The whole unit answers directly to his touch, he alone is responsible for its efficiency in the air and its behaviour on the ground."[32]

Leadership problems at the more senior ranks were more difficult to resolve, partly because the RFC remained desperately short of experienced aviators. Charles Burke, commanding Second Wing, was one of the longest-serving RFC aviators, but he was also a rigid disciplinarian and not greatly liked by his subordinates (who nicknamed him "Pregnant Percy").[33] Henderson tackled Burke privately about his behavior, but the latter pushed back against the criticism: "He [Henderson] then informed me that there were rumours of discontent in my wing owing to [the] talkings-to that I gave people. Further that it was possibly due to ill health and that if I was unwell, he could send me home for a rest. I explained the incorrectness of these statements." Four months later, Burke had to be admitted to the hospital for appendicitis, and Henderson brought in Jack Salmond (who had only recently returned to England) to replace him. Burke's departure was celebrated by many in the RFC: "Burke, the man they universally execrate is gone. We get the younger Salmond." When Burke recovered, he found that there was no place for him in France, as Henderson wanted him to go to Canada to report on flying training.[34]

Despite Trenchard's reputation for impulsive behavior, he managed his senior officers with similar caution, as his strained relationship with Hugh Dowding demonstrated.[35] Dowding was a difficult subordinate and, according to multiple accounts, an indifferent squadron commander. On the other hand, he was staff-trained, clever, articulate, dedicated, and hard-working. Dowding had little time for social niceties, as his Staff College colleagues recognized when they gave him the nickname "Stuffy." Dowding lacked the "common touch" and could appear cold and aloof, although some found him a congenial colleague. According to Archie James, "Stuffy" was an apt nickname: "In a matter of three to four weeks, having taken command of No. 16 Squadron, he reduced it to near mutiny. A more difficult, and indeed impossible man to deal with, I have never met. He was pernickety, prying and fussing to the nth degree." Another member of the squadron had much the same opinion, describing Dowding as an "old woman." On the other hand, Patrick Huskinson found Dowding "a tireless worker and a ruthless driver, his cold and somewhat intimidating manner, which earned him the nickname of 'Stuffy,' hid the gentlest, the kindest and the most generous of natures. I could not wish to be in better hands."[36] Hogg came to despise Dowding, the senior RFC officer at Fort Grange in 1916. Having asked several times for No. 23 Squadron's incompetent equipment officer to be replaced before they went to France, Hogg was fobbed off by a demand for more reports.

The final straw, however, was when Dowding informed him that he was to be reported for the loss of an equipment ledger: "I gave him the benefit of my tongue for ten minutes. He took it all like a cur. He is the most unpleasant, mean minded, inefficient and nasty creature I have had to deal with in years." Later the same year, another subordinate (Major Willie Read, commanding No. 45 Squadron) found Dowding unyielding and unsympathetic when he tried to improve the domestic accommodation for his airmen. When Read attempted to remedy the situation, Dowding complained that not enough flying was being done: "The damned old fool said I was impertinent. I was. I do not know whether I dislike him more than I despise him. There will be a big row one day and the old fool will court martial me for insubordination, and I shall deserve it."[37]

These incidents, of no great substance in isolation, echo Dowding's behavior during the 1919 Chanak crisis when he wrote to the Air Ministry complaining that Squadron Leader Arthur Tedder, commanding No. 207 Squadron, had taken more spares to Turkey than authorized. The matter was resolved, but in Tedder's opinion "Dowding was—and would remain—a petty vindictive man, without a spark of human sympathy or imagination, quite unfit for senior command." Trenchard certainly disliked Dowding's persistent pessimism ("a dismal Jimmy") and his habit of going behind his (Trenchard's) back. The antagonism seems to have been mutual, but Trenchard chose not to block Dowding's advancement either during or after the war. There is little doubt that Dowding had problems with emotions and believed that sound administration was the same as sound leadership, which may account for his failure to stop the squabbling between two of his flight commanders on No. 16 Squadron (echoing his inability to manage his group commanders in 1940). Dowding would later claim that he was sacked by Trenchard after requesting his squadrons be rested during the Somme fighting. The pair may well have argued about the issue, but Trenchard agreed to rest No. 60 Squadron, which had suffered serious casualties (although less than some other units), including the loss of their commanding officer and two flight commanders. Nevertheless, five months would pass before Dowding was posted home (on promotion). Trenchard was aware of Dowding's deficiencies, but he could ill afford to lose a senior air leader.[38]

Dowding was not a unique case, Salmond had to resolve a bitter dispute between Hogg and his predecessor as commander No. IX (Headquarters) Brigade, Brigadier General Wilfrid Freeman.[39] Salmond had asked Hogg to replace Freeman, when the latter went sick in March 1918. As the German spring offensive had just opened, time was of the essence. Freeman was sent to No. 24 General Hospital at Etaples for a complete rest, but when he returned less than a week later it was obvious that he was still unfit for work. Hogg confided to his diary that he was "not at all satisfied with Freeman: he is thoroughly sulking at having me brought in over his head to command this brigade. This is extremely foolish as he is a comparative child. I have a feeling that he is working behind my back and would take an opportunity of doing me a bad turn. A very unpleasant feeling that will probably eventuate in my asking Salmond to replace him."[40] The matter was resolved when Salmond sent Freeman back to England to attend a staff course at Greenwich. Salmond's discretion was both sensible and far-sighted. Freeman stayed with the postwar RAF and would rise to the rank of ACM, responsible for the development of many of the most important combat aircraft in World War II. According to Freeman's biographer, the decision to send him to Staff College before he was thirty showed that he was already a marked man, "one of the elite of young officers on whom the future of the RAF would depend."[41] While Freeman's selection owed more to expediency than to career planning, Salmond, as with Trenchard, was wise enough to understand that today's followers would become tomorrow's leaders.

CHAPTER 9

Delivering Airpower

AN INSPIRATIONAL LEADER DOES NOT NECESSARILY make a good commander, but Trenchard proved as good a commander as he was a leader. His enduring achievement was to make British airpower a reality in the public imagination, in political discourse, and on the battlefield. While his personal charisma played a central role in this achievement, it was built on two key pillars: organization (in the form of processes, structures, and culture) and doctrine (in the form of policies). The power of Trenchard's personality meant that these enablers were often overlooked, even though the creation of an effective air weapon demanded intellectual and management skills as much as leadership. It is not unusual to find private and public comments to the effect that Trenchard "was the RFC," as if the organization had sprung into existence fully formed, simply through his strength of will.[1]

At Trenchard's direction, the RFC flew every day, from dawn to dusk, up to twenty miles beyond enemy lines, weather permitting. Although wartime inquiries into British military aviation focused on the quality of aircraft supplied to the RFC and its general administration, concerns were raised in Parliament as early as January 1916 about whether it was necessary to cross the lines so frequently or to conduct long-distance reconnaissance in view of the high casualties involved. The criticism so troubled ministers that Haig was obliged to write to Asquith defending Trenchard's policies.[2] Such criticism largely disappeared with the end of the "Fokker Menace," and it was not until after the war that the question resurfaced, when the journalist Philip Gibbs attacked Trenchard about the human cost of the RFC's strategy during the Somme offensive.[3] "Our aircraft had grown fast, squadron upon squadron, and our aviators had been trained in the school of General Trenchard, who sent them out over the German lines to learn how to fight, and how to scout, and how to die like little gentlemen." He claimed that many young airmen, "after repeated escapes from anti-aircraft shells and hostile craft, lost their nerve, shirked another journey, found themselves crying in their tents, and were sent back home for a spell by squadron commanders, with quick observation for the breaking point; or made a few more flights and fell to earth like broken birds." A handful of RFC pilots also expressed postwar doubts, including Oliver Stewart, who thought offensive patrols were of little value; Stewart concluded that "Trenchard, regarded as a hero by many and as a 'great' man by most, did not direct the activities of the operational squadrons in France at this time in a manner which won the approval of all his operational pilots."[4]

The official historian was sufficiently concerned to use the final chapter of the air history to defend Trenchard's policies, although this did not deter Sykes, who might be described as a hostile witness, and Chamier.[5] Both men believed that the RFC's offensive strategy had been correct but that it had been employed in an unthinking and costly way. Sykes went so far as to accuse Trenchard of employing battering-ram tactics that achieved little strategic effect and resulted in grave losses. Chamier offered a slightly more balanced view:

> There will always be arguments as to whether the RFC losses were necessary. Certainly, the Verdun and Somme struggles had shown that a defensive policy was likely to be disastrous; morale must be maintained by offensive action. But the verdict of history will probably be that continuous aggressive action is unsuited to a technically weaker side; we could have combined economy with calculated offensive action and not concentrated on blind aggression.[6]

Historians have commented on Trenchard's "insatiable appetite" for new pilots that overstretched an already inadequate training program and his "unique single-mindedness bordering on stubbornness" that ensured his reputation as an uncaring commander who "threw away the lives of his men." Others have described Trenchard's driving insistence on the constant offensive as a harsh, even cruel policy that undermined morale. While it can be difficult to build a clear picture of Trenchard's views on airpower, some authors have conflated Trenchard's policies with his personality, concluding that the RFC's aggressive spirit was simply an extension of his relentless drive and pugnacious character—stubborn stupidity become dogma. "His ruthless driving spirit, and his inflexible faith in the offensive, were to reduce British air strategy to wasteful dogmatism."[7] However, there were good reasons for the strategy pursued by the RFC; moreover, it can be argued that the protection afforded to artillery cooperation machines more than justified the human and matériel cost of doing so. This is not to say that Trenchard's policies were invariably correct or that his views on airpower were always sound, but warfare involves painful trade-offs, and it is all too easy to blame a commander for choosing the least bad option or to forget that there was no previous experience to guide their decision-making.

Two interrelated factors constrained the development of British airpower in World War I: flying training and engine power. The rapid expansion of the RFC left its training organization struggling to provide adequate numbers of new pilots and observers. Unlike the French and Germans, who had established large pre-war training organizations that could be readily expanded to meet increased demand, the RFC had relied on an informal mixture of civilian and military schools, with much of the advanced training done by the front line. When all the RFC's squadrons were deployed to France on the outbreak of war, an entirely new training system had to be created—the CFS could only meet a fraction of the demand. It would take a further three years to develop a robust and effective organization with the required capacity. In the summer of 1916, pilots with fifteen hours of solo experience were being sent to France (this was raised to between twenty and twenty-eight hours shortly afterward).[8] Observers were given even less time to learn their skills. By early 1918, no pilot arrived in France with less than eighty hours of solo experience, including attendance at specialist schools in air fighting, aerial gunnery, navigation, and bomb-dropping. Higham writes that this changed when Sykes became CAS, but the transformation had taken place the previous year, initially under Charlton and then under Salmond's leadership.[9]

Even so, the training system struggled to meet the RFC's needs—a situation exacerbated by the technical superiority enjoyed by the Luftstreitkräfte. The British pre-war aeroengine industry had been almost nonexistent, and while new types were introduced, many were based on copies of German engines or were licensed French designs. Indeed, 30 percent of the engines used by the RFC during the war were purchased from overseas (largely France). These differences were most noticeable in fighter aircraft, where German engines offered better performance (top speed, rate of climb, operating ceiling, etc.) and hence a significant advantage in air combat. For much of the war the RFC had to fight for air superiority with inferior machines, which resulted in higher casualty rates, a loss of experience, and a constant need for replacement pilots. While employing more machines partially offset the RFC's technical disadvantage (quantity has a quality of its own, as long as the performance gap is not too wide), this further increased the requirement for pilots. Ideally, the RFC should have built its front line around the training system. Instead, the training system had to be built around the front line and was constantly juggling time and quality to meet demand. There was no easy answer to these problems—the air war could not be paused. As a result, manpower and engine supply issues would constrain the development of British airpower until the end of the war.[10]

Doctrine, the set of beliefs that govern an organization and its operations, is the product of a dynamic process that establishes policy based on a mixture of experience (what has been done), opportunity (what can be done), and imagination (what might be done).[11] Before 1914, there was little experience or opportunity for military aviation, but a great deal of imagination about what it could achieve. Airpower doctrine did not exist—as a unified body of thought—beyond general principles. There was certainly no agreement between the public, politicians, and generals about how aircraft might be employed in wartime. In Britain, the RFC Training Manual (Part II), first issued in draft form in January 1914, included a chapter (some thirty pages) on the employment of aircraft in war that focused on reconnaissance as the RFC's primary task.[12] British airpower doctrine evolved rapidly during the war, but it was an incremental process that produced policies based on experience and an emerging understanding of airpower principles.[13]

The RFC's offensive strategy was not an aerial version of the French army's *attaque à outrance*, or an example of Edwardian martial culture driven by the idea of the decisive battle (although both have been suggested); rather, it reflected a conceptual view on the nature of air warfare. It is certainly true that Trenchard's embrace of the offensive spirit was welcomed by Haig, but this was not the critical factor.[14] It should also be noted that the RFC's offensive strategy was not Trenchard's invention, he merely refined an existing policy first codified by Brancker, who wrote in December 1915 that "every effort must be made to obtain superiority in the air as early as possible and, once gained, to keep it.... There must be no cessation of effort ... until the enemy machines are driven from their element altogether and command of the air is complete."[15] GHQ had issued guidance to the RFC squadrons as early as January 1915 that included the statement "It is a general rule that hostile aircraft should be attacked wherever met with."[16] During 1914, 80 percent of all British airmen casualties (missing, killed, or taken prisoner) took place east of the lines. This rose to 83 percent in 1915, falling back slightly in 1916 (78 percent) and 1917 (79 percent), before rising again in 1918 (84 percent). For Henderson as well as for Trenchard and Salmond, Britain's air war lay in the enemy's battlespace.[17]

While a commitment to the offensive provided the foundation for Trenchard's airpower thinking, the most significant influence was the French air service, as he readily acknowledged: "The development of aerial methods especially in the case of aerial fighting owes a very great deal to French thought and initiative and we have based our tactics largely on their teaching."[18] Prior to October 1915, British airmen had not engaged seriously with their French counterparts, other than exchanging information, notably on artillery cooperation and aerial photography. Trenchard's appointment, and the arrival of Commandant Paul du Peuty as directeur l'aviation of the 10th Army (the most northerly of the French armies), transformed the situation.[19] Du Peuty was a small, quick, lively man who made friends easily. He was a skilled pilot who had seen air combat, whereas Trenchard was not a good pilot and never flew himself. Against the odds, Trenchard and du Peuty proved to be kindred spirits, restless, single-minded, and remorseless in their determination to defeat the enemy. Neither man spoke the other's language, but with the aid of occasional promptings from Baring, they enjoyed animated conversations.

Their discussions would result in the RFC adopting the policy of the "strategic air offensive."[20]

The Battle of Loos (25 September to 8 October 1915) was the first fought under Trenchard's command. More importantly, it was the last time the RFC employed defensive tactics. Prior to the Trenchard–du Peuty conversations, the RFC had experimented with various ways to achieve local air superiority. Henderson had initially employed "fighters" to circle specific parts of the battle area. Later, individual aircraft were stationed on or near the lines to protect army cooperation aircraft—but neither technique proved effective. At Loos, a barrage of fighters was deployed to keep enemy aircraft away from the battle area. It proved no more effective than previous techniques.

On a more positive note, Loos witnessed the RFC's first attempts to work more closely with the infantry and to attack enemy trenches. Both initiatives were introduced following conferences chaired by Trenchard. Another innovation was an Anglo-French bombing program directed at the rail network in the German rear area.[21] Although this was unsuccessful in preventing the movement of German reserves, it represented the first real attempt to use airpower to shape the battlefield. What was lacking, however, was any concentration of effort. The RFC simply didn't have the resources, even on a narrow front, to properly support the BEF's assault.[22]

After the battle, Brooke-Popham and Baring visited du Peuty's headquarters to discuss future collaboration. One of the outcomes was a decision to appoint exchange officers in their respective headquarters. Trenchard selected Captain Reginald Cooper, who had previously served in the Diplomatic Service and spoke good French and Italian.[23] His opposite number at HQ RFC was Captain Gilbert Artaud de la Ferriere. With du Peuty's encouragement, Cooper visited the Verdun front in March 1916. His subsequent report, together with documents provided by du Peuty, dramatically changed Trenchard's thinking about the nature of airpower.[24] Trenchard concluded that defensive tactics (in the form of barrages, standing patrols, or close escort) were doomed to fail and that only a constant offensive conducted on a major scale, rather than as a minor tactic, could achieve air superiority. In Brooke-Popham's opinion, "although we realised the need for air fighting and for the offensive as early as 1912, it was Trenchard who really carried this through to its logical conclusion."[25]

Trenchard decided that the RFC would employ this new approach in supporting the BEF's 1916 offensive, the first major battle under Haig's command. Conscious that success would require a maximum effort, he worked closely with Brancker to increase the number of squadrons in France and improve the RFC's capabilities in artillery cooperation, photography, infantry contact patrols, and air fighting (including creating the RFC's first dedicated fighter squadrons).[26] During the Battle of the Somme (1 July to 18 November 1916) the RFC was able to deploy nearly three times as many airplanes as it had at Loos. Much has been made of the fact that the newly arrived squadrons had had limited training, but Trenchard believed that the sheer weight of the RFC's effort would compensate for a lack of experience. In this, he was proved correct, ensuring "an almost undisputed superiority in the air" and reducing the Luftstreitkräfte (in the words of the Reichsarchiv) "to helplessness against the massed operation of enemy squadrons."[27] It would be wrong, however, to assume that Trenchard was willing to risk lives by accepting poorly trained aircrew. At his direction, Festing had authorized the return to Home Establishment of any recently arrived pilots who were identified as insufficiently trained. Trenchard also demanded that the training system now include air fighting in their syllabus.[28]

While the Somme is remembered for the huge losses suffered by the BEF, the RFC enjoyed outstanding success—at least for the first two months of fighting.[29] At the end of August, the Germans began to contest air superiority more effectively—bringing in aviation units from the Verdun sector and creating their own dedicated fighter squadrons (Jagdstaffeln) equipped with large numbers of advanced machines. RFC losses increased rapidly, as did the effectiveness of German artillery cooperation, contact patrols, and reconnaissance activities. By the end of the battle, the RFC had lost 638 machines, while the Germans had only lost around 300. But the results were not so one-sided as it appears. The RFC flew much more intensively than the Luftstreitkräfte (one RFC artillery cooperation unit flew two and half times the rate of its German counterpart). When losses are adjusted for operational effort, the difference is less marked (see appendix B).[30] More importantly, Trenchard's strategy had allowed the RFC to provide continuous support to the BEF, particularly in artillery cooperation, although the bombing of key railway stations had to be paused because of heavy losses.[31]

While the offensive was still underway, Trenchard produced a short memorandum on the rationale behind the RFC's tactics and the implications for future air policy. By any measure it was a remarkable document, inasmuch as it revealed a commander's thinking while the battle was still in progress. It was prompted by criticism at home (in Parliament and by some members of the Army Council) about the RFC's high losses. As Game was less than six months in post, the drafting fell to Baring, although the tone is 100 percent Trenchardian.[32] Written in a conversational style, the document described the purpose and rationale of the offensive strategy and considered what might transpire should the Germans follow the RFC's lead. It argued that the large numbers of German fighters, which gathered to fight the RFC's "relentless and incessant offensive," was an indication of a defensive mentality.

One critic has criticized Trenchard for believing "that the concentration of German fighters in large formations over their own territory was the reaction of an enemy gradually being beaten down rather than the efficient organization of a numerically inferior air force supporting an army on the defensive."[33] This misses Trenchard's point, which was that the RFC's strategy had prevented the Luftstreitkräfte from taking the offensive. He did not know it at the time, but none of the German attack squadrons (kampfgeschwader) brought up from Verdun could be used for day bombing operations "owing to the extremely difficult tactical situation in the air"; they all had to be employed as close escort for artillery cooperation and reconnaissance machines. Ultimately, these units were converted into dedicated protection flights (Schutzstaffeln).[34] Trenchard's greatest concern was not the growing strength of the enemy's air defenses but the possibility that the Luftstreitkräfte would use their technical superiority to take the offensive. Baring concluded his chapter on the Somme by noting that the Germans, "both by the rise of a new leader and the construction of new types of machines, did change their policy for an aggressive, and a very effectually aggressive one."[35]

The "new leader" was General Ernst von Hoeppner, appointed in October 1916 as part of a major reorganization of the Luftstreitkräfte intended to rectify the serious shortcomings revealed during the Somme fighting. Hoeppner's role was similar to Henderson's (as DGMA): it excluded operational control of the field aviation units, which remained with the field armies. He brought a new focus, however, reinvigorating German air defenses and improving training for artillery cooperation and infantry contact patrols. The impact of these advances was heightened by the technical superiority of the new German fighters and the concurrent decision to drop the policy of allocating aviation units uniformly and instead to concentrate them on the main battle fronts.

Haig's next major offensive was at Arras, where the RFC faced a far stronger enemy with improved tactics and superior equipment. Trenchard had been promised aircraft with better performance, but not before the offensive opened, and he had to fight the battle as best he could. He had the courage and honesty to tell his airmen what lay in store for them:

> I know that your machines are old in type and outclassed by the enemy's latest fighters. . . . I have worked and am continuing to work to hurry on the new machines which are being produced to replace those which you are using now. . . . In the few days that lie ahead there is going to be a battle and our aeroplanes will help largely to sway the issue with our forces on the ground. That is why I have come to see you today, to tell you of the impending attack, and to ask you to carry on and do your very best.[36]

Losses in men and machines were extremely heavy, but the RFC was still able to perform its vital artillery cooperation work in neutralizing enemy batteries and disrupting counterattacks. Hoeppner celebrated the success of his fighter pilots, but he acknowledged that the Luftstreitkräfte had been criticized for failing to support the German ground defenses.[37]

Trenchard was not resigned to the advantages enjoyed by the Germans and repeatedly urged the War Office to provide more and better machines.[38] As early as February 1916, he sent Henderson detailed operational requirements for several types of new machines. It was these designs that allowed the RFC to contest air superiority from the summer of 1917. At best, however, such improvements provided brief parity before more advanced German fighters were introduced. Unable to rely on technical superiority, the RFC's offensive strategy offered the only means to protect the critical work of the corps squadrons. This proved increasingly successful in shielding artillery cooperation machines from air attack.[39] As a result, losses from air combat fell by more than half between 1917 and 1918 (see appendix C).[40]

Notwithstanding German technical superiority, the RFC's contribution to the BEF's offensives in 1917 far exceeded that of the Somme. As Hoeppner noted, "By committing his air force en masse from the start, he [Trenchard] generally succeeded in driving back our aerial observation and diminishing the force of resistance of the German infantry during the severe struggle it had to sustain."[41] Nowhere was this more evident than in the efforts to help stem the 1918 German spring offensive. Unlike the French air service, where fighters were strictly forbidden from attacking ground targets, British fighters conducted near-continuous low-level attacks against the advancing Germans. RAF casualties on the Western Front (between April and November 1918) exceeded the total losses suffered by the RFC over the previous four years, yet these losses have not attracted the same level of criticism. The complaints leveled at Trenchard's offensive strategy appear to have had more to do with the failure of the BEF's ground offensives in 1916 and 1917 than with failure in the air.[42]

Trenchard's concerns about the criticism directed at the RFC's offensive strategy did not end with his September 1916 memorandum. The latter has been described as an enduring summary of the basic principles of air strategy, but it was aimed at informing decision-makers in Whitehall rather than setting doctrine.[43] This would have to wait until March 1917, when HQ RFC issued an expanded version of Trenchard's memorandum, titled *Fighting in the Air*. This short booklet was written by Game (at Trenchard's direction) and described the rationale for, and methods of, air fighting.[44] Unlike similar French and German documents, it bore no security or handling markings. Trenchard intended that *Fighting in the Air* should be read by as wide an audience as possible (10,000 copies were printed, and a further 10,000 of the 1918 edition). This included the wider BEF, where the lack of visible RFC machines had led to criticism that more should be done to protect the infantry; indeed, Trenchard had had to write to his fellow generals explaining that the RFC conducted wide-ranging offensive operations continuously throughout the day, from daylight to dusk, "attacking and driving back enemy aeroplanes as far from our own front lines as possible. This work is, and must be, carried out well behind the enemy's lines in order to relieve the pressure on the lines."[45] Baring played an important part in communicating the airpower message. He energetically lobbied his friends and contacts in England about the RFC's contribution to the war, but his most important contribution was in providing Trenchard with unvarnished feedback from the front line.[46] During the first week of "Bloody April," when Trenchard was laid up with bronchitis (after a bout of German measles), Baring was sent on his own to visit the squadrons to report on their morale. The next day, accompanied by a barely fit Trenchard, they visited a further eleven squadrons, where Trenchard spoke with all the pilots. It is not difficult to see Baring's influence in this spontaneous decision.

Some of the criticism faced by Trenchard after the war was driven by a belief that German airpower had shown a more rational and practical direction, but the allegation that escort duties had been replaced by offensive patrols, because Trenchard did not believe the former were sufficiently aggressive, ignored the practical difficulties involved in using fighters for close escort—a problem that the Luftstreitkräfte also encountered.[47] Another critic claimed that the Germans were responsible for almost all the major innovations on the Western Front and that the RFC lacked similar imagination, intimating that Trenchard had had to work hard to influence historians in presenting a positive view of the RFC's achievements.[48] While there was much to commend in the way the Luftstreitkräfte operated, it suffered from serious flaws. The lack of any central aviation staff at GHQ, and the absence of an aviation headquarters at army level, meant that there was little coordination or sharing of best practice until October 1916.[49] Although the German air defenses at Verdun had found that barrage flights were ineffective, the same technique was still in use five months later at the Somme.[50]

It has also been asserted that the Luftstreitkräfte managed to undertake artillery and reconnaissance tasks without the same level of effort as the RFC (or the same losses), but the picture is more complex than is suggested. German artillery cooperation was generally effective in the defensive battle, when aircraft were operating over familiar territory (although deficiencies were revealed at Arras and Third Ypres, which Hoeppner attributed to a failure by the artillery to understand air service capabilities), but they struggled to provide the same level of support during the German offensives in 1918, when the specialist ground attack units also failed to have the expected impact. By contrast, it was low-flying RFC/RAF fighter aircraft, operating in the ground attack role, that helped slow the German advance, rather than low-flying

German aircraft hastening the BEF's retreat. Indeed, German aircraft were largely absent from the ground battle after the first few days of the offensive. One RFC pilot described how they constantly attacked the advancing German columns against very little antiaircraft fire, with no interference from German fighters, and they saw only one German aircraft in four days of heavy fighting: "Our air superiority was in truth air supremacy." A German postwar analysis concluded that high casualties, supply difficulties, poor liaison, and dissipation of effort (to meet infantry appeals for air support) were responsible for the poor results.[51]

The tactics of the Luftstreitkräfte differed in important ways from those of the RFC, but there were also similarities. Instructions on the support to be provided to the field armies, issued by Hoeppner in May 1917, limited the role of the Jagdstaffeln to fighting enemy aircraft and attacking balloons. Their main task was the destruction of artillery cooperation machines. Fighter aircraft were permitted to carry out ground strafing, but they were not to carry out bombing.[52] Unlike the RFC, the bulk of German aviation units were placed under the tactical control of armies and divisions rather than under the control of a separate aviation headquarters. Another significant difference was the attitude toward operational tempo. The Luftstreitkräfte believed that it was impracticable for squadrons to operate at a high tempo for an extended period. Logistic constraints and crew morale meant that "it was even more necessary to reduce the operational tempo of flying units during quiet periods. Some personnel and equipment losses can be replaced but general depletion or exhaustion cannot be corrected." It was also stated that it was not possible to hold units in reserve for a rest period, although the RFC did rest units that had suffered badly from combat attrition.[53]

On the other hand, both air forces regarded command of the air as the precondition for their operations. It has been said that the Germans never shared the view that fighting aircraft could only be effective in an offensive role, but instructions issued to the Jagdstaffeln in October 1917 made clear that fighter aircraft were not suited to defensive actions.[54] While the Luftstreitkräfte did not pursue an offensive strategy as such, they were committed to meeting large enemy aerial forces with equally strong forces, noting that air superiority, once lost, could be regained only at a high cost. It is quite possible that Hoeppner would have pursued a more aggressive aerial policy had he been provided with the same level of resources as the Allied air services.[55]

Given that so much about airpower was unknown, or at least untested, during World War I, it is not surprising that some of Trenchard's policies were flawed or too far ahead of their time; however, there is no common thread to the criticism they have attracted, some of which is contradictory. Trenchard (like many others) had an exaggerated view of the power of aerial bombardment, both the physical effects and the psychological. Chamier was dismissive of the RFC's bombing efforts, which he felt were spread across too wide a range of targets: "It does not appear that air headquarters had fully grasped the power, or lack of power, of the bomb."[56] On the other hand, Charlton felt that Trenchard had been too subservient to Haig and had failed to exploit airpower's full potential (strategic bombing): "On the Western Front, where, after all, the war was fought and won, we adopted a systematic use of aircraft, and imposed it on our enemy, which produced an air-lock above similar to the trench-lock below." He acknowledged that the RFC had been highly successful in serving the needs of the artillery, intelligence, and General Staff, but claimed that its senior officers were army men and their brains were "clogged with two-dimensional instincts and traditions." Groves expressed similar views, arguing that the focus on the continuous offensive had distracted the RFC from realizing the true value of strategic bombing.[57]

By contrast, Stewart believed that Trenchard had one and only one measure of merit, the casualty rate, and that he and his subordinate officers "were throwing away aircraft and lives for no distinguishable purpose." Another RFC veteran felt that the problem was organizational and that wasteful flying could have been avoided if the squadrons had been answerable to the divisional or corps staffs (contradicting Charlton's argument that the RFC was too eager to fulfill the unjustified demands of the army staffs).[58] If there is a consensus, it is that the offensive strategy was justified, but not necessarily the manner in which it was implemented—a view supported by the Canadian Official History, which, while questioning Trenchard's methods, concluded that it would have been impossible for the RFC to adopt a static, defensive posture. It was only by establishing and securing air superiority that the air arm could support the BEF.[59]

Complaints by fighter pilots that they often failed to find German aircraft were justified, but they were also inevitable. Unable to locate enemy fighters in real time (other than by observation from the ground), regular offensive patrols offered the only way to counter German airpower.[60] In 1916 (when the BEF occupied some ninety miles of front), the RFC had to sweep some 3,600 cubic miles of sky to find enemy aircraft. By 1918, this had grown to nearly 5,000 cubic miles. It is hardly surprising that patrols came back empty-handed. While it is entirely reasonable to question the "wasted" effort and high casualty rates suffered by British airmen, these cannot be properly judged without considering what was achieved and whether there were realistic alternatives. For some critics, the RFC's losses represented a grave strategic miscalculation. In their view, the fact that the Luftstreitkräfte was still functioning at the Armistice meant that Trenchard's strategy must have been a costly failure.[61]

This ignores what was happening on the ground, where the German army was increasingly overwhelmed by Allied airpower.[62] While the Luftstreitkräfte developed a highly effective fighter arm, it was neither organized for, nor experienced in, high-tempo offensive operations (see appendix B). Switching from the defensive to the offensive is never easy for an army or an air force. It demands time, training, organization, logistics, and a flexible mindset, particularly the willingness to take risks. Indeed, prior to the spring 1918 offensive, Hoeppner's chief of staff had to issue advice to unit commanders about what to expect in offensive operations and mobile warfare, as so few had any relevant experience.[63] Whereas German air support faded rapidly after the offensive opened, the RFC was able to maintain a continuous effort, weather permitting—a capability that the RAF maintained during the Hundred Days campaign, when Salmond was able to pursue an aggressive and innovative air campaign, despite rapid advances on the ground and high combat attrition. In forcing their opponents into a reactive role, Henderson, Trenchard, and Salmond not only made it more difficult for the Luftstreitkräfte to take the offensive but also prevented German fighters from achieving their primary aim—the destruction of artillery cooperation machines (see appendix C).[64]

A postwar history of the Luftstreitkräfte claimed that the opening day of the Battle of Amiens (8 August 1918), described by Ludendorff as a "black day" for the German army, was a great victory because the RAF's losses far exceeded Germany's. Heavily outnumbered, and weakened by sickness and combat losses, the Luftstreitkräfte was "awarded a victory in the air that mitigated the worst outcome for the ground forces."[65] Trenchard would not have recognized this logic. As he explained to the BEF's army commanders, "The whole value of the Royal Flying Corps lies in its cooperation with the other arms, and in the assistance it can give to the conduct of operations on the ground. Fighting in the air is not an end in itself."[66] For the RFC there could be no victory in the air without victory on the ground. Locked into a defensive air battle, the Luftstreitkräfte was constrained in the level of support it could provide to the German army and increasingly unable to interfere with the RFC's ground support operations. As Hoeppner acknowledged, "Because of their numbers and their sporting audacity, the English continued to be our most dangerous adversaries and the British Front immobilised the major part of the Luftstreitkräfte."[67] This was a considerable admission from the man who, at the start of the war, had described the RFC as "non-existent as Russian airmen."

CHAPTER 10

Transforming Warfare

ESTABLISHING A NEW MINISTRY AND UNIFYING TWO separate air services to create the world's first independent air force must rank among the most challenging military transformation programs undertaken in wartime. Unfortunately, this vaulting ambition was not matched by the enabling arrangements, which faltered in the face of uncertain political priorities and the messy process of finding suitable civilian and military leaders to meet such a challenging task. The new air minister was not the government's first (or even second) choice, while his senior military adviser had previously been one of the most vociferous opponents of the whole idea.

The circumstances surrounding the creation of the RAF are complex, even if the immediate causes are not. During the summer of 1917, the Germans resumed their air attacks on England. There were eight daylight bombing raids between May and August, and two reached the capital. The material damage was not great (less than £400,000), but civilian casualties amounted to over eight hundred killed and wounded. The political impact was considerable, coming as it did on top of the growing realization that Haig's summer offensive (Third Ypres) might not deliver the anticipated success. Asquith had been forced to resign as prime minister partly because of the failure of the 1916 Somme offensive. Lloyd George was acutely aware that he might suffer the same fate and invited General Jan Smuts, who had come to London to represent South Africa at the Imperial War Conference and had subsequently been made a member of the War Cabinet, to conduct an inquiry on how Britain's air defenses might be improved and to make recommendations on the future organization and direction of the air services.[1]

Smuts started work on 11 July and produced two reports. The first, published after little more than a week, dealt with the air defense of the London area; the second, presented to the cabinet on 17 August, advocated the creation of an air ministry and a unified air service, independent of the army and Royal Navy. The two reports should not be seen as separate pieces of work. Sir John French, who met Smuts on 19 July, declared that it was only by creating a separate air service that improvements could be made in London's air defenses.[2] Underpinning Smuts' recommendations was his view that warfare would soon be transformed by the ability to conduct a sustained aerial offensive that would bring continuous and intense pressure against the enemy's chief industrial centers: "The magnitude and significance of the transformation now in progress are not easily realised."[3]

The idea of a single air service was not new. Indeed, the original RFC, with its army and navy wings, had presaged such an arrangement, which was partly why the Royal Navy had created its own air service in July 1914. Less than a week after the first zeppelin raid on Great Britain, in January 1915, Hilaire Belloc's *Land and Water* proposed that the Allies should embark on a comprehensive and sustained aerial offensive (employing a fleet of two thousand machines) as the most effective means of shortening the war and raised the question of whether military aviation should be employed solely to support the army and navy or whether it should be able to conduct operations independently, as a service in its own right.[4] The idea of an aerial offensive soon gained the support of other influential commentators, including H. G. Wells and Grey (the former believed that 10,000 airplanes would suffice, while the latter thought 20,000 was a more realistic number). It was argued that the special nature of the air necessitated the creation of an air ministry, although Wells was skeptical that the authorities could find the courage to make the necessary changes. "I am entirely with . . . the question of a big effort to bring off a sustained aerial offensive; to anyone with any imagination it is the obvious thing for us to do now. It could be done. It could end the war and it would end it decisively. But neither our politicians nor our military authorities are prepared to attempt anything so novel."

Wells concluded, presciently, that the nation would not attempt an aerial offensive "until the Germans have tried it and made a success with it. Then and only then will it appeal to them as a rational proposition."[5]

Although a comprehensive and sustained aerial offensive was never a realistic proposition (and was quite impossible in 1915), such ideas gained popular and political support as successive offensives on the Western Front failed to achieve the desired results.[6] Meanwhile, the increasing importance of military aviation resulted in the Admiralty and the War Office having to compete for limited design and manufacturing resources. This culminated, in early 1916, in the creation of an Air Board to coordinate aircraft and aeroengine production; however, the continuing difficulty in achieving any effective prioritization between the services led Lloyd George's government to promise to create an air ministry (but not, it should be pointed out, a unified air service). No progress had been made in realizing this ambition before the German bombers returned to London.

The debate about the future organization of military aviation was not uniquely British. Similar discussions had arisen in both Germany and France, although the context was rather different. While there was considerable rivalry between the German army and navy, the German army was predominant in the military establishment. In 1913, its budget was more than three times that of the navy. Of this total, some 31 million marks was allocated to military aviation, compared to just 6 million marks for naval aviation. Over the next five years, the army budget would grow exponentially, further widening the gap with the navy. As a result, the German army dominated the aircraft procurement process.[7] Of course, there were still disagreements over budgets and priorities, but these were largely within the Army High Command or between the Army High Command and the War Ministry. A similar situation existed within the French military establishment, where, if anything, the French navy was an even more junior partner to the army. Once again, disagreements about aircraft procurement and the organization of military aviation were largely confined to the Army High Command or between the high command and the War Ministry.

In Britain, the Royal Navy had occupied a preeminent position in the defense of Britain and its empire since the previous century. The naval race with Germany had seen expenditure grow to some £46 million pounds sterling in 1913, compared to just £28 million pounds sterling spent on the British Army. Nevertheless, while the Royal Navy was the leading force in the British military establishment, it did not enjoy the same level of political and budgetary dominance exercised by the German and French army high commands. Indeed, while the Royal Navy's wartime budget grew rapidly, it was quickly outstripped by the huge expansion in army expenditure.[8] Under these circumstances, it was almost inevitable that the RFC and RNAS would argue over resources. A further difficulty was that the long-established naval procurement system proved more agile and responsive in purchasing aircraft and aeroengines than the army, which had limited experience with major equipment programs or dealing with manufacturers other than the state-owned Royal Aircraft Factory. Time and again, the army staffs found that the navy had moved faster in securing manufacturing contracts. Thus, while there was no significant pressure in Berlin or Paris to change the way that aircraft were procured and operated, the same could not be said of Whitehall, where the argument grew more intense and ever more partisan as time passed.

The precise authorship of the two reports submitted by Smuts has attracted speculation, as neither he nor the committee secretary, Major Lancelot Storr (who notionally drafted them), had any significant experience of military aviation.[9] Lloyd George was not personally involved in the process (but may well have steered Smuts in the "right" direction), suggesting that the other committee members provided the creative impetus, notably David Henderson, who had been released from his duties as DGMA to work for Smuts.[10] The speed with which the reports were completed suggests that there was limited consultation and that the drafting process was a personal rather than a collective effort. Henderson had made no secret of his support for an air ministry and the creation of a unified air service, but there were other contributors to the committee's deliberations, including Lord Cowdray, John Baird, Brancker, and Hugh Cecil.[11] Irrespective of authorship, the "Smuts Report" (as it would become known) benefited from Smuts' reputation as an astute strategist and military thinker. Well educated, highly intelligent, and a staunch supporter of the empire, Smuts had sound political instincts. Churchill regarded him as one of the empire's greatest statesmen, while French and Haig, who had fought against him in the Boer War, respected Smuts as both a leader and a soldier. Smuts' recommendations could not be readily dismissed.[12]

While the War Cabinet had acted rapidly to implement the proposals for improving London's air defenses, air reorganization was a more contentious issue. It was decided to accept the recommendations "in principle" and to appoint a committee, chaired by Smuts, to investigate and report on the arrangements necessary to amalgamate the two air services.[13] Smuts' Air Reorganisation Committee was supported by a small team attached to the Air Board, including Henderson (who was replaced as DGMA by Jack Salmond), Godfrey Paine, Rear Admiral Mark Kerr (from 2 September 1917), and Brigadier General Guy Livingston (from 18 October 1917).[14] The work was complicated and required the close cooperation of the Army and Navy Departments—which harbored considerable skepticism about the entire project. Progress relied on a series of committees (there were at least four) and multiple subcommittees. Kerr, who chaired many of the subcommittees, recalled that there were at least eighteen, discussing questions ranging from discipline to uniform and titles.[15]

Trenchard was aware of the political turmoil created by the German daylight raids, although he made light of the issue, reassuring crews tasked with bombing the zeppelin shed at Gontrode, "I would like you Gentlemen to know that I have no intention of withdrawing any squadron from France because in my opinion it does politicians good to be bombed occasionally."[16] Even so, he could not prevent two fighter squadrons being sent back from France to help defend London. Both squadrons returned within a month, but it was impossible to ignore the fact that the employment of British airpower on the Western Front was as much a political as a military question. Haig recorded that Trenchard was "much perturbed" when details of Smuts' recommendations first emerged. "Perturbed," perhaps, but not surprised, as he had learned about the likely outcome as early as 8 August, when Cecil had visited HQ RFC. According to Game, Cecil was "at present working under Smuts who is going into the question of making the air service a thing apart, like the Royal Navy and Army." Cecil had also announced that Trenchard would become the First Air Lord under the reorganization.[17]

Haig's initial reaction to the Smuts Report—based on his discussions with Trenchard—was to question whether it was realistic to seek to end the war by "devastation of enemy lands and the destruction of industrial and populous centres on a vast scale." He also expressed concern about the lack of consultation with those (by this he meant Trenchard) who had practical knowledge of long-distance bombing, and he was skeptical about whether there would really be a large surplus of machines to conduct the proposed retaliatory raids—given the consistent failure to meet previous production targets. The War Cabinet was sufficiently discomforted by the last point to ask Smuts to review the long-term aircraft program. There appears to have some prior discussion on the question, as Smuts put together a briefing note the very next day that included reports from Henderson, William Weir, Brancker, and Paine recommending an acceleration of aircraft production as well as increases in aerodrome building, recruiting, and training. Smuts also referenced a conversation with Trenchard, suggesting that all sides may have seen the War Cabinet's interest as an opportunity to increase the priority afforded to military aviation.[18] In this context, it was agreed to form a further committee, the Aerial Operations Committee (also chaired by Smuts), to determine how the competing demands for military airpower could be resolved.[19]

During the last week of September there were five night-raids on London. Casualties and damage were relatively light, but munitions production was interrupted, further increasing the clamor for immediate retaliation. The question of reprisals was given to the newly formed Air Raids Committee (again chaired by Smuts) to investigate, while Trenchard was recalled from France to discuss the potential for mounting long-range counterattacks against German towns. He advised the War Cabinet that two squadrons, with over thirty machines, would be ready to bomb targets in Lorraine and the cities of Mannheim and Stuttgart before the end of the month (assuming the weather was suitable).[20] Although Trenchard, like Haig, did not believe that the war could be won by an aerial offensive, he was not opposed to attacking German cities—where there was a military objective and where it did not weaken support to the BEF. The prime minister ended the meeting by emphasizing "the importance of making a success of the forthcoming air offensive, having regard to the effect that such a success would have on the moral of the people at home." The next day, while touring some of London's bombed districts, Lloyd George made an informal comment indicating that German towns would soon be attacked, but it was a public speech by Smuts that confirmed the government's plan for air reprisals.[21]

By now the scale of the difficulties involved in creating a separate air ministry had become a matter of serious concern, just as the government was increasingly focused on the question of retaliatory bombing. Although the proposed aerial offensive did not depend on creating an air ministry, Smuts felt that a public announcement about air reorganization was required to defend against accusations of inactivity. The War Cabinet agreed, while noting that "the time might not be right for the formation of a separate air service."[22] Cowdray thought they had decided to shelve the entire idea and said as much to Kerr, who was sufficiently concerned to write a strongly worded memo on the dangers of delay, which Cowdray promptly forwarded to the War Cabinet.[23] Kerr would claim that he had spurred the prime minister to action, but the timeline suggests otherwise. When Smuts updated the War Cabinet on 15 October 1917, he could report good progress with the enabling legislation, including the draft parliamentary bill and associated pay, discipline, and other administrative regulations. The organization and functions of an Air Council (to direct the Air Ministry) had also been agreed, but there remained a great number of details to be worked out. Because of the time involved, he was concerned that it might not be possible to create a new department during the course of the war (and, by implication, to amalgamate the two air services).[24] In the discussion that followed, it was agreed that Parliament would be informed of the intention to create an air ministry but, as it might be some time before this could be achieved, to establish a further committee (yet again under Smuts' chairmanship) to coordinate air policy issues. The War Office subsequently wrote to Haig advising him that a separate air service "cannot be formed for a period of time impossible to define."[25]

All of this was too much for Lord Alfred Milner (minister without portfolio), who berated his colleagues, pointing out that the war in the air wouldn't wait for half-hearted solutions.[26] Milner, a close friend of Smuts from their time in South Africa with a reputation as Lloyd George's "enforcer," had long advocated a single unified body for the construction, training, and employment of military aviation.[27] His intervention proved decisive, nudging the War Cabinet into accepting that an air ministry should be formed even while the details were still being worked out. Having prevaricated for two months, the War Cabinet was now of the view that "public opinion was becoming very restless in consequence of the delay in forming the ministry. It appeared desirable that steps should be taken to institute the ministry at once."[28] It may be no coincidence that twenty-two Gotha bombers had attacked Dover and the eastern outskirts of London on 30 October, causing little damage but triggering further calls for retaliation. From this moment (2 November 1917) events would move quickly: the government took just six days to introduce the required legislation in Parliament.

The immediate question for Lloyd George was who should be appointed as air minister. It had been assumed that Cowdray was the preferred candidate, but the prime minister approached Lord Northcliffe, who had only recently returned from leading a highly successful war mission to the United States. Northcliffe, together with his brother Lord Rothermere (Harold Harmsworth), had founded the *Daily Mail* in 1896 and would go on to own two-thirds of the titles on Fleet Street.[29] The *Daily Mail* had been an energetic and early supporter of British aviation, sponsoring record-breaking flights, an annual Circuit of Britain air race, and a nationwide air awareness campaign. The brothers exerted considerable influence on public opinion and had campaigned vigorously for Asquith's replacement by Lloyd George.[30] Lloyd George's choice was not without merit, therefore, while also offering the possibility of more favorable press coverage. Unfortunately, Northcliffe publicly rejected the proposal, in a letter simultaneously published in *The Times*. This was the first time Cowdray knew that the prime minister had anyone else in mind. Unsurprisingly, he promptly resigned from the Air Board, leaving Lloyd George to find a new candidate. The choice fell on Northcliffe's brother, Rothermere, reputedly at Lord Beaverbrook's (Max Aitken) suggestion.[31]

Less than a week after the second reading of the Air Force Bill, it was announced that Rothermere had been appointed as air minister. Within forty-eight hours the Air Force Bill received royal assent.[32] Although Rothermere did not have the same knowledge of aviation as his brother, he had strong opinions about his new responsibilities and was determined that the Air Council should be operating as soon as possible. He immediately wrote to the Admiralty asking that Kerr and Paine be released to fill the respective posts of deputy chief of the Air Staff and master general of personnel.[33] In these and other matters, Rothermere relied on the advice of Smuts and Milner rather than existing members of the Air Board. Indeed, he was convinced that there was huge waste in the Air Department, complaining that its swollen staff was a misappropriation of military material. He was just as skeptical about the administration of the RFC and RNAS. Beyond his determination to improve efficiency, Rothermere was consumed by the belief that German morale could, and should, be broken through aerial bombing, as he explained to Almeric Fitzroy, clerk to the Privy Council, shortly after he was appointed:

> Lord Rothermere's ideas on air reprisals are not lacking in force or comprehensiveness: he is satisfied that no adequate effect will be produced in Germany unless the thing is done on a scale which, in point of thoroughness and terror, has not hitherto been dreamed of. His intention is, for every raid upon London, absolutely to wipe out one or two large German towns, either on the Rhine or in its affluent valleys.[34]

These views had been rehearsed for much of the summer in the Harmsworth newspapers, where the government's delay in launching reprisal raids had been roundly criticized. Rothermere had already announced, at a City dinner attended by the prime minister, that "it is our duty to avenge the murder of innocent women and children." He added that "it would not be long before the many criticisms which have been levelled at the Air Ministry were silenced." Although there were some critical voices (notably several bishops), Rothermere was not out of step with government policy or, indeed, with public opinion.[35] The League of Londoners congratulated the air minister "on his outspoken, courageous and emphatic speech on the question of air raid reprisals on Germany."[36]

Trenchard realized early in the air reorganization process that he was a potential candidate to head the new air service. Derby had already requested, in a confidential and personal wire sent to Haig on 14 April 1917, that Trenchard return to London to head the RFC. Haig responded the next day, arguing that the removal of Trenchard would have a serious effect on efficiency, although he floated the idea that Trenchard might return to London while retaining command in France (as Henderson had practiced). Derby rejected the suggestion, emphasizing that "it must be Trenchard or go on as we are." Haig was insistent that "the proper place for Trenchard is in actual command of the Flying Corps in the field in France." Eventually, under continuing pressure, Haig conceded that Trenchard might return home when the current offensive ended and winter began.[37] Baring's diary and notebooks make no direct reference to these matters, although he reportedly chastised Trenchard for the way he had argued with Derby about the question during one of the latter's visits to France. The issue rumbled on for the next few months, but with the appointment of Rothermere, it became urgent. The Army Council put their weight behind Trenchard, who was by far the strongest candidate. They did not want Henderson (who was seen as too independent—hence Derby's earlier efforts to replace Henderson by Trenchard), while Brancker was regarded as lacking in judgment (and too casual in his methods). While Haig did not want to lose Trenchard, the latter's presence in London offered some assurance that the future aviation needs of the BEF would be honored.[38] For his part, Trenchard wanted to stay in France. He argued that he was not good at office work and that it was best for the efficiency of the RFC that he remained responsible for its running and for "keeping the whole of it up to the mark."[39]

The selection of the new CAS was technically the prime minister's responsibility (subject to the sovereign's approval), but he appears to have left the decision to Smuts. Early in December, Salmond wrote to say that Smuts had arranged for Henderson to take the role for six months, to be succeeded by Trenchard. In the end, it was the air minister (designate) who made the final decision and selected Trenchard. The latter's role in mounting the reprisal bombing raids in October had spared the War Cabinet embarrassment and garnered him strong political support, but he was also popular with journalists. Henry Tomlinson, who reported for the *Daily News*, claimed that "the continuously superior work of our planes on the Western Front is largely the result of General Trenchard's conception of what air warfare should be and his ability to inspire young men to carry it out." Geoffrey Robinson, editor of *The Times*, visited HQ RFC in October 1916. He praised the RFC's wonderful organization and men, writing of Trenchard that "I came away with no doubt whatever that he himself was a really remarkable man. Everyone testified to the spirit which he had infused into the Flying Corps, and I was specially struck by the generous attitude towards people who must have been thorns in his side."[40] Gustave Babin, writing for *L'Illustration*, was positively effusive:

When one considers the task accomplished by General Trenchard in the midst of battle, when one considers the conditions in which he created, from the embryonic aviation body that England possessed, in 1914, this formidable air force that we see at work today, whose daily exploits we follow with passion, in front of this proud soldier, this brilliant organizer, we are aware of finding ourselves before a personality of rare temper, before a singular force.[41]

There followed an extremely long meeting between Trenchard and Rothermere, held at the Ritz (where Rothermere occupied a suite while in London). Northcliffe was also present, together with Baird, who was destined to become the air minister's Parliamentary Private Secretary (i.e., he would represent Rothermere in the House of Commons). Over the next twelve and a half hours, Rothermere and Northcliffe attempted to persuade Trenchard to accept the post. Rothermere claimed later that Trenchard was not his choice but, rather, Weir's recommendation—based on the belief that only Trenchard could properly balance the aviation needs in France with the RAF's wider commitments. Trenchard's account makes no mention of this, only that the Harmsworth brothers endeavored to recruit him to their press campaign for the removal of Robertson and Haig. Trenchard resisted but eventually agreed, even though he felt that the plans for using airpower to end the war were misguided. Trenchard's subsequent acceptance letter was positive and supportive of the planned aerial bombing offensive. His only caveat was that it should not jeopardize the Western Front. In what would prove a prophetic warning, he expressed unease that Rothermere did not know him very well and that he had "very decided views on how to run the air service and to what extent it can and must expand."[42] Trenchard's initial opposition to creating a unified air service was neither unreasonable nor misguided. Organizational change creates uncertainty as well as opportunity. Even those who recognize the latter can worry about the consequences, or at least the timing. As Prince George, the Duke of Cambridge observed, "There have been great changes in my time—great changes. But I can say this. Every change has been made at the right time, and the right time is when you cannot help it."[43] Trenchard was of this school of thought. He did not oppose the idea of a unified air service, merely whether it needed to happen at that very moment.

Historians frequently draw a straight line between the submission of the Smuts Report and the creation of the RAF on 1 April 1918. The path was anything but straight, however. At several points it looked as if the creation of an air ministry and (hence) a unified air service would not occur. The dangers inherent in embarking on such a radical reorganization in wartime were self-evident. Trenchard thought it was too big an undertaking, but later acknowledged that Henderson's vision was right and, if the creation of an independent air force had been postponed until after the war, it might never had happened. The irony is that it was Trenchard's outstanding leadership, and the evident professionalism of HQ RFC, that offered the government the confidence that the risks could be managed—risks that were further diminished when he was appointed as the first CAS.

Why did the army and Royal Navy not object more forcefully to the entire idea? The creation of an independent air service, and a separate air ministry, represented an existential threat to the status, authority, and power of the two services. Trenchard's official biographer suggested that the army was simply buying time, hoping that the plan would collapse of its own accord. There may be some truth to this, but senior figures, notably Sir John French, were enthusiastic about mounting reprisal raids and had strongly encouraged Lloyd George to create a separate air service as soon as possible.[44] The Royal Navy had less invested in aviation, but argued forcefully to be left alone, only to accept the idea when the army failed to mount a vigorous defense of the status quo. In Germany, by contrast, when the possibility of an independent air service had been suggested (at much the same time), the idea was rejected by the navy, which argued that naval aviation was distinctly different from that on land, while the army's field commanders, unwilling to lose control of their "organic" aviation, saw little reason to press the case for a third service. There was also the anomalous position of Bavaria, which created a further barrier to unification.[45] It was not until 1935 that an independent air service was established, in the form of the Luftwaffe. There was a similar debate in France, where there was a struggle between politicians and the military and, within the military, between the engineers and the artillery for control of aviation. The creation of the Division Aérienne in 1918 saw an element of military aviation (approximately 20 percent) placed under the direct control of GQG, but the bulk of frontline units remained with the respective army and corps commanders. Even this small step was resisted by parts of the military establishment, and the idea did not survive the war. It was not until 1934 that an independent air service, L'Armée de l'Air, was established.

The BEF's army and corps commanders did not regard an independent air service with the same trepidation as their French and German counterparts did. When Haig first responded to Smuts' proposals, he expressed concern that "attached" air units (i.e., "RAF" units) "could never be quite the same as if these units belonged to the Army and looked to the other arms as their comrades and the Army authorities as their true masters." He prefaced these remarks by saying that "the air services with an army in the field are now as much part of that army as are the infantry, artillery or cavalry, and the coordination and combination of the efforts of all these services must be controlled directly by the Commanders of Armies, Corps, etc., under the supreme authority of the Commander-in-Chief."

The reality was very different: neither the armies nor the corps controlled any aspect of RFC operations. Coordination and combination occurred at GOC RFC's direction, on behalf of the CinC. This had come about through a succession of organizational changes introduced by Henderson and continued by Trenchard. This was not a conscious strategy but a series of incremental steps driven by the belief that only experienced aviation officers could direct military aviation. The creation of an operational air headquarters, the establishment of RFC wings and brigades, and the successful fight to retain ownership of the corps squadrons (and kite balloons) were part of a process that separated the management of the air war from that on the ground. Unlike in the French and German armies, where senior airmen were embedded with the major operational headquarters (division, corps, and army) and exercised direct control over frontline aviation units, the British air services were under the control of HQ RFC. Indeed, there were no RFC officers with any of the BEF's operational headquarters (including GHQ). The RFC had more liaison officers with the French air service than with the BEF. The reason there was minimal opposition from the BEF's senior commanders to Smuts' proposals was that the RFC was already operating outside their command chain, a point emphasized by Cecil when the Air Force Bill was debated in Parliament:

I do not myself imagine that there would be any substantial change in the position of the Royal Flying Corps in the field, because anyone who has happened to be in France and connected with flying matters knows that the Royal Flying Corps is already a distinct service to a degree not attained in any other part of our military forces. The general control of the corps in the field, and its general management and organisation, are as independent as they can be under the conditions.[46]

The RFC's unique position had already been noted by Gustave Babin, war correspondent for *L'illustration*: "The Royal Flying Corps enjoys a large autonomy in the army. Disciplined, dedicated collaborator of the staffs, who assume the direction of operations, it is not however subordinate to them. It has its separate organization, its personal staff, its doctrines, its methods of combat or of work."[47] The BEF had come to rely on an air arm that was already "independent" in all but name. In building a headquarters capable of successfully directing air operations on the Western Front, Trenchard had created (but not planned) the preconditions for an independent air service. As Frederick Smith, the attorney general, explained in the same debate, the development of an independent air service in wartime, when the existing services were all-powerful, could not be achieved by force, only by persuading them to agree to the sacrifices involved. Trenchard's achievement was to demonstrate to the BEF's commanders that there was no sacrifice involved.[48]

CHAPTER 11

Servant of the Statesman

WHEN TRENCHARD LEFT FRANCE FOR LONDON on the afternoon of 29 December 1917, he had every reason to be uneasy about his new appointment. He was aware of the difficulties that lay ahead but felt that it was a battle he would have to fight on his own.[1] If skepticism about the government's plans for reprisal bombing and concern at the potential impact on the Western Front was not sufficient, there was the prospect of long office hours and the implication that he was abandoning the RFC in the face of an imminent German attack. There was also the matter of his lack of staff training and previous Whitehall experience. Trenchard chose not to take his senior leadership team with him to London, other than his ADC (Charles Pelham), Baring, and Simon. This ensured the continued smooth running of HQ RFC and avoided any potential clash with the existing Air Ministry staffs; however, it would prove a fateful decision. Game, who believed he should have gone as Trenchard's deputy, was jealous of Simon's advancement, although Trenchard intended to employ Simon as a high-level troubleshooter rather than as his second-in-command:

> I have been called up twice by Simon who seems to be rapidly becoming Trenchard's right-hand man. I should not wonder if he eventually regularises Simon's position which is officially nil at present and keeps him there permanently as I *expect*. Simon told me he was prepared to give up everything and stay there if necessary. Trenchard has already cast his spell on him, as he does for everyone that works for him.[2]

Simon had been with HQ RFC for less than six months, but Trenchard judged that his extensive political connections, as a long-serving Member of Parliament (MP) and an ex–cabinet minister, could prove helpful. This was almost certainly why Hugh Cecil was also asked to join his personal staff. After the turbulent discussions at the Ritz, Trenchard anticipated a politically charged environment and prepared accordingly. With Baring, Cecil, and Simon at his side, the new CAS had a ready-made political and social network that he could, and did, exploit.[3] Earlier that month, Rothermere had appointed Lieutenant Evelyn Wrench as his private secretary. Wrench had worked in journalism for one or other of the Harmsworth brothers for the previous fourteen years before volunteering for the RFC. Rothermere had asked Wrench to find two or three other able men who knew the workings of the Air Department to act as advisers. These "young colonels" included George Philippi, Euan Rabagliati, Harry Segrave, and Robert Smith-Barry. All four were fighter pilots and had seen service in France.[4]

In surrounding himself with "insiders," Rothermere may have been motivated by a desire to supplement his knowledge of military aviation, but it also revealed an incipient hostility to an organization that he believed was run by old men more interested in their status than in winning the war. He would later describe the department as a nest of intrigue where "there were all kinds of ex-infantry officers 'gunning' for high service positions to which their qualifications by no stretch of the imagination entitled them." By contrast, Rothermere expressed boundless respect for the RFC's pilots, the "supermen" who, in his opinion, possessed perfect physique, matchless bravery, and extraordinary quickness of brain.[5] The paradox was that the RFC had by far the youngest group of senior officers in the War Office, almost all pilots, including Wrench's departmental head (Conway Jenkins), who was made a brigadier general just after his thirtieth birthday.[6] Wrench admitted that his minister's preference for listening to (if not soliciting) the views of junior officers might have horrified some of the more punctilious generals and admirals, but he argued that the success of the Harmsworth brothers was based on selecting the right young men for key positions. This was more than a difference in working methods. Rothermere was determined not to indulge the War Office's system of decision-making, which he believed blocked progress and, under the guise of "good order and discipline," denied advancement to younger and (by implication) more able officers.

The new air minister's opinions reflected the influence of Major Sir Henry Norman, a Liberal MP recruited by Lloyd George to the newly created Ministry of Munitions Inventions Department in August 1915. Norman, who had been actively involved in wireless development before the war, was also a political ally of the prime minister.[7] This brought him into renewed contact with Milner (they had both worked as journalists on the *Pall Mall Gazette*) and, through Milner, with Smuts.[8] Milner had recommended Norman to Smuts based on the former's "very strong views as to the course of action that should be followed by those directing the air policy." Norman demurred, insisting that he had no specific proposals, although he acknowledged that he had provided advice on the air defense of Paris and possessed a "good deal of information" from conversations with British and French pilots. Norman's reticence proved short-lived. Over the next few months he was in regular correspondence with Rothermere, including providing a twenty-seven-page paper titled "Notes upon Our Air Service."[9] The recommendations encompassed the management of officer promotions; the appointment of air commanders; improvements to London's air defense systems, the handling of air inventions, the rationalization of airplane and aeroengine types, flying training, and manpower ratios; and the potential for a London–Paris air mail service.

Unfortunately, the document was a mixture of informed criticism, sensible suggestions, gossip, jealousy, and ignorance.[10] The sections based on Norman's direct experience, such as the management of inventions, made important points—ones he had previously raised with Milner—but others, including the organization of flying training and the perceived failure to promote talented junior officers (in contrast to "the curious histories of some officers holding commands"), owed more to score-settling on the part of his main informant: his wife's cousin Lieutenant Colonel Euan Rabagliati, assistant commandant at CFS.[11] Norman's influence was greatly increased when he was appointed to the Air Council at the end of January—a choice strongly supported by Lloyd George, who felt that Rothermere would find him a very capable assistant. Indeed, Norman claimed to have closely studied air matters for the previous six months.[12] Norman selected Major Harry Segrave as his private secretary. The pair had first met in March 1917 during the trials of the Aerial Target—the world's first drone to fly under ground control. According to Segrave, Norman would prove to be the only man on the Air Council "who considered flying problems from the actual pilot's point of view."[13]

The bitter struggle that arose between Trenchard and Rothermere has been extensively described, but almost always from a partisan perspective. What is often missed is the immense pressure on both men. The challenge of creating a new ministry, and the world's first independent air service, would have been daunting at any time, but having to do so against the expectation that airpower could bring about the enemy's defeat placed even more weight on their shoulders. Various explanations have been offered, but in the process one or other of the protagonists is portrayed as the villain. The Official History tries to avoid providing an opinion, simply noting that there were differences in temperament and in the understanding of their respective responsibilities. Rothermere and Trenchard's supporters have each criticized the other man, painting Trenchard as out of his depth and Rothermere as inexperienced and dictatorial.[14]

There is a common assumption that the trigger for their estrangement was Rothermere's determination to mount a strategic bombing campaign. The only evidence for this is Mark Kerr's statement in his memoirs that he left the Air Council after "certain differences on matters of strategy with the Chief of the Air Staff."[15] Since Kerr had campaigned for a large bomber fleet to exact reprisals on German cities, it was unlikely that he and Trenchard saw eye to eye, but the relevant correspondence between Rothermere and the Admiralty offers no hint as to the actual reason for Kerr's departure. Had the cause been Trenchard's reluctance to mount a bombing campaign, Rothermere would certainly have said so, at the time or later. Indeed, Game feared that, after just five weeks in London, Trenchard was much too positive about the bombing of Germany, complaining that this was the last thing he would have done had he remained in France.[16] If there was an argument, it was about the choice of Kerr's successor. Rothermere preferred Wing Captain Robert Groves (deputy controller of the Technical Department) but was willing to accede to Trenchard's preference for Arthur Vyell Vyvyan (assistant director of air services).[17]

Trenchard was not opposed to bombing German cities per se, nor did he believe it was his role to obstruct government policy (although Beaverbrook claimed this was exactly what Trenchard was attempting).[18] Indeed, Trenchard was more than willing to work with Rothermere to bring an independent air service into being, irrespective of his personal views, which had been well rehearsed at their Ritz meeting. For his part, Rothermere had started to understand that a bombing offensive was not as easy to organize as had been suggested: "There are of course, a large number of persons in this country who do not realize the great difficulties of aircraft production. Those of us who are engaged in the task of developing our air resources realize, however, that the building up of a great air force is one of the most difficult tasks which any country can be asked to perform."[19] Where the two men fundamentally differed was in their understanding of leadership. Trenchard's management style was vigorous and energetic but accommodated those with alternative opinions. Rothermere was equally determined, but his extraordinary business success had persuaded him to trust his own judgment and to empower those who agreed with him. For Trenchard, leadership was about mutual respect—about the journey as much as the destination. For Rothermere, leadership was about outcomes—about the destination rather than the journey.

The Air Council was formally established on 3 January 1918. Grey, normally a harsh critic of the government, warmly welcomed the event, although he claimed it was the agitation of 1915 (in which he had played a part) that was behind this happy outcome.[20] Rothermere's choice of Trenchard to head the new air service garnered almost universal approval: "No other appointment to the post could be as good for General Trenchard is the strong man of the Flying Services and has the complete trust and confidence of all of us who have served with or under him." Even Rothermere's secretary (Wrench) wrote that "everyone thinks General Trenchard's promotion as Chief of the Air Staff is a good move."[21] Trenchard's arrival coincided with the end of

Smuts' direct involvement in the air reorganization process. Lloyd George would credit Rothermere with the work to create an independent air service, but most of the major issues had been resolved by the time the Air Council was formed. Given the considerable progress that had been made, Smuts recommended that the Air Organisation Committee be dissolved, adding that the Air Ministry could deal with the few remaining questions, as they were all at an advanced state of discussion. The War Cabinet agreed, although air reorganization was immediately back on their agenda because of Rothermere's efforts to take over the British Museum for office accommodation.[22] The proposal was leaked to the press, creating a howl of indignation and the direct intervention of Lord Curzon and the archbishop of Canterbury. The idea was quickly dropped; the excuse given was that the Air Ministry's demands might have been exaggerated and alternative locations were now available. It was, perhaps, a sign of things to come.[23]

Rothermere, a tall, young-looking, thickset man in his late forties, with fair hair and a walrus moustache, friendly handshake, and strong laugh, came to the Air Ministry with a reputation as a businessman and innovator.[24] Lloyd George certainly expected the appointment to generate better treatment from the Harmsworth newspapers, but it would be wrong to conclude he had saddled the Air Ministry with a dud. Admittedly, there were those who believed that while the new air minister knew little or nothing about airplanes, what was important was not that that he could manage his department but that he could manage the public.[25] However, Rothermere had a well-earned reputation as an organizer with a flair for figures. He was also a modest man who disliked the limelight and was without political ambition (unlike his older brother). He may have lacked Northcliffe's journalistic genius and originality of mind, but those who worked closely with him testified to his considerate and generous nature and to his willingness to take subordinates into his confidence.[26] It was said that if Rothermere had a weakness, it was in overestimating the influence of money compared to ideals. Rothermere found it difficult to adjust to working in a large government department. The bureaucracy appalled him, as did the working methods and hierarchical structure.[27]

Pending the formation of the RAF, the Air Council exercised no operational control of the RFC and RNAS, which remained with their respective departments.[28] In the interim, it focused on future programs, policy, and administration, a situation that frustrated Rothermere, who was determined to build an air service that was independent, in function as well as in name, as quickly as possible. One of his early initiatives was the creation of a separate aviation medical service. Trenchard felt that this would be less efficient than relying on the existing arrangements but did not oppose his minister in this or in other areas (such as establishing separate detention centers or a chaplains' branch) where being "independent" of the army and navy was the overriding requirement, although he complained bitterly to Haig about the waste of resources.[29] When Trenchard moved to London, it was on the basis that he would retain command in France (much as Henderson had served as both DGMA and GOC RFC), at least until the air force was formed. This arrangement had been devised to give Haig reassurance that Trenchard could return in the event of a German offensive. Derby disagreed, and within a fortnight Jack Salmond was appointed to command the RFC in France. Haig was more than annoyed and moved to compare Derby to a feather pillow that "bears the marks of the last person who has sat on him."[30] The decision was likely driven by the government's concern (shared by Smuts) that if Haig was given de facto control over the bombing effort, the squadrons involved would soon be diverted to support of the BEF. The irony is that Derby's decision would later pave the way for Trenchard's return to operational command.

Derby's change of heart may have annoyed Haig, but it gave Trenchard time to focus on more immediate issues, including the establishment of effective working relationships with the army and navy staffs. Although progress was made in this and other areas, he soon came to believe that Rothermere was more interested in competing than in collaborating. In the process, their relationship moved from wary partnership to implacable hostility. This has often been described as a clash of personalities. There is some truth to the picture, but the pair had more in common than is generally recognized. Rothermere, like Trenchard, was a self-made man who had started with little but achieved success through natural ability allied to a relentless drive. Both were the product of difficult family circumstances (Rothermere's father was an unsuccessful barrister who was perennially short of money and had a fondness for alcohol). Each abhorred publicity; both were poor public speakers; both were both good with numbers and had the ability to see through a maze of detail to the heart of an issue. Just as importantly, they were outstanding organizers and generated great loyalty and affection in their personal staffs. In some ways, they were well matched.[31]

If Trenchard expected the air minister to listen patiently to his advice and act accordingly, he was gravely mistaken. Rothermere had strong, if not fixed, views about how his department should be reorganized—ideas that owed a great deal to Norman's opinions. In the process, Rothermere came to see Trenchard as a "gargantuan joke," an inflexible man of limited intellect, hostage to the traditions of the other services, and content to see the RAF settle down into a sub-arm of the war rather than "becoming a great, independent arm destined to be the determining factor in the war." For his part, Trenchard believed that Rothermere was ill informed, badly advised, and excessively sensitive to public criticism: "Every day something arose which I had to disagree with him about."[32] Under such circumstances, an explosive outcome was probably inevitable, but the damage went well beyond what might have been imagined. Within four months, seven (out of ten) members of the Air Council had submitted their resignation.[33] To understand how this "veritable human landslide" set in, we have the benefit of several firsthand accounts, although it remains remarkable that so many senior military and civilian leaders should be willing to abandon their responsibilities in wartime. Only three months earlier, Trenchard had advised Salmond (who was having a difficult time with Rothermere), "You cannot resign in war."[34]

We know something of what the pair argued about from correspondence submitted to the War Cabinet.[35] Many of the issues appear relatively innocuous, such as the plan for the *Daily Mail* to award medals to pilots. None of these were reason enough for the Air Council to implode. The fundamental problem was that Rothermere believed he had complete authority over the Air Ministry, its staffs (both civilian and military), and its operations. Trenchard acknowledged the minister's executive authority but believed that he managed the military staffs and their activities. Such issues are never entirely clear-cut and require a degree of compromise by the department's political and military heads; indeed, this was supposedly one of the functions of the Air Council. Unfortunately, neither Rothermere nor Trenchard was prepared to give ground, nor, would it appear, were they willing to ask anyone to adjudicate. Trenchard complained that he had little power and that Rothermere could veto any decisions.[36] In turn, Rothermere believed that the Air Ministry was rife with inefficiency and that Trenchard was obstructing the necessary changes.[37]

One of their more serious arguments was over flying training, an area that had been a constant challenge since the start of the war. Substantial improvements had taken place under Jack Salmond, who had led the Training Brigade (and later the Training Division) from the summer of 1916. Over the next eighteen months, the number of flying training units had been rapidly expanded, better training machines procured, and longer, more structured courses introduced—based on Robert Smith-Barry's "Gosport System." Smith-Barry had gained a reputation as one of Trenchard's more charismatic squadron commanders, although he was also "eccentric, wilful, daring, had a darting, incisive mind, delighted to scare others with his abrupt aerial antics and was a trial to his seniors."[38] Trenchard, who had been pestered by Smith-Barry about improving basic flying instruction, sent him to the training school at Gosport with a free hand to develop an entirely new approach. The Gosport System gave pilots greater confidence in their machines using dual controls and early exposure to techniques such as spinning. So successful were these changes that Smith-Barry was promoted to lieutenant colonel and given an expanded establishment, the School of Special Flying.[39] Buoyed by his success, Smith-Barry came to believe that the RFC could improve not only the quality but also the efficiency of its flying training by copying the French, who had established fewer but much larger establishments that integrated ground and air training in a single location.

Norman already believed that reform of the flying training system was essential, views strengthened by his conversations with Rabagliati, who had provided copies of internal Training Division directives issued by Ludlow-Hewitt (commanding the Northern Training Brigade) and Longcroft (Salmond's successor at the Training Division). Rabagliati's handwritten comments suggest that he had little respect for either officer. Rothermere had heard separately about Smith-Barry's ideas though his assistant private secretary, George Philippi, who had been Smith-Barry's adjutant at Gosport. At Rothermere's instigation, Norman met with Smith-Barry and Philippi.[40] Norman was impressed by their proposals and agreed to undertake a review of the flying training system. His subsequent report was highly critical, concluding that output was falling while casualties were growing. In his opinion, the situation was so alarming that it demanded urgent investigation.[41] Norman's conclusions were robustly rejected by the military members of the Air Council. Norman countered with further arguments, adding that the variation in providing returns about training deaths was scandalous. Paine (responsible for RAF training) disagreed, adding that no good purpose would be served in pursuing the correspondence further. Given that the British trained around 22,000 pilots during the war, compared to some 14,000 by the French, Paine's irritation with Norman was not entirely unjustified (see appendix D).

Rothermere decided to bring about change in a more direct manner. He first attempted to appoint Smith-Barry to command the Southern Training Brigade—on the basis that the incumbent (Dowding) was "no good." Rothermere was dissuaded, but in the New Year he appointed Smith-Barry to command the Northern Training Brigade. The first that Ludlow-Hewitt knew of his replacement was when he returned from a tour of inspection to find Smith-Barry installed in his office.[42] Paine was less than happy, particularly as Smith-Barry chose to conduct the brigade's business directly through Rothermere. Livingston, who got on well with Rothermere, and had worked with Salmond to improve the RFC's flying training system, felt that Rothermere had overreached himself:

> He had heard all about Smith-Barry and the Gosport system of training and, perhaps without fully understanding the other factors which should have been taken into consideration, had formed an opinion that in all probability he would be the most suitable man to command the Training Division. . . . In point of fact, in many ways he was entirely unsuitable, as many other qualities besides a genius for training pilots were required for such a command—in particular, knowledge of staff duties, power of organisation, etc., and it must be realised that Smith-Barry was a comparatively junior officer. Despite everything and everybody, Rothermere promoted Smith-Barry to brigadier-general and appointed him to the Training Division, thereby sowing the seeds of the final rupture between Trenchard and himself.[43]

Livingston might reasonably have added volatile temperament and pyromania to the list of Smith-Barry's unsuitable qualities.[44] It is not entirely clear whether Smith-Barry resigned or was sacked, but he was back at Gosport after only a few weeks, claiming that the existing system and conditions of training had rendered it impossible for him to produce satisfactory results. Longcroft was summoned to an interview with Rothermere and Norman, which quickly turned into a shouting match until Paine intervened. Not long afterward, Longcroft was posted to France, although Trenchard attempted to stop the move. Rothermere did not regard this as the end of the matter and, with Norman and Philippi's encouragement, continued his efforts to find a major role for Smith-Barry. "I think we've got 'em by the short hairs at last. . . . Godfrey Paine and Rothermere are hard at it next door. Shouting like the devil. [Sir Henry] Norman's running you for all you're worth this week for the All-Highest Job."[45]

By and large, these controversies stayed within the Air Ministry and were known to no more than a handful of staff. A more serious and far-reaching dispute arose from Rothermere's offer to provide the Royal Navy with four thousand aircraft for coastal patrol work. Trenchard complained that he had not been consulted, while Rothermere alleged that Trenchard had ordered the wrong type of machine.[46] The circumstances are more complex than either party was willing to admit. At this stage of the war, over 60 percent of British shipping losses were taking place within ten miles of the coast. The possibility of using land-based aircraft for antisubmarine patrols (based on French experience) had been suggested by Robert Groves in a paper forwarded by Weir to Trenchard (copied to both Rothermere and Churchill).[47] Groves had concluded that there were sufficient surplus landplanes to provide three to four thousand machines for the task within a couple of months. Rothermere took this at face value, even though Weir warned that the paper dealt with the possibilities "in much too wholesale a fashion." Trenchard was skeptical about the analysis but agreed to examine what might be done, while noting that stopping production of seaplanes in favor of landplanes would take time to achieve.[48] Unfortunately, Rothermere had already seized on the idea and advised the Admiralty that four thousand machines would soon be available.

The matter came to a head at the next Air Council meeting, although the minutes simply recorded that "some discussion followed in which doubt was thrown on the accuracy of the statements in the report."[49] When Sir Eric

Geddes (First Lord of the Admiralty) learned of the Air Ministry's concerns, he wrote to Rothermere that "it is a little disturbing to hear that General Trenchard is not quite so clear on the point as you were," precipitating a major row that led, within twenty-four hours, to Trenchard's resignation.[50] Geddes should have known that he was driving a wedge between Rothermere and Trenchard, but given that he had just sent an optimistic briefing note to the War Cabinet on the subject of land-based antisubmarine patrols, he may have been motivated by embarrassment as much as by malice.

It should be mentioned that Trenchard had little difficulty with the idea of using landplanes for antisubmarine patrols; indeed, Weir would write to Churchill that "General Trenchard has taken the matter up energetically." This did not prevent Rothermere from telling the War Cabinet quite the opposite. At Trenchard's direction two flights were immediately allocated to test the concept on Tyneside. This proved successful, and a further thirty-two flights were soon deployed at other coastal locations.[51] The Admiralty eventually conceded that only 180 machines could be made available rather than the 4,000 machines identified by Groves.[52] Rothermere was correct about the potential for land-based antisubmarine patrols, but grossly exaggerated the resources available. His unilateral decision to commit the Air Ministry to a new role without consulting his senior operational adviser reinforced Trenchard's view that the air minister preferred to listen to those "without responsibility in decisions concerning operations and the means of carrying them out."[53]

In Baird's view, Norman was the cause of many of Rothermere's problems. Norman had a good understanding of technology and, through his work with the Ministry of Munitions, a knowledge of current air inventions as well as a familiarity with French methods and innovations, but he was not one to back away from a fight—as his involvement in the 1912 Marconi scandal demonstrated. Norman was regarded as an energetic, insightful, and influential journalist, but some of his colleagues viewed him as brash and ambitious: one referred to him as a "damned ruffian" and another as a "scoundrel."[54] Norman saw himself as something of a political fixer and was determined to "weed out inefficiencies and undesirables" within the Air Ministry. Unfortunately, he had no formal role, which caused Baird to complain that "there really was no place for an irresponsible politician with no definite duties."[55] Trenchard may also have come to this view, as he pressed hard for Norman to chair the Aerodromes Committee (responsible for acquiring and developing new landing grounds), a task that Norman reluctantly accepted, but only when it was widened to include a review of flying training accidents.

None of this diminished Norman's determination to get involved in wider policy issues, notably the future development program (detailing the numbers and types of machines and engines needed to meet the RAF's requirement up to June 1919).[56] Reacting to Trenchard's proposal to include up to five hundred R.E.8 aircraft to keep the RAF's corps squadrons up to strength (as a result of production delays with the Bristol Fighter), Norman argued that a decision should be delayed, as it was such a complex matter. Trenchard, supported by Baird, pointed out that the program was the result of months of thought and deliberation, involving both Brancker and Weir's staffs. The program was approved without further debate.[57] Norman was not content to stay silent and produced a memorandum that accused the military members of scandalous behavior in approving a program that would delay the strategic bombing offensive. In this respect, he was, if anything, more ambitious than either Rothermere or Kerr. In a detailed scheme submitted on 25 March 1918, Norman described a campaign that would deliver twenty tons of bombs hourly for ten consecutive hours against selected German cities—bringing victory in sight within a month.[58] Trenchard had already advised that far fewer long-distance bombing squadrons would be available than had been forecast at the time of the Smuts Report, estimating that there would be no more than thirty-one squadrons by the end of October 1918, on the basis that "it is far better to know what can really be done so as to be able to count on it than to indulge in more generous estimates which cannot be realised." Churchill had robustly challenged Trenchard's pessimistic assessment, only for Weir and his staff to confirm the analysis.[59]

As it turned out, even Trenchard's assessment proved optimistic—just nine squadrons were available to bomb Germany by the Armistice, and rather than deliver 200 tons in a single attack, they were lucky to be able to achieve this in an entire month. Norman's plan for mounting a major bombing offensive in 1918 was simply magical thinking. It is little surprise that Trenchard believed that those who advocated such ambitious plans were "quite off their heads." Baring was already deeply skeptical about the contribution of Northcliffe and Rothermere to Britain's military effort, which he described as "Harmsworthia"—"war hysteria with a touch of megalomania. The something-must-be-done attitude, followed by suggesting something quasi-insane."[60]

Following an exchange of correspondence with Rothermere, Trenchard submitted his resignation on 19 March 1918, forty-eight hours before the German spring offensive opened.[61] Rothermere said that he was shocked by Trenchard's decision, although it cannot have been an unwelcome surprise—he would later claim that getting rid of Trenchard was the greatest thing he had done for the RAF, as "he [Trenchard] was establishing a Kitchener regime in the Air Force and gave out quite openly to his intimates that he intended to be the autocrat of the new service. I simply waited for him and tripped him up."[62] Putting their motives to one side, it seems that neither party wanted the resignation to take place immediately. By mutual agreement, the effective date was delayed a month, by which time Rothermere indicated that he would have resigned as air minister (for personal reasons), leaving his successor to decide on how to handle Trenchard's resignation. Trenchard has been criticized for his decision to resign, even by those who might be described as supporters. They argue that it was Rothermere's right to seek advice from elsewhere. In his defense, it should be said that Trenchard also recognized this principle. As he acknowledged, writing some years later for the *New York Times*, "In a democracy, because it is a democracy, the fighting man is the servant of the statesman and strategy is profoundly affected by internal and international politics. The military chiefs are the advisors on military policy and the executives through which that policy, once decided, is put into effect."[63] The red line for Trenchard was not that Rothermere consulted others (although the "quality" of their advice greatly annoyed him) but that Rothermere didn't consult him at all. His concerns were well placed: Rothermere's preference for making unilateral decisions on operational matters, without consultation and bypassing the Air Council, would soon precipitate his own resignation.

Reflecting on these events over a century later, another explanation emerges—the possibility of mutual misunderstanding. In recruiting Cecil and Simon, Trenchard believed that he was strengthening his hand for the political arguments that he would face. In fact, Rothermere was largely focused on achieving operational improvements. Trenchard's "Praetorian Guard" of politicians unsettled the air minister, who had few political friends. From Rothermere's perspective, such appointments should not have been made, as they undermined his position and spread a "false and wrong atmosphere."[64] On the other hand, in recruiting his "young colonels," Rothermere believed that he was preparing for the technical arguments that he would need to master. Rothermere's "experts" directly challenged Trenchard, who did not enjoy the same staff support that he had known in France.[65] In effect, the air minister and his chief of staff undermined each other in a misguided effort to strengthen their respective positions. While a successful relationship between soldiers and politicians requires a mutual understanding, this does not extend to playing each other's role.

What was Baring's contribution to all of this? We have little evidence, although Baring's particular skills lay in smoothing commander-to-commander and commander-to-subordinate rather than subordinate-to-commander relationships. Trenchard's dealings with Haig and Henderson had been entirely respectful, even on the rare occasions when they disagreed. The violent arguments with Rothermere represented new territory for both Trenchard and Baring. Upward mediation is extremely difficult, if not impossible—unless there is a relationship to be exploited. The only route to achieving some form of understanding between Trenchard and Rothermere would have been through mutual friends (there were none) or their respective personal staffs (Wrench, Philippi, and Segrave). Baring had previously worked with Segrave, but he may not have known Philippi.[66] There is no evidence that Baring knew Wrench (either socially or from his pre-war journalism days). The real difficulty was that Philippi was the problem rather than the solution, working actively with Smith-Barry to have his training plans implemented and, in the process, to remove Trenchard as an obstacle to progress. Rather than facilitating the smooth running of the department, Rothermere's outer office worked actively to create disharmony.[67]

Even if Baring did not mediate, did Trenchard seek his advice? The evidence suggests not. Arnold Bennett dined with Baring on the evening of 10 April and recorded their conversation. There is no hint that Trenchard (whom Baring praised effusively) was about to resign.[68] Marson, in reviewing the resignation correspondence many years later, could detect no sign of Baring's hand—the poor grammar was all Trenchard's work. When Baring and Cecil did find out, they thought that Trenchard had been outmaneuvered by Rothermere and that the resignation had been a tactical error. One person with whom Trenchard did share his concerns was Robertson, the previous Chief of the Imperial General Staff (CIGS), whose only comment was he (Trenchard) should do what his own conscience told him.[69] In this question of immense personal and professional significance Trenchard was either unwilling or unable to talk with a man that described as his only friend.[70] It reveals a barrier that was absent in France, where proximity and shared experience had forced them together. London was a larger, less intimate stage where Baring was just one of many staff officers. We catch glimpses of him from what others have written, but there are no substantial accounts.[71] Baring's place as gatekeeper was diminished, as was his role as confidant and interlocutor. There are other clues that indicate a greater distance between the two men. Baring was a prodigious letter writer, but none of his surviving correspondence covers this period, while *R.F.C. H.Q.* skips the entire episode. Baring's notebook entries stop in December 1917, only to resume in May 1918, when he returned to France. There is a similar gap in Baring's war diary. The absence of letters or diary entries may be a coincidence, but the overall impression is that Baring—the acute observer of human nature, emotion, and events—had nothing to write about or, quite possibly, had no wish to record events over which he had no control or any direct involvement.

CHAPTER 12

Resignation

ROTHERMERE KEPT THE NEWS OF TRENCHARD'S resignation to himself for nearly a month. He did not share it with any other member of the Air Council (other than Norman). Lloyd George appears to have found out on 10 April, when Rothermere tabled a memorandum at that day's War Cabinet proposing changes at the Air Ministry. The note had not been circulated in advance and was read to the meeting by the prime minister.[1] Rothermere described the absence of strategic planning in the RAF, the inefficient and ineffective flying training system, the lack of business experience in managing equipment, the ineffectual way inventions were managed, and the wasteful employment of manpower (all themes that Norman had championed). He reserved his harshest remarks, however, for "those officers that lacked the necessary elasticity of mind and were holding back the development of the Air Service," adding that he had accepted Trenchard's resignation and proposed to appoint Sykes in his place. He also intended to remove responsibility for flying training from Paine and appoint Smith-Barry (as a major general) to the new post of director of training.[2]

While Lloyd George may have been surprised by the turn of events, Milner should not have been. Norman had discussed the whole situation with him five days earlier; indeed, it was Milner who had suggested that the reorganization scheme, based on the changes in personnel proposed by Rothermere, should be submitted directly to the prime minister for his approval. Milner strongly supported the creation of a strategic council and the execution of a large-scale air offensive against German towns (while stressing the need to find ways to improve London's air defenses). It was Milner who arranged with Sir Henry Wilson (Robertson's successor as CIGS) for Sykes to return from Paris for an interview with Rothermere on the following Monday (8 April 1918).[3] Notwithstanding Milner's advance knowledge, the War Cabinet's immediate reaction was one of surprise, dispatching Smuts (who continued to deal with air matters on their behalf) to see Rothermere. The timing could not have been worse. The government had already been heavily criticized for the sacking of the chief of the Naval Staff (John Jellicoe) on 24 December 1917, followed by the CIGS (Robertson) on 18 February 1918.[4] Now, with a desperate military situation in France—underscored by Haig's "Our Backs to the Wall" order, published just three days later—a third service chief was about to depart, all within three months and all apparently because of disagreements with government ministers. Rothermere's delay, and his failure to think through the wider implications of Trenchard's resignation, had made a bad situation worse.[5] The next day Smuts lunched with Sir Maurice Hankey and Hugh Cecil to discuss what to do. Cecil vehemently defended Trenchard as a good man who had the confidence of the air service. According to Cecil, Rothermere had "without real knowledge and with a low standard both of manners and truthfulness" vexed Trenchard beyond endurance. Hankey thought that it was unwise to make such a change during a great battle and that whatever his faults, Trenchard had "created the greatest air force in the world."[6] Cecil also mentioned the bad blood that existed between Henderson and Sykes, which had resulted in the latter's abrupt departure from HQ RFC.

The next morning, the War Cabinet agreed in principle to all Rothermere's proposals. In the afternoon, Henderson met with Rothermere and Smuts to be told of Trenchard's resignation and Sykes' appointment as his successor. Henderson objected strongly and offered a very unfavorable opinion about Sykes. This unsettled Rothermere, who according to Smuts began to get cold feet.[7] Arnold Bennett encountered Rothermere in Beaverbrook's office and found him in a state of great agitation, "walking about, sitting down, standing up."[8] A further discussion took place that evening with the prime minister, during which it was decided that the Sykes' departure from France in 1915 needed to be investigated. Hankey spoke with Robertson and Smuts with Lieutenant General Sir Nevil Macready, the adjutant general. Robertson and Macready had been on French's staff in 1915 when the Sykes/Henderson argument blew up (Macready's son was Henderson's ADC at the time). Neither man could offer any reason that Sykes should not be appointed. Given the go-ahead by Smuts, Rothermere wrote to Trenchard accepting his resignation.[9] Sykes' appointment as CAS was announced the following day (Sunday, 14 April). Hearing the news, Henderson immediately announced that he was resigning his commission. Paine also resigned, although his resignation was later withdrawn when the Admiralty refused him permission to return to the Royal Navy.[10] Trenchard, incensed that Rothermere had broken their agreement, petitioned the War Cabinet. Hankey, caught in the middle, forwarded Trenchard's letter to Rothermere and offered him the right of reply.[11]

Rothermere appears to have been surprised by the fuss, but when the king also protested about Trenchard's removal, he took the unprecedented step of publishing an explanatory statement in his own newspapers. He also commissioned Norman to write an editorial for the *Daily Mail* applauding the choice of Sykes as Trenchard's successor. Rothermere's statement took the form of a letter to Colonel Walter Faber (a Conservative MP), repeating many of the complaints in the War Cabinet memorandum and citing a matter of "urgent importance" regarding the Home organization that he would rather not refer to.[12] Some questioned Rothermere's common sense in publicly criticizing his own department. If the air minister was not responsible for the activities of the Air Ministry, where he had been in charge for the last three months, who was responsible? Baird had to field at least one pointed question in Parliament about why there had been an increase in Air Ministry staffs when Rothermere believed that too many officers were engaged in filling out unnecessary forms.[13] The news of Trenchard's resignation was greeted by a howl of public protest (at least in the non-Harmsworth press). Belloc was scathing about what had transpired:

> It may at the outset be said without fear of contradiction that if efficiency and proven ability were the touchstone of office, the resignation of every other member of the Air Board would have been accepted before Sir Hugh Trenchard was permitted to retire. General Trenchard is perhaps the

most outstanding figure this war has produced; flying men regard him as the Nelson of the Air Service. He has that touch of genius both for command and brotherhood which made the British Fleet what it is today and bestowed immortality on Nelson.[14]

Trenchard would not have been surprised by such praise, written by one of Baring's closest friends, but it reflected a wider mood—even in those newspapers generally supportive of the government. The *Manchester Guardian* and *The Globe* both criticized the decision, while Cowdray's *Westminster Gazette* (which wielded considerable influence) argued that "the public gets a little uneasy in mind when it sees a procession of men like Lord Jellicoe, Sir William Robertson and Major-General Trenchard departing from positions in which they have won public confidence and in each case as the result of a difference of opinion with civilian chiefs." The *Daily News* was perhaps the most scathing:

> The Air Service knows nothing of politics, but when the man in whom above all men, it believes, relinquishes his job as the result of a conflict with someone with no technical knowledge, no administrative experience, no political standing (apart from that conferred by his own and his brother's ownership of newspapers), and a temperament reputed to be excitable, it draws its own conclusions.

The aviation journals were also largely hostile (only *Flight* trod a measured path). *The Aeroplane* decried the hidden hand that compelled the removal of any man who seemed to be in danger of winning the war, adding that the precious RAF combination, "so far from bringing unity, peace and efficiency, has only brought additional intrigue, disunion and discord." *Aeronautics* was equally robust: "If the public but knew it, Sir Hugh Trenchard won more battles for us than all our other generals combined." *Flying* asked, "Why have they gone? This is a question which will be anxiously asked by the officers of the Air Force, whose loyalty to their chiefs is a byword."[15] The collective surprise and anger echoed the views of many in the RAF. Longcroft, who received the news as he arrived in France to take up command of 3rd Brigade, wrote, "It is the most fatal thing that can possibly happen as far as the Flying

World is concerned at this time. The change will be absolutely criminal. Of course, he's too straight for these cursed politicians whose aim in life seems to be thinking out ways of losing the war as quickly as possible."[16]

Joynson-Hicks was the first MP to raise the matter in Parliament. Baird, replying for Rothermere, offered no statement beyond saying that

> the resignation resulted from the fact that General Trenchard took a view as to the powers and duties of the Chief of the Air Staff which the Secretary of State for the Royal Air Force could not accept. I am authorized by the Secretary of State to say that, personally, he yields to nobody in appreciation of General Trenchard's high qualities, and much regrets that a difference of opinion on a point of principle should have arisen.[17]

The following day, the correspondence between Rothermere and Trenchard was tabled at the War Cabinet.[18] In effect, both parties were able to make their case to the prime minister. The outcome was inevitable, although there were signs of growing disquiet. According to John Davidson, Bonar Law's private secretary, "the removal of Trenchard by Rothermere—for virtually it is that—has created consternation at home and disgust and the keenest sorrow in France. He is a born leader and absolutely honest. The trouble about the newspaper proprietors is that they are quite unfitted for the head of a great department." Trenchard was never going to win his private fight with Rothermere, but the public fight was far from over.[19]

Rothermere reveled in his apparent success, writing that he and Norman had had the time of their lives: "We simply rounded them up and then clubbed them remorselessly."[20] With Sykes in post, and Rothermere staying on as air minister, Trenchard was unwilling to take the matter any further. Pressed by Grey to explain his reasons for resigning, Trenchard replied, "You can understand that I cannot possibly discuss, and you will not expect me to, my resignation," before adding, in a handwritten postscript, "I very much hope that my going will not lead to discussion." This didn't prevent him from writing two days later to Philip Sassoon (for Haig's ear) explaining, "I resigned because the Secretary of State preferred any opinion except my own." His personal staff were also unwilling to keep silent, although Trenchard tried to dissuade them.[21] Cecil and Simon, senior MPs with considerable influence in their respective parties, were determined to raise the matter in Parliament. Their first attempt to secure an adjournment debate failed, when no one from the Air Ministry was available, although they did extract a more detailed explanation about Trenchard and Henderson's resignations. The pair returned to the attack on 22 April, when Bonar Law offered the possibility of a debate on a future (unspecified) date. Simon and Cecil's intervention was criticized because it was based on "private" information gained while on military service. Although neither had broken any rules, it was the custom that a serving MP did not use the House to discuss privileged military information or criticize the chain of command. As there were over 150 members of Parliament in the armed forces (largely with the army), this was potentially a serious issue. In Bonar Law's opinion, it was up to the good sense and good feeling of the member to decide when to speak on military matters. That was of little concern to either Cecil or Simon, as they had secured their main objective: the government had agreed to a debate. Two days later, determined to keep the government on the defensive, Simon forced Bonar Law to concede that Trenchard had resigned before the German offensive, dispelling the suggestion that he had abandoned the RAF at its time of greatest peril. Bonar Law also admitted that no member of the War Cabinet had spoken with Trenchard and that he (Trenchard) had not been informed that his resignation had been accepted, prior to the public announcement. The next day brought news of Rothermere's resignation as air minister.[22]

It might be assumed that the intervention of Cecil and Simon, the Tory and Liberal joined by their shared experience at HQ RFC and passionate in their admiration for Trenchard, had so alarmed the government that Rothermere had to go—sacrificed to secure parliamentary peace. Rothermere implied as much, loudly blaming Cecil and Simon for the grief that he had suffered in Parliament and in the press, demanding an official investigation.[23] There is an element of truth to this charge, which was repeated in Lloyd George's memoirs, but the fundamental reason for Rothermere's departure was Rothermere himself.[24] At some point, shortly before Bonar Law offered a debate in Parliament, Baird had found a copy of the memorandum submitted by Rothermere to the War Cabinet. Neither Brancker nor Paine (who were directly affected by the proposed changes) had been consulted about the contents, and certainly not Baird himself. Just as importantly, the claims of gross inefficiency (in the Air Ministry, in France, and in the RNAS generally) were strongly disputed, while the proposal to appoint Smith-Barry as director general of training was regarded with derision, placing an unstable man in a position of considerable responsibility.[25] Before the debate could be scheduled, Baird wrote to the prime minister expressing his disquiet and explaining that he could not support the air minister in Parliament. Baird's threatened resignation—because this was the inevitable result if Rothermere had remained in post—would have been catastrophic for the government. Baird was not specific in his complaints, but Brancker related the story in some detail at a dinner party attended by Repington: "Rothermere had written an extraordinary minute to the War Cabinet, saying what had been done and was to be done, without consulting Baird or his staff. Baird had seen a copy and found it both inaccurate and indefensible. So, he took it round to the departments concerned and found that they had not been consulted and disapproved of most of the things, as did Baird."[26]

Davidson said that the intemperate language used in the memorandum, particularly the criticism of Trenchard, drove Bonar Law to phone Rothermere and demand his resignation. Beaverbrook offers an alternative view, arguing that Rothermere, in poor health and still mourning the death of his sons (the most recent just two months earlier), had become incapacitated by the public attacks. However, Rothermere effectively confirmed Davidson's story when he wrote to Lloyd George, shortly after the Armistice, complaining about the coalition government's treatment of the newspaper proprietors and the indignity of being "invited on the telephone by Bonar Law to resign because he feared the criticism of Mr Austen Chamberlain and some others."[27] Whatever the exact sequence of events, it seems that Baird's complaint was the final straw for the War Cabinet. Bonar Law announced Rothermere's resignation in Parliament two days later (25 April 1918), much to the surprise of his younger brother, Cecil Harmsworth (a Conservative MP), who had known nothing of the matter.[28] Rothermere's resignation letter stressed the death of his sons, his poor health, and his belief that the work to create an independent air service was done. This was all true, but without Baird's ultimatum and the imminent debate in Parliament, Rothermere would have remained in post, which is why Lloyd

George eased the process with the promise of promotion to viscount—an advancement that the king resisted for over a year on the not unreasonable basis that the Air Ministry had only been in existence for twenty-four days and, as Bonar Law observed, some criticism could be passed on the success or otherwise of Rothermere's administration.[29]

The promised debate was held on 29 April, by which time Rothermere's departure had taken much of the sting out of the controversy. Nevertheless, the issue was serious enough for the prime minister to provide an opening statement rather than relying on Bonar Law to shoulder the government's defense.[30] Lloyd George would admit no errors and defended the reputations of all involved (including Rothermere, Sykes, and Trenchard), other than Cecil and Simon. The opening salvo for the opposition was fired by William Pringle, a Liberal backbencher and a close friend and colleague of Simon. Pringle was an able parliamentary tactician, as well as one of the most intransigent of the anti–Lloyd George Liberals. After the war, Pringle, Simon, and William Wedgewood-Benn would be described as the Liberal Party's "flying column" for the cross-party support provided to Trenchard and the RAF.[31]

It is not difficult to see Simon's hand at work, although Pringle's skills as a parliamentary tactician and persistent critic of Lloyd George needed little enhancement. Their collective intent was to expose Rothermere's incompetence and thereby salvage Trenchard's career. To do so, they sought to undermine the official explanation for Trenchard's resignation and expose what they saw as Rothermere's duplicitous behavior. Colonel Sir Harry Verney, another Liberal, joined the attack before Cecil weighed in. The latter opened his comments by dismissing the suggestion that he should not speak—on the basis that he had occupied only a lowly position in the Air Ministry (which was somewhat disingenuous).[32] A notable contribution came from Asquith, who, having overseen the creation and development of the RFC for nearly five years, refuted the government's argument about Trenchard's competence: "When people talk with that superficial and often colossal ignorance to which we are accustomed in certain of our critics, when they speak of General Trenchard as a man deficient in powers of organization, they are talking what everyone, who knows anything of the Air Force or of General Trenchard, knows to be absolute nonsense."[33] The outcome was a vote in favor of the government, but it was purchased by the prime minister's commitment during the debate to find employment for Trenchard "that would be of greatest value to the new Service."³⁴

Lloyd George's valedictory for Rothermere was not shared by the specialist aviation press. *The Aeroplane* declared that it was hard to find in Rothermere's health issues and personal loss "either the excuse or justification for his method and manner of handling the affairs of the Air Council," adding it was impossible to trace one act of his that had in any way assisted the winning of the war and that his brief career had been entirely regrettable (conveniently forgetting that four weeks earlier it had urged Rothermere not to resign and to remain in post).³⁵ Only limited criticism was directed at Trenchard about the affair. With the passage of time, however, there has been less sympathy for Trenchard's actions. The argument presented by the government and its apologists has been that he was politically naive and failed to accommodate himself to his political masters or to the ways of Whitehall. *The Times* claimed that while Trenchard had proved himself an inspiring commander in the field, it was rather unlikely that the same qualities would make him an ideal chief of staff at home.³⁶ In fact, Trenchard had no fundamental problems with politicians, as his success in working with five different secretaries of state for air (both Conservative and Liberal) between 1919 and 1929 demonstrates. Either he was a rapid learner, or his difficulties with Rothermere were unique. Trenchard was certainly forceful in manner, but he was neither a poor listener nor without a sense of humor. Charles Vane-Tempest-Stewart (Lord Londonderry), shortly to become undersecretary of state for air, met Trenchard for the first time in early 1919 when he was appointed finance member of the postwar Air Council:

> After a formal greeting, the CAS began to tell me what he intended to do with this and that. He delved among a pile of papers and found the one he wanted immediately. Then he went on with his short, decisive phrases with so much energy that I was a little taken back. After listening for a while, I ventured to remark, "But what if I don't agree with you?" He looked up in doubt: there was a moment of silence; then he laughed as energetically as he had been talking. From that moment there was a complete understanding between us.³⁷

Sir Samuel "Sam" Hoare (later Lord Templewood) served twice as secretary of state for air, for a total of nearly six years. His initial meeting with Trenchard was, by his own account, overwhelming and transformational:

> I saw at once that he was one of those men whose presence cannot be ignored, whatever be the company in which they find themselves. . . . Here was a man massive and majestic in body as well as mind. So big a man might have been mentally slow and stolid. Not so, the first Chief of the Air Staff, whose clear deep-set blue eyes were the eyes of a seer of visions and whose words were the explosions of heaped up thought that took time and fermentation to break out.[38]

None of this is to suggest that Trenchard was necessarily an easy man to work with, but it is evidence that politicians were able to hold their own with him and establish a productive relationship without surrendering their principles.

A curious incident occurred shortly after Sykes took over as CAS that offers some insight into why Trenchard failed to establish any rapport with Rothermere. The latter had decided that Livingston (Paine's deputy) was to be made air secretary (with the promise of promotion to major general and a state honor) without reference to Paine or, indeed, to the Air Council. Rothermere summoned Sykes to his office (with Livingston already present) to tell him that Livingston was authorized to communicate directly with all RAF commanders in all theaters of war in his (Rothermere's) name. Sykes was then dismissed without comment. Livingston, who admired Rothermere, felt that the minister had no comprehension of what he had done, complaining that "if you want a scapegoat for any mistakes you may make, you have succeeded admirably, and if you wished to make my position more impossible than it was before, you could not have done better."[39] There are several significant aspects to this episode. First, Sykes would have had every right to complain about Rothermere's behavior, which was not only humiliating but also undermined his authority. Sykes, not the air minister, was responsible for the direction of the air staff. We can't know what Trenchard would have done under similar circumstances, but a quiet departure would not have been one of the possibilities. Rothermere may have been motivated by the best of intentions, but his actions damaged the trust between two men who should have been working closely together.[40] Second, it is abundantly clear that Rothermere had not learned to moderate his behavior—despite the bitter rows with Trenchard. He was still sponsoring young officers, who he believed should be advanced ahead of their peers, with little regard to the impact on working relationships within the department. Finally, although Rothermere repeatedly claimed (from as early as February 1918) that he would soon resign as air minister, his bullish actions suggest a man digging in for the long term rather than someone on the cusp of resignation. Rothermere may well have been tired and burdened by personal loss, but when it was suggested only a week before that he should take a holiday, he responded, "Here's this great united air force of 170,000 men just come into existence. I can't leave the baby."[41]

Was either Trenchard or Rothermere justified in his actions? According to Londonderry, "resignation is a doubtful factor in politics. Either you resign because you feel your efforts are hopeless or because you feel the independence of your position may cause your former colleagues to be brought round to your point of view. There are few resignations which can bear examination."[42] While this may be true of politicians and political discourse in general, the resignation of a senior military commander is a different animal. Derby announced his resignation on at least three occasions. Political appointees come and go, sometimes at the wish of the prime minister, sometimes on a matter of principle, and sometimes as the result of public or private embarrassment. Service chiefs rarely resign, and when they do, it is almost always because they have been "pushed." There may be an issue of principle or policy involved, but the process is driven by the government. Trenchard's resignation was unprecedented in that he, rather than his minister, was the instigator. The impact on RAF morale proved transitory, and there is no evidence that operational effectiveness was diminished. However, the poisonous atmosphere that had developed in the Air Ministry did have an impact on the higher direction of the air effort. Timely and effective decision-making suffered, with staffs working and briefing against each other. An organization divided against itself will ultimately fail. Irrespective of where the blame lay, the departure of the two antagonists was for the best.

While Rothermere would claim that getting rid of Trenchard was a great thing for the Air Force, he didn't give up on his reorganization plans. *The*

Times carried an editorial on the day Rothermere resigned that was either written or inspired by him:

> So far, the public have heard only one side of the story—or rather they have heard nothing but the very dangerous doctrine that every popular and gallant soldier is necessarily best qualified for all the most difficult appointments and that in any case he has a prescriptive claim to the choice of them. Of the facts about this particular change the public have heard nothing authoritative at all. It is high time that the strong case for the creation of a Strategic Council of the Air and for a drastic reorganization of the new Service were better known than it is at present.[43]

Weir and Sykes did form a Strategic Council, but it met only once and was almost immediately downgraded to a committee before fading away. Rothermere's other ideas (such as separating flying training from personnel and appointing Smith-Barry as director of training) never materialized. Norman tried a few months later to stimulate interest through a question in the House but was rebuffed by Baird.[44]

It has been suggested that Trenchard's honesty, energy, and determination were no substitute for the skills required to negotiate an environment where political calculation, self-interest, personal factions, and departmental rivalry dominated. However, the evidence suggests the opposite—that Trenchard was politically astute, or at least more so than Rothermere, who had no aptitude for politics and, according to Beaverbrook, had "never gained a following in Parliament." It is fair to say that Rothermere had neither the finesse nor the patience to be able to deal with Trenchard. However, it is also true that Trenchard's response to Rothermere's ideas for operational improvements in areas such as flying training were too dismissive.[45]

Reflecting on these events, it is difficult to avoid the conclusion that if Trenchard had decided to remove his minister, he could not have chosen a more effective route. Indeed, Trenchard's private notes on the affair (written nearly forty years later) indicate that he was partly motivated by the prospect of Rothermere's resignation. Baring offered an alternative motive when he questioned what would have happened if Trenchard had not resigned. He felt that Trenchard would have faced a hostile campaign in the press that would ultimately have forced him to go. By resigning when he did, he had strengthened his position.[46] Whatever Trenchard's motives, nothing supports Beaverbrook's suggestion that he was part of a conspiracy or Sykes' claim that Rothermere had been outmaneuvered by his political opponents. This does not mean, however, that Trenchard was naive about, or uninterested in, politics. No high commander can ignore (or avoid) the political context in which they must operate. It is little wonder that Henderson, writing to Bonar Law about the reasons for his own resignation, stressed his desire "to escape from the atmosphere of intrigue and falsehood which has enveloped the Air Ministry for the last four months."[47]

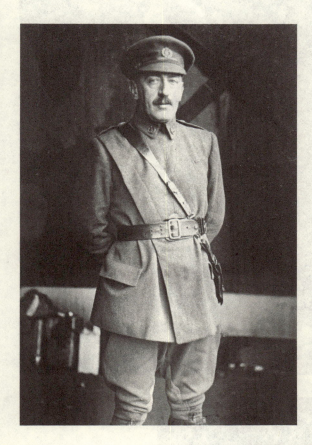

Lieutenant Maurice Baring looking uncomfortable in his RFC "Maternity Jacket" and wearing the ribbon of the Russo-Japanese War Medal, France 1916 *Author's photo*

A more relaxed Captain Maurice Baring wearing his General Staff tabs, France 1917 *Author's photo*

Major General (later Marshal of the Royal Air Force) Sir Hugh Trenchard, GOC RFC *Great War Aviation Society photo*

Major General Sir David Henderson *Great War Aviation Society photo*

Generals Edouard de Castelnau and Ferdinand Foch, France, June 1915. It was de Castelnau, rather than Foch, who extolled Baring's qualities as Trenchard's staff officer. *Great War Aviation Society photo*

Major (later Major General and Sir) Frederick Sykes shortly after the formation of the RFC. Sykes and Trenchard were bitter, lifelong rivals. *Great War Aviation Society photo*

Members of No. 22 Squadron pictured on 1 April 1918—the day the RAF was formed. Trenchard's ability to inspire his young pilots and observers was exceptional, even when they faced a superior enemy and the prospect of heavy casualties.
Great War Aviation Society photo

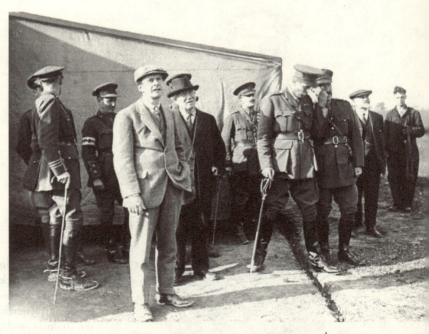

Herbert Asquith, Hugh Trenchard, and Maurice Baring at Fienvillers (Advanced HQ RFC), September 1916 *Great War Aviation Society photo*

Sir John Simon when serving as Lord Chancellor in Churchill's coalition government *Author's photo*

Sir Philip Game when serving as Commissioner Metropolitan Police, 1935–45 *Author's photo*

Lord Hugh Cecil
Author's photo

Air Commodore Lionel Charlton
Great War Aviation Society photo

HQ RFC, Chateau des Bruyeres, St-Omer, 1914–16 *Author's photo*

HQ RFC, St-Andre, 1916–18 *Great War Aviation Society photo*

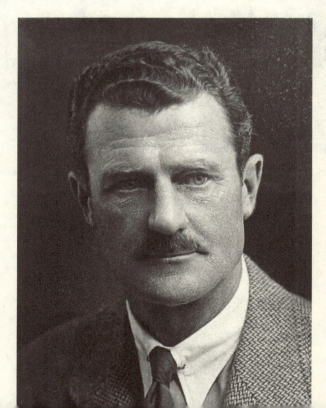

Brigadier General Francis Festing, HQ RFC, responsible for personnel and administrative activities
Author's photo

Brigadier General (later Air Chief Marshal Sir) Robert Brooke-Popham, HQ RFC, responsible for supply and logistic activities *Philip Brooke-Popham photo*

Independent airpower: fighter aircraft of No. 85 Squadron, St-Omer, September 1918 *Great War Aviation Society photo*

Trenchard hosting Queen Mary at St-Omer, June 1917. Major Claude Gould, commanding the depot's Aircraft Repair Section, is on the queen's right. *Great War Aviation Society photo*

"The RFC Interviewing Officer" (Major John Boyd). Although gently mocking Boyd's role in recruiting staff for the headquarters, the artist highlights the difficulties faced by HQ RFC in finding suitable candidates for the staff. *Author's photo*

Lord Rothermere (Harold Harmsworth) (*left*), **and his brother, Lord Northcliffe** (*right*)
Author's photo

Sir Henry Norman in uniform with staff officer tabs and wearing the rosette of the Legion d'Honneur *Author's photo*

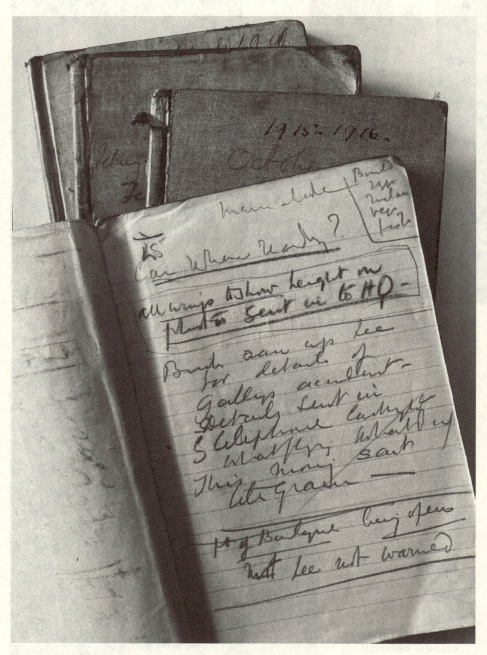

Baring's notebooks. The first volume (1915) reveals the word "marmalade" (at the top of the page), referencing Trenchard's request for marmalade at future breakfasts. Baring's handwriting did not improve over the next three years. *Author's photo*

CHAPTER 13

Regeneration

LLOYD GEORGE MOVED QUICKLY TO REPLACE Rothermere, selecting William "Willy" Weir, a cheerful, vigorous personality with strong executive skills, who would prove to be both competent and reliable. Weir was a safe choice: he had firsthand knowledge of the supply and technical aspects of aircraft production and was distinctly unpolitical.[1] Weir and Sykes worked well together, and the Air Ministry soon settled down under their calm and undemonstrative stewardship. Bullock, who worked closely with Sykes during his tenure as CAS, found him very able, with a first-class brain.[2] Weir's first test was to find a suitable post for Trenchard, which proved easier said than done. Various options were rejected based on either principle or pride. There were many, including Philip Game, who hoped that Sykes would resign: "I think it won't be long before he is found wanting as I am quite certain that he is not a big enough man to really do the job or anything like it."[3] Weir became increasingly exasperated with Trenchard's prevarication but eventually persuaded him to accept command of the RAF IF, soon to be created to undertake the strategic bombing of Germany, even though its very existence (as a separate command) offended the latter's belief in the unity of airpower. In truth, Trenchard was running out of options, notwithstanding the government's promise to find him appropriate employment. Weir was not personally hostile to Trenchard, but there was a limit to his patience in sorting out the problems caused by what he regarded as an unnecessary and unhelpful

165

resignation. Trenchard's new appointment was announced on 13 May 1918 (following several prompts in Parliament). Rothermere wrote to Northcliffe reveling in the fact that Trenchard, rather than being CAS, was now second string to Salmond. The newspapers were enthusiastic, even though the exact details took some months to emerge. Trenchard had persuaded Weir that he should report directly to Weir, rather than through Sykes. As Sykes feared Trenchard, this was probably for the best.[4]

Weir lost no time in reorganizing the Air Council and removing the staffs most directly involved in the Rothermere/Trenchard dispute. Simon was sent to France, to work for Salmond at HQ RAF, while Cecil returned to the backbenches of Parliament. Smith-Barry and Philippi (the "horrible gang," in Smith-Barry's words) were dispatched to the British Air Mission to the United States, where Smith-Barry promptly announced that he had declined a commission as a major general because "he believed he would be able to work with more freedom in a lower rank." Smith-Barry's efforts proved influential in improving American flying training methods, although only limited elements of the Gosport System were ever adopted.[5] Norman resigned, ostensibly because Weir wanted to slim down the Air Council. Harry Segrave, Norman's private secretary, was also sent to the United States, where he joined the Air Mission's staff in Washington (while continuing to correspond with Norman). Evelyn Wrench, Rothermere's private secretary, found refuge in the Ministry of Information, working for Beaverbrook. Guy Livingston was retained by the Air Ministry, but without the promised promotion and state honor. Henderson was posted to Paris, where he served as the military attaché before becoming director general of the League of the Red Cross Societies at Geneva. The Air Council was soon reduced to just seven members, with Baird as vice president (in place of Henderson). Although Groves was appointed vice chief (as Rothermere had originally intended), there was no seat for him. Sir Arthur Roberts, who had retired for reasons that remain unclear (but involved a dispute with Rothermere), was reemployed as chief financial adviser—only to resign six months later.[6]

Trenchard, accompanied by Baring and his ADC, Captain Samuel Ravenscroft, left for France and his new command on 16 May. Notwithstanding the government's enthusiasm for mounting a strategic bombing campaign, the RAF IF was largely a paper organization. None of the issues identified four months earlier by Trenchard had been resolved. While the plan was to create a force of up to sixty squadrons, based in France and England, the only operational unit was Cyril Newall's VIII Brigade, which comprised just four squadrons. This was the same organization (albeit slightly larger) that Trenchard had established in the Nancy area in October 1917.

Trenchard and Baring's first stop was their old headquarters at St-Andre, now HQ RAF, where they received a warm welcome from Jack Salmond, although Trenchard's anomalous position (reporting direct to Weir, while relying on Salmond for logistic and administrative support) would soon cause tensions between their respective staffs. There was no direct antagonism, only an incipient friction that tested both men. For his part, Baring found it a relief to be away from London, although he continued to seethe at Trenchard's treatment:

> Even now, few outside have the faintest idea of the quality and quantity of work he achieved. The work at Farnborough at the beginning and all the longsighted and carefully planned organisation and the continuous initiatives in large and small matters, the perpetual effort towards improvement and new fields of action. I remember the first struggle for effective artillery cooperation, then for bombing (where he had to fight even his own people), then for night-work, then for low-flying. In all of which things he set the pace and gave the example to the Huns long before they followed it. And yet you hear people talking that as though he a fine soldier in the field indeed but not an organiser not a man with brains!! It makes one gasp! They admit his reputation but then on what do they imagine it to be founded? What do they think he has been doing all these years? Galloping around on a horse? Or drilling people? However, it makes me too angry to think of it.[7]

For their first few weeks in France, Trenchard and Baring endured a nomadic existence, touring a succession of headquarters and meeting senior French leaders, including de Castelnau, commander of the French eastern armies, responsible for the Nancy area. A jovial, dapper little man, of quick and kindly speech, he has been described as the typical French cavalry officer. Trenchard had first encountered de Castelnau the previous year, when they had discussed the additional aerodromes needed by Newall's bombers. Trenchard and Baring returned to St-Andre on 20 May 1918 before traveling to Paris and a meeting of Inter-Allied Aircraft Committee (IAAC), established in November 1917 to coordinate Allied aircraft production.[8] They did not return to Nancy area until 2 June, only to have to drive back to St-Andre two weeks later. Each return trip involved a drive of over six hundred miles on poor roads, often in difficult weather.

The RAF IF was officially formed on 6 June 1918, the day that Trenchard and Baring took up residence in a small chateau at Autigny-la-Tour—a village of "square squat white houses and red roofs, nested on a hill and surrounded by still higher hills in the heart of the Vosges."[9] The building was smaller than St-Andre and not so busy, although Trenchard's working practices remained unchanged, including his attention to detail. "Looking around a new house with the General is a strenuous business as he insists on seeing everything and knowing everything."[10] Once installed, Trenchard still spent much of his time on the road, visiting the squadrons or attending meetings, leaving "Bos" Gordon, (previously Game's deputy) to run the headquarters for long periods, sometimes for up to a fortnight. Gordon was a familiar face and well trained in Trenchard's methods. A genial but efficient administrator, he proved an able and effective deputy, although it still took him time to get the headquarters staff to the required level of efficiency.[11] Away from London, Trenchard was reenergized by his visits to the frontline squadrons, finding a clarity and purpose in their company—even if his personality overwhelmed some: "He put the fear of God into all of us, but he was a terrific leader, and we would have done anything for him." Repington, who visited Autigny three months later, found Trenchard the "same as ever. Brilliant, full of ideas, alert, combative and a mine of information."[12] Once they had crossed the Channel, Baring had restarted his war diary and opened a new notebook. The entries are brief, single lines covering multiple days with frequent gaps, but there are still glimpses of his dry humor. When Trenchard did his first round of the frontline squadrons, Baring simply wrote, "It did not take very long."[13]

At this stage, the only significant reinforcement to Newall's brigade had been the arrival of Trenchard and his staff. As Marson explained, it was "a bit like putting the engine of a Rolls Royce in a motorcycle." Trenchard was frustrated at the lack of progress, which he credited to the decision to create a separate force that, as far as he could see, "was to employ 40 officers on the staff, about 200 men, large amount of transport, besides building huts for the headquarters, etc, in order to take the place of GHQ and HQ RAF."[14] The immediate problem, however, was the shortage of suitable aerodromes. All the well-drained sites with good approaches had been taken by the French air service. But with time and effort, even the most unpromising ground could be turned into a smooth surface of grass. The construction of additional aerodromes was already underway when Trenchard arrived, but he reenergized and expanded the program. Within three months, Gordon could report that seven aerodromes had been completed (with a capacity for forty-four squadrons) and a further four were at an advanced stage (with a capacity for a further eighteen squadrons). This represented a substantial achievement—each site required hangars, fuel and bomb stores, domestic and technical accommodation, electrical power, and sanitation. Such was the scale of the work involved that the Air Ministry sent several teams to report on the situation, although it soon became apparent that the aerodromes would be ready long before any further squadrons arrived. Weir himself came out to inspect progress, spending three hectic days with Trenchard.[15]

Trenchard and de Castelnau met regularly to discuss the RAF IF's planned operations. These were more than social events, organized to regularize decisions. Both men were conscious that the relationship between the Allies was a delicate web of shared ambitions and self-interest. The British were entirely dependent on French willingness to support the construction program and for resupply by road and rail. The prospect of additional airpower to support the eastern armies was welcome, but while the detailed arrangements could be left to their respective staffs, there were wider political and military concerns that demanded de Castelnau's personal involvement. The question of bombing German towns was a sensitive subject, in view of the (reasonable) concerns that any retaliation would target French rather than British cities. For much of the war, French bombing policy attempted to distinguish between military and civilian targets. The French government was not slow to order retaliatory bombing of German cities but had tried to avoid escalatory action. This was based on strategic, economic, geographic, and institutional factors that led them to exercise much greater restraint than the British.[16] Moreover, German cities were farther away than French cities, making it more difficult to achieve the same intensity of attacks and level of destruction—a situation complicated by the German occupation of many French towns.

Duval, Pétain's head of aviation, was not impressed by the RAF IF. To his mind, it was a distraction and a waste of resources that should be directed primarily at supporting the ground campaign rather than political objectives. As Baring noted, the RAF IF was in an extremely delicate position, and its unique and undefined status depended, as far as practical results were concerned, on the cooperation of the French: "The French had only to put the slightest spoke in our wheels, and our work became impossible, since every square inch of aerodrome, every arrangement for the transport of each gallon of petrol depended on their goodwill."[17] Trenchard admitted in his memoirs that the situation was even more finely balanced and that, without de Castelnau, the RAF IF could never have become a reality. De Castelnau was a strong believer in the value of airpower, but the key factor in securing his support was the personal bond between the two men. Baring glosses over his own role in this process: "He [de Castelnau] and the General understood each other at once after their first conversation."[18] If this was the case, it owed everything to his skills as a translator and go-between. Both Trenchard and de Castelnau would later pay tribute to Baring's role in establishing their relationship. Baring's admiration for de Castelnau was instinctive and wholehearted. For his part, de Castelnau (a well-read and cultured officer) appreciated Baring's deep knowledge of French literature and poetry. Baring's own literary reputation had yet to be established in France, but de Castelnau may have encountered *Carnet de guerre d'un officier d'état-major* (the French translation of *Translations*), which had been published in March 1918 to very positive reviews. According to the *Nouvelle revue*, it was a little masterpiece, the writing concise, elegant, and fine.[19]

De Castelnau's enthusiastic support, and the changing military situation, saw a gradual thawing of French attitudes. This was less about capabilities (which grew slowly) and more about the potential impact on domestic politics (in Paris and Berlin), once the German army's offensives had ground to a halt. These issues were debated at length in discussion papers presented by Trenchard to the IAAC. He proposed that there should be no restraint in policy, although the term "reprisals" should not be used.[20] Air superiority (particularly in daylight operations) was essential if bombing was to be effective.

But, unlike Duval, Trenchard argued that targets in Germany were of greater value than those nearer the front. Sykes supported these views, which were in line with War Cabinet policy, and argued that the RAF IF should form the core of an Allied strategic air arm. If Trenchard harbored reservations (and there is evidence that he did), he kept them to himself.[21] It was not until October 1918 that it was agreed to create an Inter-Allied Bombing Force (IABF), under Trenchard's leadership, to attack industrial and commercial sites as well as the railway system and enemy aerodromes. In deference to French concerns, Trenchard was to report to Foch, who had the authority, during periods of active operations, to prioritize the requirements of the battle over long-distance bombing. Duval remained skeptical, but Foch was supportive, advising Trenchard, "We know you have a special position; we don't mind that. Keep up the good work."[22]

Within the headquarters, Trenchard maintained his previous practice of welcoming attached staffs. This included Sir Walter Lawrence, who arrived at Autigny in July. Lawrence, an eminent Indian civil servant, had first met Trenchard in June 1916, when he visited HQ RFC and toured the squadrons.[23] Lawrence's appointment was helpful in view of the substantial numbers of Indian troops employed on aerodrome construction duties, but his presence proved particularly opportune when Prince Albert (the future King George VI) arrived in October. It says something for Trenchard's reputation that he was trusted with the care of the king's second son. Albert spent considerable time on liaison visits, often in Lawrence's company, and took the opportunity to fly with the squadrons. The prince was delighted to be in France and wrote to his father singing Trenchard's praises: "I have never seen a man more engrossed in his command. He knows more about what a squadron should have than the squadron commander. He fairly keeps everybody up to their work." Albert's praise persuaded the king to warm to Trenchard, although he had previously expressed concern about the latter's wayward hair and untidy appearance.[24] There was also an endless stream of visitors to entertain. Among them was Sir Walter Raleigh, who had been selected by the Air Council to write the Official History of the air services. Raleigh spent nearly a month in France visiting units, including Trenchard's headquarters. He talked with the staffs and toured the squadrons (but turned down the opportunity to fly on a bombing raid).[25] Raleigh, who was close to many in

Baring's social circle, already knew something of Trenchard's reputation as "a great man," and he was not disappointed. He was present when Trenchard spoke to one of the squadrons, making "courage, every word. The squadron held themselves higher when he had done."[26] Trenchard's emphasis on getting the job done might seem brutal, but it was realistic and not unappreciated, as Harold Balfour explained:

> Trenchard came round the squadron, and we thought he was going to tell us how sorry he was for our casualties and what fine chaps we were. Not a bit of it. He said: "You never finished your job, get on and do more than you are doing" and very nearly told us off. He did it in a very charming way and it was far better for morale than trying to condone the casualties and console you.[27]

During Trenchard's time as its commander, the RAF IF launched over three hundred bombing raids against German targets.[28] The first raid, during the day and night of 6/7 June, was against factories, railway sidings, and blast furnaces, and the last, during the night of 10/11 November, was against air defense aerodromes. The impact, in material terms, was modest, as postwar surveys confirmed. The limited number of aircraft employed, small bomb-loads, poor navigation, low bombing accuracy, adverse weather, and enemy action meant that the massive destruction envisaged by the War Cabinet was never close to being achieved. Trenchard acknowledged as much in his dispatch. Nevertheless, he was persuaded that the moral effect had been very much greater than the material effect. This was a widely held belief that was difficult to disprove and, in the context of Germany's eventual defeat, could not be dismissed as irrelevant. While it can be argued that if Londoners could cope with being bombed so could Berliners, it was also true that the daylight raids on London had caused a fall in munitions production and an increase (if only brief) in absenteeism.[29] The political impact had also been substantial. The British government was forced to increase the capital's anti-aircraft defenses, including temporarily redeploying fighter squadrons from the Western Front. Brigadier General Benjamin Foulois, U.S. Army Air Service, who witnessed a German air raid on London, reported that the effect on the morale of the British people from this small number of bombs "was very great in proportion to the physical damage."[30] Whether 1919 would have brought a different result (in material terms) for the RAF IF is debatable, although bombers were within days of attacking Berlin. The damage would likely have been modest, but the political effect at that stage of the war could have been significant. That said, it is difficult to believe that strategic bombing would have significantly degraded German fighting power, even when the IABF was operating at its full strength (one hundred frontline squadrons) in the summer of 1919.

As the operational tempo increased, so did the casualties. Trenchard had been severely criticized by Churchill for predicting a 40 percent monthly wastage rate, but this proved an optimistic assessment. Losses among the RAF IF squadrons amounted to closer to 50 percent. Some of this was due to technical issues beyond Trenchard's control, notably the poor performance of the D.H.9 day bomber, which meant that defensive formations were difficult to hold together and had to fly at a lower altitude than planned. On one daylight raid, No. 99 Squadron lost seven machines and fourteen officers when attacked by up to forty enemy fighters. Trenchard was greatly distressed by the news and went immediately to their base at Azelot to speak with the surviving pilots and encourage them in their continued efforts. Newall remained with the squadron until well into the evening, but they would not resume combat operations for several weeks.[31] Trenchard insisted that the Air Ministry withdraw the D.H.9 from combat operations as soon as possible. His anger at the loss of life was increased by the knowledge that he had argued a year earlier that the type would be out of date as a day bomber by the summer of 1918.[32]

Not all daylight raids were so unfortunate: No. 55 Squadron (D.H.4) fought its way to and from Frankfurt on 12 August without losing any aircraft. Even so, the losses continued including seven machines of No. 104 Squadron (D.H.9) on 22 August. The squadron had to be withdrawn from action while it was reequipped. Postwar investigations revealed that none of their bombs had hit the target. Trenchard had been up the previous night at Autreville, where he watched a successful raid by 216 Squadron (HP O/400), before returning to his HQ early in the morning. He was woken to be told the news and "was frightfully upset."[33] Trenchard found it particularly difficult to watch flying not knowing whether those involved would return safely.

Baring had Trenchard in mind when he wrote, "Of all the experiences we had in connection with aviation I thought, personally, there was none more trying, more harassing, and more hard to bear for those who were responsible than waiting for these long-distance raids to return." If the weather turned, it was the potential loss not just of a few machines, but of the whole formation.[34]

There is something rushed in Baring's account of this period, which may reflect the tensions and contradictions that he and Trenchard experienced daily: pride in the efforts and sacrifices of the squadrons, but despair at the political arguments and wasted effort. The narrative presented in *R.F.C. H.Q.* is haphazard and sometimes verges on the casual: "We started off on a long expedition either on the 18th or 19th, but I have no record of it. We went to Paris. What we did and what happened I have forgotten."[35] Baring's descriptive powers had not weakened, and he was still able to conjure up memorable scenes, such as, for example, when he and Trenchard watched night bombers take off for their targets in Germany: "It is quite uncanny to see the great monsters fly off into the sunset and disappear, and then you hear them much later humming in the darkness and circling like giant moths till they land."[36] He also affords space for a discussion of bombing policy. It is rare for Baring to touch on such issues, but he was not oblivious to the controversy about the bombing campaign, feelings shared by Trenchard, who would write in his diary, "The Force has done splendidly. It would have done just as splendidly had it remained under the command of the Expeditionary Force with half the number of officers and men it has been necessary to employ here to do the work. . . . An impossible organization was set up by politicians simply in order that they could say, 'I am bombing Germany.'"[37]

Controversial at the time, the RAF IF has continued to attract criticism—largely, it should be said, because it is seen as the genesis for the equally controversial Combined Bomber Offensive of World War II. Trenchard has been accused of exaggerating the impact of the RAF IF as part of an effort to justify the need for an independent air service, although the Air Ministry first made these claims in a report sent to the cabinet in January 1919 (when Sykes was CAS) and well before the RAF's future was in doubt.[38] There has also been criticism that Trenchard chose to attack enemy aerodromes rather than the industrial targets favored by the Air Ministry; however, this was a pragmatic response to the heavy casualties being inflicted by German fighters. Trenchard was aware that the physical damage inflicted by the bombing campaign was modest, but he genuinely believed that it had had a significant effect on German morale. In making this claim, he has been described as "fond of the totally unfounded statistic" and a man more interested in advocacy than accuracy, one who used his authority to protect his own record and his own version of the war effort in order to promote the importance of strategic bombing. By contrast, other writers have claimed that he lacked faith in aerial bombing and allowed the RAF's bombing capabilities to wither away after the war.[39] George Williams argues that Trenchard, during and after the war, exaggerated the damage inflicted and the scale of the resources diverted from the Western Front. The German Official History (published during World War II) provides a different perspective. While agreeing that the damage inflicted by Allied bombing was modest (in property destroyed and casualties inflicted), it warned that assessing the full impact was problematic in that material value did not account for aspects such as lost production. For example, the disruption caused by the attacks on the Düsseldorf steelworks had reduced output by 30 percent and curtailed night working. It was stressed that it was these effects on industrial production, and the potential shock to public morale, that justified the substantial resources committed to air defense, which, by the Armistice included 28,000 men, 768 antiaircraft guns, 102 antiaircraft machine gun platoons, 454 searchlights, 9 kite balloon sections, and 6 air defense squadrons equipped with 130 aircraft. Although the number of aircraft involved appears relatively small, it represented an unwelcome drain on the Luftstreitkräfte's limited resources. Indeed, some of these air defense units had to be withdrawn to reinforce the Western Front, in both 1917 and 1918.[40]

It is unfortunate that, in describing these events, Baring does not offer more of his personal views or touch on Trenchard's private concerns. Pride in the RAF IF's achievements sat uneasily with his resentment that it only existed for political purposes. Within days of the Armistice, Trenchard had petitioned the Air Ministry to disband his command. Weir agreed, although Salmond felt that Trenchard had acted with undue haste. For his part, Trenchard was delighted to close the door on an unhappy episode. That may explain why Baring ends *R.F.C. H.Q.* abruptly on 14 November 1918, with the announcement that the RAF IF's squadrons had come under Haig's control, an arrangement that Trenchard had always advocated and the government had previously resisted. In his eagerness to end the story, Baring fails to mention the farewell dinner hosted by de Castelnau at which the "great Frenchman" announced that Maurice Baring "was the greatest staff officer in any country in any age."[41]

CHAPTER 14

Reinstatement

WHEN TRENCHARD AND BARING LEFT AUTIGNY for the last time, they were cheered through the village streets, much to Trenchard's surprise.[1] Back in London, their first and only task was to write Trenchard's dispatch on the operations of the Independent Force. This was completed before Weir resigned as air minister in January 1919. There was something of an anticlimax to these weeks. Like thousands of other officers, Trenchard waited to discover whether his peacetime services were needed, while the government struggled to implement a phased demobilization. Reflecting on the past three years, and the privilege of serving with a "real great man," Baring committed himself to joining Trenchard wherever he went, "whether it is Abyssinia or Farnborough or West Africa or East Ham, or the Colonial Office or the War Office." In the New Year, Trenchard, accompanied by Baring, arrived at Southampton Docks to deal with a mutiny involving troops who were refusing to be sent to France. Trenchard resolved the incident through a combination of sympathy, guile, and the threat of force—while Baring was kept busy writing down hundreds of individual witness statements.[2]

A few weeks later, Trenchard was summoned to London to discuss his future with Churchill, whom Lloyd George had recently appointed war minister (the post of air minister having lapsed when Weir returned to civilian life). Churchill had decided that Trenchard should replace Sykes as the RAF's peacetime CAS.[3] Why did he select someone who had publicly embarrassed the government only ten months earlier and had caused the resignation of one of its ministers? Just as importantly, why was Churchill willing to place his trust in a man described by Beaverbrook (one of Churchill's closest friends) as self-centered and inarticulate, possessing limited ability and enjoying bitter hatreds?[4] Moreover, as Sykes was willing to continue to serve as CAS (in which role, according to Lloyd George, he had demonstrated qualities that Trenchard lacked), why did Churchill feel the need to make a change at all?[5] Trenchard was widely feted as an exceptional field commander, but the government had asserted in Parliament that he did not have the qualities needed to be an effective staff officer.

There were two reasons for the apparent change of heart. Despite Lloyd George's public statements, he knew that Rothermere was not without blame, admitting to George Riddell that while Rothermere had done the right thing at the Air Ministry, he had done so in the worst possible way.[6] It was no accident that Weir's briefing to the prime minister—in anticipation of the House of Commons debate—presented Rothermere's criticism of Trenchard as opinion rather than fact. Weir also added, in a covering note, that "owing to mismanagement, the case [for Trenchard's removal] is difficult to meet."[7] It seems that Lloyd George did not share Beaverbrook's belief that Trenchard had conspired with Jellicoe and Robertson to bring the government down, something the prime minister would have been unlikely to forget or forgive. Lloyd George might have been more skeptical, however, if he had known that two RAF brigadier generals (Ludlow-Hewitt and Newall) had met with Asquith and Sir Edward Carson, immediately prior to the House of Commons debate, to lobby for Trenchard's reinstatement.[8]

The second reason goes to the heart of the argument with Rothermere, Trenchard's willingness to speak truth to power. Churchill was wise enough to know that he needed a service chief who, while he might not always agree with him, would always be honest in his opinions. Sykes' willingness to knuckle down under Rothermere, and his indecisive nature, reflected a malleable personality. Churchill needed a credible leader who could make difficult decisions and stand by the consequences.[9] Churchill offered Sykes the post of director general of civil aviation and softened the blow by explaining that he was following Weir's advice. He did not mention that the change was popular with the other services: "I understand that Trenchard commands in a very considerable degree the confidence of the Naval flying services as well as that of the Army and that his appointment to the first place will be in every way agreeable to the Board of the Admiralty." When Trenchard's official biographer challenged Churchill to explain Trenchard's appointment, he replied, "Because I was convinced of his outstanding qualities and understood the reasons which had led him to resign in 1918."[10] Just as importantly, Lloyd George did not object, confirming that, whatever the fallout from the previous year, Trenchard had been rehabilitated—at least in some eyes.[11] Baring would later warn Trenchard that "Rothermere and Beaverbrook have it in for you. The former has never forgiven you and the latter doesn't think you're fit for your job." Rothermere's hostility led to sustained attacks by the *Daily Mirror*. One editorial would claim that "an Air Force controlled by middle-aged military men with military training is useless and expensive. The immediate need is not for more waste on unnecessary machines but younger officers with ideas and imagination."[12]

The news of Trenchard's appointment, announced on 12 February 1919, was well received, although the *Westminster Gazette* jibed that it would be welcome "to that portion of the public sufficiently informed as to the circumstances in which General Trenchard resigned his post."[13] In late February, Trenchard fell ill with influenza and then contracted pneumonia. He was laid up in his flat with only Baring to nurse him until Kitty Boyle came to their rescue.[14] For most of March, Trenchard remained in bed; he was not back at the Air Ministry before April. When he did return, he discovered that several officers who might otherwise have formed the core of the postwar air force had been allowed to retire, including Festing, and that Salmond was considering doing the same. He was able to dissuade Salmond but would always regret not being in time to prevent Festing's departure.[15] Another loss from his senior leadership team, and perhaps the most significant, was Baring. This may seem extraordinary in view of what Baring had written only a few months earlier, but the break had been at least a year in the making. The sparse entries in Baring's 1918 personal diary reflected a growing disillusionment with military life and the war in general.[16] There was a similar pattern in Baring's private correspondence, once so prolific and eclectic. He still wrote to friends and acquaintances, but by and large his letters were more serious—the playful correspondence with Lady Juliet Duff continued, but less frequently and often with a touch of sadness. Baring's commitment to Trenchard remained strong, but the man who had followed the drum for fifteen years, with a sharp eye, evocative phrases, and witty observations, had had enough of war and soldiering. The relentless and apparently never-ending death of friends, family, and colleagues had exhausted him, physically and emotionally. It is not clear whether he said as much in declining Trenchard's offer or whether he simply asked for time away to think about his future. It may have been the latter, as Trenchard approached Baring again the next year. He politely demurred, explaining that the job needed a younger, fitter man and then admitting, "I am mortally tired too; tired by and of the war," adding later, "You don't realise what has happened to me in the last three years. It is simply this: the main spring is broken. . . . It is torn out by the roots and has been for three years ever since the war."[17]

Major Maurice Baring, Officer of the British Empire (awarded for his services in France), was transferred to the Unemployed List on 1 April 1919, receiving a Mention in Despatches for his work with the Independent Force.[18] His successor (Marson) was extremely capable, but Trenchard missed Baring's insights, intuition, and writing skills. He had to turn to Brooke-Popham and Game (both of whom had decided to stay with the peacetime RAF) to undertake any drafting work.[19] Before the war, Baring had lived with the Herberts at Old Queen Street, but Nan Herbert (now Lady Lucas) had given this up following Bron's death and moved to Bell House, Dulwich. Part of the estate included Pickwick Cottage, which Baring rented for the next three years. It was here that he wrote the first draft of what would become *R.F.C. H.Q.* as well as several other works, including his autobiography, *The Puppet Show of Memory*.

R.F.C. H.Q. is an important work in the historiography of British airpower—offering a firsthand view of the RFC's senior leadership on the Western Front. It is, nevertheless, a personal account. When Baring came to write the story, there were no published sources to draw on, other than the official despatches. The first volume of the air history, *The War in the Air*, was at least two years away, and the final volume would not emerge until 1937.[20] Baring had a handful of official documents, but otherwise constructed the narrative around the cryptic "action" lists preserved in his notebooks, his personal diary, private letters, and memory, which helps explain the patchwork feel to the finished work. Short bursts of evocative prose sit next to reports on technical matters (transcribed without any apparent pretense at understanding) and eulogies to friends killed in action. A scattering of French or classical Greek, playful exchanges, and ironic commentary offer a smorgasbord of style, content, and emotion. It is tempting to see Baring's private contradictions reflected in this mix—a man of culture and refinement playing a pivotal role in a brutal war, deeply moved by the loss of friends but frivolous with his confidants, out of step with the modern world yet excited and strangely inspired by technology. Baring produced his manuscript in less than two months, but the first publisher approached (Chatto & Windus) rejected it, in part because they already had his book *Round the World in Any Number of Days* waiting for publication, but largely because of a negative reader's report advising that its length and character precluded commercial success:

> If one is interested in Maurice Baring, one presumably will be interested to know with whom he had tea and with whom he dined every day of the war, and whether all the crockery was broken at dinner or not and what he read all the time. But apart from its personal interest, and, of course, its unintentional spotlight upon the kind of life lived by staff officers attached to GHQ, the manuscript has little interest.[21]

George Bell and Sons were more receptive, and by the autumn Baring had signed a contract, although he resisted attempts to remove some of the more prosaic elements that the publisher believed "would not be of very much interest excepting perhaps to flying men themselves."[22] This suggests that the juxtaposition of the mundane with the dramatic was a deliberate technique rather than an accident or owed to expediency. Originally Baring had titled the manuscript *War Diary*, and he toyed with changing it to *R.F.C. G.H.Q., 1914–1918* before settling on *R.F.C. H.Q. 1914–1918*—a choice endorsed by Trenchard.[23] For the 1930 edition (and all subsequent editions) the title was altered to the less cryptic *Flying Corps Headquarters, 1914–1918*.[24]

The unusual structure and erratic style of Baring's narrative has made it difficult to criticize *R.F.C. H.Q.* as either literature or history. A close reading of Baring's sources confirms the main elements of his account, but it also reveals that key details have been omitted. As a result, we are presented with a headquarters populated by a happy band of brothers that functions without confusion or disagreement. No student of human nature, let alone anyone who has ever worked in an operational headquarters, could believe that this is an accurate picture. Marson, who should have been in a position to know, claimed that Baring had wanted to write a different book, but Trenchard complained that there was too much about him and not enough on the subject.[25] Andrew Boyle says that Baring turned down the opportunity to write the Official History because of his own project to write a memoir covering this period, apparently mistaking the 1930 edition of *R.F.C. H.Q.* for the first edition.[26] He adds that Baring had produced some draft chapters by 1934 but that Trenchard did not like them, as they contained personal praise. It is difficult to know quite where the truth lies, but there was very little opportunity in the two months that it took Baring to produce the manuscript for Trenchard to make significant changes. It seems likely that the decision about what to include, and what to exclude, rested largely with Baring.

Important discussions that don't appear in *R.F.C. H.Q.* include the debate in October 1914 about the future organization of the RFC and the argument in the spring of 1915 about the employment of fighter aircraft. The full extent of the Trenchard–du Peuty conversations in late 1915 and the long-running discussions about parachutes are also omitted. Other aspects, such as the air agitation of early 1916, and the plan for Henderson to replace Trenchard as GOC RFC in January 1916, are mentioned, but without revealing his deep anxieties. Only in his private letters do we discover that Baring was struggling with "awkward and disagreeable things," that he felt Pemberton Billing was doing serious harm to the Flying Corps, and that Trenchard was "sick and yellow with worry."[27] Most significantly, for someone with uncanny insight, Baring has nothing to say about Trenchard's moods (and, indeed, his own moods). He left it to others to describe the "punishment" regime he inflicted on Trenchard when the latter transgressed.

By presenting Trenchard as an Olympian figure, incapable of mistakes or of changing his mind, Baring did a disservice to the person he admired above all others. Trenchard was undoubtedly a great man, not because he was infallible or avoided human frailties, but because he was able to overcome the defects, weaknesses, and failures that would have proved fatal in other leaders. Baring's work gained a new lease of life when it was republished, with a foreword and supplementary notes, to mark the RAF's fiftieth anniversary. The new edition received glowing reviews. Humphrey Wynn, assistant editor of *Flight*, cited *Flying Corps Headquarters 1914–1918* as a "classic of air warfare," while celebrating Baring's "luminous, highly personal style."[28] Wing Commander Raphael "Raph" Preston (an RFC veteran) wrote that "no other book could present a more intriguing, witty and penetrating picture of the day to day activities of those big men who brought the Royal Flying Corps into being and instilled into it the traditions which it has been able to hand on to the Royal Air Force."[29] In Air Commodore Christopher Paul's view, Sir Walter Raleigh and Baring had much in common, "not least a profound understanding of the spirit that animated the first commanders of the RFC and which, because they were great men, they were able to instill into the Service which they created."[30]

The Armistice saw the breakup of Trenchard's senior leadership team, but not the RAF—although its survival as an independent air service was touch and go for at least ten years. Trenchard's energy and determination saw repeated attempts by the army and navy to dismember, if not disband, the new service. For his spirited defense, Trenchard became known as "the Father of the RAF," although he insisted that the title properly belonged to David Henderson (who had died suddenly at Geneva in 1921).[31] Trenchard served as CAS for ten years, before retiring in 1930. He then served as commissioner of the Metropolitan Police until 1935. Elevated to the House of Lords in 1930, he remained an important influence on the RAF before and during World War II. Trenchard died in 1956, aged eighty-three, a much-respected figure and universally recognized as a major force in the development of airpower.

Festing left the RAF to pursue a career in civil aviation. He was appointed manager of the world's first scheduled airline (operating between London and Paris), but this failed in 1920. He subsequently worked for Frederick Sykes in the Civil Aviation Department before joining Blackburn Aviation in 1924 as a consultant, but none of his subsequent ventures prospered. He rejoined the RAF in 1940 but retired for reasons of ill health in 1942 and died in 1948, aged seventy-one. Brooke-Popham enjoyed a full career in the RAF, retiring as an ACM in 1936 to become the governor of Kenya. He rejoined the RAF in 1939 and played an important role in setting up the Empire Air Training Scheme in Canada and South Africa. He was appointed CinC Far

East in 1940, responsible for the air and land forces based in Malaya, but was replaced shortly after the Japanese attack in December 1941: becoming a convenient scapegoat for the military disaster that culminated in the fall of Singapore. Brooke-Popham died in 1953, aged seventy-five. Game left the RAF in 1929 to serve as governor of New South Wales before succeeding Trenchard as commissioner of the Metropolitan Police. He retired in 1945 and died aged eighty-four in 1961, the last survivor of Trenchard's senior leadership team.

Trenchard's political colleagues in the Air Ministry enjoyed long careers. Baird, whom Beaverbrook labeled as a Trenchard supporter, occupied a wide variety of ministerial posts. He was elevated to the House of Lords as Lord Stonehaven in 1925, and served as governor-general of Australia until 1930. He died in 1941, aged sixty-seven.[32] Simon served in a range of important government appointments over the next thirty years, finally retiring when Churchill lost the 1945 election. He is the only man to have held all five of the most important offices of state—attorney general, Chancellor of the Exchequer, foreign secretary, home secretary, and Lord Chancellor. He died in 1954, aged eighty. Cecil retired as an MP in 1937 and became provost of Eton, where he was commonly regarded as intransigent, exasperating, and eccentric.[33] Churchill elevated his old friend to the House of Lords in 1941, where he sat as Lord Quickswood. Cecil died in 1956, aged eighty-seven. Weir, elevated to the House of Lords as Baron Weir, went back to being a leading industrialist, chairing the engineering firm G. and J. Weir until 1953. Alert, nimble, and highly capable, he was regarded as one of the most effective businessmen ever brought into government. Weir remained influential in aviation matters and was behind the creation of the shadow aircraft factories that proved so important during World War II. He died in 1959, aged eighty-two.[34]

De Castelnau remained on close terms with Trenchard and attended the fourth annual reunion of the RAF IF in 1922 as Trenchard's guest. A member of the Imperial War Graves Commission's Anglo-French committee, he joined Trenchard at the unveiling of the British Air Services Memorial at Arras in 1932, commemorating the nearly one thousand British and Commonwealth airmen with no known grave who fell on the Western Front. Their last known meeting was in 1935, when, along with Baring, they attended a dinner party in London hosted by the French ambassador. De Castelnau was a major political figure in interwar France, establishing a right-wing, pro-clerical party that at one point had over 2 million members. He also agitated against the continuing threat posed by a resurgent Germany. As early as 1923, he chaired a meeting at the Sorbonne, with three thousand attendees, to discuss the danger of German airpower. During World War II, de Castelnau was extremely critical of Pétain (once his subordinate, then his superior) and the actions of the Vichy regime. It is said that when a priest brought a message from his cardinal asking de Castelnau to moderate his criticism, he replied, "So your cardinal has a tongue? I thought he had worn it out licking Pétain's arse."[35] De Castelnau died in 1944, aged ninety-two, the only French general to have served in operational command from the start to the end of World War I. There is little doubt that he deserved to have been made the fourth Marshal of France (after Joffre, Foch, and Pétain). That this never happened seemed to be of little concern to him.

What of Trenchard's protagonists? Harold Harmsworth (Lord Rothermere) never held political office again, although he continued to be active in politics. It was said that he was always better at pointing out failings than at finding solutions.[36] When his elder brother died in 1922, Rothermere purchased his newspapers to add to his own, creating Amalgamated Holdings and becoming the most powerful press baron of the interwar period. Rothermere supported rearmament and campaigned tirelessly to redress what he saw as the RAF's weakness in bomber strength, going so far as to sponsor his own design (the Bristol Blenheim).[37] Paradoxically, he was an enthusiastic admirer of Adolph Hitler.[38] *The Times*, as might be expected, published a glowing obituary that highlighted Rothermere's many business successes but avoided mentioning the flirtation with fascism, although it did add that he might have been too prone to act on his impulses and that his political interventions were not always successful. Of Rothermere's time at the Air Ministry, it was said that "he encountered strenuous departmental resistance to the sweeping reforms he hoped to carry out."

Norman returned to his liaison post with the Ministry of Munitions, running their Paris office until 1919. He remained close to Lloyd George, assisting with his successful 1918 election campaign, and, together with Rothermere (and Livingston), helped plan John Alcock and Arthur Brown's successful transatlantic flight. Norman remains best known for his work in developing wireless communications before and after the war. He died in 1939, aged eighty.[39] Smith-Barry left the RAF, although he retained his links with aviation. He rejoined the RAF in 1939 as a flying instructor, where he continued to advocate innovative training schemes, only to be told that his ideas didn't fit the modern RAF.[40] He died in South Africa in 1949, aged sixty-three. Philippi, who met his future wife in New York when part of the British Air Mission, retired to run his father's estates at Crawley Court as an important country sports venue. The family lost much of their fortune in the financial crisis of 1929 and had to sell the Crawley estate in 1931. Philippi died in 1953, aged sixty-three. Segrave returned to his pre-war passion, motor racing, and was knighted after setting several world land speed records. He was killed in 1930, aged thirty-three, when his boat crashed shortly after setting a new water speed world record.

And Maurice Baring? The publication of *R.F.C. H.Q.* did not mark the end of his relationship with Trenchard or the RAF. He was Trenchard's best man at his wedding to Kitty Boyle in 1920. There appears to be no surviving record of his speech—it would have made interesting reading. Trenchard's final words at the train station, as the happy couple were about to leave on their honeymoon, were "All right, Baring, You may go. This is a journey I shan't want you on."[41] Two years later, Trenchard asked him to take over the writing of the official air history, after Sir Walter Raleigh's sudden death, but Baring declined—preferring to focus on his blossoming career as a novelist. There was, however, a brief reunion during the General Strike of 1926. Trenchard recruited Baring and Festing to join Brooke-Popham and Game in the Air Ministry crisis cell, coordinating the RAF's contribution to the government response. Diana Cooper recalled how delighted Baring was to be back in uniform and at Trenchard's side. After a week, however, the strike collapsed, and normal life resumed.[42]

Baring proved to be a successful author, although his reputation has diminished over the last fifty years. His novels (twelve were published between 1921 and 1935) faithfully re-create the Edwardian world of privilege and class. They are beautifully crafted, but his elegant and nuanced writing tends to linger over the journey rather than the destination. One reader went so far as to claim that Baring had "discovered how to leave out his entire story and write nothing but the connecting passages." Even those who regarded Baring as an outstanding novelist admitted that it sometimes seemed he wrote many books but only one story.[43] The simplicity of his writing has been applauded, but he leaves the reader to do much of the heavy lifting. Some have complained that his work is too lifelike. Characters arrive and depart with no explanation, others abruptly die, and there are no sudden revelations or catastrophic events. The books are well-written, austere, beautifully crafted novels that lack only a plot—a sort of Raymond Chandler without the crime or the wisecracks. This may explain why Baring's fiction has always been more warmly received in France, where method is as important as meaning, and where the reader is expected to work as hard as the author. Baring didn't lack imagination, but he found it difficult to write about what he had not seen or experienced, admitting that "he would not dare to write of a world in which he had not lived." As a staff officer, however, his meticulous eye and emotional detachment made him the perfect recorder of people and events: "I have tried to make it my business to discover, understand and explain the points of view of the people with whom I have met; with some of these views I sympathise, with others I do not, but I have attempted to understand even what repelled me."[44] Critics have had plenty to say about Baring the novelist, poet, and playwright but have paid little attention to his wartime work, preferring to see it as a temporary phase where he found employment as an "odd-jobs man."[45]

The last years of Baring's life were extremely difficult. He was increasingly incapacitated by Parkinson's disease, largely unable to write but still dictating correspondence to his many friends, including Marson, whom he addressed as "Grandpa," a name bestowed by the young pilots of No. 56 Squadron when Marson served as their recording officer.[46] Baring bore his illness with patience and fortitude. Unable to look after himself, he was evacuated to Scotland in 1940 to stay at Beaufort Castle with his friend Lady Laura Lovat and her family. Bedridden, frequently delirious but uncomplaining, Baring died at Beaufort in 1945, aged seventy-one. Trenchard was unable to attend the funeral, but "Grandpa" represented him and the RAF.

We may never entirely resolve the enigma that was Maurice Baring. One critic concluded that everything about him was "quite impossible," while another simply asked, "What was Maurice Baring *for*?"[47] Yet there is no question that Baring was an exceptional staff officer. He was the perfect foil to

Trenchard, providing support and guidance and, most importantly, giving him a "voice": two complex and elusive personalities in perfect harmony. It is difficult to disagree with de Castelnau's assessment that "there never was a staff officer in any country, in any nation, in any century like Major Maurice Baring," but perhaps we should leave the last word to the man himself. In September 1916, as the RFC fought for, and secured, air superiority over the devastation that was the Somme battlefield, he wrote to his great friend G. K. Chesterton that "this is the only time in my life when I have been of the slightest use to anyone."[48]

CHAPTER 15

Reconstruction

THE IMMEDIATE POSTWAR YEARS PROVED EXTREMELY difficult for the RAF. Trenchard was faced with the challenge of dismantling a wartime force and reconstructing it as an affordable but still effective peacetime organization—while the army and Royal Navy circled, waiting for an excuse to eliminate what they saw as a misguided and wasteful experiment. By 1920, the RAF had shed 90 percent of its personnel and a similar proportion of its aircraft. Trenchard was the first to admit that, in the haste to achieve immediate economies, mistakes were made. Men were demobilized without much inquiry, while land and buildings were disposed of at a faster pace than the other services. It may have been the price of survival, but Trenchard would always regret that he had "wiped out a lot of the great Flying Corps."[1]

The blueprint for the postwar air force, Trenchard's memorandum on the "Permanent Organization," was published in December 1919.[2] The bulk of the drafting was undertaken by Game and Brooke-Popham, assisted by Bullock, although the conceptual core was largely Trenchard's. A key thread running through the document was an emphasis on training and education. Hugh Cecil, who had recruited so many young pilots to the RFC in 1915 and later joined Trenchard and Baring at HQ RFC, chaired the committee that defined the qualities needed by officers in the new service.[3] The establishment of the recruit depot at Uxbridge, the cadet college at Cranwell, and the apprentice training school at Halton provided the new service with its key building blocks. Additional structure was provided by the creation of the Staff College at Andover, but these organizational developments, important though they were, were not sufficient. As the "Permanent Organization" explained, "To create an Air Force worthy of the name, we must create an air force spirit, or rather foster this spirit which undoubtedly existed in a high degree during the war, by every means in our power."[4] Trenchard never defined what the "air force spirit" comprised. The closest example can be found in his autobiographical notes, where he describes the different type of courage needed by an airman compared to an infantryman. It is purely "Trenchardian," in its fractured grammar, misspelling, and tortuous wording, but offers some idea of what he had in mind: "There were no parachutes, and whenever you were hit you came down in flames. You were by yourself with nothing to keep up your courage; machine engines were always going wrong yet how magnificently these young men did their work. They were attached [sic] in the air by Germans, shot at by anti-aircraft guns badly, but just as much alarmingly."[5]

Trenchard didn't have to labor over what he meant by the "air force spirit," because it lived in the shared experience of those who had served in the war. What was important, however, was that the peacetime RAF retained officers capable of managing the reconstruction effort while sustaining a culture that embodied the traditions forged in World War I. Although Trenchard was not directly involved in the detail of the demobilization process, he took a personal interest in selecting the RAF's senior leadership team. There is no direct evidence about how officers were chosen for a permanent commission, but some general principles can be deduced.[6] A good war record was important, but so was achieving a balance between ex-RFC and ex-RNAS personnel. Professional skills weighed heavily—more so, perhaps, than conformance to social norms. It might have been assumed that those with a checkered personal history might be weeded out, but Trenchard seems to have shown little concern about an individual's private life. AVM "Jack" Higgins was appointed director of personnel at the Air Ministry, even though he had featured in divorce proceedings that were widely reported in December 1918.[7] When the RAF had been formed, its senior leadership comprised forty-five general officers (including Higgins), the most senior being Henderson. This would increase to over sixty general officers by the Armistice, although the number was inflated by those holding honorary rank and by senior army and navy officers (with no aviation background) recruited to fill administrative appointments. By the time the "Permanent Organization" was published, Trenchard had reduced the size of the RAF's senior leadership to just twenty air officers (one star and above), of whom around 60 percent had seen service on the Western Front. Eight were former members of the RNAS (a slightly higher proportion than the size of the RNAS in April 1918 might have justified). They were all relatively young, with ages ranging from thirty-six to forty-eight years. This would subsequently cause problems in succession planning, although it was probably unavoidable in such a young organization. Trenchard was largely content with the outcome, although he regretted that some officers, such as Festing, had left for civilian employment before he could get them to change their mind.

When Trenchard retired in 1929, fourteen members of these "founding leaders" were still serving. Two had died in flying accidents (Edward Maitland and Robert Groves), three had retired at their own request, and one (Charlton) had resigned his commission. The remainder could properly claim to have laid the foundations for the modern RAF.[8] Beyond this cadre was a more diverse and looser group of individuals, many of whom had been flight or squadron commanders on the Western Front. These "follower-leaders," who included "Bert" Harris, Trafford Leigh-Mallory, Keith Park, "Peter" Portal, Sholto Douglas, and Arthur Tedder, would fill many of the RAF's senior command appointments during World War II. As commanders on the Western Front, they had exhibited leadership of the highest order under difficult conditions. As airmen, they had had to find the determination, courage, and self-leadership to cope with high casualty rates while fighting an enemy that was often superior in equipment and tactics. The impact of these experiences did not diminish with time; if anything, it hardened with the continued attacks on the RAF's independence and as rapid advances in technology gave airpower ever greater potential to transform warfare.

It was this sense of modernity, of representing the future, that sustained the RAF's leaders during the interwar period. Although the RAF owed its existence to the efforts of army and naval aviators during World War I, it was not the natural heir to the long history and traditions of their parent services. This was partly the result of a determined effort to demonstrate a distinct identity and partly the result of its reputation for attracting the "wrong sort" of people. Admittedly, the RAF possessed a successful wartime record and contained officers of distinction, but there was a view in polite society that it was brash and socially inept.[9] This sense of insecurity, coupled with concerns about the RAF's independence, encouraged a defensive mentality: "A young service, offering something new to the world, has to be able to face those who criticise its youth, its natural exuberance, the order of its new approach to old problems, everything that shakes the old idea."[10] The RAF was torn between embracing the "new" and claiming the "old." The revolutionary credentials adopted by the new service sat uneasily with its desire to be accepted as the equal of the army and navy and to enjoy the same public esteem. Notwithstanding Trenchard's assertion that these issues were only of the past, the RAF continued to display a sensitivity about its professional credentials and social status throughout the interwar years.[11] Of course, there is a danger in making too much of this sense of social and professional isolation, but the vehemence of the arguments about airpower that raged through the interwar years, and the RAF's difficult relationship with its sister services, owed as much to a sense of institutional inadequacy as to professional rivalry.

We need, however, to take care not to claim too much for RAF culture, as distinct from military culture. The postwar RAF was undoubtedly "modern" in the context of its time, but it was also of its time. It comprised white males (the color bar, suspended at the start of the war, was quietly reimposed after the Armistice), and most of its new officers were public school–educated. Young men could join as apprentices and (by selection) go on to attend the cadet college at Cranwell, but these were the exception. The RAF reflected the social and cultural world in which it operated. It was, however, a young organization in its equipment, its attitudes, and the way it waged war. It was therefore more in step with contemporary society than the other services, which were burdened by centuries of tradition. It was also led by men who had seen the potential of military aviation before it was fashionable—even if it might cost them their careers. It is no coincidence that the syllabus for the first RAF staff course at Andover addressed the need to embrace, rather than fear, intellectualism and the importance of innovation. It also stressed the need to respect specialists and celebrate collective endeavors. As Brooke-Popham explained, the RAF needed officers who could think and act quickly:

"We must have a mobile brain. This does not mean changing one's mind but that one must be receptive of new ideas, envisage their effect on air operations and foresee future developments." He also warned that merely wearing a blue uniform and employing novel titles was not enough, and that a severe mental effort was required to grasp what this new power meant. There were limits, however, as S. P. B. "Petre" Mais, who had been a member of the Cecil Committee, soon discovered. Mais was the first professor of English at Cranwell, but the appointment ended in controversy when he was dismissed because of student essays that it was claimed verged on the "pornographic." Mais made the mistake of failing to set any boundaries in attempting to teach his students how to think, rather than what to think.[12]

From the very start of his tenure as CAS, Trenchard was concerned about how to create a distinct identity for an organization that had existed for barely eight months. There was very little detail in his acceptance letter to Churchill, but he spent time stressing the need to sustain RAF traditions in organization and nomenclature, to "keep discipline and a good tone."[13] He was also determined to show that the RAF needed leaders and not managers, even if fighting in the air involved only a fraction of its personnel. The bulk of the RAF's "airmen" never left the ground or the vicinity of their home stations. How, then, to convey the idea of a fighting service, when most those wearing "air force blue" came no closer to the enemy than the civilian population they were defending? It was a concept that many outside the RAF found challenging, most obviously in the debate about recognizing the efforts of Bomber Command ground crew in World War II. "Bert" Harris, CinC of Bomber Command, who believed passionately that those who serviced the bombers (often at risk to their own lives) deserved public recognition, was unable to secure a specific award.[14]

Trenchard's tribute to the "tone of service" that Baring had brought into the RFC was part of his wider effort to build an identity that embraced everyone who served "to help other men and save lives in the Army on the land and in the Navy at sea." It may seem surprising that Trenchard should offer Baring, who possibly never fired a shot in anger, as an example of the ethos that should motivate a fighting service. The reference to supporting the army and navy was a nod to contemporary accusations that the RAF had failed to support the other services (Trenchard was never one to miss an opportunity to have a dig at his critics), but what did he mean by "tone," and why did he set so much store by it? The first point to make is that the terms "ethos," "spirit," and "tone" can be interchangeable, depending on the context. They are all integral to what would now be described as "organizational culture." Leaders play a critical role in shaping an organization's culture, but strong leadership is not the only influence. Social, political, institutional, technological, and environmental factors are also involved.[15] Moreover, culture is dynamic rather than static. This is particularly true where young organizations are involved. We know that Trenchard repeatedly referred to the "air force spirit" without providing any clarification, but a degree of mystique can be helpful when creating new traditions and the associated rituals, artifacts, and symbols. Indeed, referencing the modern to the past is a powerful tool in establishing cohesion, legitimizing the institution, and inculcating beliefs.[16] The subjective nature of this process was highlighted by James, one of the first instructors at Cranwell, who believed that the postwar RAF spirit was created "bit by bit as they went along," adding that the one element binding everything together was Trenchard and the "memory of the wartime discipline combined with freedom."[17]

There is little doubt that Trenchard's service on the Western Front provided the spiritual foundation for the RAF, but it was Baring who had framed how Trenchard processed this experience. Baring was literally Trenchard's eyes and ears, interpreting events and explaining motives, providing the emotional lens through which he understood the war. It was Baring who enabled Trenchard to comprehend the needs, anxieties, and fears of his young airmen, mourning their loss and celebrating their achievements. In the process, Trenchard came to believe that Baring's sense of service, selflessness, and dedication to a greater purpose were the very qualities that should motivate the RAF, even if Baring was the most unexpected of role models. *The Tatler*, usually interested only in society gossip, had already noticed how war had brought poetry and the writers of poetry to the forefront, including Baring, "erstwhile *litterateur* and poet but now a member of General Trenchard's staff." It went on to reflect on the benefits to public life of thinkers as well as doers.[18] More recent writers have found Baring no less unusual:

> He was an original, a man who cannot be neatly pigeon-holed by social background, profession, nationality, or time-period. Steeped in the classics

he delved deeply into the literatures, music and art of Europe and Russia. By character and personality, moreover he was extraordinarily well tuned to the little nuances and big perspectives of civilization. His was an unusual combination of scholarly disinterest and passionate aesthetic commitment, of strong moral assertion and cultural receptivity and tolerance.[19]

The choice of Baring as a role model might be considered even more surprising because of questions about his sexuality. That Baring never married and was not known to have had affairs with any of his many female friends (although there is some uncertainty about this) has led to speculation that he was, like his great friend Eddy Marsh, a homosexual who was "celibate" or (like many of the characters in his novels) simply unlucky in love. A sense of unhappiness, if not melancholy, certainly pervades Baring's novels, but while this may reflect an inner turmoil, it could just as easily reflect his wartime experiences.[20] Baring's sexual preferences are part of the wider mystery of his character, but from Trenchard's perspective, they were of little account. Army officers generally married late in life, as regulations barred them from marrying until they reached the rank of captain. Many did not marry until much later in their careers, including Trenchard and Brooke-Popham, who were still single in their forties. Homosexuality was not unknown in the British Army before, during, or after World War I. At least 230 members of the British Army (including officers and other ranks of the RFC) were sentenced in connection with homosexual offences between 1914 and 1918.[21] Considering that the strength of BEF had grown to nearly 1.4 million men by 1918, this seems an improbably small number. It can be assumed that the wartime authorities had more pressing issues than prosecuting homosexual acts.

There was also a greater tolerance of homosexuality than is commonly assumed—where there was no threat to good order and discipline. It is difficult to believe that no one in the RFC's senior leadership neither knew nor suspected that Charlton and E. B. Ashmore, both senior and very successful RFC officers, were gay.[22] Charlton's autobiography makes little effort to hide his sexuality. Writing in the third person, he described his dislike of women and made it clear that his interests lay elsewhere. This included hosting "special friends" in the privacy of his home, including young RFC officers straight from the leave boat. Charlton's friend J. R. Ackerley confirmed

Charlton's homosexuality and his assertion that Ashmore "had also indulged in homosexual practices, but furtively, screening himself by marriage and by denouncing and punishing the same practice in the ranks of his command."[23] Ashmore's cosmopolitan social life, including the musical parties he hosted and his intimate friendship with Noël Coward, suggest that the claim is true.

None of this would have carried weight with Trenchard unless public scandal was involved. Trenchard and Brancker's plans for promoting Hogg were disrupted in the summer of 1917 because of the latter's romantic involvement with a married woman. Their concern was not about the morality of the relationship but about the potential press interest when her criminal case (involving theft and the use of drugs) went to court. Hogg's career didn't suffer from the controversy (which eventually blew over), and he proved to be an outstanding brigade commander.[24] Trenchard was no more interested in Baring's politics or religion than in his sexuality. He valued Baring's friendship, his many talents, and particularly his sense of duty. Baring could easily have avoided military service, but he had committed himself to helping the war effort in any capacity—without preference or expectation for personal advancement. Baring's loyalty to Henderson, and subsequently Trenchard, was wholehearted, uncompromising, and unswerving. As an outsider, with no pretense to an army career, Baring was neither a threat nor an embarrassment to his fellow officers. His spontaneous and impulsive behavior did not reflect adversely on Trenchard or the RFC. If anything, it indicated that the Flying Corps was different from the rest of the army and that individualism could be cherished without impeding military effectiveness. It was this irrepressible spirit, as much as his selfless dedication, that Trenchard had in mind when he described the "tone of service" that Baring had brought into the RFC.

When Trenchard wrote of Baring, he often described someone much closer to a father figure than to a confidant. Baring made light of this, referring to Trenchard as "the child" in his private letters while also joking, "Generals are like children, they need a lot of looking after," following the incident when Trenchard threw a teapot out of the breakfast room window (after the lid fell off into his cup one too many times).[25] Baring would not be the first to speak truth in jest. How else to explain the punishments inflicted by Baring on Trenchard when he transgressed? Indeed, why should Trenchard be willing to indulge Baring in this manner? That Baring accepted responsibility for Trenchard's actions, and apologized to his victims, suggests a personal (if not paternal) obligation. Although Baring remained the junior officer, their relationship was more familial than deferential, allowing Baring to redress Trenchard in a public setting (with a humorous put-down) without appearing disrespectful or overreaching.

Trenchard was not shy about publicizing the RFC's achievements, partly because he needed to educate the army and partly because he understood the importance of informing and (hopefully) influencing politicians and the public at home. HQ RFC published regular communiques, irreverently known as "comic cuts," detailing the week's air fighting as well as issuing monthly statistical bulletins. However, he vigorously resisted celebrating the achievements of individual "aces," unlike the French air service. In Trenchard's eyes, the air war was a collective endeavor. Although the RAF's postwar officer corps was based on pilots, Trenchard made no distinction, at least in spiritual terms, between individual members of the organization—officers, noncommissioned officers, apprentices, and enlisted men. For Trenchard, the RAF was as indivisible as the air. The "air force spirit" imbued everyone who served, and no one's efforts were more worthy than another's. What was important was that everyone who served shared a common ethos, whether they flew or worked in a support role, whether they were fighter pilots or engine fitters. In citing Baring as the embodiment of "service," Trenchard was not only articulating his fundamental belief about airmen and air warfare but also acknowledging the debt he owed to the man who had supported him throughout the war.

CHAPTER 16

Conclusions

A WORLD WAR, THE ADVENT OF MILITARY AIRPOWER, and the creation of an independent air service were exceptional events, but so too was the transformation of an abrasive, inarticulate infantry officer, lacking social skills and with few visible qualities, into an outstanding leader and respected commander. When leadership is discussed, Trenchard is the exception that makes the rule. He lacked so many of the elements traditionally associated with successful leaders that we need to adopt a broader definition of what leadership comprises. In Trenchard's case, any assessment must also include the contribution of those who surrounded him and, just as importantly, the role of friendship in allowing him to function as an effective commander and inspirational leader.

There is considerable variety in the character, personality, motivation, and style of military officers. Senior commanders are no more likely to adhere to institutional norms than their subordinates. These differences offer alternative perspectives, stimulate innovation, and enhance the quality of decision-making, but they can also cause division. We may like to think that disagreements between senior commanders are rare and that, if they do occur, they are due to professional differences, but they are just as likely to be the result of personality clashes. Jealousy, antipathy, and personal enmity are always to be found in any group of ambitious, highly competitive individuals—even at the highest ranks. War widens rather than closes such fault lines.

The senior leadership directing British military aviation in World War I suffered from all these issues, yet it also oversaw the creation of a highly effective air arm, based on enduring principles that made a significant contribution to Allied victory. The development of airpower in World War I was an erratic, sometimes haphazard process, as the protagonists experimented and steadily learned how to fight an air war. The British air services possessed a visionary commander in David Henderson and a relentless executor of that vision in Hugh Trenchard. Both men were outstanding leaders, but Trenchard possessed the spark of greatness that inspired his pilots, impressed his allies, and persuaded politicians that an independent air service was both desirable and practicable. Trenchard instinctively understood that the devolved nature of air leadership needed a different sort of commander, one who needed to engage closely with his airmen. He also realized that air superiority required sustained, concentrated, offensive effort and that this could be achieved only through innovation and logistic efficiency. Just as importantly, he created a learning organization that was open to bottom-up ideas. However, while much is owed to both individuals, the organizational arrangements that enabled airpower to develop separate from the army were arrived at more by accident than design. The divergent command strategies adopted by the British, French, and German armies meant that it was the British, the smallest of the air arms at the outbreak of World War I, that established the world's first independent air service.

The characteristics of good leadership—integrity, vision, humility, moral courage, honesty, drive, consistency, and loyalty—are universal and timeless, but no leader can possess all these qualities or deploy them to the same degree. We forget that leaders, like all human beings, have faults and so overlook the important question about how they overcame these deficiencies. Moreover, the stress, worry, and isolation of command require leaders to find some form of social support if they are to cope with such relentless pressure. Self-awareness is fundamental to the exercise of leadership. Leaders who do not know themselves cannot know those they lead. The most successful military commanders have surrounded themselves with staff who can help them handle the extraordinary demands of wartime. In some cases this has involved specific skills or abilities, but in others it has extended as far as friendship. Trenchard was acutely aware of his inability to articulate his thoughts, conduct a clear conversation, or explain his decisions. He recruited a senior leadership team who compensated for these weaknesses and were also willing to challenge him. Trenchard inherited Maurice Baring as his assistant with the intention of firing him, only to discover Baring's value as a personal staff officer, mentor, counselor, and friend.

Trenchard and Baring's relationship during World War I was not unprecedented, but it was nonetheless extraordinary. Both men were flawed, but they were also immensely gifted. Well matched in character, they possessed very different personalities. They shared the same motivation and ambitions but interacted with the world in very different ways. Both had experienced a difficult, if not traumatic, adolescence made worse by financial embarrassment and successive academic failures that left them uncertain and underconfident. Trenchard, driven by shame and frustration, found his refuge in the army, while Baring, having toyed with several careers, had yet to find his calling. Without the outbreak of war, their respective paths would probably never have crossed.

The relationship between commanders and their personal staffs can vary greatly; some staff members are kept at arm's length, while others enjoy a more privileged position. Working and living together doesn't necessarily engender friendship. It is a question not of loyalty, respect, or competence but of chemistry. Proximity and shared dangers provide the opportunity, but there must be openness, honesty, and a willingness to share personal thoughts and private turmoil. Willingness to speak truth to power is much lauded, but it is the quickest way to a rapid departure and a new appointment unless the recipient is willing to listen. There are few staff officers who can be honest with their commander, and even fewer commanders prepared to be honest with their staff officers. It is an issue partly of fear and partly of ambition (the two are not mutually exclusive). Trenchard was a good listener, but his personality could overawe otherwise self-confident and assured officers. The twenty-eight-year-old George Griffith, an artillery officer and pre-war pilot, who had served in France in the early months of the war, arrived on promotion at St-Omer in January 1916 having worked successfully for Brancker at the War Office. Griffith had been selected to take over the management of the RFC's stores, but within a few weeks was back in England because Trenchard scared him.[1] Even Baring could be taken aback by Trenchard's single-mindedness: "I'm sure he is a descendant of a bastard of Peter the Great when

Peter the Great was in England learning shipbuilding. He is exactly like him in face, tall and dark, electrically energetic and quick, quite ignorant of everything that had never affected him in work, seeing right through people and judging people and things in space."[2]

The friendship between Trenchard and Baring was genuine, but it emerged slowly. At the beginning there was an element of hero worship on Baring's part: "I should like to tell you without any exaggeration I consider General Trenchard, who commands the RFC at present out here, one of the biggest men I have ever come across, with something very like genius for getting work done and inspiring those under him."[3] Trenchard admired Baring's erudition, literary abilities, and outstanding language skills, but tolerated his showmanship. At some point the two must have realized (or at least sensed) that they shared the same insecurities. Baring makes no direct mention of such an understanding, but there is a revealing passage that alludes to their personal empathy in a letter he wrote to Ethel Smyth:

> I think I understand what he [Trenchard] is driving at better than most people and I sympathise with the background and the overtones of his mind and character. He is one of these people who have such a swift intelligence, such a lightning-like grasp, that they don't make themselves clear when they write. I mean they jump to the end of their sentence when they have hardly got the first word out of their mouth . . . and he knows exactly what you are thinking. I have never, in man or woman, met intuition to beat his.[4]

Paradoxically, it was Trenchard, a man famous for being unable to say what he thought, and chronically incapable of expressing his feelings, who made clear to the world the deep emotional bond he shared with Baring. Trenchard's letter to *The Times* on Baring's death in 1945 may have surprised some of its readers, but not those who had witnessed their relationship firsthand. Among them was Ludlow-Hewitt, who provided Trenchard's biographer with a finely observed picture:

> Baring was an astonishing personality. His duet with Trenchard was even more astonishing. The two, so oddly dissimilar, were perfectly suited and

understood one other perfectly. Baring had a metaphysical mind, perceptive, sharp, detached. He knew the heart of a problem, by logic if you like. Trenchard knew it just as surely by a baffling, barely expressed, intuition. Trenchard and Baring's minds met here and never failed to. If their outlook on life was especially different, one (Baring's) was broad and deep, the other narrow but fiercely concentrated, they seemed to have the gift of mutual comprehension. They shared in common a basic respect for men and human life and (and from different viewpoints) a great understanding of LIFE. Baring was the playboy, the wit, the raconteur loved by others and Trenchard, belying appearances, was the soul of indiscrete toleration.[5]

Sholto Douglas also spoke of Baring's role and his closeness to Trenchard: "He was the very last whom one would have expected ever to make any impact on the Flying Corps; his delicate touch and sensitive imagination, one would have thought, would have been entirely out of place among the somewhat brash youngsters of the squadrons."[6]

Trenchard and Baring lived long before personality tests became popular, but they would probably have been assessed as opposites. Trenchard was an introvert who perceived the world intuitively, made decisions based on thinking, and took a structured, organized approach to dealing with external events. Baring was an extrovert who perceived the world through his senses, made decisions based on feeling, and took a flexible, spontaneous approach to external events.[7] Personality tests can be more entertaining than informative, but they indicate that Trenchard chose someone who not only thought differently but also emoted differently. Trenchard was charismatic, with boundless energy and relentless determination, but he struggled with self-regulation and performed poorly in managing relationships with others. On the other hand, he was aware of these weaknesses and had the open-mindedness to find someone who could provide the emotional and social competencies he lacked. While emotional intelligence can be learned, the Trenchard-Baring relationship suggests that a collective persona can offer the basis for effective leadership.[8]

It is no coincidence that Trenchard referred to Baring as his guide and mentor. Baring enabled Trenchard, who had a natural tendency to an authoritative, if not coercive, style of leadership to find a more affiliative and sometimes democratic approach. Together, they reached a level of emotional intelligence that, as individuals, they could never have achieved, including the ability to deploy different, if not contradictory leadership styles in a dynamic, changing environment. As Gary Sheffield has observed, "Natural, inspirational leaders do not necessarily have the ability to become good commanders."[9] Baring nurtured Trenchard's self-confidence and emotional health, while enabling him to develop the trust and mutual understanding with his subordinates that are essential to command. In a war when "command recognition" (the degree to which an ordinary soldier knows his senior officers) was low, Trenchard stands head and shoulders above his fellow generals. Trenchard was convinced that the RFC's offensive strategy was the best way to defeat the German army, but he had to confront the price of that strategy in every visit he made to the squadrons. Baring provided the psychological anchor and emotional resilience that Trenchard needed as their commander and leader. Baring could not stop Trenchard from making mistakes, but he was able to soften the impact—at least while they served on the Western Front. Once in London, however, Baring could no longer play this role. It is arguable that the absence of key subordinates, and Baring's diminished influence, lay at the heart of Trenchard's missteps during his first term as CAS.

In peacetime, the selection of personal staff officers is carefully managed, and appointments are usually reserved for individuals with high potential who could benefit from the broadening experience. The senior commander concerned may have the final decision on selection, following an interview or a personal recommendation, or they may simply inherit an existing appointment, but it is likely that the candidates will all share similar characteristics. In wartime, commanders have an opportunity to gather round them individuals with very different personalities.[10] This is not a guarantee of success: witness Rothermere and de Castelnau's staffs, who adopted an aggressive approach in championing their respective principal. Rather than working to smooth relationships, they encouraged friction and, in the process, harmed the very interests they sought to protect. Trenchard's staff in France avoided falling into this trap, but military organizations tend to attract, recruit, and employ people with similar characteristics—partly because of a desire to maintain "institutional values" and partly because of unconscious (implicit) bias.[11] It is highly unlikely that Baring would have volunteered, been accepted, and found productive employment as a soldier without the extraordinary circumstances of a world war. The same might be said of Rawlins, Sassoon, and Hansen—none of whom were destined for military careers.

Contemporary military organizations might be better advised to find a different method for selecting personal staff for senior commanders, one that recognizes the importance of contrasting personalities as well as of career development. There can be no better example than Baring, so different from Trenchard yet so close emotionally that they functioned as one. Baring may not have been exceptional in the support he gave his commander, but he was undoubtedly unusual in the range of attributes he brought to the task. He exhibited the compassion and concern of Rawlins, the networking and language skills of Sassoon, the loyalty and literary skills of Hansen, and the hard work and exuberance of de Guingand. What was unique, however, was Trenchard's willingness to acknowledge Baring's contribution. Great leaders have great flaws, as if excellence in one area must have a counterbalance in another. The most successful leaders find someone to meet their emotional, social, and intellectual needs, but it takes a truly remarkable leader to declare their flaws and admit how much of their success they owed to their friend.

APPENDIX A

Maurice Baring's War Diary and Notebooks

BARING REFERS TO A PERSONAL DIARY AS EARLY as 1906. The context suggests that this was something he maintained when overseas, perhaps with a view to future books. There is no indication that he kept a diary on a day-to-day basis beyond these periods. The Berg Collection holds a typed copy of his war diary from 30 June 1914 to 16 November 1918. There are handwritten corrections and minor additions. This document provided the framework (and original title) for *Headquarters RFC*—with additional content sourced from his letters and the notebooks. Baring's notebooks comprise fourteen copies of Army Book 136. Each six-by-four-inch notebook consists of some ninety lined pages. Eight are card-covered, and the remainder have paper covers. Two are account books; the earliest ink entries are in a different (and neater) hand than the pencil scrawl that appears from January 1915 onward, when Baring took over the running of the mess, a task made more difficult than it should have been because of his chronic innumeracy. Baring would record that it took one sergeant, one corporal, and two clerks to help him complete the mess accounts.[1]

The notebooks have been dated (in pencil) on their covers, probably by Baring himself. The first book (volume 1) opens in August 1915, when Baring began writing notes at Trenchard's request. At the very top of the page is a scribbled reference to marmalade, in response to Trenchard's comment that he liked Oxford Marmalade, and the occasion for Trenchard's remark that Baring had a memory which he would make use of. The last book (volume XII) closes in November 1918. Volume VI, covering the period August to October 1916, is missing, although there are several pages toward the end of volume I labeled "Sep 16." As volume V is the last notebook with hard covers, it appears that Baring's supply of fresh notebooks had been exhausted pending arrival of the softback version of Army Book 136, forcing him to recycle some of the earlier volumes. All the notebooks feature a series of short, densely written action points. There are occasional passages of shorthand and draft letters as well as narrative accounts (such as his interviews with the No. 56 Squadron pilots involved in shooting down a German ace, Werner Voss, in September 1917). The latter appears, largely unchanged, in *Headquarters RFC*. Someone (presumably Baring) has used the inside of the covers to practice with their censor's red ink stamp and to doodle—faces and heads are the most popular.

The notebooks are difficult to read, as Baring's handwriting is often illegible; this point is also noted by Jocelyn Hillgarth and Julian Jeffs, who edited Baring's collected letters, although they added that when he used a typewriter, "he hit the keys in such a haphazard way that the result was often little better." A second challenge is that Baring used a private language in writing to his family or intimate friends. The "Expressions" had been created by the Baring-Ponsonby family and vested words and phrases with specific meaning. For example, "Heygate" meant "second-rate" or "jobsworth." "Padlock" meant "secret," and "Deep Padlock" meant "Very Secret."[2] Thus, Maurice wrote to Nan Herbert about Trenchard's efforts to get him promoted. "Deep Padlock: He recommended me to be made a Captain, as he said I was doing a Captain's work, but the Heygates at GHQ won't do it as they said they'd have to do it for the others. He says it will be done later."[3]

APPENDIX B

Operational Tempo

THE RFC'S OPERATIONAL STRATEGY WAS BASED ON the principle of maximum effort during major ground offensives. During the Battle of the Somme, No. 9 Squadron (equipped with eighteen airplanes) was employed on artillery cooperation, infantry support, and photography. In the first month of the offensive (July 1916) they flew 835 sorties (some twenty-seven sorties per day), equivalent to forty-six sorties per machine per month. By comparison, Fliegerabteilung Artillerie 221 (FA(A) 221), a German artillery cooperation unit (equipped with an average of six airplanes), flew forty-eight sorties (roughly two sorties per day) in the same month and in the same battle, equivalent to eight sorties per machine per month—a fraction of No. 9 Squadron's rate (figures 1 and 2). The key to the RFC's greater operational effort was the ready supply of replacement crews and machines. The relative operational tempo between the two units varied during the war, but No. 9 Squadron was able to operate at a consistently high level for extended periods, although this came at a price: the squadron lost 67 machines to enemy action and 119 in accidents between January 1916 and the Armistice, whereas FA(A) 221 lost just 10 machines to enemy action and 34 in accidents over the same period. If No. 9 Squadron's casualties are adjusted for the greater number of total sorties flown, the loss rate is virtually the same as that experienced by FA(A) 221. Between June 1916 and November 1918 (some thirty months), FA(A) 221 completed 2,917 sorties and employed a total of 89 machines, whereas No. 9 Squadron completed 12,624 sorties and employed a total of 281 machines—equivalent to 36 percent more sorties per airplane.[1]

FA(A)221's peak effort occurred in September 1917 during the fighting at Third Ypres; by March 1918 and the German spring offensive, however,

APPENDIX B

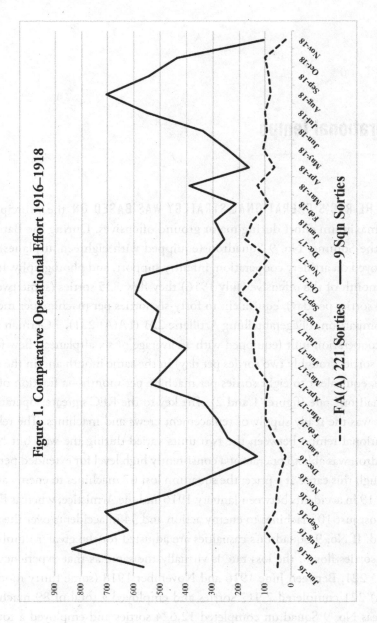

Figure 1. Comparative Operational Effort 1916–1918

it was unable to match this level. Although this comparison offers a narrow window on the question of relative operational effort, the picture is consistent with other evidence pointing to the RFC's higher operational tempo and logistic efficiency. By way of comparison, the American 24th Aero and

91st Aero squadrons (employed in a similar role) flew 243 and 186 operational sorties, respectively, in October 1918—an average of 11 and 8.5 sorties per machine, similar to FA(A) 221, but substantially less than No. 9 Squadron.[2]

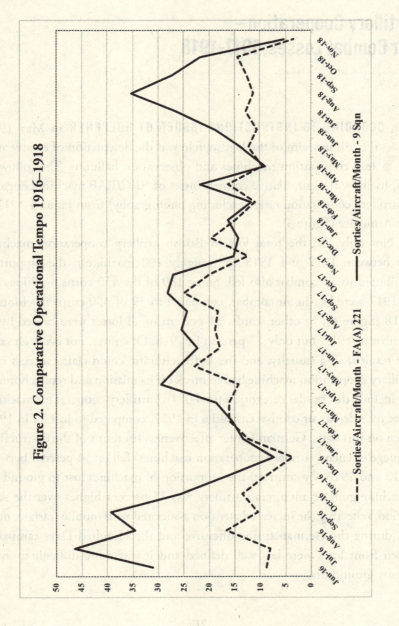

Figure 2. Comparative Operational Tempo 1916–1918

APPENDIX C

Artillery Cooperation— Air Combat Losses, 1917-1918

ACCORDING TO INSTRUCTIONS ISSUED BY HOEPPNER in May 1917, the primary aim of the Jagdstaffeln was the destruction of enemy artillery cooperation machines and observation balloons. The following graphs show the cumulative combat losses of RFC/RAF machines engaged in artillery cooperation tasks (excluding photography) from January 1917 to the Armistice (figure 3).

Not only did the total loss in British artillery cooperation machines fall between 1917 and 1918 (by roughly 100 machines); the proportion attributed to air combat also fell. Some 139 of the 450 corps machines lost in 1917 were lost in air combat, compared to 59 of 350 corps machines in 1918 (figure 4). In other words, 31 percent of all losses were caused by air combat in 1917, but only 17 percent in 1918. Of course, not every air combat resulted in a casualty, and the Luftstreitkräfte could claim success if an artillery cooperation machine had to break off its mission and return home. If we include this border category, a total of 162 artillery cooperation machines were recorded as air combat casualties in 1917, compared to just 74 in 1918. Even on this basis, German fighter effectiveness (in terms of the destruction/ damage of enemy artillery cooperation machines) fell by 54 percent between 1917 and 1918. By contrast, the proportion of machines lost to ground fire (machine gun) or antiaircraft artillery was 33 percent higher over the same period, reflecting the increased attrition associated with mobile warfare, notably during the German spring offensive and the Hundred Days campaign, when front lines were less well defined and it was more difficult to avoid enemy ground fire.

ARTILLERY COOPERATION–AIR COMBAT LOSSES | 211

As the primary aim of Trenchard's continuous offensive was to protect the RFC's support operations from the German fighter force, the data indicates that this strategy was increasingly successful through 1917 and 1918—a remarkable achievement when one considers the technical advantages that the Luftstreitkräfte enjoyed for much of the war.

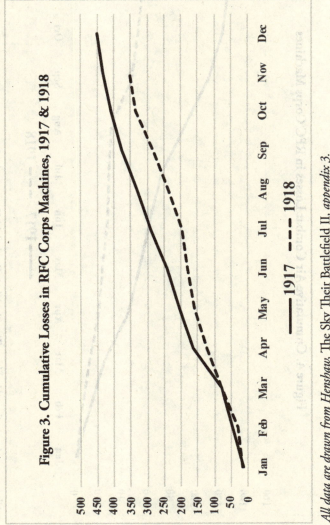

Figure 3. Cumulative Losses in RFC Corps Machines, 1917 & 1918

All data are drawn from Henshaw, The Sky Their Battlefield II, appendix 3.

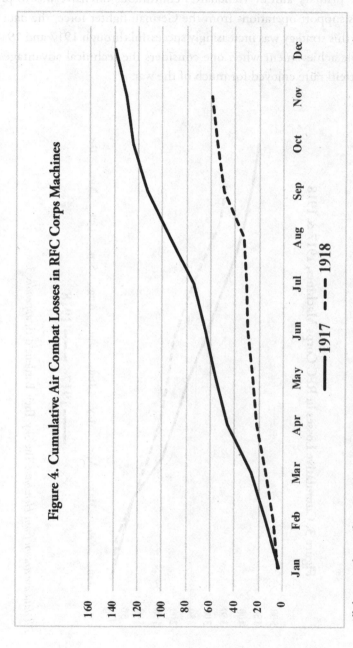

All data are drawn from Henshaw, The Sky Their Battlefield II, *appendix 3.*

APPENDIX D

Operational Wastage

FROM THE SUMMER OF 1918 ONWARD, THE Luftstreitkräfte found itself increasingly short of pilots, planes, and petroleum—the three P's that determine airpower capability. Many Jagdstaffeln were only manned to 75 percent of establishment (and some to only 50 percent), while replacement pilots lacked the training and operational experience of their predecessors.[1] Frontline aircraft numbers fell by approximately one thousand between March and November 1918, while aviation fuel became increasingly scarce. The Allied economic blockade was partly to blame, but the root cause lay in a failure to anticipate the level of attrition that an intensified air war would bring, and the high wastage associated with offensive air operations. By contrast, the British and French had greatly expanded their pilot training and aircraft production capacity in 1916, well before Germany embarked on a similar but more tentative expansion. At the Armistice, the British and French had collectively produced more than 123,000 airframes and 126,000 aeroengines, almost three times those produced by Germany (43,931 airframes and 40,449 aeroengines).[2] They had also trained nearly 36,000 pilots, almost four times more than Germany (10,000). By the end of the war, Britain was producing new pilots at a rate of 1,200 per month, compared to around 360 graduating per month from the German flying schools.[3]

Detailed information on the losses suffered by the Luftstreitkräfte is limited, as the German Official History acknowledges, but the available data indicate that the wastage in frontline flying personnel posed a significant problem from as early as 1917 and became acute after Third Ypres, necessitating special recruiting measures and the reluctant imposition of changes designed to speed the training of fighter pilots.[4] Flying personnel casualties

214 | APPENDIX D

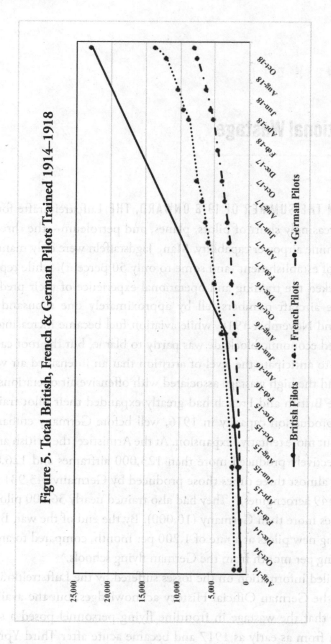

Figure 5. Total British, French & German Pilots Trained 1914–1918

(pilots, observers, and air gunners) from all causes, at home and at the front, from August 1914 to November 1918 amounted to approximately 11,000 personnel. Pilot losses represented 52 percent of this total, averaging 200 per month in 1917 and 400 per month in 1918.[5] The actual shortfall is likely to have been even greater. British experience indicates that noncombat losses (including fatigue, illness, and unsuitability) may have accounted for nearly half of all wastage.

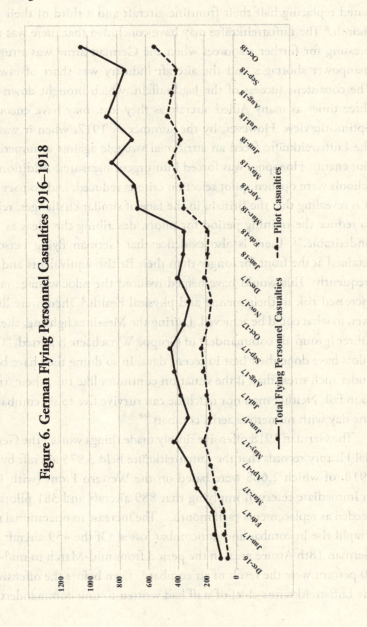

Figure 6. German Flying Personnel Casualties 1916–1918

The Germans recognized the need to compensate for wastage if they were to contest air superiority, and they planned to replace one-third of the aircraft committed at the front and one-seventh of the crews each month. However, these figures are substantially lower than those of the British, who anticipated replacing half their frontline aircraft and a third of their pilots each month.[6] The Luftstreitkräfte may have concluded that there was no value in pressing for further resources when the German army was struggling with manpower shortages and the aircraft industry was short of raw materials. The consistent success of the Jagdstaffeln, which brought down two if not three times as many Allied aircraft as they lost, may have encouraged this optimistic view. However, by the summer of 1917, when it was clear that the Luftstreitkräfte faced an attritional struggle against a numerically superior enemy, Hoeppner was forced into urgent measures. Additional training schools were opened, pilot selection criteria reduced, and courses shortened. It is revealing that the British, in the face of similar challenges, rejected calls to reduce the training period for pilots, describing the ideas as "extremely undesirable."[7] There is also evidence that German flying personnel were retained at the front for longer than their British equivalents and rested less frequently. This would have helped reduced the pilot wastage rate—but at increased risk to their mental and physical health.[8] There were limits, however, to what could be achieved. During the Messines fighting, the Gruppenführer (group air commander) of Gruppe Wytschaete reported, "Our fighter pilots have done their best in recent days. In so doing they have been placed under such stress that, if the situation continues like this, their strength will soon fail. Neither man nor machine can survive five to six combat sorties in one day with numerous aerial combats."[9]

The German 1918 offensive simply made things worse. The German Official History records that the Luftstreitkräfte held 3,975 aircraft by 21 March 1918, of which 2,668 were based on the Western Front (with 1,000 held in immediate reserve), implying that 889 aircraft and 381 pilots would be needed as replacements each month.[10] The increase in operational tempo saw a rapid rise in combat and noncombat losses. Of the 459 aircraft lost in the German 18th Armee area, in the period from mid-March to mid-May, only 40 percent were the result of air combat.[11] Even before the offensive opened, the Luftstreitkräfte's chief of staff had written to unit commanders about the high losses suffered in December 1917 (which were around three times the level experienced in December 1916), demanding that greater fighter protection be provided to close reconnaissance machines and more attention paid to the potential impact of weather on air combat.[12] Although the German aircraft industry failed to deliver the 2,000 aircraft and 2,500 engines per month envisaged by the Amerika program, aircraft and engine deliveries still averaged around 1,700 and 1,641 per month, respectively, during 1918. On the other hand, the flying schools were only producing an average of 360 pilots a month.[13] We do not know the exact monthly wastage in pilots and aircraft, but while the supply of replacement aircraft may have been sufficient to cope with wastage, the pilot situation was much less satisfactory, a problem exacerbated by the decision to increase the number of frontline units rather than improving the sustainability of existing ones.[14]

Notes

INTRODUCTION

1. James covered some of this ground nearly thirty years ago, but he had little to say about the character, behavior, or interactions of senior leaders. J. James, *The Paladins* (London: Macdonald & Co., 1990).
2. Sir Dermot Boyle, the first graduate of RAF College Cranwell to become CAS.
3. ACM Dowding (1882–1970) was CinC RAF Fighter Command, 1936–40. R. Wright, *Dowding and the Battle of Britain* (London: Macdonald & Co., 1969), 77.
4. The idea that RAF leadership is somehow exceptional and that Dowding's actions during the Battle of Britain offer positive leadership lessons is based on slim evidence but is still cited in contemporary literature. J. Jupp, *Rise Above: Leadership Lessons from the RAF* (Harlow: Pearson, 2021).
5. See Philip Joubert de la Ferté's history of the RAF, *The Third Service* (London: Thames & Hudson, 1955).
6. AFBSC (02)4, "Strengthening RAF Ethos," 26 April 2002; AFBSC (03)2, "Developing Excellence in Leadership," February 2003.
7. Major General J. F. C. "Boney" Fuller (1878–1966) served in the Tank Corps during World War I and became a noted military theorist. Air Commodore L. E. O. Charlton (1879–1958) served as a brigade commander in World War I. He was replaced as chief staff officer in Iraq in 1923 when he raised objections to the RAF's policy of aerial policing. He resigned his commission three years later to write on airpower issues.
8. There is conflicting research on the behavioral preferences of senior military officers. R. Moffett and N. Hein, "Homogeneity in Behavioural Preferences among U.S. Army Leaders," *Group Dynamics Theory Research and Practice* 1, no. 3 (1997): 222–30; J. Pierce, *Is the Organizational Culture of the U.S. Army Congruent with the Professional Development of the Senior Level Officer Corps?* (Carlisle, PA: USAWC Press, 2010); J. Newcomer and D. Connelly, "Personality and Leadership—The Potential Impact to Future Strategic Thinking," *Air and Space Power Journal*, Summer 2020, 36–54.
9. P. Dye, "Leading Change," RAF Leadership Forum, HQ Personnel and Training Command, September 2002; D. Anderson, *Leadership in Defence* (Shrivenham: Defence Leadership Centre, 2004), 74.
10. Field Marshal Sir William Robertson (1860–1935) was a senior soldier and businessman. ACM Sir Keith Williamson, who became CAS in 1982, started his RAF career as a Halton apprentice, but never "served" in the ranks.

11. *RUSI Journal*, August 1996, 9–12.
12. R. Graves and L. Hart, *T. E. Lawrence, Letters to His Biographers* (London: Cassell, 1963), 123.
13. Graves and Hart, 53.
14. MRAF Sir Hugh Trenchard (1873–1956) was a soldier, airman, police commissioner, and businessman.
15. The air secretary is responsible for the RAF's personnel management, including postings, promotions, and career development of officers and other ranks.
16. Relevant works include H. A. Jones, *The War in the Air*, vol. 6 (Oxford: Clarendon, 1937); J. A. Chamier, *The Birth of the Royal Air Force* (London: Sir Isaac Pitman & Sons, 1943); H. St. George Saunders, *The Rise of British Air Power 1911–1939* (London: Oxford University Press, 1944); H. R. Allen, *The Legacy of Lord Trenchard* (London: Cassell & Co., 1976); B. D. Powers, *Strategy without Slide-Rule* (London: Croom Helm, 1976); M. Dean, *The Royal Air Force and Two World Wars* (London: Cassell, 1979); M. Cooper, *The Birth of Independent Air Power* (London: Allen & Unwin, 1986); and R. Overy, *The Birth of the RAF 1918* (London: Allen Lane, 2018).
17. J. Black, *The Battle of Waterloo* (London: Icon Books, 2010), 220.
18. The Combined Bomber Offensive was the joint American/British strategic bombing campaign, mounted between 1943 and 1945, aimed at the progressive destruction and dislocation of the German military, industrial, and economic systems and the undermining of the morale of the German people.
19. TNA AIR 1/119/15/40/69, Brancker to Sykes, 8 September 1913.
20. M. Paris, "The Rise of the Airmen: The Origins of Air Force Elitism, c. 1890–1918," *Journal of Contemporary History* 28, no. 1 (1993): 123–41.

CHAPTER 1. AN UNLIKELY SOLDIER–AN UNLIKELY PARTNERSHIP

1. The Honourable Maurice Baring (1874–1945), the eighth child and fourth son of Edward Baring, 1st Baron Revelstoke, was a diplomat, journalist, staff officer, and writer, with over seventy works to his name.
2. P. Fussell, *The Ordeal of Alfred M. Hale: The Memoirs of a Soldier Servant* (London: Leo Cooper, 1975).
3. M. Baring, *R.F.C. H.Q. 1914–1918* (London: G. Bell & Sons, 1920), 10–11. Conrad Russell (1878–1947) was a civil servant, soldier, farmer, and letter writer. Bron Herbert (1874–1916) and his sister Nan (1880–1958) were Baring's closest and dearest friends. Herbert had reported on the Boer War (where he lost a leg) and was later private secretary to Richard Haldane, secretary of state for war, before being appointed a minister in the Liberal government. He resigned when the coalition government was formed in May 1915 and volunteered for the RFC.
4. Albums of Nan Herbert (ANH), Private Diary, 9 August 1914.
5. "Obituary, Mr Maurice Baring—Poet, Essayist and Novelist," *Times*, 17 December 1945, 6. Conrad Russell, writing to Diana Cooper, indicated that her husband (Duff Cooper)

had written Baring's obituary. G. Blakiston, ed., *Letters of Conrad Russell* (London: John Murray, 1987), 256.

6. "Mr Maurice Baring—An Appreciation," *Times*, 18 December 1947, 7. A further recollection was contributed by Ettie Grenfell (Lady Desborough), *Times*, 19 December 1945, 14. See also R. Davenport-Hines, *Ettie: The Intimate Life and Dauntless Spirit of Lady Desborough* (London: Weidenfeld & Nicolson, 2008), 359–60.

7. L. Lovat, *Maurice Baring: A Postscript* (London: Hollis & Carter, 1947), 17.

8. General Edouard de Castelnau (1851–1944) served twice as Joffre's chief of staff (1911–14 and 1915–16). A fervent Catholic and royalist, he lost three sons during the war. Strongly anti-German and anti-Communist, de Castelnau became a prominent figure in postwar right-wing politics, leading the short-lived Fédération Nationale Catholique, which at one stage boasted over 2 million members. *Times*, 9 October 1915, 6, and 23 March 1944, 7.

9. *The Observer*, 26 March 1916. For a discussion of the frequent (and complex) changes in the French High Command during World War I, see R. A. Doughty, *Pyrrhic Victory—French Strategy and Operations in the Great War* (Cambridge, MA: Belknap Press of Harvard University Press, 2005).

10. De Castelnau's strong faith and belief in the offensive meant that he was known throughout the French army as *le capuchin botte* (the fighting friar). La Ferriere, the French liaison officer at HQ RFC, claimed that the only criticism that could be made of de Castelnau was that he was an able man.

11. *London Gazette*, 31 December 1918.

12. Baring, *R.F.C. H.Q.*, 273–74.

13. C. Van Schaick Mitchell, *Letters from a Liaison Officer 1918–1919* (Princeton, NJ: Princeton University Press, 1920), 99–100; H. Asquith, *Memories and Reflections 1852–1927* (London: Cassell & Co., 1928), 2:57; D. Lloyd George, *War Memoirs*, vol. 1 (London: Odhams, 1934), 93–94; *Times*, 1 October 1915, 1.

14. *The Aeroplane*, 21 June 1922, 437–38; R. Las Vergnas, "Un écrivain catholique anglais: M. Maurice Baring," *Revue des deux mondes*, 15 October 1936, 917–43; L. Chaigne, *Maurice Baring* (Paris: J. De Gigord, 1932), 43–44. De Castelnau may have read some of Baring's work, as the French edition of *Translations* had been published in March 1918. M. Baring, "Carnet de guerre d'un Officier d'État-Major, Fête Galante, La Rose Bleue," *Les cahiers britanniques et américains*, no. 4 (Paris: C. Georges-Bazile, 1918).

15. Trenchard chose Thomas Marson, who had served on the Western Front with No. 56 Squadron and the RAF IF. Marson remained Trenchard's private secretary for ten years. Marson, or "Grand Pa," and Baring would become good friends. J. Hillgarth and J. Jeffs, *Maurice Baring Letters* (Norwich: Michael Russell, 2007), 129; E. Letley, *Maurice Baring—A Citizen of Europe* (London: Constable, 1991), 189–90.

16. Baring's first two novels, *Passing By* (1921) and *Overlooked* (1922), could be described as "experimental" in that neither follows established form and both tackle questions that owe more to his World War I experiences than their Edwardian setting. *Passing By* is a love story told from two different perspectives, presented in the form of diary entries and

letters (the same technique employed in *H.Q. R.F.C.*). It leaves the reader to decide which is true or whether both accounts can be true. *Overlooked* is also a love story, but it centers on how observation and imaginative speculation are inadequate to understanding an individual's motives. It is not difficult to see this as an allegory about Trenchard and the private man hidden behind the public figure.

17. *Times*, 19 July 1920, 9.
18. F. Fox, *GHQ—Montreuil-sur-Mer* (London: Philip Allan & Co., 1920); C. de Pierrefeu, *French Headquarters 1915–1918* (London: Geoffrey Bles, 1924).
19. *The Aeroplane*, 19 May 1920, 983–85. *The Spectator* was content to recommend the book, "though it reveals no wonderful secrets, tells no scandal, blasts no reputations and contains no vigorous indictment of those in authority." *Spectator*, 17 July 1920, 85–86.
20. *Flight*, 24 June 1920, 670; J. Sweetman, "Crucial Months for Survival: The Royal Air Force, 1918–1919," *Journal of Contemporary History* 19, no. 3 (1984): 529–47.
21. M. Baring, *The Puppet Show of Memory* (London: Heinemann, 1922); Chaigne, *Maurice Baring*; E. Smyth, *Maurice Baring* (London: Heinemann, 1938); and Letley, *Maurice Baring*; L. Liggera, "In Such Fortitude: Major the Hon. Maurice Baring, OBE," *Stand To*, no. 58 (April 2000): 34–35.
22. T. J. Binyon, "Round Things," review of *Maurice Baring: A Citizen of Europe*, by Emma Letley, *London Review of Books*, 24 October 1991, 20–22.
23. Blakiston, *Letters*, 256. Charles Grey (1875–1953) was the founder-editor of *The Aeroplane*, an influential aviation journal published weekly from 1911. Grey was a controversial figure with pronounced right-wing views who made enemies as easily as friends. *The Aeroplane*, 19 May 1920, 983; T. James, "Charles Grey and His Pungent Pen," *Aeronautical Journal*, October 1969, 839–52; M. Lochhead, "Maurice Baring's Books," *Blackfriars* 28, no. 326 (1947): 210–14.
24. Winston Churchill, "The Russian Enigma," BBC, 1 October 1939: "I cannot forecast to you the action of Russia. It is a riddle, wrapped in a mystery, inside an enigma; but perhaps there is a key. That key is Russian national interest." Churchill was a close friend of Hugo Baring (Maurice's younger brother). They served together in the same regiment—until Hugo had to leave because of financial problems stemming from the family banking crisis. R. Churchill, *Winston S. Churchill*, companion vol. 1, part 1: *1896–1900* (London: Heinemann, 1967), 927–28.
25. Many of the expressions had a false derivative. Thus *Robespierre*, who was a dandy, meant "shabby," while *Ibsen* meant "ordinary" (what everybody has always said or thought). On the other hand, *Floater* meant anything that gave rise to an awkwardness or distaste (scatological).
26. Hillgarth and Jeffs, *Letters*, 121. Baring's military service papers recorded that he was fluent in seven languages (including Danish and Greek).
27. Letley, *Maurice Baring*, 168; Baring, *Puppet Show*, 118–37.
28. Baring once again failed at arithmetic, but his French essay was judged so good that the Civil Service Commissioners granted him an overall pass.

29. Baring's dispatches were published as *With the Russians in Manchuria* (London: Methuen, 1905), and, in expanded form, as *What I Saw in Russia* (London: Thomas Nelson, 1913).
30. Lovat, *Maurice Baring*, 9.
31. *Times*, 10 December 1912, 7; Baring, *With the Russians*, ix, 162–70.
32. Edmund Gosse (1849–1928) was an influential writer and critic; Ethel Smyth (1858–1944), a suffragette, writer, and composer.
33. Edward Marsh (1872–1953), polymath, civil servant, and strong supporter of the arts. Marsh devoted a chapter to Baring in his autobiography, *A Number of People* (London: Harper & Brothers, 1939). According to Marsh's biographer, Baring had considerable personal charm. "His letters, with their private language, obtuseness and darting turns of thought, may perplex the casual reader but, for the intended recipient, were resonant with his personality." C. Hassall, *Edward Marsh—A Biography* (London: Longmans, 1959), 50–51. Baring's letters to Marsh can be found in the Henry W. and Albert A. Berg Collection of English and American Literature, New York Public Library.
34. George Grahame (1873–1940) was a diplomat, ambassador at Brussels and Madrid; Hilaire Belloc (1870–1953), a writer and historian; Raymond Asquith (1878–1916), a barrister, leading figure in the group of intellectuals known as "The Coterie," and eldest son of the British prime minister; John Buchan (1875–1940), a writer, politician, and diplomat; Gilbert Chesterton (1874–1936), a writer, philosopher, theologian, and critic; Evan Charteris (1864–1940), a barrister, biographer, and patron of the arts; Juliet Duff (1881–1965), a socialite and hostess; Ettie Grenfell (1867–1952), a socialite, hostess, and member of the royal household; and H. G. Wells (1866–1946), a writer and futurist.
35. Davenport-Hines, *Ettie*, 359.
36. Marsh, *A Number of People*, 65.
37. Hillgarth and Jeffs, *Letters*, 112, Baring to Marsh, 18 September 1916; ANH, Baring to Nan, 20 September 1916; Lovat, *Maurice Baring*, 58, Baring to Ethel Smyth, 20 September 1916.
38. Trenchard has been the subject of two authorized biographies, neither entirely satisfactory, although for different reasons. Andrew Boyle's *Trenchard—Man of Vision* is comprehensive but presents a one-sided picture and rarely offers criticism of his subject. Russell Miller's *Boom* draws on a wider range of sources but is thin in places and rarely delves into Trenchard's character or motives. A. Boyle, *Trenchard—Man of Vision* (London: Collins, 1962); R. Miller, *Boom—The Life of Viscount Trenchard, Father of the Royal Air Force* (London: Weidenfeld & Nicolson, 2016).
39. Sandhurst offered entry to the "best" infantry and cavalry regiments while Woolwich offered entry to either the Royal Engineers or the Royal Artillery.
40. *West Somerset Free Press*, 1 June 1889, 1; *Western Gazette*, 12 July 1889, 7, and 2 August 1889, 7; *Chard and Ilminster News*, 5 August 1889, 5, and 17 August 1889, 5.
41. Boyle, *Trenchard*, 21–23.
42. *Times*, 29 April 2022.
43. CUL Add 9429/1B/1218(iv).

44. Boyle, *Trenchard*, 46. There is no record that Trenchard ever returned to Taunton. When he came to choose his title on entering the House of Lords, he selected Wolfeton, the ancient Trenchard family seat in Dorset, rather than the Somerset town where he had been born and brought up.
45. Boyle, *Trenchard*, 376.
46. Lorraine was killed in a flying accident in May 1912.
47. IWM 27, "Interview with Cecil Reginald King." Edward Ling, who encountered Trenchard while on sentry duty, also recalled the terrifying sound of Boom's voice. *Daily Telegraph*, 9 April 1962.
48. *The Aeroplane*, 8 January 1914, 40.

CHAPTER 2. LEADERSHIP AND FRIENDSHIP

1. V. J. Gray, *Xenophon's Mirror of Princes* (Oxford: Oxford University Press, 2011); C. Krebs and J. Moles, eds., "Aspects of Leadership in Xenophon," *Histes Supplement 5* (2016): 51–83; R. F. Buxton, "Xenophon on Leadership: Commanders as Friends," in M. Flower, ed., *The Cambridge Companion to Xenophon* (Cambridge: Cambridge University Press, 2017), 323–37. The British Defence Academy references Xenophon's writings on leadership but makes no mention of the importance of friendship. Anderson, *Leadership in Defence*, A-4.
2. A. Silard and S. Wright, "The Price of Wearing (or Not Wearing) the Crown: The Effects of Loneliness on Leaders and Followers," *Leadership* 16, no. 4 (2020): 405.
3. According to the British Defence Academy, the attributes of a military leader comprise Integrity; Vision; Communication; Decision Taking; Innovation; Humility; and Professional Knowledge. Anderson, *Leadership in Defence*, 21–23.
4. S. P. Huntington, *The Common Defense* (New York: Columbia University Press, 1961).
5. Human beings require social and emotional connections to be able to function effectively. The more a commander is isolated, both emotionally and socially, the more their performance is compromised. R. Ashkenhas, "How to Overcome Executive Isolation," *Harvard Business Review*, 19 March 2014; Silard and Wright, "Price of Wearing (or Not Wearing) the Crown."
6. W. Goerlitz, *The German General Staff* (New York: Frederick Praeger, 1953), 180–82.
7. R. Parkinson, *Tormented Warrior—Ludendorff and the Supreme Command* (London: Hodder & Stoughton, 1978), 174–75; R. Asprey, *The German High Command at War* (New York: William Morrow, 1991), 462–63.
8. Asprey, *High Command*, 464.
9. N. Dixon, *On the Psychology of Military Incompetence* (London: Jonathan Cape, 1976), 19, 52.
10. Even "good" generals are not immune to stress—as General George Patton's "slapping" incidents indicate. C. D'Este, *A Genius for War* (New York: HarperCollins, 1995), 538–39.
11. N. Boyd and R. Taylor, "A Developmental Approach to the Examination of Friendship in Leader/Follower Relationships," *Leadership Quarterly* 9, no. 1 (1998): 1–25; P. Bregan, B. Laker, et al., "What to Do When You Become Your Friend's Boss," *Harvard Business*

Review, 24 September 2020; K. Unsworth, D. Kragt, and A. Johnston-Billings, "Am I a Leader or a Friend? How Leaders Deal with Pre-existing Friendships," *Leadership Quarterly* 28, no. 6 (December 2018): 674–85.

12. Socrates defined friendship as the exchange of benefits for mutual eudaemonia (happiness). It is mutual, instinctive, and affective.
13. F. de Guingand, *Generals at War* (London: Hodder and Stoughton, 1964), 15.
14. De Pierrefeu, *French Headquarters*, 43–44; R. Blake, ed., *The Private Papers of Douglas Haig: 1914–1919* (London: Eyre & Spottiswoode, 1952), 159. Major Francois Camus (1871–1921) was an engineer and a staff officer with General de Castelnau, 1914–16; Field Marshal (later 1st Earl) Sir Douglas Haig (1861–1928) was CinC BEF, 1915–18.
15. P. Gibbs, *Realities of War* (London: Heinemann, 1920), 200.
16. Brian Holden Reid offers the proposition that "behind every successful commander stands an able chief of staff: intuitive, energetic, gifted with foresight and tact; but above all, devoted to his chief." B. Holden Reid, "The Commander and His Chief of Staff: Ulysses S. Grant and John A. Rawlins," in G. Sheffield, ed., *Leadership and Command: The Anglo-American Military Experience since 1861* (London: Brassey's, 1997), 17.
17. General Hiram Ulysses Grant (1822–85), a soldier and politician, was president of the United States from 1869 to 1877. Grant's life has been the subject of numerous studies. Among the most recent are H. Bands, *The Man Who Saved the Union—Ulysses Grant in War and Peace* (New York: Anchor Books, 2013); R. White, *American Ulysses—A Life of Ulysses S. Grant* (New York: Random House, 2016); and R. Chernow, *Grant* (New York: Penguin Press, 2017).
18. John Aaron Rawlins (1831–69) was a lawyer, soldier, and politician. Rawlins has been the subject of two full-length biographies, published over a hundred years apart. J. Wilson, *The Life of John A. Rawlins* (New York: Neale, 1916); A. Ottens, *General John A. Rawlins—No Ordinary Man* (Bloomington: Indiana University Press, 2021).
19. G. Farnum, "John Rawlins, Country Lawyer and Grant's Lieutenant," *American Bar Association Journal* (1943): 650–51, 657; Reid, "Commander and His Chief of Staff," 17–36.
20. Farnum, "John Rawlins," 651. Rawlins would also write, "I love him [Grant] as a father." Wilson, *The Life*, 71.
21. U. S. Grant III, "Civil War: Fact and Fiction," *Civil War History* 2, no. 2 (1956): 29–40; Chernow, *Grant*, 84.
22. White, *American Ulysses*, 139; Bands, *Man Who Saved the Union*, 246; Wilson, *The Life*, 378.
23. B. Catton, *Grant Takes Command* (Boston: Little, Brown, 1969), 4.
24. Catton, 135; Wilson, *The Life*, 378; Reid, "Commander and His Chief of Staff," 32.
25. Grant's prejudices have led to accusations that he was a nativist. T. Anbinder, "Ulysses S. Grant, Nativist," *Civil War History* 43, no. 2 (1997): 119–41.
26. J. Y. Simon, "The Paradox of Ulysses S. Grant," *Register of the Kentucky Historical Society* 81, no. 4 (1983): 366–82; Catton, *Grant Takes Command*, 136; U. S. Grant, *Personal Memoirs of U. S. Grant* (New York: Charles Webster & Co., 1885), 1:152.

27. Wilson, *The Life*, 21; Reid, "Commander and His Chief of Staff," 32; Ottens, *General John A. Rawlins*, 545.
28. Sir Philip Sassoon (1888–1939) was a soldier, politician, and patron of the arts.
29. Baring and Sassoon would work together on the war artists scheme, encouraging William Orpen to draw several of the RFC's fighter "Aces." M. Baring, *Dear Animated Bust—Letters to Lady Juliet Duff, France 1915–1918* (Salisbury: Michael Russell, 1981), Baring to Duff, 14 December 1915.
30. P. Stansky, *Sassoon: The Worlds of Philip and Sybil* (New Haven, CT: Yale University Press, 2003); D. Collins, *Charmed Life—The Phenomenal World of Philip Sassoon* (London: Collins, 2016). Sassoon was, like Baring, a regular correspondent with Ettie Desborough.
31. Brigadier General John Charteris (1877–1946) was a professional soldier, chief of intelligence of the BEF (1915–18), and politician. Charteris was something of a court jester and a member of Haig's inner circle. Stansky, *Sassoon*, 71; Collins, *Charmed Life*, 62; J. Beach, *Haig's Intelligence* (Cambridge: Cambridge University Press, 2013), 271.
32. Lord Northcliffe (1865–1922) was Britain's foremost press baron. Geoffrey Robinson (1874–1944) was a civil servant, journalist, and editor of *The Times*, 1912–19 and 1923–41. Robinson changed his surname to Dawson in 1917. Such informal correspondence was helpful to all sides. Haig was not above using Sassoon to convey his personal views.
33. D. Cooper, *Haig*, vol. 2 (London: Faber & Faber, 1936), 431.
34. Blake, *Private Papers of Douglas Haig*, 30.
35. Stansky, *Sassoon*, 51.
36. G. J. De Groot, *Douglas Haig 1861–1928* (London: Unwin Hyman, 1988), 220, Douglas Haig to Doris (Lady) Haig, 16 June 1918; Stansky, *Sassoon*, 58; G. Sheffield, *The Chief* (London: Aurum, 2011), 134–35.
37. Stansky, *Sassoon*, 59, 75; Collins, *Charmed Life*, 28–31.
38. Stansky, *Sassoon*, 52.
39. Lloyd George had previously believed that Sassoon could be part of a pro-Asquith conspiracy. Stansky, *Sassoon*, 71; Collins, *Charmed Life*, 61.
40. Stansky, *Sassoon*, 89.
41. Lieutenant General (later Field Marshal, 1st Viscount, Sir) Bernard Montgomery (1887–1976) was a professional soldier and chief of the General Staff. Brigadier (later Major General Sir) Francis "Freddie" de Guingand (1900–1979) was a professional soldier and businessman.
42. B. Montgomery, *The Memoirs of Field-Marshal Montgomery* (London: Collins, 1958), 67.
43. De Guingand, *Generals at War*, 121.
44. B. Montgomery, *The Path to Leadership* (New York: Putnams, 1959), 54.
45. R. Lewin, *Montgomery as Military Commander* (New York: Stein and Day, 1971), 15–16.
46. Lewin, *Montgomery*, 244–45; D. K. R. Crosswell, *Chief of Staff—The Military Career of General Walter Bedell Smith* (Westport, CT: Greenwood, 1991), 293.
47. Montgomery, *Memoirs*, 98.
48. Lewin, *Montgomery*, 51.

49. Lewin, 11, 52.
50. Montgomery, *Memoirs*, 166–67.
51. Lewin, *Montgomery*, 51.
52. Lewin, 1–4.
53. Second-Lieutenant (later Lieutenant Colonel) Chester "Chet" Hansen (1917–2012) was a journalist, military officer, author, and public relations officer. *New York Times*, 25 October 2012.
54. S. Ossad, *Omar Nelson Bradley: America's GI General, 1893–1981* (Columbia: University of Missouri Press, 2017), 7.
55. J. Lavoie, *The Private Life of General Omar N. Bradley* (Jefferson: McFarland, 2015), 78; O. Bradley and C. Blair, *A General's Life* (New York: Simon & Schuster, 1983), 105, 200.
56. Lavoie, *Bradley*, 176.
57. J. Eisenhower, *Soldiers and Statesmen—Reflections on Leadership* (Columbia: University of Missouri Press, 2012), 128.
58. D. Feldmann, "Fixing One's History: George S. Patton's Changes in His Personal Diary," *War in History* 28, no. 1 (2021): 166–83.
59. Lavoie, *Bradley*, 64, 176.
60. Eisenhower, *Soldiers*, 115.
61. Bradley and Blair, *General's Life*, 381; A. Axelrod, *Bradley* (New York: Palgrave Macmillan, 2008), 313.
62. *New York Times*, 24 October 2012.
63. O. Bradley, *A Soldier's Story* (New York: Henry Holt, 1951).
64. Bradley, 5.
65. *Social Intelligence—Introduction and Overview for the Army's Human Dimension Initiative*, HDCDTF, Fort Leavenworth, February 2016.

CHAPTER 3. AMBITION, JEALOUSY, AND DIVISION

1. Sir David Henderson (1862–1921) was an expert in in field intelligence and reconnaissance. It is sometimes claimed that Henderson prevented the RFC from developing more offensive capabilities, but the RFC was experimenting with both aerial bombing and artillery cooperation well before the outbreak of war—within a limited budget. M. Paris, *Winged Warfare: The Literature and Theory of Aerial Warfare in Britain 1859–1917* (Manchester: Manchester University Press, 1992), 163; F. Prins, "Forgotten Founder," *The Aeroplane*, April 2012, 60–63, and May 2012, 36–38; W. S. Brancker, "The Allocation of Royal Flying Corps Units to Subordinate Commands," *Royal Artillery Journal* 42 (June 1915): 113–24; J. O'Brien, "Mobilising the BEF August 1914," *Stand To*, no. 78 (January 2007): 6–9.
2. Henderson had previously served as French's staff officer in 1908, when the latter had been appointed inspector general of forces. It was French who recommended that Henderson be appointed to chair the military aviation subcommittee, which ultimately led to the creation of the RFC.

3. Trenchard Family Papers (TFP), Brooke-Popham to Saunders, 25 July 1951.
4. Both the French and Germans believed that command appointments in their army air services could be held by senior officers from any background. Examples include Lieutenant General Ernst von Hoeppner (1860–1922), a cavalrymen appointed to command the Luftstreitkräfte in 1916, and Brigadier General Maurice Duval (1869–1958), an infantryman appointed director of aviation at the French General Headquarters in 1917.
5. Baring, *R.F.C. H.Q.*, 8; Baring, *Puppet Show*, 170; Letley, *Maurice Baring*, 157–59. Baring had been a lodger in the Herbert household since 1911.
6. Other guests included Raymond Asquith, James Barrie, Hilaire Belloc, Evan Charteris, William Orpen, Conrad Russell, Lady Ettie Desborough, and Lady Juliet Duff.
7. Berg Collection, Baring's War Diary, 6 August 1914; Baring, *R.F.C. H.Q.*, 8.
8. While it was intended that the RFC would operate like an independent cavalry brigade, it was organized as army troops reporting directly to GHQ. W. Raleigh, *The War in the Air*, vol. 1 (Oxford: Oxford University Press, 1922), 288.
9. Colonel (later Lieutenant General Sir) George Macdonagh had recently been appointed as the BEF's GSO1 (Intelligence). Macdonagh served as the army's director of military intelligence from 1916 to 1918. Sir Philip Sassoon (1888–1939) served as a staff officer at GHQ before becoming Haig's private secretary.
10. Baring, *With the Russians*, 204; Lovat, *Maurice Baring*, 40; M. Baring, *Lost Lectures* (London: William Heinemann, 1932), 114–37; Baring, War Diary, 6 August 1914.
11. Lovat, *Maurice Baring*, 45–47; Baring, *With the Russians*, 205; Blakiston, *Letters*, 256. Baring was immensely proud of the Russo-Japanese War Medal (awarded for distinguished service during combat operations) and wrote from Moscow to get the king's license to accept it. TNA FO 372/28.
12. *Field Service Regulations Part II* (London: War Office, 1909), 37–43. The other staff comprised Lieutenant Colonel (later Major General Sir) Frederick Sykes (1877–1954); Major (later ACM Sir) Robert Brooke-Popham (1874–1953); Captain (later ACM Sir) Geoffrey Salmond (1878–1933); and Lieutenant (later Major) Basil Barrington-Kennett (1885–1915). F. Sykes, *From Many Angles* (London: George Harrap, 1942), 122; E. Ash, *Sir Frederick Sykes and the Air Revolution 1912–1918* (London: Frank Cass, 1999), 50–51.
13. F. Sykes, *Aviation in Peace and War* (London: Edward Arnold, 1922), 27. Gollin asserts that this was the start of the mutual hostility between Henderson and Sykes. A. Gollin, *The Impact of Air Power on the British People* (London: Macmillan, 1989), 312.
14. IWM Documents 11963, "Private Papers of Wing Commander Sir Archibald James." "Archie" James (1893–1980) was a cavalryman, observer, pilot, diplomat, and MP. R. Pigot, "Some Memories of the Earliest Days of Military Aviation in England," *RAF Quarterly*, Spring 1973, 51–57. Not all of Sykes' contemporaries found him disagreeable. Geoffrey de Havilland likened Sykes to a scholar or a university don, with a slim build, soft voice, and great charm. G. de Havilland, *Sky Fever* (Shrewsbury: Airlife, 1979), 77; E. Ash, "Air Power Leadership: A Study of Sykes and Trenchard," in P. Gray and S. Cox, eds., *Airpower Leadership and Practice* (London: HMSO, 2002), 160–77.

15. E. L. Spears, *Liaison 1914* (London: Heinemann, 1930), 416.
16. J. Salmond, "Forged and Tempered," *Blackwood's* 295, no. 1782 (April 1964): 289–304; Baring, War Diary, 26 August 1914.
17. ANH, Baring to Nan, 18 August 1914. Murat was well liked and proved particularly helpful with billeting problems. H. Stewart, *From Mons to Loos, Being the Diary of a Supply Officer* (Edinburgh: William Blackwood & Sons, 1916), 29.
18. HQ RFC spent most of the war in two locations. From October 1914, it was located at Château des Bruyères, on the hill between the town of the St-Omer and the aerodrome, and (from March 1916) at L'abbaye Saint-André-aux-Bois, near Gouy.
19. By May 1918, Luftstreitkräfte headquarters comprised sixty officers and three hundred men, compared to approximately thirty officers and two hundred men on the establishment of HQ RAF. National Archives, RG 45, box GHQ, SS 407 "Composition of Headquarters British Armies in France," November 1918.
20. The eight squadrons were calculated based on one for each army headquarters and one for each corps headquarters. TNA AIR 1/143/15/40/316, Secretary of State to CIGS, 21 December 1914.
21. *London Gazette*, 9 September 1914, 7192; *London Gazette*, 19 October 1914, 8376.
22. Major (later AVM Sir) Sefton Brancker (1877–1930), Staff College trained, proved an able administrator and field commander. After the war, he became the director of civil aviation but died in the R-101 disaster, along with the air minister, Lord Thomson.
23. Spears, *Liaison*, 520.
24. RAFM MFC 77/13/22, Henderson to Brancker, 13 November 1914; TNA AIR 1/128/15/40/173, Brancker to CIGS, 18 November 1914.
25. Sykes, *From Many Angles*, 143–45. Burke, commanding No. 2 Squadron RFC, attached to 1st Corps, wrote that it was useless trying to explain aviation affairs to Haig. Burke, Personal Diary, 8 October 1914, https://rafmontrose.org.uk/burke/; RAFM MFC 77/13/22, HQ RFC to CIGS, 30 October 1914.
26. Boyle, *Trenchard*, 125.
27. French and Henderson had a particularly close friendship that only strengthened as the war progressed. J. Pugh, *The Royal Flying Corps, the Western Front and the Control of the Air, 1914–1918* (London: Routledge, 2017), 119–20.
28. Baring, War Diary, 30 November 1914.
29. TNA WO 95/589/1, SO 1st Corps to OC 1st Division, 30 November 1914.
30. Baring, War Diary, 13 and 22 November 1914.
31. J. Morrow, *The Great War in the Air* (Shrewsbury: Airlife, 1993), 91; J. R. Cuneo, *Winged Mars: The Air Weapon 1914–1916* (Harrisburg, PA: Military Service Publishing, 1947), 166. HQ RFC moved to L'abbaye Saint-André-aux-Bois in March 1916 when GHQ relocated to Montreuil.
32. Cuneo, *Winged Mars*, 163–65.
33. The lack of aviation staff officers proved particularly damaging to the effective employment of the German aircraft sections. M. Bowden, *The Great War's Finest—An Operational*

History of the German Air Service (Reno: Aeronaut Books, 2017), 274; Cuneo, *Winged Mars*, 144.
34. Morrow, *Great War in the Air*, 104. Unlike the French air service, where the artillery and engineers provided a substantial proportion of the officer cadre, the composition of the RFC largely reflected that of the BEF. Of the 97 RFC officers (exclusive of attached officers), who deployed to France in August 1914, the majority came from infantry regiments (59 percent). The remainder were drawn from the Royal Artillery (16 percent), the Royal Engineers (7 percent), the Cavalry (5 percent), and direct entrants through the RFC special Reserve Scheme (13 percent).
35. Major (later AVM Sir) Charles Longcroft (1883–1958) was a pre-war pilot and senior RAF officer.
36. N. Macmillan, *Sir Sefton Brancker* (London: Heinemann, 1935), 64, 96–108.
37. Henderson's ADC was Lieutenant (later Lieutenant General Sir) Gordon Macready (1891–1956).
38. Macmillan, *Brancker*, 106–7.
39. Henderson had moved his advanced headquarters to Hazebrouck during the Neuve Chapelle fighting but spent the entire week unwell in bed.
40. Henderson died suddenly in 1921, just after his fifty-ninth birthday.
41. Richard Pope-Hennessy, a close friend of Brooke-Popham's, who had joined HQ RFC in March 1915, found Sykes a congenial boss, although "he is very much disliked and astonishingly young to be a full colonel, but he is quick and intelligent." Cooper acknowledges that there is no firm evidence for the supposed intrigue against Henderson, while Ash argues that the popular interpretation of Sykes' downfall is erroneous. Cooper, *Birth of Independent Air Power*, 22; Ash, *Sir Frederick Sykes*, 66–67; Ash, "Air Power Leadership," 160–77.
42. W. Beaverbrook, *Men and Power 1917–1918* (London: Hutchinson, 1956), 378–79. Neville Jones has claimed that the Admiralty was unaware of Sykes' appointment, but this is a misreading of the relevant documents. N. Jones, *The Origins of Strategic Bombing* (London: William Kimber, 1973), 69; S. Roskill, *Documents Relating to the Naval Air Service 1908–1918* (Bromley: Navy Records Society, 1969), 223–24.
43. ANH, Henrietta Henderson to Nan, August 1914.

CHAPTER 4. BUILDING A LEADERSHIP TEAM

1. Baring, War Diary, 18 November 1914; *Times*, 29 April 1933, 16.
2. B. Smythies, "Experiences during the War, 1914–1918," in *AP 956—A Selection of Lectures and Essays from the Work of Officers Attending the First Staff Course at the Royal Air Force Staff College 1922–1923* (London: Air Ministry, 1923), 74–90.
3. According to Baring, Trenchard "must have someone at his elbow *all day*." ANH, Baring to Nan, 6 September 1915.
4. For his part, Pope-Hennessy had little time for Trenchard, whom he accused of creating a horrible atmosphere round him that made both work and social relations quite intolerable for his staff. IWM Documents 12641, "Private Papers of Major-General L.H.R.

Pope-Hennessy," Private Diary, 13 May 1916; TFP, Brooke-Popham to Saunders, 16 August 1951.
5. Brigadier General (later AVM Sir) Philip Game (1876–1961) later served as governor of New South Wales and commissioner of the Metropolitan Police. P. Dye, *The Man Who Took the Rap* (Annapolis, MD: Naval Institute Press, 2018), 41–42.
6. Brigadier General Francis Festing (1877–1948) later served as director of the Air Personnel Services RAF, managing director of Air Transport and Travel, controller of the Aerodromes Civil Aviation Department, foreign representative for Blackburn Aircraft Co., and adviser to Gloster Aircraft Co. "Brigadier-General Festing," *The Aeroplane*, 4 and 19 November 1948.
7. Baring, War Diary, 30 January 1916; TFP, Brooke-Popham to Saunders, 16 August 1951.
8. Game Papers, Philip Game to Clara Game, 21 August 1916.
9. James spent several spells attached to HQ RFC and was greatly impressed by the senior members of Trenchard's staff, describing them as "an efficient and harmonious body." IWM 11963.
10. Brooke-Popham Family Papers, Philip Game to Opal, 25 October 1953.
11. J. Simon, *Retrospect: The Memoirs of the Right Honourable Viscount Simon* (London: Hutchinson, 1952), 113–14.
12. Festing's responsibilities included training, casualties, medical and welfare issues, chaplaincy, prisoners of war, honors and awards, disciplinary matters, allowances, and pay. The scale of this task was substantial but not as difficult as finding competent and qualified personnel to fill flying and technical appointments. Attrition, and the relatively small pool of potential candidates, made selecting the right individuals with the right professional and leadership skills a continuous challenge.
13. RAFM MFC 76/1/8, Trenchard to Brancker, 4 December 1916; RAFM MFC 76/1/9, Trenchard to Brancker, 18 January 1917.
14. CUL Add 9429/1B/209/iv. Trenchard's approach was not entirely hands-off. The frontline squadrons were required to complete a wide range of statistical forms that were forwarded to HQ RFC, via wings and brigades. Pugh, *Royal Flying Corps*, 78.
15. Trenchard's phrase "Make a note of that, Baring" became famous throughout the RFC and provides the epigraph for *R.F.C. H.Q.*
16. A. A. Nicod, "Memories of 60 Squadron R.F.C.," *Popular Flying*, January 1935, 540.
17. N. Macmillan, *Into the Blue* (Norwich: Jarrolds, 1969), 112–13.
18. According to Cyril Falls, while visits to the trenches by British commanders were not frequent, they were more common than in the French army. C. Falls, "Contacts with Troops: Commanders and Staffs in the First World War," *Army Quarterly* 88 (1964): 173–80; P. Liddle, *The Airman's War* (Poole: Blandford, 1987), 63; E. Johnstone, *Naval Eight* (London: Arms & Armour, 1972), 13–14; James, *Paladins*, 58–59.
19. Samuel (later 1st Viscount Templewood) Hoare (1880–1959) was a politician, diplomat, and intelligence agent. S. Hoare, *Empire of the Air* (London: Collins, 1957), 44; D. Jordan, "The Battle for the Skies: Sir Hugh Trenchard as Commander of the Royal Flying

Corps," in M. Hughes and M. Seligmann, eds., *Leadership in Conflict* (Barnsley: Leo Copper, 2000), 71–72.
20. Sykes, *From Many Angles*, 105; D. Jordan and G. Sheffield, "Douglas Haig and Airpower," in Gray and Cox, *Airpower Leadership and Practice* (London: HMSO, 2002), 264–82.
21. RAFM MFC 76/1/61; *Daily Telegraph*, 26 March 1962; Cooper, *Haig*, 2:410. Nicodemus was a rich Pharisee, a wise, well-respected religious teacher, who debated with Jesus about his teachings. Silenus was a god of contradictions who enjoyed drink, music, dance, and sleep but was also a wise prophet and the bearer of terrible wisdom.
22. RAFM MFC 76/1/104, Brooke-Popham to Trenchard, 10 December 1929.
23. P. Gribble, *The Diary of a Staff Officer (Air Intelligence Liaison Officer) at Advanced Headquarters North B.A.F.F. 1940* (London: Methuen, 1941), 30.
24. Trenchard would be described as a "nonlinear" thinker (holistic, intuitive, timeless, and nonverbal) as opposed to a "linear" thinker (analytic, rational, and time-orientated). TFP, Brooke-Popham to Saunders, 6 July 1951; CUL Add 9429/1B/1268(iii), Bullock to Boyle, 14 August 1961.
25. This was still the case ten years later, when Trenchard was CAS. G. Gibbs, *Survivor's Story* (London: Hutchinson, 1956), 50.
26. ANH, Baring to Nan, 13 September 1915.
27. Bates stayed with Trenchard until after the war. He received Mention in Despatches awards twice (in 1917 and 1919) and was also awarded the Meritorious Service Medal in 1917.
28. Charles added, "I never knew a man carrying greater strain, and I never knew a man with such a wonderful power of making other people want to do things that he had in mind." IWM 8585, Hubert Noel Charles, Oral History.
29. The U.S. Army's liaison officer at de Castelnau's headquarters in Nancy commented on the force and brusqueness of Trenchard's letters. Van Schaick Mitchell, *Letters from a Liaison Officer*, 100; Lovat, *Maurice Baring*, 20.
30. The "Air Agitation" campaign was led by an industrialist and ex-RNAS officer, Noel Pemberton Billing (1881–1941), who was elected as an independent MP in March 1916. His allegations about mismanagement at the Royal Aircraft Factory and administrative failures by the RFC led the government to set up two inquiries (the Burbidge and Bailhache Committees) that reported in August 1916 and January 1917, respectively. Hillgarth and Jeffs, *Letters*, 90–91, Baring to Ettie Desborough, 1 October 1915.
31. Spenser Wilkinson (1853–1937) was the drama critic, and then editor, of the *Morning Post* when Baring was one of the newspaper's foreign correspondents. "Mr Spenser Wilkinson—The History and Policy of War," *Times*, 1 February 1937, 16; Berg Collection, Baring to Marsh, 26 February 1916.
32. *Times*, 25 March 1916; Hillgarth and Jeffs, *Letters*, 95–104, Baring to Marsh, 26 January 1916, and Baring to Wilkinson, 23 March 1916.
33. TFP, H. Saunders, "Notes on Chapter 2"; Spears, *Liaison 1914*, 25.
34. By contrast, Major General Sir Francis de Guingand, COS of the Eighth Army, believed that Montgomery became more dictatorial, and less compromising, the more he was

isolated from his headquarters. F. de Guingand, *Operation Victory* (London: Hodder and Stoughton, 1947), 192.

35. Captain Hugo Baring (1876–1949) served in the Tirah Campaign and the Boer War (where he was wounded) before leaving the army. He reenlisted on the outbreak of World War I, joining the BEF in September 1914. Another brother, Everard Baring (1862–1932), served as a brigade commander in France. For an assessment of the role of a staff officer at GHQ, see Anonymous, "The Staff. The Myth? The Reality?," *Stand To*, no. 15 (Winter 1985): 44–51.

36. R. Speaight, *The Life of Hilaire Belloc* (New York: Farrar, Straus & Cudahy, 1957), 289.

37. H. Belloc, "Our Air Service," *Land and Water*, 10 February 1916, 3. When Belloc's eldest son, Louis, wanted to transfer to the RFC as a fighter pilot, Belloc enlisted Trenchard's help. Louis was killed in action in August 1918. Baring, *R.F.C. H.Q.*, 293.

38. For example, B. Fellows, "The Rise of the RFC," *Land and Water*, 2 August 1917, 24–25.

39. In writing to Nan, Baring invariably referred to the GOC as "David." Biddle, citing Higham, claims that Trenchard had cultivated important professional and social relationships, including members of the royal family; however, other than his meetings with Kitchener, these were no more than casual encounters. T. Biddle, *Rhetoric and Reality in Air Warfare* (Princeton, NJ: Princeton University Press, 2002), 27; R. Higham, *The Military Intellectuals in Britain, 1918–1939* (New Brunswick, NJ: Rutgers University Press, 1966), 32–134.

40. Raymond Asquith and Baring had been members of "The Coterie," a fashionable pre-war set of aristocrats and intellectuals who were well known for their extravagant parties and also took pride in their erudition and learning. After Lloyd George became prime minister, Marsh returned to work for Churchill at the Ministry of Munitions. He continued to serve Churchill and other government ministers for the next twenty years, before retiring in 1937. Lovat, *Maurice Baring*, 20.

41. J. F. C. Fuller, *Memoirs of an Unconventional Soldier* (London: Ivor Nicholson & Watson, 1936), 192. Charteris ran his billet at a "ruinous rate," providing sumptuous teas that included sardines, honey, jam, and cakes. Baring, War Diary, 1 March 1915; *Times*, 19 November 1940, 9.

42. Hugh Gascoyne-Cecil (1869–1956), fifth son of the 3rd Marquess of Salisbury, was a politician, committed Anglican, and provost of Eton College. He served as a Unionist MP from 1895 to 1906 and again from 1910 to 1937. Cecil was one of a small group of young reactionary Conservative MPs (including Winston Churchill) known as the "Hughligans." He was later best man at Churchill's wedding. Cecil was an outstanding orator and has been described as "possibly the greatest parliamentarian never to hold ministerial office." Cecil was created the 1st Baron Quickswood in 1941 on Churchill's recommendation. *Daily Telegraph*, 11 December 1956; R. Rempel, "Lord Hugh Cecil's Parliamentary Career, 1900–1914: Promise Unfulfilled," *Journal of British Studies* 11, no. 2 (May 1972): 104–30.

43. C. Lewis, *Sagittarius Rising* (London: Peter Davies, 1936), 9–10.

44. IWM 11963.
45. Sir John Simon (1873–1954), a highly successful barrister and politician, remains the only man to have served as home secretary, foreign secretary, Chancellor of the Exchequer, and Lord Chancellor. C. Messenger, *Call-to-Arms: The British Army 1914–1918* (London: Weidenfeld & Nicholson, 2005), 153; Simon, *Retrospect*, 111.
46. *Times*, 25 October 1917, 3.
47. IWM Documents 10986, "Private Papers of Air Vice-Marshal Sir Philip Game," Philip Game to Gwendolen, 22 June 1918; G. Garro-Jones, *Ventures and Visions* (London: Hutchinson, 1935), 205.
48. Cecil and Simon, although from different political parties, had been on close terms since before the war. K. Rose, *The Later Cecils* (London: Weidenfeld and Nicolson, 1975), 257; J. Charteris, *At G.H.Q.* (London: Cassell, 1931), 241–42.
49. B. Roberts, *Sir John Simon—Being an Account of the Life and Career of John Allesbrook Simon* (London: Robert Hale, 1938), 127.
50. Simon, *Retrospect*, 114.

CHAPTER 5. FUNCTIONING AS A TEAM

1. By November 1918 there were 226 active RAF aerodromes in France and Belgium. TNA AIR 1/1135/204/5/2222.
2. RAFM MFC 76/1/8, Trenchard to Brancker, 8 October 1916, and Brancker to Trenchard, 11 October 1916.
3. Edward Corballis (1890–1967) was a pre-war pilot, RAF officer, and businessman. Collingwood Ingram (1880–1981) was a staff captain, ornithologist, gardener, and expert in the Japanese flowering cherry. C. Ingram, *Wings over the Western Front*, ed. E. Pollard and H. Strouts (Charlbury: Day Books, 2014).
4. Hansard, HC Debate, 29 April 1918.
5. Anonymous, "The Staff. The Myth?," 44–51; P. Harris, "Soldier Banker: Lieutenant-General Sir Herbert Lawrence as the BEF's Chief of Staff in 1918," *Journal of the Society for Army Historical Research* 90 (2012): 44–67. "GHQ lived, said our guest, in a world of its own, rose-coloured, remote from the ugly things of war. They had heard of the trenches, yes, but as the West End hears of the East End—a nasty place where common people lived. Occasionally they visited the trenches as society folk go slumming and came back proud of having seen a shell burst, having braved the lice and the dirt." Gibbs, *Realities*, 161.
6. By the summer of 1916, the RFC in France comprised some 11,000 personnel—including six brigadiers (with an average age of thirty-nine). The rapid advancement available to a handful of officers in the RFC gave rise to criticism. Brooke-Popham (age thirty-seven) was one of the youngest brigadiers in the BEF, but even his friend Pope-Hennessy raged, "What damned rot it was having these ridiculous Flying Corps generals commanding two men and a boy, and they themselves children in war." IWM 12641, Diary, 13 May 1916.
7. Brancker, "Allocation of Royal Flying Corps Units."

8. General Andre Voisin was a French army aviation officer who wrote extensively on airpower issues based on his World War I experience. Voisin was not shy about identifying what he saw as operational weaknesses or missteps. In his opinion, the critical error was to believe that the increasing strength of the air force should correspond to a new doctrine of greater scope, while the practical range of its machines still limited aviation's role to that of an auxiliary force, fighting within the framework of the armies. Voisin gained wider attention with the publication, in 1932, of *La doctrine de l'aviation française de combat (1915–1918)*. Voisin's criticism cannot be entirely divorced from the contemporary debate in France on the need for an independent air service and the role of strategic bombing. A. Voisin, *La doctrine de l'aviation française de combat au cours de la guerre (1915–1918)* (Paris: Berger-Levrault, 1932); 61.
9. The working group members were, in more detail, Lieutenant Colonel (later Air Commodore Sir) John Chamier, Major (later Wing Commander) Charles Mackay (1895–1931), and Major (later ACM Sir) George Pirie (1896–1980). S.S. 131, "Aircraft Cooperation with Artillery," and S.S. 132, "Aircraft Cooperation with Infantry."
10. Major (later ACM Sir) Trafford Leigh-Mallory (1892–1944). No. 8 Squadron was allocated to this task and made great strides in improving cooperation between aircraft and tanks. TNA AIR 69/3; TNA WO 95/95/4/05; TNA AIR 1/1074/204/5/1665.
11. TNA AIR 1/2390/228/11/124.
12. H. Griffith, *R.A.F. Occasions* (London: Crescent, 1941), 2–3.
13. Brooke-Popham acknowledged that this was a difficult balancing act and sometimes meant that partially trained pilots had to be used to keep squadrons at their full establishment, with a concomitant increase in casualties. T. Henshaw 'British Squadron Aircraft Establishments, 1914-1918', Cross and Cockade International Journal 50 (Spring 2024), 32-41.
14. James Birley (1884–1934) was a doctor, consulting physician, and RAF medical officer. J. Birley, "Medical Science and Military Aviation," *The Lancet*, 29 May 1920, 1147–51; 5 June 1920, 1205–12; and 12 June 1920, 1252–57. No. 60 Squadron was rested after suffering very heavy casualties during the Somme fighting. TFP, Brooke-Popham to Saunders, 2 August 1951; L. Shaw Cobden, "Nerves Flying and the First World War," *British Journal for Military History* 4, no. 2 (February 2018): 121–42; D. Jones, "Flying and Dying in WW1: British Aircrew Losses and the Origins of U.S. Military Aviation Medicine," *Aviation, Space and Environmental Medicine* 79, no. 2 (February 2008): 139–46. Only limited medical support was provided for the squadrons, in the form of a single medical orderly who attended aircraft crashes and organized the transportation of casualties to hospital.
15. Boyle, *Trenchard*, 145.
16. R. Heussler, "Maurice Baring and the Passing of the Victorian Age," *Biography* 7, no. 2 (Spring 1984): 134–57; Lovat, *Maurice Baring*, 107–12; Berg Collection, Baring to Marsh, 20 September 1937.
17. Baring reprimanded Nan for referring to No. 13 Squadron as the "13th Squadron." ANH, Baring to Nan, 20 October 1915. When Marsh wrote to him at the "British

Mission," Copenhagen, rather than the "British Legation," Baring complained that it made him appear to be part of a Wesleyan society for informing the Danish royal family. Berg Collection, Baring to Marsh, undated (ca. 1900); Harry Ransom Archive, Maurice Baring Collection, Trenchard to Baring, 29 December 1921.

18. *Who's Who, 1934* (London: A & C Black, 1934); J. Epstein, "Maurice Baring and the Good High-Brow," *New Criterion* 11, no. 2 (October 1992); Lovat, *Maurice Baring*, 64, Baring to Hart Davies, 29 March 1925; R. Storrs, "Maurice Baring: A Recollection," *The Atlantic*, October 1947, 111–14.

19. Baring, *R.F.C. H.Q.*, 66.

20. Although "Uncle Maurice" had never met Frankie Festing, they corresponded regularly. Berg Collection, Baring to Marsh, 7 September 1916; B. Delany, *Blackfriars* 27, no. 312 (March 1946): 1; Storrs, "Maurice Baring."

21. IWM 10986, Philip Game to Gwendolen, 26 January 1918.

22. "The Problems of Flying to Mars," *The Economist*, 23 February 2019; J. C. Johnson, L. A. Palinkas, and J. S. Boster, *Informal Social Roles and the Evolution and Stability of Social Networks* (Washington, DC: National Academies Press, 2003). Thomas Trenchard believed that his father's first biographer (Boyle) had overlooked his father's humorous side and ready smile. RAF CASPS, "Interview with Thomas Trenchard," YouTube video, 50:54, posted 31 March 2018, https://www.youtube.com/watch?v=ZO7RbSknmkE.

23. Orpen thought it "one of the greatest poems ever written and by far the greatest work of art the war has produced." W. Orpen, *An Onlooker in France* (London: Williams and Norgate, 1921), 29. T. E. Lawrence wrote, "It takes me each time I read it absolutely by the throat—so simply sincere, and grievous and splendid." Lovat, *Maurice Baring*, 7–8; M. Baring, *Poems 1914–1918* (London: Martin Secker, 1920); E. Gosse, *Some Diversions of a Man of Letters* (London: Heinemann, 1920), 273–75.

24. IWM 10986, Philip Game to Gwendolen, 18 April 1916.

25. CUL Add 9429/1B/207(i).

26. H. A. Jones, *The War in the Air*, vol. 2 (Oxford: Clarendon, 1928), 156; V. Orange, *Park: The Biography of Air Chief Marshal Sir Keith Park* (London: Methuen, 1984), 17.

27. Major (later Wing Commander) Bernard Smythies (1886–1930) served as a squadron commander (No. 64 Squadron) on the Western Front for over a year. Smythies, "Experiences," 74–90.

28. ANH, Baring to Nan, 3 December 1916, and Trenchard to Nan, 4 December 1916; IWM 11963; CUL Add 9429/1B/126(iii).

29. D. Cooper, *The Rainbow Comes and Goes* (London: Rupert Hart-Davis, 1958), 90.

30. ANH, Private Diary, 25 December 1914.

31. Orpen, *An Onlooker*, 53.

32. Nowhere is this more difficult than poetry, where the translator must convey aesthetic and expressive values while maintaining the same meters and rhymes. Baring was an acknowledged genius in this task.

33. In Brooke-Popham's words, "The combination of the two men was unequalled," although, as du Peuty was much smaller than Trenchard, they made for an incongruous pairing. TFP, Brooke-Popham to Saunders, 16 August 1951.
34. Personal correspondence with Louis Jebb, 28 August 2021.
35. V. Maclean, "Maurice Baring, the Final Years," *Chesterton Review* 19, no. 1 (February 1988): 109–16.
36. J. Jefford, "NCO Pilots in the RFC/RAF 1912–18," *RAF Air Power Review* 7, no. 2 (Summer 2004): 89–99.
37. Paris claimed that the RFC's refusal to issue parachutes to pilots was the result of Trenchard's quest for moral superiority. Paris, *Winged Warfare*, 246. The Air Ministry eventually placed orders in September 1918 for one thousand parachutes to two designs, but none had been issued before the war ended. A. Gould Lee, *No Parachute* (London: Jarrolds, 1968), 305–12.
38. RAF Museum, MFC 76/1/9, Trenchard to Brancker, 6 January 1917.

CHAPTER 6. AN AIRPOWER VISIONARY

1. Pugh, *Royal Flying Corps*, 165–68.
2. IWM 12641.
3. TNA AIR 1/529/16/12/70, Army Secretary to CinC BEF, 27 August 1915; TNA AIR 1/529/16/12/70, CinC BEF to Army Secretary, 13 September 1915. This did not stop Trenchard from grumbling that he had to seek the War Office's approval in making appointments or removing unsuitable officers. RAFM MFC 76/1/76, Trenchard to Brancker, 7 March 1917.
4. TNA AIR 1/529/16/12/70, War Office to CinC BEF, 25 August 1915. Dowding, who had taken command of the Ninth Wing in June, was replaced in January 1917.
5. H. A. Jones, *The War in the Air*, vol. 4 (Oxford: Clarendon, 1934), 140–41; Baring, *Dear Animated Bust*, 18; TFP, Brooke-Popham to Saunders, 6 July 1951; RAFM MFC 76/1/7, Brancker to Trenchard, 17 August 1916; Macmillan, *Brancker*, 142.
6. TNA AIR 1/752/204/4/61; Jones, *War in the Air*, 2:148.
7. Trenchard appointed Lieutenant Colonel (later MRAF Sir) Cyril Newall (1886–1963) to command the Headquarters Wing in December 1916. Newall, a special favorite of Trenchard's, was later sent to organize the RFC bombing force in the Nancy area. He became CAS in 1937.
8. Trenchard appears to have had this development in mind as early as the autumn of 1916. When GHQ issued instructions detailing the organization, command, and employment of the RFC, the role of the Headquarters Wing (or Brigade) included offensive action against the enemy's aircraft and vulnerable points, in addition to the existing reconnaissance and special missions for GHQ. TNA AIR 1/529/16/12/70. Major General (later MRAF Sir) Jack Salmond (1881–1968) was a pre-war pilot and senior RAF officer.
9. Jones, *War in the Air*, 4:129, 135; Jones, *War in the Air*, 6:402–12; D. Jordan, "The Royal Air Force and Air/Land Integration in the 100 Days," *RAF Air Power Review* 11, no. 2

(2008): 12–29; J. Boff, "Air Land Integration in the 100 Days: The Case of Third Army," *RAF Air Power Review* 12, no. 3 (2009): 7–88.
10. The backbone of HQ RFC's communication system was the Despatch Rider Letter Service (DRLS). A fleet of motorcycles (generally equipped with a sidecar) was employed to move reports, documents, and photographs between units. By the end of 1917, a regular program had been established comprising a daily inbound journey to St-Andre from brigades and depots and at least five return journeys between St-Andre and GHQ. The brigades, wings, and squadrons also communicated by DLRS, their schedule coordinated with the daily run to and from HQ RFC. Every day, irrespective of the weather, over two hundred dispatch riders were to be found on the roads of northern France keeping the RFC's paperwork flowing.
11. James claimed that the brigade structure added very little value to the RFC. IWM 11963.
12. TNA AIR 1/725/97/2, Notes on Corps Squadron Work, August 1918; J. Slessor, *Air Power and Armies* (London: Oxford University Press, 1936), 151–53; Jordan, "Royal Air Force and Air/Land Integration," 15.
13. A low-key example of this was Trenchard's insistence that the headquarters be placed on a proper footing, rather than continuing to live on a temporary basis in basic conditions. Henderson had always advocated that something be done to improve matters, but it took Trenchard to make them happen. TFP, Brooke-Popham to Saunders, 28 August 1951. Michael Howard believed that while Trenchard end up as a visionary, it was no sudden conversion. His ideas expanded with his responsibilities rather than the other way around. M. Howard, "Reluctant Apostle of Air Power," *The Observer*, 25 March 1962, 27.
14. Pugh, *Royal Flying Corps*, 74–76.
15. This data relates to operations by the Division Aérienne (May–November 1918). It is unlikely that other French aviation units fared any better. National Archives, RG 165, "General Organization of the French Air Service—A Report by Captain Pierre Boal." P. Dye, *The Bridge to Airpower* (Annapolis, MD: Naval Institute Press, 2015), 136–39, 169; TFP, Brooke-Popham to Saunders, 2 August 1951.
16. Morrow, *Great War in the Air*, 345–47; National Archives, RG 165, "Distribution of Service Planes as Related to Military Policies." The War Department analysis included the RAF's Bristol F2b Fighter (a two-seat reconnaissance/cooperation aircraft) as a pursuit machine but excluded the German equivalents. It also excluded the German navy's Marineflieger fighter squadrons on the Channel coast. For the RAF (including the Independent Force) the proportions were roughly 42 percent fighters, 29 percent observation, and 30 percent bombers. Such comparisons are always fraught with difficulties and should be regarded as merely indicative, but several sources confirm that the proportion of fighter aircraft quoted for the French air service (34 percent) is correct.
17. Chamier, *Birth of the Royal Air Force*, 177; M. Cooper, "The Development of Air Policy and Doctrine on the Western Front, 1914–1918," *Aviation Historian* 28, no. 1 (1981): 38–51.
18. TFP, Brooke-Popham to Saunders, 25 July 1951.

19. D. Mechin, "The Air Division in Combat," *Cross and Cockade International Journal* 50 (Summer 2019): 108–13; C. Thollon-Pommerol, "La Division du General Duval (May–November 1918)," *Icare*, no. 248 (March 2019): 20–185; Baring, *R.F.C. H.Q.*, 294; National Archives, RG 165, "General Organization of the French Air Service—A Report by Captain Pierre Boal."
20. Before the attack, it would seek to destroy the enemy air force by provoking it with incursions into its lines and the bombardment of its land; during the attack, it would act en masse, in the air against the enemy air force, against the combatants on the ground by machine gun and bomb; by night, it would carry out repeated and violent bombardments on the organization of the enemy's rear. *Les armées françaises dans la Grande Guerre*, tome 6, vol. 2 (Paris: Ministere de la Guerre, 1935), 55–56.
21. Voisin, *La doctrine de l'aviation*, 88.
22. TNA AIR 1/529/16/12/70, HQ RFC to GHQ, 25 September 1916.
23. Lieutenant General (later General, 1st Baron) Sir Henry Rawlinson (1864–1925), one of Haig's more successful subordinates, was later CinC in India.
24. One of the artillery officers who regarded this move as a mistake was Lieutenant Colonel (later Field Marshal, 1st Viscount Alanbrooke) Sir Alan Brooke (1883–1963), CIGS. A. Brooke, "Evolution of Artillery in the Great War," *Journal of the Royal Artillery* 53, no. 1 (1926): 76–93.
25. TNA AIR 1/752/204/4/61.
26. L. E. O. Charlton, *Charlton* (London: Faber & Faber, 1931), 286–87.
27. L. A. Strange, *Recollections of an Airman* (London: John Hamilton, 1933), 123–29.
28. M. Smith, *British Air Strategy between the Wars* (Oxford: Oxford University Press, 1984), 20–57.
29. CUL Add 9429/13/207(i), Trenchard Personal Memoir. Trenchard made the same point to Hankey, about the importance of listening to criticism, and at his eightieth birthday celebratory dinner, attended by Winston Churchill. TREN 1, Trenchard to Hankey, 15 September 1939; CUL Add 9429/1B/215(v), Speech, 3 February 1957.
30. Jordan, "Battle for the Skies," 73; Baring, War Diary, 19 October 1915. These suggestions included ideas for new gun mountings and an innovative trigger mechanism. TNA AIR 1/1320/204/11/2, "Improved Gun Mountings"; E. Rowell, *In Peace and War—Tyneside, Naples and the Royal Flying Corps* (Otley: E. R. Rowell, 1996), 134.
31. TFP, Brooke-Popham to Saunders, 16 August 1951. Brooke-Popham convened regular meetings at HQ RFC with squadron commanders and technical NCOs to review technical issues. G. Babin, "Le Royal Flying Corps," *L'illustration*, 23 February 1918, 184.
32. Baring, *R.F.C. H.Q.*, 171.
33. Charles de Tricornot de Rose (1876–1916) was an aviator and fighter pilot who instigated the French offensive tactics employed successfully at Verdun. Oswald Boelcke (1891–1916) was an aviator and fighter pilot who pioneered the tactics of air fighting; he was also the driving force behind the creation of the Jagdstaffeln. Major Lanoe Hawker (1890–1916) was an aviator and pioneer fighter pilot. J.-P. Dumond, *Le Commandant*

de Rose, créateur de l'aviation de chasse—héros méconnu de la Grande Guerre, 1876–1916 (Paris: Ste Ecrivans, 2007). According to Spears, de Rose was an outstanding officer, outspoken and independent of mind. Spears, *Liaison 1914*, 48.

34. Boff, "Air Land Integration in the 100 Days," 85.
35. J. Ferris, ed., *The British Army and Signals Intelligence during the First World War* (Stroud: Alan Sutton, 1992), 14–15; Jones, *War in the Air*, 2:328.
36. The RFC's first attempt at SEAD took place on 25 September 1916, when three enemy aerodromes were attacked in the vicinity of Libercourt, while a separate bombing attack was carried out on Libercourt Station. Jones, *War in the Air*, 2:328–29; TNA AIR 69/41.
37. GQG 3rd Bureau issued a series of "Secret" instructions on air operations in early 1918 that sought to define combat roles. Fighter aircraft were barred from low-level bombing of ground targets. *Instruction sur l'organisation et l'emploi de l'aéronautique aux armées—titre II, aviation de combat*, GQG 3rd Bureau et Aéronautique, March 1918; *Instruction sur l'organisation et l'emploi de l'aéronautique aux armées—titre III, aviation de bombardement*, GQG 3rd Bureau et Aéronautique, March 1918.
38. National Archives, RG 45, Box 145, Intelligence Bulletin, 19 September 1918; "Aerodrome Strafe, 1918 Style," *Aircraft Illustrated*, June 1971, 218–19.
39. By "air strategic policy" Slessor appears to mean policies driven by the view that airpower would become a decisive strategy in warfare. J. Slessor, foreword to H. Montgomery Hyde, *British Air Policy between the Wars* (London: Heinemann, 1976).

CHAPTER 7. AN INSPIRATIONAL LEADER

1. IWM 10986, Philip Game to Gwendolen, 26 July 1918; CUL Add 9429/1B/1268(iii), Bullock to Boyle. Sir Christopher Bullock (1891–1972) was an RFC pilot, senior civil servant, and industrialist. Jack Salmond wrote that Trenchard possessed "the masterful imaginative touch of the natural leader." RAFM B2621, "Salmond Draft Autobiography," 138.
2. De Havilland, *Sky Fever*, 105; TFP, Brooke-Popham to Saunders, 16 August 1951. According to Thomas Trenchard, his father never held a driving license. RAF CASPS, "Interview with Thomas Trenchard"; C. à Court Repington, *The First World War* (London: Constable, 1920), 1:536. Sir Walter Raleigh described Trenchard as "the most single-minded man I ever knew." L. G. Raleigh, *Letters of Sir Walter Raleigh*, 2 vols. (London: Methuen, 1926), 1:512.
3. RAF CASPS, "Interview with Thomas Trenchard."
4. F. C. Bartlett, *Psychology and the Soldier* (Cambridge: Cambridge University Press, 1927), 138.
5. *The Aeroplane*, 17 April 1918.
6. Baring, *R.F.C. H.Q.*, 267; *The Aeroplane*, 21 June 1922.
7. J. Howard-Williams, "Book Reviews: Trenchard, Man of Vision (Boyle)," *Flight*, 17 May 1962.
8. *Daily Telegraph*, 26 March 1962.

9. Allen, *Legacy*, 29.
10. A. Lieblich, *Transition to Adulthood during Military Service* (New York: State University of New York Press, 1989), 149–66.
11. CUL Add 9429/15/1218(i).
12. *Times*, 18 December 1947.
13. Bullock and Moore-Brabazon both felt that marriage "softened" Trenchard, while Marson recalled an incident where he persuaded Trenchard not to send in a resignation letter until he had slept on the matter. The next morning Trenchard tore it up. CUL Add 9429/1B/1218(i); CUL Add 9429/1B/1216(vi).
14. CUL Add 9429/1B/1219.
15. Hillgarth and Jeffs, *Letters*, 116, Baring to Gilbert Chesterton, 29 September 1916.
16. Lord Robert Cecil (1864–1958) was a lawyer, politician, and diplomat; Arthur (1st Earl) Balfour (1848–1930) was a statesman and politician. C. Alston, "Russian Liberalism and British Journalism: The Life and Work of Harold Williams (1876–1928)" (PhD diss., Newcastle University, 2004), 129.
17. The Anglo-Russia Bureau was intended to improve Russian attitudes toward its ally. Baring's contacts in Russia, knowledge of the language, and well-known affection for the country made him an ideal candidate. R. Beaseley, *Russomania: Russian Culture and the Creation of British Modernism, 1881–1922* (Oxford: Oxford University Press, 2020), 379; Baring, *R.F.C. H.Q.*, 126–28; NHA, Nan to Bron, 24 January 1916. Sir Edward Grey (1862–1933) was the secretary of state for foreign affairs from 1905 to 1916.
18. CUL Add 9429/1B/1218(iv); Miller, *Boom*, 240.
19. I. Boyd, "Maurice Baring's Early Writing," *Downside Review* 92, no. 308 (1974): 160–70.
20. IWM 10986, Philip Game to Gwendolen, 26 January 1918.
21. Lord Brabazon, *The Brabazon Story* (London: Heinemann, 1956), 96; *Daily Telegraph*, 26 March 1962; Boyle, *Trenchard*, 139; Miller, *Boom*, 116, 227.
22. IWM 10986, Philip Game to Gwendolen, 28 January 1917. "Bos" Gordon was Major (later Brigadier General) E. B. Gordon (1877–1963). Game's technique echoes that adopted by de Guingand in "managing" Montgomery. De Guingand, *Operation Victory*, 189–90.
23. TFP, Brooke-Popham to Saunders, 25 July 1951. Captain Spenser Ellerton (1894–1978) later became air commodore.
24. IWM 11963.
25. Smyth, *Maurice Baring*, 184–217, 313–40. Other letters can be found in Lovat, *Maurice Baring*; Baring, *Dear Animated Bust*; and Hillgarth and Jeffs, *Letters*—each adjusted in style, tone, and content to suit their intended recipient.
26. ANH, Bron to Nan, 21 October 1916.
27. T. Marson, *Scarlet and Khaki* (London: Jonathan Cape, 1930), 160–62. According to Brooke-Popham, the punishments were slightly different and ranged from humming to opening and (ultimately) breaking a window.
28. Bartlett, *Psychology*, 138–39.

29. G. Taylor, *Sopwith Scout 7309* (London: Cassell, 1968), 162; TNA AIR 1/520/16/11/2. Edward Stanley, Lord Derby (1865–1948) was a soldier, politician, and diplomat.
30. TNA AIR 1/2390/228/11/129.
31. Sholto Douglas, *Years of Combat* (London: Collins, 1963), 182.
32. Marson, *Scarlet and Khaki*, 158–59.
33. "Sammy" Maynard was Flight Commander (later AVM) F. H. M. Maynard (1893–1976). TNA AIR 1/2387/228/11/49.
34. No. 46 Squadron had suffered significant casualties in low-flying patrols during the Cambrai offensive. Gould Lee, *No Parachute*, 249–50.
35. The nature of "distant" as opposed to "close" leadership varies according to social interaction. Anderson, *Leadership in Defence*, 13–14. Hunt offers a different leadership model, based on a multilevel hierarchy: "Direct," "Organizational," and "Systems," each with a different time horizon and cognitive complexity. Trenchard, as GOC RFC, operated at the "Organizational" level on a two- to ten-year time span but also could, and did, operate at the "Direct" level. J. Hunt, *Leadership: A New Synthesis* (Newbury Park, CA: Sage, 1991).
36. Sholto Douglas, *Years of Combat*, 183–85; H. Balfour, *An Airman Marches* (London: Hutchinson, 1933), 123–24.
37. Sir William Hugh Stobart Chance, C.B.E., "Experiences of Sir William Chance, Part 3," accessed 24 January 2024, http://www.worcestershireregiment.com/wr.php?main=inc/whs_chance_1; Chance was a pilot with No. 27 Squadron at Fienvillers in 1916.

CHAPTER 8. FOLLOWERS AS LEADERS

1. It was only officers (with a few exceptions) who flew aircraft or manned the kite balloons. The majority (more than 90 percent) of the RFC's personnel on the Western Front served in support and logistic roles.
2. Air Commodore Ernest Howard-Williams (1895–1942) was a pilot and author. E. Howard-Williams, *The Air Is the Future Career* (London: Hutchinson, 1939), 254.
3. Howard-Williams, 255.
4. Since Trenchard's arrival in France, the RFC had grown from an organization comprising just under 3,000 personnel (all ranks) to one of over 42,000—of which some 1,800 were combatants (pilots and observers).
5. G. D. Sheffield, *Leadership in the Trenches* (London: Macmillan, 2000).
6. Griffith, *R.A.F. Occasions*, 5.
7. J. Leonard and P. Leonard-Johnson, *The Fighting Padre* (Barnsley: Pen & Sword, 2010).
8. W. Coppens, *Days on the Wing* (London: Aviation Book Club, 1935), 107, 118–19.
9. IWM 10986, Philip Game to Gwendolen, 14 April 1916.
10. Marson, *Scarlet and Khaki*, 136–37. Garro-Jones, who served in the RFC during the war and later introduced measures to control alcohol in the RAF, nevertheless attested to the moderate drinking he had encountered. Garro-Jones, *Ventures and Visions*, 226–27.
11. Smythies, "Experiences," 75–89.

12. ACM "Bert" Harris, Air Officer Commanding-in-Chief of the RAF Bomber Command (1942–45), rarely visited his frontline units but was still able to offer effective leadership to his bomber crews, even though their overall loss rate was higher than that experienced by the RFC on the Western Front. The difference, however, was that by World War II, the RAF had an established identity, traditions, and a binding ethos. Just as importantly, Harris could rely on a large cadre of experienced subordinate commanders. H. Probert, *Bomber Harris: His Life and Times* (Barnsley: Frontline Books, 2016), 199–201; Anderson, *Leadership in Defence*, A-4.
13. Baring, *Dear Animated Bust*, 130–31, Baring to Juliet Duff, 25 May 1917.
14. D. Winter, *The First of the Few* (London: Allen Lane, 1982), 177.
15. Brigadier General (later ACM Sir) Edgar Ludlow-Hewitt (1886–1973) was a senior RAF officer. A. Insall, *Observer—Memoirs of the RFC 1915–18* (London: Kimber, 1970), 136. Ludlow-Hewitt's paper would provide the basis for S.S. 132, "Aircraft Cooperation with Infantry."
16. Charlton, *Charlton*, 237–38; P. Playfair, *"Pip" Playfair—A Founding Father of the RAF* (Ilfracombe: Arthur Stockwell, 1979), 49–57; RAFM, Hogg Diary.
17. IWM 11963.
18. C. Cole, *McCudden V.C.* (London: William Kimber, 1967), 106.
19. E. Richards, *Australian Airmen—A History of the 4th Squadron Australian Flying Corps* (Melbourne: Bruce & Co., 1922), 53–58.
20. TNA AIR 1/818/204/130; TNA AIR 1/686/21/13/2252; P. Dye, "The Aviator as Superhero?," *Air Power Review* (Winter 2004): 65–74.
21. TNA AIR 1/683/21/13/2234.
22. P. Dye, "The Intrepid Airman: The Physiology of Air Warfare," in R. Mahoney, ed., *First World War in the Air* (London: RAF Museum, 2015), 77–81.
23. TNA AIR 10/973.
24. Winter, *First of the Few*, 174–91.
25. S. K. Taylor, "Mum's the Word: An Evening Major W Sholto Douglas, MC, DFC, Would Prefer to Forget," *Cross and Cockade International Journal* 37, no. 2 (2006): 116–19.
26. M. Westrop, *A History of No 10 Squadron Royal Naval Air Service in World War I* (Atglen: Schiffer, 2004), 81–82.
27. S. Wise, *Canadian Airmen and the First World War—The Official History of the Royal Canadian Air Force* (Toronto: University of Toronto Press, 1980), 1:174–75. Commodore (later AVM Sir) Charles Lambe (1875–1953) commanded the Royal Navy's Dover Command, which included the RNAS air station at Dunkirk.
28. TNA AIR 1/2387/228/11/49.
29. Wise, *Canadian Airmen*, 175.
30. CUL Add 9429/18/207.
31. TNA AIR 1/1515/204/58/56.
32. Smythies, "Experiences," 85.

33. An image alluded to by Baring in his *R.F.C.Alphabet*: "M is for Maurice, too slender for Burke."
34. This effectively marked the end of Burke's RFC career. He rejoined his parent regiment but was killed in action during the Battle of Arras. Burke, Personal Diary, 3 May 15; ANH, Bron to Nan, 15 August 1915.
35. The issue is not helped by partisan writing about the nature and timing of Dowding's retirement (or "dismissal") in 1940.
36. RAFM, Hogg Diary, 4 March 1916; IWM 11963; D. Grinnell-Milne, *Wind in the Wires* (London: Hurst and Blackett, 1933), 59; C. Shelley, "A Popular Memoir of the First World War Casually Critiqued by One of Its Characters," *Canadian Air Historical Society Journal* 55, no. 3 (2017): 110–22; G. Ellis, *Toolbox on the Wing* (Shrewsbury: Airlife, 1983), 44–45; P. Huskinson, *Vision Ahead* (London: Werner Laurie, 1949), 26. Air Commodore Patrick Huskinson (1897–1966) was a fighter pilot and senior RAF officer.
37. C. G. Jefford, *The Flying Camels* (High Wycombe: Flying Camels, 1995), 9–10.
38. V. Orange, *Tedder: Quietly in Command* (London: Routledge, 2012), 68–69; RAFM MFC 76/1/7, Trenchard to Brancker, 19 August 1916, and Brancker to Trenchard, 21 August 1916; Wright, *Dowding and the Battle of Britain*, 32–35; Shelley, "A Popular Memoir," 119. The idea that Dowding was punished for opposing Trenchard's bloody-minded insistence on offensive action during the Somme fighting continues to find favor with historians. A. Cumming, "The Air Marshal versus the Admiral: Air Chief Marshal Sir Hugh Dowding and Admiral of the Fleet Sir Charles Morton Forbes in the Pantheon," *History* 94, no. 2 (2009): 203–28.
39. Brigadier General (later ACM Sir) Wilfrid Freeman (1888–1953) was vice chief of the Air Staff, Chief Executive of the Ministry of Aircraft Production, and a businessman.
40. RAFM, Hogg Diary, 28 March 1918, 3 April and 8 April 1918.
41. A. Furse, *Wilfrid Freeman—The Genius behind Allied Survival and Air Supremacy 1939 to 1945* (Staplehurst: Spellmount, 2000), 46.

CHAPTER 9. DELIVERING AIRPOWER

1. Sir Walter Raleigh, the official historian of the RFC, declared that "what is said of General Trenchard is said of the Flying Corps." Raleigh, *War in the Air*, 1:417; Jones, *War in the Air*, 2:472–75.
2. *Times*, 21 January and 25 January 1916; Blake, *Private Papers of Douglas Haig*, 126. Baring wrote to Marsh on the same day, rebutting the criticism and suggesting a coordinated effort. Berg Collection, Baring to Marsh, 26 January 1916.
3. The "Fokker Menace" was the period between July 1915 and March 1916 when the German Fokker monoplane, equipped with a synchronized forward-firing machine gun, dominated air fighting. The losses encountered during the Somme fighting were far higher, but not until Gibbs' book was there any public criticism. Gibbs, *Realities*, 286.
4. O. Stewart, *Words and Music for a Mechanical Man* (London: Faber & Faber, 1967), 134; A. Gould Lee, *Open Cockpit* (London: Jarrolds, 1969), 139–41. Harold Balfour, another

fighter pilot, was also critical about effort wasted in offensive patrols. H. Balfour, *Wings over Westminster* (London: Hutchinson, 1973), 39–40.
5. Henry Albert Jones (1893–1945), an RFC observer and civil servant, took over the writing of the official air history after Sir Walter Raleigh's death. Sir John Chamier (1883–1974) was an air commodore. Hillgarth and Jeffs, *Letters*, 95–96, Baring to Marsh, 26 January 1916; Jones, *War in the Air*, 6:552–58; Sykes, *From Many Angles*, 220–21; Chamier, *Birth of the Royal Air Force*, 116; Biddle, *Rhetoric and Reality*, 28; Stewart, *Words and Music*, 131–34; Gibbs, *Realities*, 317.
6. Chamier, *Birth of the Royal Air Force*, 117.
7. Biddle, *Rhetoric and Reality*, 28; P. Meilinger, *Paths of Heaven* (Maxwell Air Force Base, AL: Air University Press, 1997), 44–45; Wise, *Canadian Airmen*, 175; Paris, *Winged Warfare*, 237; M. Cooper, "A House Divided: Policy, Rivalry and Administration in Britain's Military Air Command 1914–1918," *Journal of Strategic Studies* 3, no. 2 (1980): 178–201.
8. Chamier says that pilots were still being sent overseas with an average of 17.5 hours solo in the spring of 1917, although this had risen to 48.5 hours by the autumn. Chamier, *Birth of the Royal Air Force*, 162.
9. G. Livingston, *Hot Air in Cold Blood* (London: Selwyn & Blount, 1933), 89–106; Sykes, *From Many Angles*, 220–21; TNA AIR 1/1288/204/11/53; R. Sturtivant, "Flying Training in World War I," *Aviation News*, 14 October 1977, 4; Higham, *Military Intellectuals in Britain*, 158.
10. Jones, *War in the Air*, 6:28; TNA AIR 1/678/21/13/2100.
11. B. Posen, *The Sources of Military Doctrine—France, Britain and Germany between the World Wars* (Ithaca, NY: Cornell University Press, 1984).
12. TNA AIR 1/785/204/4/558. Just one hundred copies were produced. When the revised edition (December 1915) was published, six thousand copies were ordered.
13. Reviewing operational papers written between 1910 and 1917, Brooke-Popham observed that the RAF's doctrine (as regards the air offensive) had steadily developed since the days of the Air Battalion "following a logical and consistent sequence." While there is always a danger (in working backward from a received 'truth') of selecting evidence that builds toward the desired outcome, Brooke-Popham was uniquely qualified to comment on how the RFC's doctrine had evolved. LHCMA BP 9/9/37, Brooke-Popham to Garrod, 6 December 1949.
14. Biddle, *Rhetoric and Reality*, 27. Trenchard readily acknowledged that Haig had imbued him with the right spirit—of attacking the enemy. RAFM MFC 76/1/18, Trenchard to Sassoon, 24 March 1918.
15. LHCMA BP 9/9/37, "Development of RAF Offensive Doctrine," Brooke-Popham to Garrod, 6 December 1949. Strictly speaking, the statement originated with the January 1914 draft of the RFC Training Manual. TNA AIR 1/785/204/4/558, War Office, RFC (Military Wing) Training Manual Part II, Correspondence and Proofs.
16. TNA AIR 1/2251/209/54/3, "Notes on Air Reconnaissance."

17. T. Henshaw, *The Sky Their Battlefield II* (London: Fetubi Books, 2014), 346. Comparative figures for the Luftstreitkräfte are not readily available, but over the course of the war it is likely that no more than a quarter of casualties on the Western Front occurred over Allied lines. Figures for the French air service indicate that two-thirds of their casualties occurred west of the lines and only one-third over German lines. National Archives, RG 165.
18. TNA AIR 1/522/16/12/5, "Secret Memorandum on the French Air Services," Trenchard to GHQ BEF, 28 August 1917.
19. Commandant Paul du Peuty (1878–1918) was a pre-war cavalry officer who joined the aviation service early in the war. Following General Nivelle's appointment as CinC in December 1916, he replaced Colonel Barès as head of aviation at GQG. TFP, Brooke-Popham to Saunders, 16 August 1951.
20. Jones, *War in the Air*, 2:164–65.
21. One of Trenchard's earliest actions was to convene a meeting with the Belgian and French air services at HQ RFC on 7 August 1915 to review the effectiveness of aerial bombing. It was concluded that attack against trains, rather than the railway system in general, were likely to be most effective way to interrupt the enemy's movements of troops, ammunition, and supplies. Direct liaison between the RFC and the French 10th Army continued through September before a formal plan was submitted to Foch for his approval. TNA AIR 1/752/204/4/61.
22. TNA AIR 69/1; TFP, Brooke-Popham to Saunders, 6 July 1951; TNA AIR 1/8/15/1/13, Reichsarchiv to AHB, 13 October 1923. HQ RFC issued a "lessons learned" note on bombing attacks once the offensive had concluded. Jones, *War in the Air*, vol. 2, appendix 6.
23. Lieutenant Colonel R. A. Cooper (1885–1965) had joined the diplomatic service in 1912 but resigned on the outbreak of war and, after flying training, joined the RFC in France. Baring, War Diary, 13 June 1915.
24. TNA AIR 1/1303/204/11/169, Trenchard to War Office, 15 May 1916; TNA AIR 1/1585/204/82/41; TNA AIR 1/1303/204/11/169.
25. TFP, Brooke-Popham to Saunders, 25 July 1951; Jones, *War in the Air*, 2:164–68.
26. RAFM MFC 76/6/61, "Trenchard Autobiographical Narrative," 79.
27. TNA AIR 1/8/15/1/13, Reichsarchiv to AHB, 13 October 1923. General Fritz von Below, commander of the First Army, wrote, "The beginning and the first few weeks of the Somme battle were marked by a complete inferiority of our own air forces." TNA AIR 69/3.
28. TNA AIR 1/993/204/5/1218; TNA AIR 1/138/15/40/281.
29. The German IV Corps reported that "the numerical superiority of the enemy's airmen and the fact that their machines were better, were made disagreeably apparent to us, particularly in their direction of the enemy's artillery fire and in bomb-dropping. . . . The enemy's airmen were often able to fire successfully on our troops with machine guns by descending to a height of a few hundred metres." "Experiences of the IV German Corps in the Battle of the Somme during July 1916," S.S. 478, GHQ, 30 September 1916.
30. Henshaw, *Sky Their Battlefield II*, appendix 3.

31. Asked to lead this effort, James told Trenchard that the idea was suicidal. Another officer was selected, and the attacks went ahead. As predicted, enemy fighters focused on the lone machines, which, without an observer, could not defend themselves. Trenchard immediately stopped these lone missions, and thereafter bombing was only carried out with escorts. James felt that Trenchard never held his decision against him. IWM 11963; Jones, *War in the Air*, 2:278–79.
32. Writing privately to Spenser Wilkinson some six months earlier, Baring wrote persuasively and at length about the operational constraints faced by the RFC. Hillgarth and Jeffs, *Letters*, 96–104. Boyle says that the document was all Baring's work—based on Trenchard's thoughts. Boyle, *Trenchard*, 86–189.
33. V. Orange, *Churchill and His Airmen* (London: Grub Steer, 2013), 47–48.
34. TNA AIR 1/8/15/1/13, Reichsarchiv to AHB, 13 October 1923; R. Duiven and D.-S. Abbott, *Schlacht-Flieger—Germany and the Origins of Air/Ground Support 1916–1918* (Atglen: Schiffer, 2006), 17–33. The French air service resurrected day bombing in 1918, under Duval's leadership, when the Division Aérienne was formed to provide greater firepower in support of ground operations. Pétain declared that aerial bombing was the "direct extension of the artillery. . . . All efforts should converge on the essential act: the battle."
35. Baring, *R.F.C. H.Q.*, 179–84.
36. Macmillan, *Into the Blue*, 112–13.
37. E. Hoeppner, *Deutschlands Krieg in der Luft* (Leipzig: Koehler, 1921), 100–105; M. Bechthold, "Bloody April Revisited: The Royal Flying Corps at the Battle of Arras, 1917," *British Journal for Military History* 4, no. 2 (February 2018): 50–69.
38. De Havilland, *Sky Fever*, 107.
39. E. R. Hooton, *War over the Trenches—Air Power and the Western Front Campaigns 1916–1918* (Hersham: Ian Allen, 2010), 179.
40. Jordan, "Royal Air Force and Air/Land Integration," 15; Dye, *Bridge to Airpower*, 69. Of the 450 RFC/RAF corps machines engaged in artillery cooperation and recorded as casualties in 1917, 139 were due to air combat compared to 59 (of 350) recorded in 1918. This equates to 31 percent of casualties in 1917 and just 17 percent in 1918. Not only was the total loss in artillery cooperation aircraft lower in 1918 compared to 1917 (by one hundred machines), but the proportion due to enemy fighters was also lower (17 percent compared to 31 percent). Not every air combat resulted in a casualty and the Luftstreitkräfte could also claim success if an artillery cooperation machine had to break off and return home because of damage. If we include this broader category, a total of 162 artillery cooperation machines were recorded as casualties in 1917, compared to 74 in 1918. In other words, German fighter effectiveness (in terms of the destruction/disruption of the BEF's artillery cooperation machines) fell by 54 percent between 1917 and 1918.
41. The RFC flew nearly 120,000 hours during the Third Ypres offensive, compared to 83,000 hours during the Somme. Dye, *Bridge to Airpower*, 105; Hoeppner, *Deutschlands Krieg in der Luft*, 104–5; OHL, *Vorschriften für den Stellungskrieg für alle Waffen*, Teil 13: *Einsatz von Jagdstaffeln*, Chef des Generalstabe des Feldheeres, 25 October 1917, 4.

42. During the Hundred Days campaign (8 August–11 November 1918), the RAF suffered a loss rate only exceeded by Bloody April. Henshaw, *Sky Their Battlefield II*, 346.
43. Boyle, *Trenchard*, 188–89.
44. *Fighting in the Air* is a mixture of instruction and propaganda. A second edition was published in April 1918. The document was unclassified, unlike the French and German equivalents, which were classified as either Secret or Confidential and were not to be taken into aircraft or the trenches.
45. TNA AIR 1/524/16/12/26. When Trenchard was appointed CAS, he asked both Brooke-Popham and Game for papers on specific topics, like those he had commissioned from them in France. It is possible that all the policy papers produced by HQ RFC in 1916 and 1917 were drafted in this way. "I know I am asking you for a lot, but you used to do this sort of thing for me in France and I submitted them, although they were really your own." RAFM MFC 76/1/140/1, Trenchard to Brooke-Popham 10 May 1919; RAFM MFC 76/1/189/1, Trenchard to Game, 16 February 1919.
46. Hillgarth and Jeffs, *Letters*, 95–104, Baring to Marsh, 26 January 1916, and Baring to Spenser Wilkinson, 23 March 1916. Gould Lee describes a conversation with a "perceptive" Baring in November 1917 when they discussed the army's ignorance about the help that the RFC was providing to operations on the ground. Gould Lee, *Open Cockpit*, 140.
47. Stewart, *Words and Music*, 124–34. Stewart says that Trenchard banned escort patrols, forcing recce and other machines to venture over enemy territory without protection, but HQ RFC was only opposed to "close escort." It was extremely difficult for the higher-performance single-seat fighters to remain close to the slower two-seaters without becoming targets themselves. Jordan is more measured in his criticism. D. Jordan, "The Army Cooperation Missions of the Royal Flying Corps/Royal Air Force 1914–1918" (PhD diss., University of Birmingham, 1997), 36–37. At least one day bomber pilot claimed that an unescorted formation fared better than one with escorts. M. Moore, 'No 45 Squadron, 1916-1917', The Hawk, December 1928, 102; OHL, *Vorschriften für den Stellungskrieg für alle Waffen*, Teil 13, 5.
48. Paris, *Winged Warfare*, 4–5.
49. TNA AIR 1/8/15/1/9, Reichsarchiv to AHB, 6 October 1921.
50. TNA AIR 1/8/15/1/19, Reichsarchiv to AHB, 13 October 1923. Describing the lessons learned on the Somme, the Reichsarchiv stated that "it was no longer possible, by purely defensive action to keep the enemy reconnaissance aircraft over their own lines and hermetically to barricade the front lines."
51. "With an Army Cooperation Squadron during the German Attacks of 1918," *The Hawk*, 1931, 20–27. Another RFC pilot recalled that the roads packed with British vehicles and retreating troops represented "one of the finest targets for machine guns and light bombs presented during the war." B. Smythies, "The German Air Service on the Western Front," *RUSI Journal* 69, no. 473 (1924): 126–37; J. R. Cuneo, "Preparation of German Attack Aviation for the Offensive of March 1918," *Military Affairs* 7, no. 2 (1943): 69–78; Hooton, *War over the Trenches*, 208–15.

52. J. S. Corum, "From Biplane to Blitzkrieg: The Development of German Air Doctrine between the Wars," *War in History*, no. 1 (January 1996): 85–101; J. S. Corum and R. Muller, *The Luftwaffe's Way of War: German Air Force Doctrine 1911–1945* (Baltimore: Nautical and Aviation Publishing, 1998), 48–65; J. S. Corum, "The Luftstreitkräfte Builds a Bomber Doctrine," *RAF Air Power Review*, Spring 2003, 61–77.
53. Corum and Muller, *Luftwaffe's Way of War*, 52. See appendix B for an analysis of operational tempo.
54. Interestingly, Hoeppner, like Trenchard, believed that heavy losses in aircraft and personnel would have a demoralizing effect on the enemy as well as encouraging one's own troops. OHL, *Vorschriften für den Stellungskrieg für alle Waffen*, Teil 13, 3.
55. P. Neumann, *Die deutschen Luftstreitkräfte im Weltkriege* (Berlin: Mittler & Son, 1923), 277–79.
56. Chamier, *Birth of the Royal Air Force*, 177.
57. L. E. O. Charlton, *War from the Air—Past, Present, Future* (London: Thomas Nelson & Sons, 1935), 45–47; P. R. C. Groves, *Behind the Smoke Screen* (London: Faber and Faber, 1934), 287; E. J. Kingston-McCloughry, *Winged Warfare: Air Problems of Peace and War* (London: Jonathan Cape, 1937), 5–22. These views have been contested on the basis that concentration on support to the army was more in harmony with actual capabilities. M. Cooper, "Blueprint for Confusion: The Administrative Background to the Formation of the Royal Air Force, 1912–1919," *Journal of Contemporary History* 22, no. 3 (1987): 437–53. Groves remained close to Lord Rothermere and wrote regularly on airpower matters for his newspapers.
58. R. R. Money, *Flying and Soldiering* (London: Ivor Nicholson & Watson, 1936), 93–95.
59. Although Trenchard's methods were questioned, it was acknowledged that his strategy provided freedom of action for the RFC's artillery, recce, and ground support activities. Wise, *Canadian Airmen*, 315–420. Other historians of the air war have come to the same conclusion. Jordan, "Battle for the Skies," 80.
60. It eventually proved possible to locate German artillery cooperation machines from their wireless signals, but this required that dedicated interceptors be constantly ready on the ground within reach of the target before it disappeared.
61. For example, see Corum, "From Biplane to Blitzkrieg," 87; Cooper, "Development of Air Policy," 47, and "House Divided," 197. Cooper's argument is reminiscent of the reasoning found in at least one German postwar history that claimed the Luftstreitkräfte was never defeated, as "until the end of the war, German reconnaissance aircraft and attack aircraft flew far into enemy territory. Until the last day, German fighter pilots shot down their enemies. On the last night of the war, German airmen were still trying to bomb the enemy's barracks and accommodation." E. von Loewenstern, *Eine falsche englische Rechnung, die Fliegerschlacht von Amiens am 8. August 1918* (Berlin: Bernard & Graese, 1938), 12.
62. Fliegerabteilung 221 flew less than half the number of artillery cooperation sorties between August and October 1918 as it did in the same three-month period of 1917. A. Koch, *Die Flieger-Abteilung (A) 221* (Berlin: Gerhard Starling, 1925), 189–90.

63. Bundesarchiv, PH 17-I/19/0003, "Hinweise für die Führung einer Fliegerabteilung in der Angriffsschlacht und im Bewegungskrieg" (Advice for Leading a Fliegerabteilung in Offensive Battles and Mobile Warfare), 10 February 1918.
64. Cooper, *Birth of Independent Air Power*, 75; Corum and Muller, *Luftwaffe's Way of War*, 55; OHL, *Vorschriften für den Stellungskrieg für alle Waffen*, Teil 13, 3.
65. Von Loewenstern, *Eine falsche englische Rechnung*, 12.
66. TNA AIR 1/520/16/11/2.
67. Corum and Muller, *Luftwaffe's Way of War*, 55; Hoeppner, *Deutschlands Krieg in der Luft*, 43, 93, 175–78. The editor of the French edition was moved to add, "It is undeniable that the English airmen, because of their traditions and training, were more combative than the French and German airmen. But it must not be forgotten that the front held by the British Army was very narrow and that consequently, the proportion of troops in line and of fighter squadrons, was extremely high there. The Allied fighter aircraft therefore presented a maximum density in the English sector to which a similar distribution corresponded on the German side." Hoeppner, *Allemagne et la guerre de l'air* (Paris: Payot, 1923), 147. The more combative nature of the RFC was also acknowledged by German commanders. Boff, "Air Land Integration in the 100 Days," 84.

CHAPTER 10. TRANSFORMING WARFARE

1. TNA CAB 23/3/29.
2. R. Holmes, *The Little Field Marshal* (London: Jonathan Cape, 1981), 319–20.
3. H. A. Jones, *The War in the Air*, vol. 6: *Appendices* (Oxford: Clarendon, 1937), 8–12.
4. *Land and Water*, 23 January, 30 January, 24 April, and 3 July 1915.
5. H. G. Wells, "Imagination in the Air War," *Land and Water*, 26 June 1915.
6. F. Lanchester, "The Failure of the Derby Committee," *Land and Water*, 20 April 1916, 12.
7. J. Morrow, *Building German Airpower, 1909–1914* (Knoxville: University of Tennessee Press, 1976), 8.
8. In 1913, naval expenditure represented 63 percent of Britain's defense budget, whereas in Germany it represented 27 percent and in France 23 percent. D. Stevenson, *Armaments and the Coming of War* (Oxford: Clarendon, 1996), 1–9.
9. The Joint War Committee had been created in February 1916 to coordinate the design and supply of materials for the two air services. Like its successor, the Air Board, it proved a failure. Major (later Lieutenant Colonel Sir) Lancelot Storr (1874–1944) was assistant secretary of the War Cabinet (and later the Imperial War Cabinet).
10. Smuts had seen the influence of airpower during the German East Africa Campaign. *London Gazette*, 20 June 1916; Boyle, *Trenchard*, 231.
11. Weetman Pearson, 1st Viscount Cowdray (1856–1927), an engineer, industrialist, and Liberal politician, was appointed president of the Air Board in January 1917. Major (later Sir) John Baird, Lord Stonehaven (1874–1941), a Conservative MP, had joined Lloyd George's government in December 1916 as parliamentary secretary to

the Air Board. Baird had no aviation background but proved an able and effective administrator.
12. TNA AIR 1/718/29/9, Maurice to Trenchard, 2 September 1917; Roskill, *Documents Relating to the Naval Air Service*, 564–69; TNA AIR 1/718/29/9, Cecil to Trenchard, 26 August 1917; J. Spaight, *The Beginnings of Organised Air Power* (London: Longmans, Green & Co., 1927), 142; Parliamentary Archives (PA) LG/F/45/9/12, Smuts to Lloyd George, 11 July 1917.
13. TNA CAB 23/3/38; TNA CAB 23/3/71.
14. Rear-Admiral Sir Godfrey Paine (1871–1932) was a pre-war aviator appointed to command the Central Flying School in 1912. Admiral Mark Kerr (1864–1944), a pre-war aviator, was the first British flag officer to learn to fly. Brigadier General Guy Livingston (1881–1950) was a regular soldier closely connected with pre-war aviation.
15. M. Kerr, *Land, Sea and Air* (London: Longmans, Green & Co., 1927), 291–92; TNA CAB 24/29/60, GT 2360. Smuts recognized that the proliferation of committees may have been confusing, noting that some had subsumed the work of previous committees or simply changed their name. The four committees were Air Raids; Air Reorganisation; War Priorities; and Air Policy.
16. Liddle, *Airman's War*, 181.
17. Game Papers, Philip Game to Gwendolen Game, 9 August 1917; TNA CAB 24/26/58, CIGS to Haig, 24 August 1917, and Haig to CIGS, 15 September 1917; TNA AIR 1/718/29/9, Cecil to Trenchard, 26 August 1917, Maurice to Trenchard, 2 September 1917, and Trenchard to Haig, 6 October 1917. Cecil's visit appears to have triggered Trenchard's offer to see Smuts in company with Captain Charles Lambe (his RNAS counterpart). P. Elliott, "Sir David Henderson, the Smuts Report and the Birth of Independent Air Power," in R. Mahoney, ed., *First World War in the Air* (London: RAF Museum, 2015), 125–29.
18. Sir William (later 1st Viscount) Weir (1877–1959), an engineer, industrialist, and politician, was appointed director general of aircraft production in 1917. TNA CAB 24/26/62, Smuts to War Cabinet, 18 September 1917.
19. TNA CAB 23/4/11; TNA CAB 24/27/78.
20. TNA CAB 23/13/19; TNA CAB 23/4/18.
21. *Times*, 4 October and 5 October 1917.
22. TNA CAB 24/28/22, GT 2222; TNA CAB 23/4/20.
23. TNA CAB 24/28/84, GT 2284; Kerr, *Land, Sea and Air*, 289–91.
24. TNA CAB 23/4/23.
25. TNA CAB 24/29/79, GT 2242, War Office to Haig, 18 October 1917.
26. Alfred Lord Milner (1854–1925) was a journalist, statesman, and colonial administrator and one of the most influential members of Lloyd George's War Cabinet. TNA CAB 24/30/9, GT 2409.
27. E. Wrench, *Alfred Lord Milner—The Man of No Illusions* (London: Eyre & Spottiswoode, 1958), 308.

28. TNA CAB 23/4/35 and CAB 23/4/38.
29. Harold Harmsworth (1868–1940) was a leading British newspaper proprietor and pioneer of popular journalism. Harmsworth, who was raised to the peerage as Baron (later Viscount) Rothermere in 1914, shared ownership of Associated Newspapers (which included *The Times*, the *Daily Mail*, the *Evening News*, and the *Daily Mirror*) with his older brother Alfred Harmsworth (1865–1922), who became Baron (later Viscount) Northcliffe in 1905. By 1914, they controlled nearly 47 percent of the circulation of London's daily newspapers and enjoyed considerable political influence. J. M. McEwen, "The National Press during the First World War: Ownership and Circulation," *Journal of Contemporary History* 17, no. 3 (July 1982): 471.
30. S. Taylor, *The Great Outsiders—Northcliffe, Rothermere and the Daily Mail* (London: Weidenfeld & Nicolson, 1996), 119–27.
31. *Times*, 17 November 1917. Lloyd George was incensed by Northcliffe's behavior. "He has no sense of loyalty and there is something of the cad about him." J. McEwen, ed., *The Riddell Diaries 1908–1923* (London: Athlone, 1986), 205; A. J. P. Taylor, *Beaverbrook* (New York: Simon and Schuster, 1972), 131.
32. *Times*, 27 November 1918.
33. TNA ADM 116/1602, Rothermere to Geddes, 28 November 1917. Godfrey Paine was one of the most experienced naval aviators and Trenchard's commanding officer at CFS before the war.
34. A. Fitzroy, *Sir Almeric Fitzroy, Memoirs* (London: Hutchinson, 1925), 2:666–68.
35. *Times*, 16 June 1917.
36. The League of Londoners had been formed in July 1917 to persuade the government to intern more enemy aliens and adopt a policy of reprisal air raids. *Times*, 24 July, 10 October, 15 October, 15 December, and 18 December 1917; *The Aeroplane*, 19 December 1917, 1804–6.
37. TNA AIR 1/520/16/11/2; Boyle, *Trenchard*, 242; Jones, *War in the Air*, 6:23–24.
38. TNA CAB 23/4/18.
39. TNA AIR 1/718/29/9.
40. Brigadier General William "Billy" Mitchell, U.S. Army Air Service, visited Trenchard at St-Andre in May 1917 and later wrote, "His judgement inspired my immediate confidence and his whole personality my deep respect." W. Mitchell, *Memoirs of World War I* (New York: Random House, 1960), 104–5.
41. G. Babin, "Le Royal Flying Corps," *L'illustration*, 23 February 1918, 182–85.
42. Boyle, *Trenchard*, 251–53.
43. Prince George (1819–1904) was CinC of the British Army for thirty-nine years. G. St Aubyn, *The Royal George 1819–1904* (London: Constable, 1963), 329.
44. Boyle, *Trenchard*, 241; G. Riddell, *Lord Riddell's War Diary 1914–1918* (London: Ivor Nicholson & Watson, 1933), 254–55.
45. H. Boog, "The Problem of Independence of Airpower in Germany," in C. Carlier, ed., *Adaptation de l'arme aérienne aux conflits contemporains et processus d'indépendance des*

armées de l'Air des origines à la fin de la Seconde Guerre Mondiale (Paris: Institute d'Histoire des Conflits Contemporains, 1985), 131–51; M. Spivak, "Les problèmes posés à l'armée de Terre par la création du ministère de l'Air et les perspectives d'indépendance de l'armée de l'Air, 1928–1934," in Carlier, *Adaptation*, 131–51.
46. Hansard, HC Debate, 12 November 1917.
47. G. Babin, "Le Royal Flying Corps," *L'illustration*, 16 February 1918, 153.
48. Hansard, HC Debate, 12 November 1917.

CHAPTER 11. SERVANT OF THE STATESMAN
1. IWM 10986, Philip Game to Gwendolen, 27 January 1918.
2. Game hoped that he could join Trenchard in London—once Salmond had found his feet. IWM 10986, Philip Game to Gwendolen, 12 and 16 January 1918. Although Rothermere was suspicious about Simon's role, Trenchard used him as a roving emissary rather than as a political fixer. J. Simon, "Gott mit uns—An Impression of the Critical Days of March 1918," *Blackwood's* 204 (July–December 1918): 771–74.
3. Trenchard would later consider recruiting Sir Harold Baker (1877–1960), another Liberal MP and a friend of Simon, who had served as financial secretary to the War Office in the Asquith government.
4. Lieutenant (later Major Sir) Evelyn Wrench (1882–1966) was an entrepreneur, author, and journalist. Recruited by Lord Northcliffe in 1904, he later founded the English-Speaking Union and the British Overseas League. E. Wrench, *Struggle* (London: Ivor Nicholson & Watson, 1935), 271. Captain (later Lieutenant Colonel) George Philippi (1890–1933) won the Military Cross with No. 60 Squadron in 1916. Lieutenant Colonel Euan Rabagliati (1892–1978) was a pre-war pilot who won the Military Cross with No. 5 Squadron in 1915. He raced cars after the war and later joined the Secret Intelligence Service. Major (later Sir Henry) Segrave (1896–1930) was a land and water world speed record holder. Major Robert Smith-Barry (1886–1949) was an early pilot and pioneer flying instructor, "inventor" of the Gosport System.
5. Wrench, *Struggle*, 282–88.
6. Brigadier General Conway Jenkins (1888–1933) was head of the Air Board's Aircraft Acceptance Department.
7. Sir Henry Norman (1858–1939) was a crusading journalist and politician. Norman held several minor ministerial posts before the war and was made a privy councilor in 1918. He was a member of the War Office Wireless Committee before joining the Ministry of Munitions, where he served on the Instruments subcommittee and the General Purposes subcommittee as well as acting as the department's liaison officer with the French Ministry of Inventions. IWM Documents 9887, Private Papers of Sir Henry and Lady Norman.
8. IWM 9887, Lane to Norman, 6 September 1917.
9. IWM 9887, Norman to Rothermere, 1 January 1918.
10. For example, Norman raised concerns about the suitability of an officer of the Central India Horse, extolled the utility of the French anilite explosive, which had been

withdrawn from use because it lacked explosive power, and quoted data on the RFC's manpower to frontline aircraft ratio that was nearly four times worse than the actual position. Jones, *War in the Air*, 6:28.

11. Norman's second wife, Priscilla McLaren, was related to Euan Rabagliati through her aunt, Helen Rabagliati (née McLaren).
12. IWM 9887, Lloyd George to Rothermere, undated note; author's collection, Norman to Donald, 29 January 1918.
13. U. Bloom, *He Lit the Lamp—A Biography of Professor A.M. Low* (London: Burke, 1958), 75–80; S. Mills, *The Dawn of the Drone* (Haverton: Casemate, 2019), 212–13; IWM 9887, Segrave to Norman, 7 May 1918. Norman was equally effusive about Segrave's qualities, writing, "There seems no aspect of the air service with which you are not intimately acquainted." C. Posthumus, *Sir Henry Segrave* (London: Batsford, 1961), 39–40.
14. See, for example, Beaverbrook, *Men and Power*, 218–42; Boyle, *Trenchard*, 266–88; Livingston, *Hot Air*, 133–51; Jones, *War in the Air*, 6:26–27, D. Lloyd George, *War Memoirs*, vol. 2 (London: Odhams, 1936), 1113–15; Macmillan, *Brancker*, 184–88; Powers, *Strategy without Slide-Rule*, 102–3; Repington, *First World War*, 2:283–85; W. J. Reader, *Architect of Air Power—The Life of the First Viscount Weir* (London: Collins, 1968), 67–68; S. Roskill, *Hankey: Man of Secrets* (London: Collins, 1970), 518–19; Simon, *Retrospect*, 114–20; Spaight, *The Beginnings*, 188–90; Taylor, *Great Outsiders*, 230–32; and Wrench, *Struggle*, 285–97.
15. Kerr, *Land, Sea and Air*, 294. Kerr was appointed to command the South-Western Area (a large operational command comprising over sixty units engaged in convoy protection and antisubmarine operations) in March 1918.
16. TNA ADM 116/1807, Geddes to Weir, 20 May 1918; IWM 10986, Philip Game to Gwendolen, 26 January 1918.
17. Captain (later AVM Sir) Vyell Vyvyan (1875–1935) and Brigadier General (later Air Commodore) Robert Groves (1880–1920). The matter was overtaken by Trenchard's resignation and the decision was left to Sykes, who selected Groves. Robert Groves should not be confused with Brigadier General Percy Groves (1878–1959), who was appointed director of flying operations in May 1918.
18. Beaverbrook, *Men and Power*, 220–21.
19. *New York Times*, 1 February 1918, 3.
20. The members were Rothermere (president); Trenchard (chief of the Air Staff); Baird (parliamentary undersecretary); Henderson (vice president); Kerr (deputy chief of the Air Staff); Paine (master general of personnel); Brancker (comptroller general of equipment); Weir (director general of aircraft production); and Sir John Hunter (administrator of works and buildings). Two additional members, Sir Henry Norman and Sir Arthur Roberts, were appointed later in January. *Times*, 3 January 1918, 6; C. G. Grey, *The Air Ministry* (London: George Allen & Unwin, 1940), 41, 82.
21. *The Aeroplane*, 9 January 1918, 1720; Wrench, *Struggle*, 283.

22. TNA CAB 24/37/97, GT 3197; Lloyd George, *War Memoirs*, 2:1114. Outstanding issues included pay and transfer of technical control. TNA CAB 24/38/53, GT 3252; TNA CAB 23/5/10.
23. Lord Curzon (1859–1925) was a statesman, politician, and writer.
24. *New York Times*, 1 February 1918, 3.
25. *The Aeroplane*, 13 February 1918, 638. In his defense, Rothermere had served as director general of the Royal Army Clothing Department from 1916 to 1917, introducing important reforms and demonstrating an ability to cut bureaucracy and improve performance.
26. Wrench, *Struggle*, 275–76, 279; Garro-Jones, *Ventures and Visions*, 141.
27. Wrench, *Struggle*, 279.
28. TNA CAB 24/39/41.
29. TNA CAB 24/40/78; G. Sheffield and J. Bourne, eds., *Douglas Haig War Diaries and Letters 1914–1918* (London: Weidenfeld & Nicolson, 2005), 373. Beaverbrook regarded these private comments as an example of Trenchard's lack of loyalty.
30. Sheffield and Bourne, *Douglas Haig*, 371–72.
31. Wrench, *Struggle*, 281. Rothermere never forgot how little money his mother had for food when he was growing up, and the deep shock that he experienced when a neighboring family was made bankrupt and all died by suicide. Taylor, *Great Outsiders*, 5. Rothermere and Trenchard's contrasting personalities are regularly cited to explain their conflict: for example, P. Phillips, "Decision and Dissension—Birth of the RAF," *Aerospace Historian* 18, no. 1 (1971): 33–39.
32. TNA CAB 23/14/11; R. Pound and C. Harmsworth, *Northcliffe* (London: Cassell, 1959), 638; Wrench, *Struggle*, 282; Sheffield and Bourne, *Douglas Haig*, 373.
33. This includes Admiral Mark Kerr (vice chief of the Air Staff) and Sir Arthur Roberts, who resigned on 24 April 1918 because of a disagreement with Rothermere. He later rejoined the Air Ministry to work for the new air minister.
34. Spaight, *Beginnings of Organised Air Power*, 188; Boyle, *Trenchard*, 253; Cooper, "House Divided," 192.
35. TNA CAB 24/49/21, GT 4231.
36. Boyle, *Trenchard*, 264. Trenchard attended twenty-four meetings of the Air Council before his resignation. Even allowing for the "sanitizing" nature of official minutes, nothing controversial appears to have been discussed. TNA AIR 6/12.
37. Sanders claims that it was Rothermere's determination to create new squadrons, at the expense of maintaining the strength of existing squadrons, that was the primary cause for the Rothermere-Trenchard estrangement. J. Ramsden, ed., *Real Old Tory Politics—The Political Diaries of Sir Robert Sanders, Lord Bayford, 1910–1935* (Gloucester: Alan Sutton, 1984), 104.
38. Robert Smith-Barry had learned to fly before the war and became one of the earliest members of the RFC. He was famous for his innovative training methods as well as his eccentricities. "Robert Smith-Barry," *The Aeroplane*, 13 May 1949, 540; "Robert Smith-Barry,"

Flight, 5 May 1949, 541; "He Taught the World to Fly," *RAF Flying Review*, February 1963, 33.
39. H. A. Jones, *The War in the Air*, vol. 5 (Oxford: Clarendon, 1935), 429–34; Livingston, *Hot Air*, 98–102; Boyle, *Trenchard*, 202–3.
40. F. Tredrey, *Pioneer Pilot—The Great Smith-Barry Who Taught the World to Fly* (London: Peter Davies, 1976), 81–83. The Training Brigade had issued a pamphlet titled *General Methods of Teaching Scout Pilots* in October 1917 that embodied Smith-Barry's ideas. TNA AIR 1/2126/207/77/3; IWM 9887, Norman to Rothermere, 2 January 1918.
41. IWM 9887, Norman to Rothermere, 21 February 1918; Norman to Rothermere, 14 March 1918; Norman to Rothermere, 26 February 1918.
42. D. Spiers and J. Buckley, eds., *The Dowding Papers* (Farnborough: FAST, 2020), 75–76; CUL Add 9429/1B/1217(v); CUL Add 9429/1B/1215(ii).
43. Livingston, *Hot Air*, 135–36.
44. Smith-Barry had a long track record of burning anything that annoyed him, whether it was a visiting aircraft, squadron record books, or staff files. Tredrey, *Pioneer Pilot*, 74–83, 144–45.
45. Tredrey, *Pioneer Pilot*, 74–83; Boyle, *Trenchard*, 262–66; Library and Archives Canada, MG 30 A 72, vol. 9, file 9: "S.E. Parker, Memoirs of Major S.E. Parker"; Spiers and Buckley, *Dowding Papers*, 75–76.
46. TNA AIR 8/167; Boyle, *Trenchard*, 268.
47. Such matters were properly the responsibility of the naval air staff rather than the Directorate of Aircraft Production, but Groves raised the question as a design policy issue. CHAR 15/58, Weir to Trenchard, 4 March 1918.
48. Groves' analysis not only exaggerated the number of suitable surplus machines but also skated over the operational difficulties. CHAR 15/58, "Notes on Marine Aircraft—Construction and Design Policy," 1 March 1918.
49. TNA AIR 6/12.
50. CHAR 15/58, Geddes to Rothermere, 18 March 1918.
51. J. Bruce, *British Aeroplanes 1914–1918* (London: Putnam, 1957), 188–89; TNA AIR 1/400/15/231/41. There was an element of bluff involved, as the aircraft employed (the D.H.6 two-seat trainer) was underpowered and could not carry an observer as well as a load of bombs. Only one German submarine was found and attacked (unsuccessfully). CHAR 15/58, Weir to Churchill 9 April 1918.
52. Geddes noted that the original number had emerged as a result of a meeting with Rothermere and Churchill that took place on the evening of 15 March. Geddes also stressed that there should be no reduction in the production of float seaplanes (supporting Trenchard's analysis). TNA CAB 24/48/13, GT 4123; TNA CAB 24/45/44, GT 3944.
53. TNA CAB 24/49/21, GT 4231.
54. The Marconi scandal, which broke in 1912, involved allegations of insider trading in Marconi shares by highly placed members of Asquith's administration aware of an

imminent lucrative government contract. Norman played a prominent role in the subsequent parliamentary inquiry. E. P. Oppenheim, *The Pool of Memory* (London: Hodder and Stoughton, 1941), 213; A. Havinghurst, *Radical Journalist: H. W. Massingham* (Cambridge: Cambridge University Press, 1974), 74–84.
55. Author's collection, Henry Norman to Robert Donald, 29 January 1918; NAL, Grey Correspondence, Wood to Grey, 6 April 1918; PA BL/83/2/19, Baird to Bonar Law, 18 April 1918.
56. TNA AIR 6/12.
57. Trenchard's decision to maintain large production orders for the R.E.8 proved sound as its replacement was considerably delayed by engine problems. Norman resented the presumption that the Air Council could not question any plans agreed by Brancker, Trenchard, and Weir. CHAR 15/58, Weir to Rothermere, 25 March 1918.
58. IWM 9887, Norman to Rothermere, 25 March 1918. This was based on a force of 250 bombers attacking individual cities in relays of 25 bombers per hour that would exhaust the defenses.
59. CHAR 15/58A, Trenchard to Churchill, 18 January 1918. Churchill questioned Trenchard's methodology and assumptions, including wastage rates and workup period; however, Weir and Sir John Watson Gibson (Controller Aircraft Requirements) confirmed their validity.
60. Jones, *War in the Air*, vol. 6: *Appendices*, 22–26; Blake, *Private Papers of Douglas Haig*, 273; Hillgarth and Jeffs, *Letters*, 87–88, 119, Baring to Gilbert Chesterton, 24 May 1915, 119, and Baring to MacCarthy, 14 April 1917; Berg Collection, Baring to Marsh, 26 January 1916.
61. TNA CAB 24/49/21.
62. Pound and Harmsworth, *Northcliffe*, 638.
63. Maurice Dean, who admired Trenchard, felt that he should not have opposed government policy or complained when his minister sought advice elsewhere. Dean, *Royal Air Force and Two World Wars*, 29; *New York Times*, 28 January 1942.
64. TNA CAB 24/49/21.
65. Jack Salmond believed that Rothermere didn't think Trenchard was a good staff officer because Trenchard couldn't write or express himself well—showing "the shallow judgement of a journalist." CUL Add 9429/1B/1217(v).
66. Baring, *Dear Animated Bust*, 133.
67. Sidney Parker, who worked closely with Smith-Barry, has provided a memoir of this period. It contains several factual inaccuracies but confirms that Philippi had Rothermere's ear, and that Philippi and Smith-Barry worked together to have Longcroft and Trenchard replaced to facilitate Smith-Barry's plan for an "Invincible Air Force." Library and Archives Canada, MG 30 A 72, vol. 9, file 9, "S.E. Parker, Memoirs of Major S.E. Parker, Additions by L.B. Rochester."
68. N. Flower, ed., *The Journals of Arnold Bennett 1911–1921* (London: Cassell & Co., 1932), 226.
69. CUL Add 9429/1B/1216(iv); Miller, *Boom*, 197; Boyle, *Trenchard*, 269.

70. CUL Add 9429/1B/209/iv.
71. Livingston, *Hot Air*, 133–34; IWM 10986, Philip Game to Gwendolen, 26 January 1918. Marson believed that whenever a big decision was involved, Trenchard would become secretive and go into his shell. CUL Add 9429/1B/1216(iv).

CHAPTER 12. RESIGNATION

1. TNA CAB 23/14/9. As neither the Air Council nor the Navy Board was represented at the meeting, the circulation of the minutes caused some anxiety. There is an earlier version of Rothermere's letter among Norman's papers, suggesting that Norman was directly involved in its drafting.
2. TNA CAB 23/14/11. Additional proposals included the creation of a "Strategic Committee" and appointment of Brigadier General Robert Groves as deputy chief of the Air Staff.
3. Lieutenant General (later Field Marshal) Sir Henry Wilson (1864–1922), CIGS. IWM 9887, Norman to Rothermere, 5 April 1918. Sykes was unaware as to the true reason for his recall.
4. Admiral of the Fleet Lord Sir John Jellicoe (1859–1935) was a senior naval officer and later governor-general of New Zealand.
5. *Times*, 13 April 1918.
6. Rose, *Later Cecils*, 259; Roskill, *Hankey*, 518.
7. Roskill, *Hankey*, 519.
8. Flower, *Journals of Arnold Bennett*, 227.
9. PA, Smuts to Lloyd George, 13 April 1918; Rothermere to Trenchard 13 April 1918. Rothermere's letter left little doubt that he was glad to see the back of Trenchard.
10. Library and Archives Canada, MG 30 A 72, vol. 9, file 9, "S.E. Parker, Memoirs of Major S.E. Parker," 40. The exact timing of Paine's resignation remains uncertain.
11. Boyle, *Trenchard*, 271; PA, Henderson to Rothermere, 14 April 1918, Trenchard to Hankey, 14 April 1918. Trenchard stated that he was told on 10 April that his resignation had been accepted; however, it seems that this occurred on 12 April, the day the War Cabinet accepted Rothermere's proposal. Hansard, HC Debate, 24 April 1918; *The Aeroplane*, 24 April 1918.
12. *Daily Mail*, 15 April 1918. Colonel Walter Faber (1857–1928) was a Conservative politician and soldier. Faber had been a leading figure in the "Air Agitation" of 1916, asserting that RFC pilots were being "murdered." *Daily Mirror*, 15 April 1918.
13. Hansard, HC Debate, 18 April 1918; *Flying*, 24 April 1918.
14. H. Belloc, *Land and Water*, 25 April 1918.
15. *Manchester Guardian*, 15 April 1918; *Globe*, 16 April 1918; *Westminster Gazette*, 16 April 1918; *Daily News*, 20 April 1918; *The Aeroplane*, 17 April 1918; *Aeronautics*, 17 April 1918; *Flying*, 24 April 1918; McEwen, "National Press during the First World War."
16. NAL, Grey Correspondence, Longcroft to Grey, 15 April 1918.
17. Hansard, HC Debate, 15 April 1918.

18. TNA CAB 24/49/21, GT 4321.
19. J. C. C. (later 1st Viscount) Davidson (1889–1970) was a civil servant and Conservative politician. J. R. Rhodes, *Memoirs of a Conservative—J.C.C. Davidson's Memoirs and Papers 1910–1937* (London: Weidenfeld & Nicolson, 1969), 68; *Times*, 19 April 1918.
20. Wrench, *Struggle*, 324.
21. While this may be true, it did not prevent Trenchard from supplying Cecil and Simon with copies of his private correspondence with Rothermere or thanking them later for their intervention. Rose, *Later Cecils*, 262; NAL, Grey Correspondence, Trenchard to Grey, 17 April 1918; Simon, *Retrospect*, 119; Stansky, *Sassoon*, 91.
22. Hansard, HC Debate, 18, 22, 24, and 25 April 1918.
23. Rothermere was incensed by Cecil's actions, and the pair exchanged a series of increasingly ill-tempered letters, which led Rothermere to relieve him of his staff duties. Rose, *Later Cecils*, 259–62.
24. J. Grigg, *Lloyd George: War Leader* (London: Penguin, 2003), 483; Lloyd George, *War Memoirs*, 2:1113.
25. Trenchard was unable to convince Rothermere and Norman about the large number of ground personnel required to keep a squadron operational. RAFM T/76/1/4, Memorandum, 17 April 1918.
26. Repington refers to "General X," but Brancker was the only RAF general with whom he regularly dined. Repington, *First World War*, 2:283; PA F/44/5/5, Baird to Lloyd George, 22 April 1918.
27. CHAR 2/103/73, Rothermere to Lloyd George, 14 November 1918.
28. Rhodes, *Memoirs of a Conservative*, 68–69; A. Thorpe and R. Toye, eds., *The Diaries of Cecil Harmsworth, MP, 1909–1922* (Cambridge: Cambridge University Press, 2016), 269.
29. Beaverbrook, *Men and Power*, 241–43; Grigg, *Lloyd George*, 483.
30. Hansard, HC Debate, 29 April 1918. Rothermere's resignation meant that the promised debate in the House of Lords was never held. *New York Times*, 26 April 1918.
31. *The Spectator*, 16 February 1924.
32. Hansard, HC Debate, 29 April 1918.
33. *The Aeroplane*, 1 May 1918.
34. *Times*, 30 April 1918.
35. *The Aeroplane*, 3 April and 1 May 1918.
36. *Times*, 22 April 1918.
37. Londonderry, *Wings of Destiny* (London: Collins, 1943), 9.
38. Hoare, *Empire of the Air*, 39–41.
39. Livingston, *Hot Air*, 140–42.
40. Livingston was never promoted to major general, nor was he awarded the promised state honor.
41. Rothermere's rumored departure had been raised in Parliament. *The Aeroplane*, 27 February 1918; Flower, *Journals of Arnold Bennett*, 227.

42. Londonderry, *Wings of Destiny*, 95.
43. *Times*, 26 April 1918; Wrench, *Struggle*, 294; Beaverbrook, *Men and Power*, 236.
44. Hansard, HC Debate, 9 May 1918.
45. P. Ferris, *The House of Northcliffe* (New York: World Publishing, 1972), 215; Beaverbrook, *Men and Power*, 218.
46. NAL, Grey Correspondence, Baring to Grey, 29 May 1918; *The Aeroplane*, 24 April 1918, 1493.
47. Grigg, *Lloyd George*, 258; Henderson to Bonar Law, 26 April 1918; Beaverbrook, *Men and Power*, 222–23; Sykes, *From Many Angles*, 217.

CHAPTER 13. REGENERATION

1. Weir had proved extremely effective in rationalizing aeronautical supply. Reader, *Architect of Air Power*, 57–68; C. Addison, *Politics from Within, 1911–1918* (London: Herbert Jenkins, 1924), 2:174. Both the king and his younger son, Prince Albert (serving at RAF Cranwell), were concerned at the effect of Trenchard's resignation. J. Wheeler-Bennett, *King George VI—His Life and Reign* (New York: St. Martin's, 1958), 111–12.
2. Bullock felt that Sykes, in terms of academic intellect, was a cleverer man than Trenchard. CUL Add 9429/1B/1269(ii).
3. IWM 10986, Philip Game to Gwendolen, 1 May 1918.
4. Pound and Harmsworth, *Northcliffe*, 638, Rothermere to Northcliffe, 20 May 1918; *The Aeroplane*, 15 May and 25 September 1918; *Westminster Gazette*, 18 June 1918; IWM 10986, Philip Game to Gwendolen, 29 June 1918.
5. *Boston Globe*, 6 August 1918; R. H. Cameron, *Training to Fly: Military Flight Training 1907–1945* (Washington, DC: Air Force History & Museums Program, 1999), 127–28.
6. Roberts' departure only served to increase the criticism directed at Rothermere. *New York Times*, 26 April 1918.
7. NAL, Grey Correspondence, Baring to Grey, 29 May 1918.
8. De Pierrefeu, *French Headquarters*, 43; P. Armengaud, *Le renseignement aérien, sauvegarde des armées* (Paris: Librairie Aéronautique, 1934), 7–15; Baring, War Diary, 9 November 1917; Blake, *Private Papers of Douglas Haig*, 135; Baring, *R.F.C. H.Q.*, 276. The IAAC met monthly in Paris to coordinate aircraft production following the United States' entry into the war. By May 1918 it had evolved into a forum for strategic planning.
9. Baring, *R.F.C. H.Q.*, 277.
10. Baring, 272.
11. Evelyn Boscawen Gordon (1877–1963) was a soldier, land agent, and farmer. *St George's Gazette*, 31 December 1963, 246.
12. Liddle, *Airman's War*, 181; Repington, *First World War*, 2:389.
13. *R.F.C. H.Q.* covers the next six months in just thirty pages. Baring, *R.F.C. H.Q.*, 272.
14. Montgomery Hyde, *British Air Policy*, 43.
15. TNA AIR 1/72/15/9/136; TNA AIR 1/490/15/312/288, Gordon to Groves, 1 September 1918.

16. A. Barros, "Strategic Bombing and Restraint in 'Total War,' 1915–1918," *Historical Journal* 52, no. 2 (2009): 413–31.
17. Baring, *R.F.C. H.Q.*, 274.
18. Baring, 273.
19. *Les cahiers britanniques et américains*, no. 4, March 1918; *La nouvelle revue*, May–June 1918.
20. Barros, "Strategic Bombing," 424; Baring, *R.F.C. H.Q.*, 280.
21. Trenchard believed in the efficacy of aerial bombing but had little faith in the campaign envisaged by the War Cabinet. He felt there were better and more effective ways to end the war than by expanding the size of the RAF IF. RAFM C1/10/3, Private Diary, 26 May–11 November 1918; Repington, *First World War*, 2:390, 470; Montgomery Hyde, *British Air Policy*, 9–43.
22. Baring, *R.F.C. H.Q.*, 285.
23. Sir Walter (later 1st Baronet) Lawrence (1857–1940) was a civil servant in India, private secretary to Lord Curzon (Viceroy India), and commissioner for sick and wounded Indian soldiers in France and England, 1914–16. Baring, *R.F.C. H.Q.*, 152; British Library India Office Records MSS Eur F143/103, Sir Walter Lawrence Correspondence and Papers (1916–19).
24. Wheeler-Bennett, *King George VI*, 116–17; CUL Add 9429/1B/1426(xiv).
25. Sir Walter Raleigh (1861–1922) was a professor of English at Oxford University. TNA AIR 6/12. Visitors to Autigny included Hilaire Belloc, Sir Maurice Bonham Carter, Lord Curzon, and David Henderson, whose son Ian, a pilot, had been killed a few weeks earlier. Baring had known Ian Henderson in 1917, when he was a member of No. 56 Squadron, with seven aerial victories to his name.
26. Raleigh, *Letters* 2:499, 512, and 1:417.
27. Liddle, *Airman's War*, 56.
28. Jones, *War in the Air*, 6:152–65; *London Gazette*, 31 December 1918, 133–38. The RAF IF also provided bombing support for the American St-Mihiel offensive in September 1918.
29. Overy, *Birth of the RAF*, 29.
30. Office of Air Force History, *The U.S. Air Service in World War I*, vol. 2 (Washington: Government Printing Office, 1978), 161–63, Foulois to Harbord, 23 December 1917.
31. Twelve aircraft set out to bomb Mainz. Three aircraft dropped out with engine trouble, but another seven were lost to enemy fighters to and from the target. K. Rennles, *Independent Force* (London: Grub Street, 2002), 71–73.
32. Jones, *War in the Air*, 6:142.
33. Baring, *R.F.C. H.Q.*, 290–91.
34. Baring, *R.F.C. H.Q.*, 288; Baring, War Diary, 7 November 1915.
35. Baring, *R.F.C. H.Q.*, 285.
36. Baring, *R.F.C. H.Q.*, 283.
37. Montgomery Hyde, *British Air Policy*, 44–45.

38. *Synopsis of British Air Effort through the War*, Air Ministry, 1 January 1919; G. Williams, *Biplanes and Bombsights: British Bombing in World War I* (Maxwell Air Force Base, AL: Air University Press, 1999), v.
39. M. Cooper, "The British Experience of Strategic Bombing," *Cross and Cockade International Journal* 17, no. 2 (1986): 49–61; Orange, *Churchill*, 57; Smith, *British Air Strategy*, 61.
40. The number of searchlights and antiaircraft guns dedicated to homeland air defense represented 60 percent and 30 percent, respectively, of the total available in the West. The number of single-seat fighters dedicated to homeland air defense represented approximately 11 percent of total frontline strength. Williams, *Biplanes and Bombsights*, 203–6; R. Hammer, *Der militärische Heimatluftschutz im Weltkriege, 1914 bis 1918* (Berlin: Mittler & Son, 1943), 105–6, 111–12; Hoeppner, *Deutschlands Krieg in der Luft*, 159.
41. CUL Add 9429/1B/207(ii).

CHAPTER 14. REINSTATEMENT

1. Boyle, *Trenchard*, 315; Baring, *R.F.C. H.Q.*, 301.
2. Hillgarth and Jeffs, *Letters*, 129–13, Baring to Trenchard, 23 December 1918; Boyle, *Trenchard*, 313–23.
3. *Times*, 12 February 1920.
4. Beaverbrook, *Men and Power*, xxv.
5. Hansard, HC Debate, 29 April 1918.
6. McEwen, *Riddell Diaries*, 227, Diary Entry 12 May 1918.
7. WEIR 1/6, Weir to Lloyd George, 27 April 1918.
8. CUL Add 9429/1B/1215(ii).
9. Eric Ash, Sykes' biographer, has described Trenchard as a more pragmatic, tactical, short-term thinker and Sykes as more visionary, idealistic, and strategically orientated. To create an affordable air force, Churchill needed a pragmatist rather than a visionary. Ash, "Air Power Leadership," 160–77.
10. CHAR 16/4, Churchill to Sykes, 9 February 1919, and Churchill to Walter Long, 8 February 1919; CUL Add 9429/1B/221(ii), Churchill to Saunders, 7 June 1951.
11. Lloyd George's pragmatism was helped by the fact that Trenchard's plans for the postwar RAF were more affordable than those submitted by Sykes. RAFM MFC 76/1/189/1, Game to Trenchard, 20 February 1919.
12. Boyle, *Trenchard*, 356; *The Aeroplane*, 19 July 1922.
13. Boyle, *Trenchard*, 329–30; *Westminster Gazette*, 12 February 1919, 2.
14. Boyle, *Trenchard*, 334–36.
15. Churchill may also have had an appointment in mind for Festing. CHAR 16/15A-B, Churchill to Seely, 10 January 1919.
16. Baring covers the events of 1918 in a mere thirty pages, less than half the space afforded to either 1917 or 1916.
17. Letley, *Maurice Baring*, 207, Baring to Grahame, 23 March 1920.

18. *London Gazette*, 7 June 1918, 6695, and 30 May 1919, 7040.
19. *Cmd 467—Permanent Organization of the Royal Air Force* (London: HMSO, 1919); Boyle, *Trenchard*, 350.
20. *London Gazette*, 1 January 1919. Baring may have had an opportunity to read Raleigh's draft introduction, which was completed early in 1919. H. A. Jones, *Sir Walter Raleigh and the Air History* (London: Edward Arnold, 1920), 8–9.
21. Frank Swinnerton (1884–1982) was a critic and novelist. Reading CW RR/7/174. Baring knew Swinnerton through Arnold Bennett, but as the review suggests, they were not particularly close.
22. Reading MS 1640/151/18, Bickers to Baring, 3 November 1919.
23. An alternative was "Make a Note of That," but this was felt to be either too frivolous or too unintelligible for the general public.
24. M. Baring, *Flying Corps Headquarters 1914-1918* (London: Heinemann, 1930).
25. N. Parton, "Historical Book Review, RFC Headquarters 1914–1918," *Air Power Review* 10, no. 1 (2007): 119–22; CUL Add 9429/1B/1216(iv).
26. Boyle, *Trenchard*, 14.
27. Henderson was more relaxed about the potential damage, writing that "while striving to do evil, I think Mr Billing has done some good, for the Government must take some steps to put the two services on a better footing." RAF Museum, MFC 76/1/76(2), Henderson to Trenchard, 20 April 1916.
28. *Flight*, 16 May 1967.
29. R. Preston, "Review of Maurice Baring, *Select Flying Corps Headquarters, 1914–1918*," *Aeronautical Journal* 72, no. 691 (July 1968): 629.
30. *Air Pictorial*, July 1968.
31. Henderson's obituary was titled "Maker of the RAF." *Times*, 19 August 1921, 11.
32. Beaverbrook, *Men and Power*, 227.
33. D. Fraser, *War and Shadows: Memoirs of General Sir David Fraser* (London: Allen Lane, 2002), 20.
34. Addison, *Politics from Within*, 174.
35. De Castelnau actively supported the Resistance, while two grandsons fought with the Free French.
36. Addison, *Politics from Within*, 169.
37. Rothermere was supported in this effort by Percy Groves, who wrote extensively on the need for a stronger bomber force, revisiting the arguments employed fifteen years earlier.
38. *Times*, 27 November 1940.
39. *Times*, 5 June 1939. Norman's interest in aviation was continued by his son (who helped found Airwork Services) and grandsons (one of whom cofounded Britten-Norman).
40. Balfour, *Wings over Westminster*, 45.
41. Boyle, *Trenchard*, 375. Wedding guests included Lord Hugh Cecil, Winston Churchill, General Maurice Duval, Sir David Henderson, Sir Walter Lawrence, Sir John Simon, and Sir Frederick Sykes.

42. J. Norwich, *The Duff Cooper Diaries* (London: Weidenfeld & Nicolson, 2005), 214.
43. *Chicago Daily Tribune*, 28 August 1933; P. Horgan, *Maurice Baring Restored* (London: Heinemann, 1970), 24.
44. Lovat, *Maurice Baring*, 3; Las Vergnas, "Un écrivan catholique," 917–43; S. Ezban, "Maurice Baring et la France," *Proceedings of the Modern Language Association* 60, no. 2 (June 1945): 503–16; Lovat, *Maurice Baring*, 108; Hillgarth and Jeffs, *Letters*, 11; M. Baring, *A Year in Russia* (London: Methuen, 1907), xix.
45. Epstein, "Maurice Baring and the Good High-Brow."
46. Cole, *McCudden V.C.*, 106.
47. J. B. Downing, "Baring's Collapse," *New Criterion* 39, no. 8 (April 2008); Epstein, "Maurice Baring and the Good High-Brow"; P. P. Read, "What's Become of Maurice Baring?," *The Spectator*, 13 October 2007; P. Ziegler, *Times Literary Supplement*, 20 September 1991.
48. Miller, *Boom*, 255; Hillgarth and Jeffs, *Letters*, 115–16, Baring to Chesterton, 29 September 1916.

CHAPTER 15. RECONSTRUCTION

1. The RAF's strength fell from a wartime strength of 291,170 officers and men to 60,000 by 1 October 1919 and to 26,000 by 1920. I. Philpott, *The Royal Air Force—The Trenchard Years 1918 to 1929* (Barnsley: Pen and Sword Aviation, 2005), 269–70.
2. Cmd 467.
3. TNA AIR 2/100/A13339.
4. Cmd 467.
5. CUL Add 9429/1B.
6. Joubert de la Ferté, *Third Service*, 70–71, 82–89.
7. *Western Times*, 3 December 1918; *Yorkshire Telegraph and Star*, 2 December 1918; *Illustrated Police News*, 12 December 1918.
8. Longcroft and Brooke-Popham (respectively the first commandants at the Cadet College and the Staff College) were immensely influential in shaping the ethos and traditions of the service. The other twelve included the Salmond brothers (Jack and Geoffrey) and Ellington (all would serve as CAS), three ex-RNAS officers (Charles Lambe, Edward Masterman, and John Steel), Jack Higgins, Philip Game, Duncan Pitcher, Francis Scarlett, Oliver Swan, and Tom Webb-Bowen.
9. Brooke-Popham alluded to this in drafting CAS's address at the Staff College in March 1921. Trenchard agreed "except with regard to the point that we are said to be impossible socially. This used to be said, but it is not said nearly so much now. Really, it is the aftermath of what was formally said from which we are suffering now, and also the fact that, because we are new, our behaviour must be better than that of the older services." RAFM MFC 76/1/140/1, Trenchard to Brooke-Popham, 30 March 1922.
10. Howard-Williams, *Air Is the Future Career*, 231.
11. RAFM MFC 76, Trenchard to Brooke-Popham, 30 March 1922.

12. S. B. Mais, *All the Days of My Life* (London: Hutchinson, 1937), 83–117; M. Robson, An *Unrepentant Englishman* (Rotherham: King's England Press, 2005), 65–81.
13. CHAR 16/4, Trenchard to Churchill, 5 February 1919.
14. A. Harris, *Bomber Offensive* (London: Collins, 1947), 267–68; Probert, *Bomber Harris*, 346–48.
15. J. Black, *War and the Cultural Norm* (Cambridge: Polity, 2012), 1–43, 101–4.
16. E. Hobsbawm and T. Ranger, *The Invention of Tradition* (Cambridge: Cambridge University Press, 1983), 1–14.
17. Joubert de la Ferté, *Third Service*, 86; James interview, CUL Add 9429/1B/1214(ii).
18. *The Tatler*, 30 October 1918, 116.
19. Heussler, "Maurice Baring and the Passing of the Victorian Age," 134–57.
20. Writing to Eddy Marsh, Baring observed that "it was a little foolish to quarrel with one of the few friends he had left." Berg Collection, Baring to Marsh, 13 April 1917.
21. A. D. Harvey, "Homosexuality and the British Army during the First World War," *Journal of the Society for Army Historical Research* 79 (2001): 313–19.
22. According to E. M. Forster, Charlton was "living with a young ex-aircraftsman [and] carrying this fact off among his fellow officers with great insouciance." P. Furbank, *E. M. Forster: A Life* (London: Martin Secker & Warburg, 1977), 2:36. Major General E. B. Ashmore (1872–1953) was a pre-war pilot and brigade commander.
23. J. R. Ackerley, *My Father and Myself* (London: Bodley Head, 1968), 201.
24. RAFM MFC 76/1/9, Brancker to Trenchard, 26 July 1917; C. Hallam, *White Drug Cultures and Regulation in London 1916–1960* (London: Palgrave Macmillan, 2018), 25–27; *Times*, 30 November 1917, 10.
25. CUL Add 9429/1B/1219; ANH, Baring to Nan, 20 March 1916; Baring, *Dear Animated Bust*, Baring to Juliet Duff, 30 July 1918.

CHAPTER 16. CONCLUSIONS

1. TFP, Brooke-Popham to Saunders, 16 August 1951.
2. ANH, Baring to Nan, 13 September 1915.
3. Hillgarth and Jeffs, *Letters*, 103.
4. Miller, *Boom*, 150.
5. CUL Add 9429/1B/1215(ii).
6. Sholto Douglas, *Years of Combat*, 183.
7. Under the Myers-Briggs Type Indicator methodology, Trenchard would probably be categorized as an INTJ and Baring an ESFP. I. Myers and M. McCaulley, *Manual: A Guide to the Development and Use of the Myers-Briggs Type Indicator* (Palo Alto: Consulting Psychologists Press, 1985).
8. The need for military commanders to accommodate different behavioral styles has been described as "Janusian" thinking. J. Hunt and R. Phillips, "Leadership in Battle and Garrison: A Framework for Understanding the Differences and Preparing for Both," in R. Gal and D. Mangelsdorff, eds., *Handbook of Military Psychology* (Chichester: Wiley,

1991), 411–29; and D. Goleman, *Emotional Intelligence* (London: Bloomsbury, 1995) and *The Emotionally Intelligent Leader* (Boston: Harvard Business School Publishing, 2019), 48.
9. Sheffield, *Leadership and Command*, 9–10.
10. Examples include Dwight Eisenhower and Walter Bedell "Beetle" Smith, George Patton and Hugh Gaffey, William Simpson and James Moore, and Edwin Rommel and Alfred Gause. J. Vermillion, "The Pillars of Generalship," in L. Matthews and D. Brown, eds., *The Challenge of Military Leadership* (London: Brassey's 1989), 59–73.
11. L. Wong, P. Bliese, and D. McGurk, "Military Leadership: A Context Specific Review," *Leadership Quarterly* 14, no. 6 (December 2003): 673.

APPENDIX A. MAURICE BARING'S WAR DIARY AND NOTEBOOKS

1. Baring, War Diary, 2 March 1915.
2. Letley, *Maurice Baring*, 238.
3. ANH, Baring to Nan, 13 September 1915.

APPENDIX B. OPERATIONAL TEMPO

1. A. Koch, *Die Flieger-Abteilung (A) 221* (Berlin: Gerhard Starling, 1925), 89–190; TNA AIR 1/1241/204/6/54-57.
2. Library of Congress, LOT 3068.

APPENDIX D. OPERATIONAL WASTAGE

1. A. Imrie, *Pictorial History of the German Army Air Service* (London: Ian Allan, 1971), 50–55.
2. Morrow, *Building German Airpower*, 203–9; Jones, *War in the Air*, vol. 6: *Appendices*, 154.
3. The British produced a total of 21,957 pilots (and just over 2,000 were killed in training accidents), while the French issued some 14,000 pilot certificates. By comparison, the Germans issued around 7,000 pilot certificates, and the Bavarians 950. A postwar report claimed that 10,000 pilots had been trained during the war. TNA AIR 1/686/21/13/2252; P. Pletschacher, *Die königlich bayerischen Fliegertruppen, 1912–1919* (Stuttgart: Motorbuch Verlag, 1978), 172; Morrow, *Great War in the Air*, 367; N. Franks, F. Bailey, and R. Duiven, *Casualties of the German Air Service 1914–1920* (London: Grub Street, 1999), 8; Spaight, *Beginnings of Organised Air Power*, 291–93; *Flugsport*, 22 January 1919, 2–3.
4. Hoeppner, *Deutschlands Krieg in der Luft*, 143–44; Reichsarchiv, *Die militärische Operationen zu Lande*, Band 14: *Die Kriegführung an der Westfront im Jahre 1918* (Berlin: Mittler und Sohn, 1944), 720–24; Imrie, *Pictorial History*, 53–55.
5. By 1918, the Luftstreitkräfte was operating fourteen flying schools, each of which, together with two Bavarian schools, could train around 275 pilots per year (equivalent to an overall output of some 360 pilots per month). TNA AIR 1/2117/207/58/3; TNA AIR 1/14/15/1/57; Franks, Bailey, and Duiven, *Casualties of the German Air Service*.

6. Imrie, *Pictorial History*, 50–53; Reichsarchiv, *Die militärische Operationen zu Lande*, Band 14, 720–24; Neumann, *Die deutschen Luftstreitkräfte*, 586; TNA AIR 1/686/21/13/2252.
7. Jones, *War in the Air*, 4:426.
8. No. 9 Squadron RFC employed 47 percent more flying personnel than its equivalent (FA 221) between January 1916 and November 1918.
9. Reichsarchiv, *Die militärische Operationen zu Lande*, Band 12: *Die Kriegführung im Frühjahr 1917* (Berlin: Mittler und Sohn, 1939), 440–41.
10. Reichsarchiv, *Die militärische Operationen zu Lande*, Band 10: *Die Operationen des Jahres 1916* (Berlin: Mittler und Sohn, 1936), 622–25; Reichsarchiv, *Die militärische Operationen zu Lande*, Band 12, 8–10.
11. Imrie, *Pictorial History*, 55. Only 5,569 of 11,000 German flying personnel casualties were the result of air combat. TNA AIR 1/14/15/1/57.
12. Bundesarchiv, PH 17-I/76/0002, Thomsen to Unit Commanders, 2 February 1918.
13. Under the Amerika program (to achieve victory in 1918 before American forces could intervene on the Western Front), Hoeppner invested substantial resources in expanding his fighter force. By April 1918, although the Luftstreitkräfte was more than twice as strong as the year before (across all fronts), this was largely due to a nearly threefold expansion in the number of single-seat fighters. P. Groz, "Frontbestand," *WWI Aero*, no. 107 (December 1985): 60–66, and "Frontbestand," *WWI Aero*, no. 108 (February 1986): 66–69; Morrow, *Building German Air Power*, 202–7.
14. Reichsarchiv, *Die militärische Operationen zu Lande*, Band 14, 720–24. A situation confirmed by a postwar German review that stated the severe shortage of trained pilots was the Luftreitkräfte's primary wartime problem. J. Corum, *The Luftwaffe: Creating the Operational Air War, 1918–1940* (Lawrence: University Press of Kansas, 1997), 62.

Selected Bibliography

BOOKS AND BOOK CHAPTERS
Ackerley, J. R. *My Father and Myself.* London: Bodley Head, 1968.
Addison, C. *Politics from Within, 1911–1918.* Vol. 2. London: Herbert Jenkins, 1924.
Allen, H. R. *The Legacy of Lord Trenchard.* London: Cassell & Co., 1976.
Anderson, D. *Leadership in Defence.* Shrivenham: Defence Leadership Centre, 2004.
Armengaud, P. *Le renseignement aérien, sauvegarde des armées.* Paris: Librairie Aeronautique, 1934.
Ash, E. *Sir Frederick Sykes and the Air Revolution 1912–1918.* London: Frank Cass, 1999.
———. "Air Power Leadership: A Study of Sykes and Trenchard." In P. Gray and S. Cox, eds., *Airpower Leadership and Practice.* London: HMSO, 2002.
Balfour, H. *An Airman Marches.* London: Hutchinson, 1933.
———. *Wings over Westminster.* London: Hutchinson, 1973.
Bands, H. *The Man Who Saved the Union.* New York: Anchor Books, 2013.
Baring, M. *With the Russians in Manchuria.* London: Methuen, 1905.
———. *Lost Diaries.* London: Duckworth & Co., 1913.
———. *What I Saw in Russia.* London: Thomas Nelson, 1913.
———. *R.F.C. Alphabet.* London, Ballantyne Press, 1915.
———. *Round the World in Any Number of Days.* London: Chatto & Windus, 1919.
———. *Poems 1914–1918.* London: Martin Secker, 1920.
———. *R.F.C. H.Q. 1914–1918.* London: G. Bell, 1920.
———. *The Puppet Show of Memory.* London: Heinemann, 1922.
———. *Hildesheim.* London: William Heinemann, 1924.
———. *Flying Corps Headquarters, 1914–1918.* London: Heinemann, 1930.
———. *Lost Lectures.* London: William Heinemann, 1932.
———. *Dear Animated Bust—Letters to Lady Juliet Duff, France 1915–1918.* Salisbury: Michael Russell, 1981.
Beach, J. *Haig's Intelligence.* Cambridge: Cambridge University Press, 2013.
Beaseley, R. *Russomania: Russian Culture and the Creation of British Modernism, 1881–1922.* Oxford: Oxford University Press, 2020.
Beaverbrook, W. *Men and Power 1917–1918.* London: Hutchinson, 1956.
Biddle, T. *Rhetoric and Reality in Air Warfare.* Princeton, NJ: Princeton University Press, 2002.
Black, J. *The Battle of Waterloo.* London: Icon Books, 2010.
———. *War and the Cultural Norm.* Cambridge: Polity, 2012.

Blake, R., ed. *The Private Papers of Douglas Haig: 1914–1919*. London: Eyre & Spottiswoode, 1952.
Blakiston, G., ed. *Letters of Conrad Russell*. London: John Murray, 1987.
Bloom, U. *He Lit the Lamp—A Biography of Professor A.M. Low*. London: Burke, 1958.
Boog, H. "The Problem of Independence of Airpower in Germany." In C. Carlier, ed., *Adaptation de l'arme aérienne aux conflits contemporains et processus d'indépendance des armées de l'Air des origines à la fin de la Seconde Guerre Mondiale*. Paris: Institute d'Histoire des Conflits Contemporains, 1985.
Bowden, M. *The Great War's Finest—An Operational History of the German Air Service*. Reno: Aeronaut Books, 2017.
Boyle, A. *Trenchard—Man of Vision*. London: Collins, 1962.
Brabazon. *The Brabazon Story*. London: Heinemann, 1956.
Bradley, O. *A Soldier's Story*. New York: Henry Holt, 1951.
Bradley, O., and C. Blair. *A General's Life*. New York: Simon & Schuster, 1983.
Bruce, J. *British Aeroplanes 1914–1918*. London: Putnam, 1957.
Cameron, R. H. *Training to Fly: Military Flight Training 1907–1945*. Washington, DC: Air Force History & Museums Program, 1999.
Catton, B. *Grant Takes Command*. Boston: Little, Brown, 1969.
Chaigne, L. *Maurice Baring*. Paris: J. De Gigord, 1932.
Chamier, J. A. *The Birth of the Royal Air Force*. London: Sir Isaac Pitman & Sons, 1943.
Charlton, L. E. O. *Charlton*. London: Faber & Faber, 1931.
———. *War from the Air—Past, Present, Future*. London: Thomas Nelson & Sons, 1935.
———. *More Charlton*. London: Longmans, Green, 1940.
Charteris, J. *At G.H.Q.* London: Cassell, 1931.
Chernow, R. *Grant*. New York: Penguin Press, 2017.
Churchill, R. *Winston S. Churchill, Companion*. Vol. 1, part 1, *1896–1900*. London: Heinemann, 1967.
Cole, C. *McCudden V.C.* London: William Kimber, 1967.
Collins, D. *Charmed Life—The Phenomenal World of Philip Sassoon*. London: Collins, 2016.
Cooper, D. *Haig*. Vol. 2. London: Faber & Faber, 1936.
———. *The Rainbow Comes and Goes*. London: Rupert Hart-Davis, 1958.
Cooper, M. *The Birth of Independent Air Power*. London: Allen & Unwin, 1986.
Coppens, W. *Days on the Wing*. London: Aviation Book Club, 1935.
Corum, J.S. *The Luftwaffe: Creating the Operational Air War, 1918–1940*. Lawrence: University Press of Kansas, 1997.
Corum, J. S., and R. Muller. *The Luftwaffe's Way of War, German Air Force Doctrine 1911–1945*. Baltimore: Nautical and Aviation Publishing Co., 1998.
Cresswell, D. K. R. *Chief of Staff—The Military Career of General Walter Bedell Smith*. Westport, CT: Greenwood, 1991.
Cuneo, J. R. *Winged Mars: The German Air Weapon 1870–1914*. Harrisburg, PA: Military Service Publishing, 1942.

———. *Winged Mars: The Air Weapon 1914–1916*. Harrisburg, PA: Military Service Publishing, 1947.
Davenport-Hines, R. *Ettie: The Intimate Life and Dauntless Spirit of Lady Desborough*. London: Weidenfeld & Nicolson, 2008.
Dean, M. *The Royal Air Force and Two World Wars*. London: Cassell, 1979.
de Guingand, F. *Operation Victory*. London: Hodder and Stoughton, 1947.
———. *Generals at War*. London: Hodder and Stoughton, 1964.
de Havilland, G. *Sky Fever*. Shrewsbury: Airlife, 1979.
de Pierrefeu, C. *French Headquarters 1915–1918*. London: Geoffrey Bles, 1924.
D'Este, C. *A Genius for War*. New York: HarperCollins, 1995.
Dixon, N. *On the Psychology of Military Incompetence*. London: Jonathan Cape, 1976.
Doughty, R. A. *Pyrrhic Victory—French Strategy and Operations in the Great War*. Cambridge, MA: Belknap Press of Harvard University Press, 2005.
Douglas, Sholto. *Years of Combat*. London: Collins, 1963.
Duiven, R., and D.-S. Abbott. *Schlacht-Flieger—Germany and the Origins of Air/Ground Support 1916–1918*. Atglen: Schiffer, 2006.
Dumond, J.-P. *Le Commandant de Rose, créateur de l'aviation de chasse—héros méconnu de la Grande Guerre, 1876–1916*. Paris: Ste Ecrivans, 2007.
Dye, P. *The Bridge to Airpower*. Annapolis, MD: Naval Institute Press, 2015.
———. "The Intrepid Airman: The Physiology of Air Warfare." In R. Mahoney, ed., *First World War in the Air*. London: Royal Air Force Museum, 2015.
———. *The Man Who Took the Rap*. Annapolis, MD: Naval Institute Press, 2018.
Eisenhower, J. *Soldiers and Statesmen—Reflections on Leadership*. Columbia: University of Missouri Press, 2012.
Elliott, P. "Sir David Henderson, the Smuts Report and the Birth of Independent Air Power." In R. Mahoney, ed., *First World War in the Air*. London: RAF Museum, 2015.
Ferris, J., ed. *The British Army and Signals Intelligence during the First World War*. Stroud: Alan Sutton, 1992.
Ferris, P. *The House of Northcliffe*. New York: World, 1972.
Fitzroy, A. *Sir Almeric Fitzroy, Memoirs*. Vol. 2. London: Hutchinson, 1925.
Flower, N., ed. *The Journals of Arnold Bennett 1911–1921*. London: Cassell, 1932.
Fox, F. *GHQ—Montreuil-sur-Mer*. London: Philip Allan & Co., 1920.
Franks, N., F. Bailey, and R. Duiven. *Casualties of the German Air Service, 1914–1920*. London: Grub Street, 1999.
Fraser, D. *War and Shadows: Memoirs of General Sir David Fraser*. London: Allen Lane, 2002.
Fuller, J. F. C. *Memoirs of an Unconventional Soldier*. London: Ivor Nicholson & Watson, 1936.
Furse, A. *Wilfrid Freeman—The Genius behind Allied Survival and Air Supremacy 1939 to 1945*. Staplehurst: Spellmount, 2000.
Fussell, P. *The Ordeal of Alfred M. Hale*. London: Leo Cooper, 1975.
Garro-Jones, G. *Ventures and Visions*. London: Hutchinson, 1935.

272 | SELECTED BIBLIOGRAPHY

Gibbs, G. *Survivor's Story*. London: Hutchinson, 1956.
Gibbs, P. *Realities of War*. London: Heinemann, 1920.
Gibson, C. *Behind the Front: British Soldiers and French Civilians, 1914–1918*. Cambridge: Cambridge University Press, 2014.
Goerlitz, W. *The German General Staff*. New York: Frederick Praeger, 1953.
Gosse, E. *Some Diversions of a Man of Letters*. London: Heinemann, 1920.
Gould Lee, A. *No Parachute*. London: Jarrolds, 1968.
———. *Open Cockpit*. London: Jarrolds, 1969.
Grant, U. S. *Personal Memoirs of U. S. Grant*. Vol. 1. New York: Charles Webster, 1885.
Graves, R., and L. Hart. *T. E. Lawrence, Letters to His Biographers*. London: Cassell, 1963.
Gray, V. J. *Xenophon's Mirror of Princes*. Oxford: Oxford University Press, 2011.
Grey, C. G. *The Air Ministry*. London: George Allen & Unwin, 1940.
Gribble, P. *The Diary of a Staff Officer (Air Intelligence Liaison Officer) at Advanced Headquarters North B.A.F.F.* 1940. Reprint, London: Methuen, 1941.
Griffith, H. *R.A.F. Occasions*. London: Crescent, 1941.
Grigg, J. *Lloyd George: War Leader*. London: Penguin, 2003.
Groves, P. R. C. *Behind the Smoke Screen*. London: Faber and Faber, 1934.
Hallam, C. *White Drug Cultures and Regulation in London 1916–1960*. London: Palgrave Macmillan, 2018.
Harris, A. *Bomber Offensive*. London: Collins, 1947.
Hassall, C. *Edward Marsh—A Biography*. London: Longmans, 1959.
Havinghurst, A. *Radical Journalist: H. W. Massingham*. Cambridge: Cambridge University Press, 1974.
Henshaw, T. *The Sky Their Battlefield II*. London: Fetubi Books, 2014.
Higham, R. *The Military Intellectuals in Britain, 1918–1939*. New Brunswick, NJ: Rutgers University Press, 1966.
Hillgarth, J., and J. Jeffs. *Maurice Baring Letters*. Norwich: Michael Russell, 2007.
Hoare, S. *Empire of the Air—The Advent of the Air Age 1922–1929*. London: Collins, 1957.
Hobsbawm, E., and T. Ranger. *The Invention of Tradition*. Cambridge: Cambridge University Press, 1983.
Holmes, R. *The Little Field Marshal*. London: Jonathan Cape, 1981.
Hooton, E. R. *War over the Trenches—Air Power and the Western Front Campaigns 1916–1918*. Hersham: Ian Allen, 2010.
Horgan, P. *Maurice Baring Restored*. London: Heinemann, 1970.
Howard-Williams, E. *The Air Is the Future Career*. London: Hutchinson, 1939.
Huntington, S. *The Common Defense*. New York: Columbia University Press, 1961.
Ingram, C. *Wings over the Western Front*. Edited by E. Pollard and H. Strouts. Charlbury: Day Books, 2014.
Insall, A. *Observer—Memoirs of the RFC 1915–18*. London: Kimber, 1970.
James, J. *The Paladins*. London: Macdonald & Co., 1990.
Jefford, C. G. *The Flying Camels*. High Wycombe: Flying Camels, 1995.

Johnson, J. C., L. A. Palinkas, and J. S. Boster. *Informal Social Roles and the Evolution and Stability of Social Networks.* Washington, DC: National Academies Press, 2003.
Johnstone, E. *Naval Eight.* London: Arms & Armour Press, 1972.
Jones, H. A. *Sir Walter Raleigh and the Air History.* London: Edward Arnold, 1920.
Jones, N. *The Origins of Strategic Bombing.* London: William Kimber, 1973.
Jordan, D., and G. Sheffield. "Douglas Haig and Airpower." In P. Gray and S. Cox, eds., *Airpower Leadership and Practice.* London: HMSO, 2002.
Joubert de la Ferté, P. *The Third Service.* London: Thames and Hudson, 1955.
Kerr, M. *Land, Sea and Air.* London: Longmans, Green, 1927.
Kingston-McCloughry, E. J. *Winged Warfare: Air Problems of Peace and War.* London: Jonathan Cape, 1937.
Koch, A. *Die Flieger-Abteilung (A) 221.* Berlin: Gerhard Starling, 1925.
Lavoie, J. *The Private Life of General Omar N. Bradley.* Jefferson: McFarland, 2015.
Letley, E. *Maurice Baring—A Citizen of Europe.* London: Constable, 1991.
Lewin, R. *Montgomery as Military Commander.* New York: Stein and Day, 1971.
Lewis, C. *Sagittarius Rising.* London: Peter Davies, 1936.
Liddle, P. *The Airman's War.* Poole: Blandford, 1987.
Lieblich, A. *Transition to Adulthood during Military Service.* New York: State University of New York Press, 1989.
Livingston, G. *Hot Air in Cold Blood.* London: Selwyn & Blount, 1933.
Lloyd George, D. *War Memoirs.* Vol. 1. London: Odhams, 1934.
———. *War Memoirs.* Vol. 2. London: Odhams, 1936.
Londonderry. *Wings of Destiny.* London: Collins, 1943.
Lovat, L. *Maurice Baring: A Postscript.* London: Hollis & Carter, 1947.
Macmillan, N. *Sir Sefton Brancker.* London: Heinemann, 1935.
———. *Into the Blue.* London: Jarrolds, 1969.
Mais, S. B. *All the Days of My Life.* London: Hutchinson, 1937.
Marsh, E. *A Number of People: A Book of Reminiscences.* London: Harper & Brothers, 1939.
Marson, T. B. *Scarlet and Khaki.* London: Jonathan Cape, 1930.
McEwen, J., ed. *The Riddell Diaries 1908–1923.* London: Athlone, 1986.
Meilinger, P. *Paths of Heaven.* Maxwell Air Force Base, AL: Air University Press, 1997.
Messenger, C. *Call-to-Arms: The British Army 1914–1918.* London: Weidenfeld & Nicolson, 2005.
Miller, R. *Boom—The Life of Viscount Trenchard, Father of the Royal Air Force.* London: Weidenfeld & Nicolson, 2016.
Mills, S. *The Dawn of the Drone.* Haverton: Casemate, 2019.
Mitchell, W. *Memoirs of World War I.* New York: Random House, 1960.
Money, R. R. *Flying and Soldiering.* London: Ivor Nicholson & Watson, 1936.
Montgomery, B. *The Memoirs of Field-Marshal Montgomery.* London: Collins, 1958.
———. *The Path to Leadership.* New York: Putnams, 1959.
Montgomery Hyde, H. *British Air Policy between the Wars 1918–1939.* London: Heinemann, 1976.

Morrow, J. *Building German Airpower, 1909–1914*. Knoxville: University of Tennessee Press, 1976.
———. *The Great War in the Air*. Shrewsbury: Airlife, 1993.
Norwich, J. *The Duff Cooper Diaries*. London: Weidenfeld & Nicolson, 2005.
Occleshaw, M. *Armour against Fate—British Military Intelligence in the First World War*. London: Columbus Books, 1989.
Oppenheim, E. P. *The Pool of Memory*. London: Hodder and Stoughton, 1941.
Orange, V. *Churchill and His Airmen*. London: Grub Steer, 2013.
Orpen, W. *An Onlooker in France*. London: Williams and Norgate, 1921.
Ossad, S. L. *Omar Nelson Bradley: America's GI General, 1893–1981*. Columbia: University of Missouri Press, 2017.
Ottens, A. *General John A. Rawlins—No Ordinary Man*. Bloomington: Indiana University Press, 2021.
Overy, R. *The Birth of the RAF 1918*. London: Allen Lane, 2018.
Paris, M. *Winged Warfare: The Literature and Theory of Aerial Warfare in Britain 1859–1917*. Manchester: Manchester University Press, 1992.
Parkinson, R. *Tormented Warrior—Ludendorff and the Supreme Command*. London: Hodder & Stoughton, 1978.
Philpott, I. *The Royal Air Force—The Trenchard Years 1918 to 1929*. Barnsley: Pen and Sword Aviation, 2005.
Playfair, P. *"Pip" Playfair—A Founding Father of the RAF*. Ilfracombe: Arthur Stockwell, 1979.
Posen, B. *The Sources of Military Doctrine—France, Britain and Germany between the World Wars*. Ithaca, NY: Cornell University Press, 1984.
Pound, R., and C. Harmsworth. *Northcliffe*. London: Cassell, 1959.
Powers, B. D. *Strategy without Slide-Rule*. London: Croom Helm, 1976.
Raleigh, L. G., ed. *Letters of Sir Walter Raleigh*. Vol. 2. London: Methuen, 1926.
Ramsden, J., ed. *Real Old Tory Politics—The Political Diaries of Sir Robert Sanders, Lord Bayford, 1910–1935*. Gloucester: Alan Sutton, 1984.
Reader, W. J. *Architect of Air Power—The Life of the First Viscount Weir*. London: Collins, 1968.
Rennles, K. *Independent Force*. London: Grub Street, 2002.
Repington, C. à Court. *The First World War 1914–1918*. 2 vols. London: Constable, 1920.
Rhodes, J. R. *Memoirs of a Conservative*. London: Weidenfeld & Nicolson, 1969.
Richards, E. *Australian Airmen—A History of the 4th Squadron Australian Flying Corps*. Melbourne: Bruce & Co., 1922.
Riddell, G. *Lord Riddell's War Diary 1914–1918*. London: Ivor Nicholson & Watson, 1933.
Roberts, B. *Sir John Simon—Being an Account of the Life and Career of John Allesbrook Simon*. London: Robert Hale, 1938.
Robson, M. *An Unrepentant Englishman*. Rotherham: King's England, 2005.
Rose, K. *The Later Cecils*. London: Weidenfeld and Nicolson, 1975.
Roskill, S. *Documents Relating to the Naval Air Service 1908–1918*. Bromley: Navy Records Society, 1969.

———. *Hankey: Man of Secrets*. London: Collins, 1970.
Rowell, E. *In Peace and War—Tyneside, Naples and the Royal Flying Corps*. Otley: E. R. Rowell, 1996.
Sheffield, G., ed. *Leadership and Command: The Anglo-American Military Experience since 1861*. London: Brassey's, 1997.
———. *The Chief*. London: Aurum, 2011.
Sheffield, G., and J. Bourne, eds. *Douglas Haig War Diaries and Letters 1914–1918*. London: Weidenfeld & Nicolson, 2005.
Simon, J. *Retrospect—The Memoirs of the Right Honourable Viscount Simon*. London: Hutchinson, 1952.
Slessor, J. *Air Power and Armies*. London: Oxford University Press, 1936.
———. Foreword to H. Montgomery Hyde, *British Air Policy between the Wars*. London: Heinemann, 1976.
Smith, M. *British Air Strategy between the Wars*. Oxford: Oxford University Press, 1984.
Smyth, E. *Maurice Baring*. London: William Heinemann, 1938.
Smythies, B. "Experiences during the War, 1914–1918." In *AP 956—A Selection of Lectures and Essays from the Work of Officers Attending the First Staff Course at the Royal Air Force Staff College 1922–1923*. London: Air Ministry, 1923.
Spaight, J. *The Beginnings of Organised Air Power*. London: Longmans, Green, 1927.
Speaight, R. *The Life of Hilaire Belloc*. New York: Farrar, Straus & Cudahy, 1957.
Spears, E. *Liaison 1914*. London: Heinemann, 1930.
Spiers, D., and J. Buckley, eds. *The Dowding Papers*. Farnborough: FAST, 2020.
Spivak, M. "Les problèmes posés à l'armée de Terre par la création du ministère de l'Air et les perspectives d'indépendance de l'armée de l'Air, 1928–1934." In C. Carlier, ed., *Adaptation de l'arme aérienne aux conflits contemporains et processus d'indépendance des armées de l'Air des origines à la fin de la Seconde Guerre Mondiale*. Paris: Institute d'Histoire des Conflits Contemporains, 1985.
Stansky, P. *Sassoon: The Worlds of Philip and Sybil*. New Haven, CT: Yale University Press, 2003.
St Aubyn, G. *The Royal George 1819–1904*. London: Constable, 1963.
Stevenson, D. *Armaments and the Coming of War*. Oxford: Clarendon, 1996.
Stewart, O. *Words and Music for a Mechanical Man*. London: Faber & Faber, 1967.
St George Saunders, H. *The Rise of British Air Power 1911–1939*. London: Oxford University Press, 1944.
Strange, L. A. *Recollections of an Airman*. London: John Hamilton, 1933.
Sykes, F. *Aviation in Peace and War*. London: Edward Arnold, 1922.
———. *From Many Angles*. London: George Harrap, 1942.
Taylor, A. J. P. *Beaverbrook*. New York: Simon and Schuster, 1972.
Taylor, S. J. *The Great Outsiders—Northcliffe, Rothermere and the Daily Mail*. London: Weidenfeld & Nicolson, 1996.
Terraine, J. *Douglas Haig—The Educated Soldier*. London: Leo Cooper, 1963.
———. *Essays on Leadership and War*. Reading: Western Front Association, 1998.

Thorpe, A., and R. Toye, eds. *The Diaries of Cecil Harmsworth, MP, 1909–1922*. London: Cambridge University Press, 2016.
Tinsley, A. B. *One Rissole on My Plate*. Braunton: Merlin Books, 1984.
Tredrey, F. *Pilot's Summer: A Central Flying School Diary*. London: Duckworth, 1939.
———. *The House of Blackwood*. Edinburgh: William Blackwood & Sons, 1954.
———. *Pioneer Pilot—The Great Smith-Barry*. London: Peter Davies, 1976.
Udet, E. *Ace of the Black Cross*. London: Newnes, 1937.
Van Schaick Mitchell, C. *Letters from a Liaison Officer 1918–1919*. Princeton, NJ: Princeton University Press, 1920.
Voisin, A. *La doctrine de l'aviation française de combat au cours de la guerre (1915–1918)*. Paris: Éditions Berger-Levrault, 1932.
von Hoeppner, E. *Deutschlands Krieg in der Luft*. Leipzig: Koehler, 1921. French translation: *Allemagne et la guerre de l'air*. Paris: Payot, 1923.
Westrop, M. *A History of No 10 Squadron Royal Naval Air Service in World War I*. Atglen: Schiffer, 2004.
Wheeler-Bennett, J. *King George VI—His Life and Reign*. New York: St. Martin's, 1958.
White, R. *American Ulysses*. New York: Random House, 2016.
Who's Who, 1934. London: A & C Black, 1934.
Williams, G. *Biplanes and Bombsights: British Bombing in World War I*. Maxwell Air Force Base, AL: Air University Press, 1999.
Wilson, J. *The Life of John A. Rawlins*. New York: Neale, 1916.
Winter, D. *The First of the Few*. London: Allen Lane, 1982.
Wrench, E. *Struggle*. London: Ivor Nicholson & Watson, 1935.
———. *Geoffrey Dawson and Our Times*. London: Hutchinson & Co., 1955.
———. *Alfred Lord Milner—The Man of No Illusions*. London: Eyre & Spottiswoode, 1958.
Wright, R. *Dowding and the Battle of Britain*. London: Macdonald & Co., 1969.

ARTICLES

Anbinder, T. "Ulysses S. Grant, Nativist." *Civil War History* 43, no. 2 (1997): 119–41.
Anderson, H. "Lord Horne as an Army Commander." *Journal of the Royal Artillery* 56, no. 4 (1930).
Anonymous. "The Staff. The Myth? The Reality?" *Stand To*, no. 15 (Winter 1985): 44–51.
Ashkenhas, R. "How to Overcome Executive Isolation." *Harvard Business Review*, 19 March 2014.
Babin, G. "Le Royal Flying Corps." *L'illustration*, 16 and 23 February 1918.
Baring, M. "Carnet de Guerre d'un Officier d'État-Major, Fête Galante, La Rose Bleue." *Les cahiers britanniques et américains*, no. 4 (1918).
Barros, A. "Strategic Bombing and Restraint in 'Total War,' 1915–1918." *Historical Journal* 52, no. 2 (2009): 413–31.
Bechthold, M. "Bloody April Revisited: The Royal Flying Corps at the Battle of Arras, 1917." *British Journal for Military History* 4, no. 2 (February 2018): 50–69.
Belloc, H. "Our Air Service." *Land and Water*, 10 February 1916.

SELECTED BIBLIOGRAPHY | 277

Binyon, T. J. "Round Things." Review of *Maurice Baring: A Citizen of Europe*, by Emma Letley. *London Review of Books*, 24 October 1991, 20–22.

Birley, J. "A Lecture on the Psychology of Courage Delivered at the Royal Air Force Staff College." *The Lancet*, 21 April 1923.

———. "Medical Science and Military Aviation." *The Lancet*, 29 May 1920, 1147–51; 5 June 1920, 1205–12; and 12 June 1920, 1252–57.

Blin Desbleds, L. "The Aeroplane on the Offensive—A Potent Quality Hitherto Unrecognised." *Land and Water*, 23 January 1915.

———. "The Influence of Air Power—The Aerial Dilemma: A Solution." *Land and Water*, 24 April 1915.

Boff, J. "Air Land Integration in the 100: The Case of Third Army." *RAF Air Power Review* 12, no. 3 (2009): 7–88.

Brancker, W. S. "The Allocation of Royal Flying Corps Units to Subordinate Commands." *Royal Artillery Journal* 42 (June 1915): 113–24.

Bregan, P., B. Laker, et al. "What to Do When You Become Your Friend's Boss." *Harvard Business Review*, 24 September 2020.

Cooper, M. "A House Divided: Policy, Rivalry and Administration in Britain's Military Air Command 1914–1918." *Journal of Strategic Studies* 3, no. 2 (1980): 178–201.

———. "The Development of Air Policy and Doctrine on the Western Front, 1914–1918." *Aerospace Historian* 28, no. 1 (1981): 38–51.

———. "The British Experience of Strategic Bombing." *Cross and Cockade International Journal* 17, no. 2 (1986): 49–61.

———. "Blueprint for Confusion: The Administrative Background to the Formation of the Royal Air Force, 1912–1919." *Journal of Contemporary History* 22, no. 3 (1987): 437–53.

Corum, J. S. "From Biplane to Blitzkrieg: The Development of German Air Doctrine between the Wars." *War in History*, no. 1 (January 1996): 85–101.

———. "The Luftstreitkräfte Builds a Bomber Doctrine." *RAF Air Power Review*, Spring 2003, 61–77.

Cumming, A. "The Air Marshal versus the Admiral: Air Chief Marshal Sir Hugh Dowding and Admiral of the Fleet Sir Charles Morton Forbes in the Pantheon." *History* 94, no. 2 (2009): 203–28.

Cuneo, J. R. "Preparation of German Attack Aviation for the Offensive of March 1918." *Military Affairs* 7, no. 2 (1943): 69–78.

Delany, B. *Blackfriars* 27, no. 312 (March 1946): 1.

Downing, J. B. "Baring's Collapse." *New Criterion* 39, no. 8 (April 2008).

Dye, P. "The Aviator as Superhero?" *Air Power Review* (Winter 2004): 65–74.

Epstein, J. "Maurice Baring and the Good High-Brow." *New Criterion* 11, no. 2 (October 1992).

Ezban, S. "Maurice Baring et la France." *Proceedings of the Modern Language Association* 60, no. 2 (June 1945): 503–16.

Falls, C. "Contacts with Troops: Commanders and Staffs in the First World War." *Army Quarterly* 88 (1964): 173–80.

SELECTED BIBLIOGRAPHY

Feldmann, D. "Fixing One's History: George S. Patton's Changes in His Personal Diary." *War in History* 28, no. 1 (2021): 166–83.
Fellows, B. C. "The Rise of the RFC." *Land and Water*, 2 August 1917, 24–25.
Gibson, C. "The BEF in France, 1914–18: Billeting." *The Poppy and the Owl*, no. 14 (October 1994).
Grant, U. S., III. "Civil War: Fact and Fiction." *Civil War History* 2, no. 2 (1956): 29–40.
Gray, C. "New Year's Honours." *The Aeroplane*, 8 January 1914.
———. "On Making a Note of It." *The Aeroplane*, 19 May 1920.
Groz, P. "Frontbestand." *WWI Aero*, no. 107 (December 1985): 60–66.
———. "Frontbestand." *WWI Aero*, no. 108 (February 1986): 66–69.
Harris, P. "Soldier Banker: Lieutenant-General Sir Herbert Lawrence as the BEF's Chief of Staff in 1918." *Journal of the Society for Army Historical Research*, no. 90 (2012): 44–67.
Harvey, A. D. "Homosexuality and the British Army during the First World War." *Journal of the Society for Army Historical Research* 79 (2001): 313–19.
Henshaw T, 'British Squadron Aircraft Establishments, 1914-1918', *Cross and Cockade International Journal* 50 (Spring 2024): 32-41.
Heussler, R. "Maurice Baring and the Passing of the Victorian Age." *Biography* 7, no. 2 (1984): 134–57.
Howard, M. "Reluctant Apostle of Air Power." *The Observer*, 25 March 1962, 27.
———. "The Armed Forces and the Community." *RUSI Journal*, August 1996.
Howard-Williams, J. "Book Reviews: Trenchard, Man of Vision (Boyle)." *Flight*, 17 May 1962.
James, T. "Charles Grey and His Pungent Pen." *Aeronautical Journal*, October 1969, 839–52.
Jefford, J. "NCO Pilots in the RFC/RAF 1912–18." *RAF Air Power Review* 7, no. 2 (Summer 2004): 89–99.
Jones, D. "Flying and Dying in WW1: British Aircrew Losses and the Origins of U.S. Military Aviation Medicine." *Aviation, Space and Environmental Medicine* 79, no. 2 (February 2008): 139–46.
Lanchester, F. "The Failure of the Derby Committee." *Land and Water*, 20 April 1916, 12.
Las Vergnas, R. "Un écrivain catholique anglais: M. Maurice Baring." *Revue des Deux Mondes*, 15 October 1936, 917–43.
Liggera, L. "In Such Fortitude: Major the Hon. Maurice Baring, OBE." *Stand To*, no. 58 (April 2000): 34–35.
Lochhead, M. "Maurice Baring's Books." *Blackfriars* 28, no. 326 (1947): 210–14.
Maclean, V. "Maurice Baring, the Final Years." *Chesterton Review* 19, no. 1 (February 1988): 109–16.
McEwen, J. "The National Press during the First World War: Ownership and Circulation." *Journal of Contemporary History* 17, no. 3 (July 1982).
Mechin, D. "The Air Division in Combat." *Cross and Cockade International Journal* 50 (Summer 2019): 108–13.
Moore, M. "No 45 Squadron, 1916-1917." *The Hawk*, 1928, 101-104
Nicod, A. "Memories of 60 Squadron R.F.C." *Popular Flying*, January 1935, 540.

O'Brien, J. "Mobilising the BEF August 1914." *Stand To*, no. 78 (January 2007): 6–9.
Paris, M. "The Rise of the Airmen: The Origins of Air Force Elitism, c. 1890–1918." *Journal of Contemporary History* 28, no. 1 (1993): 123–41.
Parton, N. "Historical Book Review, *RFC Headquarters 1914–1918*." *Air Power Review* 10, no. 1 (2007): 119–22.
Phillips, P. "Decision and Dissension—Birth of the RAF." *Aerospace Historian* 18, no. 1 (1971): 33–39.
Pigot, R. "Some Memories of the Earliest Days of Military Aviation in England." *RAF Quarterly*, Spring 1973, 51–57.
Preston, R. "Review of Maurice Baring, *Flying Corps Headquarters, 1914–1918*." *Aeronautical Journal* 72, no. 691 (July 1968): 629.
Prins, F. "Forgotten Founder." *Air Enthusiast* 47 (September–November 1992).
———. "Forgotten Founder." *The Aeroplane*, April 2012, 60–63.
Read, P. P. "What's Become of Maurice Baring?" *The Spectator*, 13 October 2007.
Rempel, R. "Lord Hugh Cecil's Parliamentary Career, 1900–1914: Promise Unfulfilled." *Journal of British Studies* 11, no. 2 (May 1972): 104–30.
Salmond, J. "Forged and Tempered." *Blackwood's Magazine*, 295, no. 1782 (April 1964): 289–304.
Shaw Cobden, L. "Nerves Flying and the First World War." *British Journal for Military History* 4, no. 2 (February 2018): 121–42.
Simon, J. "Gott mit uns—An Impression of the Critical Days of March 1918." *Blackwood's* 204 (July–December 1918): 771–74.
Simon, J. Y. "The Paradox of Ulysses S. Grant." *Register of the Kentucky Historical Society* 81, no. 4 (1983): 366–82.
Smythies, B. "The German Air Service on the Western Front." *RUSI Journal* 69, no. 473 (1924): 126–37.
Sturtivant, R. "Flying Training in World War I." *Aviation News*, 14 October 1977, 4.
Sweetman, J. "Crucial Months for Survival: The Royal Air Force, 1918–1919." *Journal of Contemporary History* 19, no. 3 (1984): 529–47.
Taylor, S.K. `Mums The Word,' *Cross and Cockade International Journal* 37 (Summer 2006): 116-119.
Thollon-Pommerol, C. "La Division du General Duval (May–November 1918)." *Icare*, no. 248 (March 2019): 20–185.
Wells, H. G. "Imagination in the Air War." *Land and Water*, 26 June 1915.
"With an Army Cooperation Squadron during the German Attacks of 1918." *The Hawk*, 1931, 20–27.

DISSERTATIONS AND INTERVIEWS

Alston, C. "Russian Liberalism and British Journalism: The Life and Work of Harold Williams (1876–1928)." PhD diss., Newcastle University, 2004.
Jordan, D. "The Army Cooperation Missions of the Royal Flying Corps / Royal Air Force 1914–1918." PhD diss., Birmingham University, 1997.

280 | SELECTED BIBLIOGRAPHY

Trenchard, T. "Interview with Lord Trenchard." YouTube video, 50:54, posted 31 March 2018. https://www.youtube.com/watch?v=ZO7RbSknmkE.

PERIODICALS/NEWSPAPERS
Aeronautics
The Aeroplane
Aircraft Illustrated
Air Pictoria
Boston Globe
Chard and Ilminster News
Chicago Daily Tribune
Daily Mirror
Daily News
Daily Telegraph
The Economist
Flight
Flying
Illustrated Police News
Manchester Guardian
New York Times
The Observer
RAF Flying Review
The Spectator
The Tatler
The Times
Western Gazette
Western Times
Westminster Gazette
West Somerset Free Press
Yorkshire Telegraph and Star

PAPERS
AFBSC (02)4. "Strengthening RAF Ethos." 26 April 2002. Reissued as PTC/113358/DP&T Pol, 30 June 2003.
AFBSC (03)2. "Developing Excellence in Leadership." February 2003.

OFFICIAL HISTORY/PUBLICATIONS
Air Publication 956: War Experiences. London: Air Ministry, 1923.
GHQ. "S.S. 478, Experiences of the IV German Corps in the Battle of the Somme during July 1916." September 1916.
———. "S.S. 214, Tanks and Their Employment—Cooperation with Other Arms." August 1918.

———. "S.S. 407, Composition of Headquarters British Armies in France." November 1918.
GQG. *Instruction sur l'organisation et l'emploi de l'aéronautique aux armées—Titre II, Aviation de combat.* March 1918.
———. *Instruction sur l'organisation et l'emploi de l'aéronautique aux armées—Titre III, Aviation de bombardement.* March 1918.
Hansard. HC Debate. 12 November 1917.
———. 21 February 1918.
———. 15 April 1918.
———. 18 April 1918.
———. 22 April 1918.
———. 24 April 1918.
———. 25 April 1918.
———. 29 April 1918.
———. 9 May 1918.
Jones, H. A. *The War in the Air.* Vol. 2. Oxford: Oxford University Press, 1928.
———. *The War in the Air.* Vol. 4. Oxford: Clarendon, 1934.
———. *The War in the Air.* Vol. 5. Oxford: Clarendon, 1935.
———. *The War in the Air.* Vol. 6. Oxford: Clarendon, 1937.
———. *The War in the Air.* Vol. 6, *Appendices.* Oxford: Clarendon, 1937.
Les armées françaises dans la Grande Guerre. Tome VI, vol. 2. Paris: Ministere de la Guerre, 1935.
London Gazette
Office of Air Force History. *The U.S. Air Service in World War I.* Vol. 2. Washington, DC: Government Printing Office, 1978.
OHL. *Vorschriften* für den *Stellungskrieg* für alle Waffen. Teil 13, *Einsatz von Jagdstaffeln.* Chef des Generalstabe des Feldheeres, 25 October 1917.
Raleigh, W. *The War in the Air.* Vol. 1. London, Oxford University Press, 1922.
Synopsis of British Air Effort through the War. Air Ministry, 1 January 1919.
U.S. Army. *Social Intelligence—Introduction and Overview for the Army's Human Dimension Initiative.* Fort Leavenworth: HDCDTF February 2016.
War Office. *Field Service Regulations Part II.* London: War Office, 1909.
———. *RFC (Military Wing) Training Manual Part II*, 1914.
———. *Fighting in the Air*, 1917.
Wise, S. *Canadian Airmen and the First World War.* Toronto: University of Toronto Press, 1980.

ARCHIVES

Berg Collection of English and American Literature
Maurice Baring, War Diary, 30 June 1914–16 November 1918
Edward Marsh Letters

282 | SELECTED BIBLIOGRAPHY

British Library
India Office Records MSS Eur F143/103, Sir Walter Lawrence Correspondence & Papers

Cambridge University Library
CUL Add 9429/1B/1218(iv)
CUL Add 9429/13/207(i)
CUL Add 9429/15/1218(i)
CUL Add 9429/15/1218(ii)
CUL Add 9429/1B/1215(ii)
CUL Add 9429/1B/1216(iv)
CUL Add 9429/1B/1217(v)
CUL Add 9429/1B/1218(iv)
CUL Add 9429/1B/1268(iii)
CUL Add 9429/1B/209/iv
CUL Add 9429/1B/221(ii)
CUL Add 9429/1B/1219
CUL Add 9429/1B/126(iii)
CUL Add 9429/1B/209/iv
CUL Add 9429/1B/215(v)
CUL Add 9429/1B/1215(ii)
CUL Add 9429/1B/1426(xiv)

Churchill Archive
CHAR 2/103/73
CHAR 15/58
CHAR 15/58A
CHAR 16/15A-B
CHAR 16/4
TREN 1
WEIR 1/2
WEIR 1/6

Houghton Hall
Sassoon Papers

Imperial War Museum
IWM 8585
IWM 9887
IWM 10868
IWM 10986

SELECTED BIBLIOGRAPHY | 283

IWM 11963
IWM 12641

Library & Archives Canada
MG 30 A 72, Vol. 9, File 9: "S.E. Parker, Memoirs of Major S.E. Parker"

Liddell Collection
LHCMA BP 9/9/37
LHCMA BP/9/1/3
LHCMA BP/1/5/3

Montrose Museum
Burke, Personal Diary

National Aerospace Library
C. G. Grey Correspondence

National Archives and Records Administration (College Park, MD)
Record Group (RG) 45
RG 54
RG 165

The National Archives (Kew, London)
TNA ADM 116/1602
TNA ADM 116/1807
TNA AIR 1/8/15/1/13
TNA AIR 1/8/15/1/19
TNA AIR 1/8/15/1/9
TNA AIR 1/72/15/9/136
TNA AIR 1/119/15/40/69
TNA AIR 1/128/15/40/173
TNA AIR 1/138/15/40/281
TNA AIR 1/143/15/40/316
TNA AIR 1/163/15/136/1
TNA AIR 1/522/16/12/5
TNA AIR 1/524/16/12/26
TNA AIR 1/529/16/12/70
TNA AIR 1/675/21/13/1726
TNA AIR 1/678/21/13/2100
TNA AIR 1/718/29/9
TNA AIR 1/725/97/2

SELECTED BIBLIOGRAPHY

TNA AIR 1/727/152/5
TNA AIR 1/752/204/4/61
TNA AIR 1/785/204/4/558
TNA AIR 1/993/204/5/1218
TNA AIR 1/1068/204/5/1621
TNA AIR 1/1138/204/5/2253
TNA AIR 1/1159/204/5/2459
TNA AIR 1/1241/204/6/54–57
TNA AIR 1/1288/204/11/53
TNA AIR 1/1303/204/11/169
TNA AIR 1/1585/204/82/41
TNA AIR 1/1590/204/82/87
TNA AIR 1/1997/204/273/245
TNA AIR 1/2117/207/58/3
TNA AIR 1/2126/207/77/3
TNA AIR 1/2170/209/12/8
TNA AIR 1/2399/280/1
TNA AIR 2/100/A13339
TNA AIR 6/12
TNA AIR 8/167
TNA AIR 18/1/18
TNA AIR 69/1
TNA AIR 69/3
TNA AIR 69/41
TNA CAB 23/3/29
TNA CAB 23/3/38
TNA CAB 23/3/71
TNA CAB 23/4/11
TNA CAB 23/4/18
TNA CAB 23/4/20
TNA CAB 23/4/23
TNA CAB 23/4/35
TNA CAB 23/4/38
TNA CAB 23/5/10
TNA CAB 23/13/19
TNA CAB 23/14/9
TNA CAB 23/14/11
TNA CAB 24/26/58
TNA CAB 24/26/62
TNA CAB 24/27/78
TNA CAB 24/28/22

TNA CAB 24/28/84
TNA CAB 24/29/60
TNA CAB 24/30/9
TNA CAB 24/37/97
TNA CAB 24/38/53
TNA CAB 24/39/41
TNA CAB 24/40/78
TNA CAB 24/45/44
TNA CAB 24/48/13
TNA CAB 24/49/21
TNA FO 372/28

Parliamentary Archives
Parliamentary Archives BL/83/2/19
Parliamentary Archives F/44/5/5
Parliamentary Archives LG/F/45/9/12

Private Collections
Brooke-Popham Family Papers
Nan Herbert Albums
Trenchard Family Papers

RAF Museum
RFC/RAF Casualty Forms
RAFM C1/10/3
RAFM MFC 76/1/4
RAFM MFC 76/1/7
RAFM MFC 76/1/8
RAFM MFC 76/1/9
RAFM MFC 76/1/18
RAFM MFC 76/1/61
RAFM MFC 76/1/76
RAFM MFC 76/1/104
RAFM MFC 76/1/140/1
RAFM MFC 76/1/189/1
RAFM MFC 77/13/22

University of Reading Special Collections
CW RR/7/174
MS 1640/151/18

Index

Ackerley, J.R. "Joe", 195
Admiralty. *See* Royal Navy
aerial bombing. *See* air operations
Aerial Operations Committee, 127. *See also* Smuts
aerial photography. *See* air operations
Aerial Target (world's first ground-controlled drone), 139
Aerodromes Committee, 148
aerodromes, 55, 63, 83, 91, 98, 102, 127, 148, 168–169, 170–172, 174, 231n6, 234n1
Aeronautics, 155
Aeroplane, 14, 23, 58, 86, 155, 160
Air Board, 124, 126, 130, 154, 250n11
air casualties, 69–70, 72, 97, 99, 106, 107, 111, 116, 118, 144, 172–174, 207, 210, 213–215, 235n13, 246n17, 267n11
air combat, 9, 96, 110–111, 115, 210–212, 216–217, 247n40. *See also* air operations
Air Council, 128–129, 139–141, 143, 145–146, 149, 152, 160–161, 166, 171, 255n36, 257n57
Air Department. *See* Air Ministry
Air Force Bill, 129, 134–135
"air force spirit", 97, 100, 183, 190, 194, 197
air minister, 122, 129–131, 141, 143, 147, 149–150, 154, 156–158, 161–162, 177. *See also* Harmsworth, Harold; Weir, William
Air Ministry, 33, 64, 105, 123–125, 128, 130, 133, 136, 141, 143–144, 146–147, 152, 154, 157–159, 162, 164, 165–166, 169, 173–175, 178–179, 184–186, 190
Air Operations Committee, 141
air operations: aerial bombing, 9, 69, 72, 79, 83, 99, 112–114, 118–119, 126, 170, 227n1, 246n21, 247n31, 247n34; aerial photography, 9, 42, 53, 82, 111, 113, 207; air reconnaissance, 40, 42, 44, 69, 72, 75, 77–78, 101, 107, 110, 113–114, 117, 217, 248n50, 249n61; air-to-ground and ground-to-air communications, 96; aircraft-tank cooperation, 82; antitank gun suppression, 82, 66; artillery cooperation, 9, 42, 66, 72, 74, 77–80, 82, 101, 109, 111,113-115, 117–118, 120, 167, 207, 210, 227n1, 247n40; contact patrols, 100, 113, 115; OCA (offensive counter-air), 82; SEAD (suppression of enemy air defences), 83, 240n36
air organization: agility, 26, 75, 80; command arrangements, 3, 6, 26, 41–42, 44–48, 50, 54, 58, 65, 99–100, 103–104, 135, 142, 165, 174, 199; flexibility, 45, 53, 82; innovation, culture of, 82, 192, 198–199
Air Policy Committee, 128, 251n15. *See also* Smuts
Air Raids Committee, 127. *See also* Smuts
air reconnaissance. *See* air operations
Air Reorganisation Committee, 126, 251n15. *See also* Smuts
air superiority, 77, 110, 112–113, 115, 118-119, 170, 188, 199, 216
aircraft and aeroengine production: coordination of allied aircraft production, 168; British, 75, 110, 124, 127, 140, 146, 148, 165; French, 110, 213; German; 216–217; superiority of French and German aeroengines, 110
aircraft-tank liaison. *See* air operations
aircraft: communications with, 96; comparative performance of, 110; frontline

strength, 39–40, 46, 66, 75, 78, 189, 213, 216; serviceability and wastage, 77; supply and production, 63, 66, 75, 107, 124–125, 189, 216, 217
airfields. *See* aerodromes
airpower: British doctrine, 65, 79, 107–111, 116, 126, 135, 180, 245n13; concentration and, 78, 112, 114; development in World War 1, 8–9, 83; founding tenet of, 73; French doctrine, 79, 83, 111, 235n8; German doctrine, 78, 83, 118, 210; Haig's understanding of, 55; importance of organizational model and, 39; influence on World War II, 8; three-dimensional warfare and, 9, 119. *See also* Henderson; RFC; Trenchard
Aitken, Max (Lord Beaverbrook), 129, 140, 153, 158, 163–164, 166, 178–179, 184
Alcock, John, 185
Allen, "Dizzy", 87
Amalgamated Holdings, 185
American Civil War, 19. *See also* Grant
Amerika programme. *See* Luftstreitkräfte
Amiens, Battle of, 76, 120
Andover (staff college), 190, 192
Anglo-American alliance (World War 2), 34
antitank gun suppression. *See* air operations
Archbishop of Canterbury, 141
Armistice. *See* World War 1
Army Council, 40, 74, 114, 131
Arras, Battle of, 75, 93, 115, 117, 244n34
artillery cooperation. *See* air operations
Ashmore, Edward "Splash", 195–196, 265n22. *See also* homosexuality
Asquith, Raymond (son of Herbert), 18, 60, 223n34, 228n6, 233n40
Asquith, Herbert: administration of, 61, 256n54; assessment of de Castelnau, 13; concern about RFC casualties, 107; death of Raymond, 18; defence of Trenchard, 159, 178; high opinion of Baring, 60; meeting with Trenchard, 60; press campaign against, 129; resignation of, 122
Asquith, Katharine, 71
Atkinson, Percy, 103

Australia, 184, 93, 97. *See also* Royal Australian Air Force
Autigny (Autigny-la-Tour), 168, 171, 177, 261n25
Autreville, 173
aviation fuel (petroleum), 63, 169, 213
aviation logistics. *See* RFC
Azelot, 173

Babin, Gustave, 131–132, 135
Bailhache Committee investigation, 30n232, 58
Baird, John, 125, 132, 147–148, 154, 156–158, 163, 166, 184, 250n11, 254n20
Balfour, Arthur, 58, 89, 241n16
Balfour, Harold, 172, 241n16, 244n4
Balkans, the, 17
Bank of England, 16
Bares, Joseph, 46–47, 246n19. *See also* French Air Service
Baring-Ponsonby private language, 16, 206, 222n25
Baring, Edward, 16, 220n1
Baring, Hugo, 59, 222n24, 233n35
Baring, John, 59
Baring, Maurice: adopts role of 'clown' and 'storyteller' within HQ RFC, 68–70; assumes role of personal staff officer (PSO), 47; autobiography, 15, 180; character and personality of, 15–16, 41, 194–195, 201–202; chastises Trenchard, 92, 131, 196, 241n27; de Castelnau's opinion of, 13–14, 176; diplomatic service, 16–17; early life, 16; friendship with Bron and Nan Herbert, 11–12, 18, 40, 43, 52, 69–70, 90–92, 180, 206, 220n3; helps nurse Trenchard, 179; Henderson, relationship with, 40, 43, 45–47, 49–50; Belloc, friendship with, 11, 18, 58–59; final illness and death, 12–13, 18, 187, 201; importance of Catholic faith, 18; influence on Trenchard, 71, 88–89, 94, 102, 117, 194–195, 203; joins HQ RFC, 11, 40, 43; knowledge of Trenchard's resignation, 150–151, 163, 167; move to

London, 136–137; natural empathy of, 9; nicknamed Nicodemus by Haig, 54; obituary, 12, 220n5; Oxford marmalade and, 205; personal faults of, 67; partial portrait of Trenchard, 181–182; Pickwick Cottage, resident at, 180; post-war career of, 186–188; published works, 4, 12, 14, 170, 181, 186; proposed posting to Russia, 89–90, 241n17; reasons for joining RFC, 41, 241n17; reputation within RFC, 92, 94–95; return to France, 166, 168; Russo-Japanese war and, 17, 41, 228n11; sexuality of, 195–196; state honours, 180; skill as an interpreter, 13, 52, 71, 111, 170; Trenchard and, 10, 14, 51–61, 90–91, 99, 114, 116–117, 174–175, 177, 179–180, 200–204; Trenchard's eulogy, 12, 193–197; war diary and notebooks, 205–206; work as a journalist, 17, 150
Barrington-Kennett, Basil, 43, 228n12
Bartlett, Frederick, 86
Bates, Tom, 57
Bavaria, anomalous position, 133
Beaufort castle, Scotland, 13, 187
Beaverbrook. *See* Aitken, Max
Belgian Air Service, 98, 246n21
Belgium, 18
Belgrade, 17
Bell House, Dulwich, 180
Belloc, Hilaire, 11, 18, 58–59, 123, 154, 223n34, 228n6, 233n37, 261n25
Bennet, Arnold, 153, 263n21
Berg Collection, 205
Berlin, 170, 172-173
Binyon, T.J. 15, 222n22
Birley, James, 67, 235n14
Black, Jeremy, 8
Bloody April, 117, 248n42
Boelcke, Oswald, 239n33
Boer War. *See* South African War
Bomber Command. *See* RAF
Bonar Law, Andrew, 156–59, 164
Bonham-Carter, Maurice, 60, 261n25
Boulogne, 11, 51
Bow and Arrow Brigade, 7

Boyle, Andrew, 182, 223n38, 236n22
Boyle, Kitty. *See* Trenchard, Kitty
Bradley, Omar, N., 35–38
Brancker, Sefton, 44–45, 47, 49, 53, 61, 64–65, 72, 75, 104, 111, 113, 125, 127, 131, 148, 157–158, 196, 200, 229n22, 254n20
Bristol Fighter, two-seat fighter, 148
Britain, Battle of, 2
British Air Services Memorial, Arras, 184
British airpower. *See* airpower; Henderson; RFC; Trenchard
British Army/BEF (British Expeditionary Force): Army Council, 40, 114, 131; CIGS (chief of the imperial general staff), 151, 153; command and seniority in, 42; conscription and, 11, 61–62; deployment to France, 39; expenditure on, 124–125; GHQ (General Headquarters), 28; intelligence and, 32, 55, 80, 82, 226n31, 227n1, 228n9; leadership philosophy of, 97; strength of, 41, 47, 195. *See also* RFC
British Museum, 141
British Parliament: House of Commons, 132, 178; House of Lords, 6, 183–184, 224n44
British War Cabinet, 75, 123, 126–128, 131, 141, 143, 147, 152–154, 156–158, 171–172
Bromet, Geoffrey, 55
Brooke-Popham, Robert "Brookham": career of, 183–184, 228n12; character of, 53; comment on manning policy, 235n13; relationship with Game, 53; CinC Far East (1940), 184; comments on importance attached to logistics by Trenchard, 77; criticism of army commanders, 78; discusses Trenchard's influence on RFC, 82, 83, 112; drafting work for Trenchard, 180, 189, 248n45; du Peuty's influence, 112, 237n33; Empire Air Training Scheme and, 183; evolution of RAF doctrine, 245n13; General Strike and, 186; importance of listening to bottom-up ideas, 81–82; influence on

290 | INDEX

RAF ethos, 264n8; marriage of, 195; Pope-Hennessy and, 230n41, 234n6; relationship with Trenchard, 51, 54, 56, 69, 91, 102; replaces Sykes as chief of staff, 49; responsibilities at HQ RFC, 52–53, 64, 66, 239n31; RAF staff college and 192–193
Brown, Arthur, 185
Buchan, John, 18, 60, 223n34
Bullock, Christopher, 85, 165, 189, 240n1, 241n13, 260n2
Burbidge Committee investigation, 232n30
Burke, Charles, 74, 104, 229n25, 244n34

Cambridge (Trinity College), 16, 18
Camus, Francois, 28
Canada, 97, 104, 183
Carson, Edward, 178
Castelnau, Edouard de: Baring's opinion of, 13; comments about Baring, 15, 170, 176, 221n14; mistaken for Foch, 12–13; criticism of personal staff, 28, 203; Petain and, 13, 185; post-war career, 184–185, 221n8; relationship with Trenchard, 13–15, 167, 169–170, 184; reputation of, 13, 221n8, 221n10; Verdun, Battle of, 13
Cecil Committee, 189, 193
Cecil, Hugh: career of, 233n42; character, 61–62; death of, 184; joins HQ RFC, 61; joins Trenchard in London, 137, 149; Smuts committee and, 125–126; Trenchard's resignation and, 151, 153, 156–159, 166; relationship with Simon, 234n48; 259n21; views on RAF independence, 134–135
Cecil, Robert, 89, 241n16
CFS (Central Flying School). See flying training
CIA (Central Intelligence Agency), 37
Chamberlain, Austen, 158
Chamier, John, 65, 108, 119, 235n9, 245n8
Chard & Ilminster News, 19
Charles, Hubert, 57
Charlton, Lionel: Battle of Amiens and, 76; concern about RAF's air control policy,
80; criticism of Trenchard's offensive strategy, 119; homosexuality and, 195–196, 265n22; military 'outsider', 3; post-war career, 191, 219n7; responsibilities as brigade commander, 100; work of training brigade, 100, 109
Charteris, Evan, 18, 40, 61, 223n34, 228n6, 233n41
Charteris, John, 32, 226n31, 234n48
Chatto & Windus, 181
Chesterton, Gilbert "G.K.", 18, 60, 188, 223n34
CAS (chief of the air staff). See RAF
CIGS (chief of the imperial general staff). See British Army
Churchill, Winston: appointed war minister, 177; coastal patrol argument, 146–147; criticises Trenchard on wastage rates, 148, 173; Eddy Marsh and, 233n40; friendship with Beaverbrook, 178; Hugh Cecil and, 184, 233n42; Hugo Baring and, 222n24; loses 1945 election, 184; Maurice Baring and, 60; opinion of Jan Smuts, 125; Trenchard's 80th Birthday, 239n29; selects Trenchard as CAS, 177–179, 193, 262n9; Soviet Union, description of, 16, 222n24
Civil Aviation Department, 178, 183, 229n22, 231n6
command of the air. See air superiority
conscription. See British Army
Conservative Party, 64, 154, 158, 160, 233n42, 250n11, 258n12, 259n19
Constantinople, 17
contact patrols. See air operations
constant offensive. See Henderson; RFC; Trenchard
Cooper, Diana, 70, 186, 220n5
Cooper, Duff, 220n5
Cooper, Malcom, 249n61
Cooper, Reginald, 112, 246n23
Copenhagen, 17, 235n17
Coppens, Willy, 98
Corballis, Edward "Teddy", 64, 234n3
Coward, Noel, 196
Cowdray, Lord. See Weetman, Pearson

INDEX | 291

Cranwell (Cadet College), 189, 192–194, 219n2
Crawley Court, 186
Curzon, George, 58, 141, 255n23, 261n23

D.H.4, day bomber, 173
D.H.6, trainer, 256n51
D.H.9, day bomber, 173
Daily Mail, 129, 143, 154
Daily News, 131, 155
Dardanelles, 49
Davidson, John, 156, 158, 259n19
Dawson, Geoffrey. *See* Robinson, Geoffrey
DMA (Department Military Aeronautics), 44, 74
Derby, Lord. *See* Stanley, Edward
Desborough, Ettie. *See* Grenfell, Ettie
Diplomatic Service, 16–17, 112, 246n23
DOP (distant observation patrols), 94
Division Aérienne. *See* French Air Service
Dixon, Norman, 26–27
doctrine. *See* airpower
Douglas, Sholto, 93–94, 101–102, 191, 202
Dover, 129, 12n27
Dowding, Hugh: failure to control subordinates, 2; leadership during Battle of Britain, 2, 219n4; reputation for being difficult, 104–105; retirement (1940), 244n35; strained relationship with Trenchard, 80, 105–106 , 244n38; training role, 145; work on Western Front, 75
Duff, Juliet, 18, 60, 91, 179, 223n34, 228n6
Duke of Cambridge. *See* Prince George
Duke of York. *See* King George VI
Dunkirk, 102, 243n27
Düsseldorf, 175
Duval, Maurice, 78–79, 170–171, 228n4, 239n19, 263n41. *See also* French Air Service

East Ham, 177
Eisenhower, Dwight, 34, 266n10
Ellerton, Spenser, 91, 241n23
Empire Air Training Scheme, 183
Estrée Blanche, 70

Etaples (24 General Hospital), 67, 106
Ethelred the Unready, 62
ethos: definition of, 194; fighting service and, 193, 197, 243n12, 264n8; organizational, 1, 3, 81; RFC squadrons, 97. *See also* "air force spirit"
Eton, 16, 18, 184, 233n42

Faber, Walter, 154, 258n12
Farnborough, 43, 45, 167, 177
Ferriere, Gilbert Artaud de la, 112, 221n10
Festing, Francis, 52–53, 66, 68, 113, 179, 183, 186, 191, 231n6, 231n12, 262n15
Fienvillers, 60, 76
Fighter Command. *See* RAF
Fighting In The Air, booklet, 116, 248n44
Fitzroy, Almeric, 130
fliegerabteilung. *See* Luftstreitkräfte
Flight, 155, 183
Flying Corps Headquarters 1914–1918 (Baring). *See R.F.C H.Q. 1914–1918*
flying training: American, 166; British, 108–110, 113, 127, 138, 144–146, 148, 150, 152, 158, 163, 183, 186, 213, 250n67, 256n40; comparison between air services, 109, 213, 266n3; French, 145, 213; German, 114–115, 120, 213–217
Flying, 155
Foch, Ferdinand, 12–13, 15, 171, 185, 246n21
Fokker menace, 69, 107, 244n3
foreign secretary, 62, 184, 234n45
Fort Grange, 105
Foulois, Benjamin, 172
France, attitude to bombing cities, 169-170
Frankfurt, 173
Freeman, Wilfrid, 106, 244n39
French Air Service: aircraft serviceability, 77; aircraft strength of, 46; air reorganization, and 124; celebration of fighter aces, 197; commander of, 46, 78; bombing policy, 169–170; creation of Division Aérienne, 65, 78–79, 83, 133–134, 238n15, 247n34; distribution of aircraft roles, 238n16; dominance of artillery and

engineer officers, 230n34; establishment of an independent air service (L'Armée de l'Air), 134; influence on RFC, 82, 111; liaison with RFC, 112, 134, 246n21; operational wastage, 77; organizational model, 44; proportion of casualties over German lines, 246n17; restrictions on employment of fighter aircraft, 116; support for RAF IF, 160, 169
French Army: *attaque à outrance*, 111; Eastern Army Group, 13; GQG (Grand Quartier General), 28, 47, 133, 240n37, 246n19; Second Army, 13, Tenth Army, 111; Lorraine offensive, 13; use of anilite explosive, 253n10; view on air service independence, 134. *See also* French Air Service
French, John, 11, 31, 39, 44, 50, 55, 59, 123, 133, 154, 227n2
friendship. *See* leadership
Fuller, J.F.C. "Boney", 3, 219n7

Game, Philip: Baring and, 68–69; comments on air reorganization, 126; compares Salmond to Trenchard, 85; criticism of Trenchard's changed views on bombing, 139; drafting work for Trenchard, 114, 116, 180, 189, 248n45; management of Trenchard, 90–91, 241n22; post-war career, 184, 231n5; recruitment as chief of staff, 52; reluctance to stay at HQ RFC, 52–53, 98; relationship with Brooke-Popham, 53; role in 1926 General Strike, 186; Simon, relationship with 62, 136; views on Sykes, 165; work as chief of staff, 53, 64–66, 168
Geddes, Eric, 147, 256n52. *See also* Royal Navy
GOC RFC (General Officer Commanding) RFC. *See* Henderson; Trenchard
General Strike, 33, 186
generalship: command recognition, 203; commanders as leaders, 203; contribution of senior leadership team, 3, 6–7, 25, 53; demands placed on wartime commanders, 1, 9, 26–27, 29–38; isolation and , 26–29; relationship with personal staffs, 37–38, 57, 88, 200, 203; rivalry between commanders, 31, 47–48, 198; impact of commanders on organizations, 4; importance of friendship, 25–27, 38, 198; variation in personality and interests of senior leaders, 1, 27, 33, 35. *See also* leadership
Geneva, 166, 183
George Bell and Sons, 181
German Air Service. *See* Luftstreitkräfte
German Army: Amiens, Battle of, 120; attempt to outflank BEF, 42; budgetary dominance over German navy, 125; control of aviation assets, 134; general staff, 26; importance of seniority for promotion, 47; limited support from Luftstreitkräfte, 121; Marne, First battle of, 42; manpower shortages, 216; Oberste Heeresleitung (OHL), 26, 47, 124; overwhelmed by Allied airpower, 120; rivalry with navy, 124; RFC strategy to defeat, 203; Somme lessons, 246n27, 248n50; spring offensive, 75, 106, 116–117, 149, 170, 207, 210; views on air service independence, 134; war ministry and, 124. *See also* Luftstreitkräfte; Ludendorf
Gibbs, Philip, 28, 64, 108, 234n5, 244n3
Globe, 155
Gontrode, 126
Gordon, "Bos", 91, 168-169, 241n21, 260n11
Gosport (*Gosport System*), 144–146, 166, 253n4
Gosse, Edmund, 18, 223n32
Gotha, bomber, 129
Gould Lee, Arthur, 72, 94, 248n46
Grahame, George, 18, 223n34
GQG (Grand Quartier General). *See* French Army
Grant, Ulysses S., 29–31, 38, 225n17
Great Britain, 8, 123
Greenwich (staff college), 106
Grenfell, Ettie, 18, 58, 60, 221n6, 223n34, 228n6

INDEX | 293

Grey, Charles, 14–15, 123, 140, 156, 222n23
Grey, Edward, 241
Gribble, Philip, 56
Griffith, George, 200
Griffith, Herbert, 97
Groves, Percy, 119, 249n57, 263n37
Groves, Robert, 140, 146–147, 191, 254n17, 258n2, 256n47
Guingand, Freddie de, 33–36, 204, 226n41, 241n22

Haig, Douglas, 28, 31–33, 38, 44, 45, 55–56, 62, 79, 93, 107, 11, 119, 125–128, 130–132, 134, 142, 150, 225n14
Haldane, Richard, 40, 220n3
Halton (training school), 189
Hankey, Maurice, 153–154, 239n29, 254n14, 258n6, 258n11
Hansen, Chester, "Chet", 35–37, 204, 227n53
Harmsworth, Alfred (Lord Northcliffe), 32, 129, 132, 149, 166, 226n32, 252n29
Harmsworth, Harold (Lord Rothermere): appointed air minister by Lloyd George, 129; arguments with Trenchard, 139–140, 142–148, 179; attacked by Cecil and Simon, 156–157; correspondence with war cabinet, 152, 154; creates Amalgamated Holdings, 185; forms air council 129–130, 140; helps found the *Daily Mail*, 129; influence of Sir Henry Norman, 138–139, 143–146, 148; recruits 'young colonels', 137; reputation and career, 141, 252n39; resignation as air minister, 157–160, 162–164; respect for RFC pilots, 137; selects Trenchard as chief of the air staff, 132, 140; similarities with Trenchard, 142–143; sponsors Bristol Blenheim bomber, 185; supports non-stop Trans-Atlantic flight, 185–186; Trenchard's resignation, 149–151, 154; views on reprisal raids, 130–131; working methods, 138, 140–41, 161–162
Harmsworthia, 148
Harris, "Bert", 191, 193, 243n12

Hawker, Lanoe, 82, 239n33
Hazebrouck, 76, 230n39
HQ RFC. *See* RFC
Henderson, David: airpower visionary, 73–74, 199; appointed to command 1st Division, 44–45; character of, 43; relationship with Baring, 2, 40, 45, 47–49; Bron Herbert and, 40; career of, 227n1; constant (relentless and incessant) offensive, 111, 120; creation of forward air headquarters, 76; death of son (Ian), 261n25; described by Trenchard as 'Father of the RAF', 183; DGMA (Director General Military Aeronautics), 39, 49, 125; distances RFC from army commanders, 134; Evan Charteris and, 61; fights for control of kite balloons, 80; GOC RFC, 39, 44–45, 50, 51; handling of senior air commanders, 104; lack of senior officers, 47; membership of air council, 254n20; objects to Sykes' appointment as chief of the air staff, 153–154, 164; persistent ill health of, 49; posted to Paris, 166; potential chief of the air staff, 131; relationship with Douglas Haig, 150; relationship with John French, 39, 43; removal of Sykes as chief of staff, 50; RFC organizational model and, 39, 43–44, 46, 50, 75; society friends, 59; Sykes and, 41, 44, 49; selects Brooke-Popham as chief of staff, 50–51; Trenchard and, 42, 45–46, 49, 64, 115, 182, 199, 263n41; work for Smuts, 125–127
Herbert, Bron, 11, 18, 40, 69–70, 91–92, 220n3
Herbert, Nan, 12, 43, 52, 90–91, 180, 206, 220n3
Higgins, Jack, 190, 264n8
Hildesheim, 16–17, 60
Hillgarth, Jocelyn, 206
Hispano engine, 55
Hitler, Adolph, 185
Hoare, Sam, 55, 161, 231n19
Hoeppner, Ernst von, 114–118, 120–121, 210, 216, 228n4, 249n54, 250n67, 267n13. *See also* Luftstreitkräfte

Hogg, Rudolph "Rudi", 75, 100, 105–106, 196
home establishment, 97, 103, 117
home secretary, 61, 184
homosexuality, 32, 195–196
Horne, Henry, 79–80
Howard-Williams, Ernest, 96, 242n2
HP O/400, night bomber, 173
Hundred Days campaign, 75, 76, 82, 120, 210, 248n42
Huntington, Samuel, 26
Huskinson, Patrick, 105

Illinois, 29
Imperial War Conference, 122
Imperial War Graves Commission, 184
Independent Force. *See* RAF IF
India, 21–22, 102
Indian troops, 171, 261n23
Information, Ministry of, 166
Ingram, Collingwood, 64, 234n3
innovation. *See* air organization
Inter-Allied Aircraft Committee (IAAC). *See* Trenchard
Inter-Allied Bombing Force (IABF). *See* Trenchard
Ireland, 23

jagdstaffeln (Jasta). *See* Luftstreitkräfte
James, "Archie", 61, 70, 100, 105, 194, 228n14, 231n9, 247n31
James, Baron, 82
Japan. *See* Russo-Japanese war
Jeffs, Julian, 206
Jellicoe, John, 153, 155, 178, 258n4
Jenkins, Conway, 137, 253n6
Joffre, 28, 42, 44. *See also* French Army
Joint Chiefs, U.S., 37
Joint War Committee, 250n9
Joynson-Hicks, William, 64, 156

kampfgeschwader, 114
Kenya, 183
Kerr, Mark, 126, 128–129, 139, 148, 251n14, 254n15, 254n20, 255n33
King George V, 59, 171. *See also* Trenchard

King George VI, 60, 171, 260n1
King's Hussars, 42
Kitchener, Herbert, 22, 43–45, 49, 58–59, 233n39
kite balloons, 80, 99, 118, 134, 210, 242n1
Kluck, Alexander von, 42, 43

L'Armée de l'Air. *See* French Air Service
L'illustration, 131–132, 135
Lambe, Charles, 102, 151n17, 243n27, 264n8
Land and Water, 59, 123
Landon, Herman, 44
Lawrence, Herbert, 234n5
Lawrence, T.E. "Lawrence of Arabia", 4–5, 60, 95, 220n12, 236n23
Lawrence, Walter, 171, 261n23, 263n41
leadership: characteristics of a good leader, 2, 25–26, 199; friendship and; 25, 27, 37–38; importance of contrasting personalities in small teams, 35, 38, 68–69; military compared to aviation, 2; organizational culture and, 81, 194; RFC's leadership model, 96–97, 101, 103–104, 198–199; self-awareness in senior leaders, 2, 6, 34, 81, 86, 199; wartime demands on leaders, 26–27, 38, 99. *See also* Trenchard
League of Londoners, 130, 252n36
Leigh Mallory, Trafford, 66, 191, 235n10
Leith-Thomsen, Hermann von der, 46–47
Lewis, Donald, 82
Liberal Party, 61, 138, 157, 159–160
Lincoln, Abraham, 30–31
Livingston, Guy, 126, 145, 161, 166, 185, 251n14, 259n40
Lloyd George, David, 13, 33, 60, 75, 122, 124–125, 127–129, 133, 138–139, 141, 152, 157–160, 177–179, 185, 262n11
Lloyds, of London, 16
logistics. *See* RFC
Lomax, Samuel, 44
London, 14, 17, 50, 61, 68, 89, 102, 122, 132, 138, 151, 167–168, 177, 183, 185, 203

London: air defense of, 12, 123, 126; bombing of, 124, 127, 129–130, 172. *See also* Luftstreitkräfte
Londonderry, Lord. *See* Vane–Tempest–Stewart, Charles
Longcroft, Charles, 47, 144, 146, 155, 230n35, 257n67, 264n8
Loos, Battle of, 112–113
Lorraine, Eustace, 23
Lovat, Laura, 13, 187
Lowther, Juliet. *See* Duff, Juliet
Lucas, Lord. *See* Herbert, Bron
Lucas, Nan. *See* Herbert, Nan
Ludendorff, Erich von, 26, 120
Ludlow-Hewitt, Edgar, 100, 144–145, 178, 201, 243n15
Luftstreitkräfte: ability to concentrate fighter assets, 78; amerika programme, 217, 267n13; Battle of Amiens and, 120–121; Battle of Arras and; 115; Battle of Messines and, 216; Battle of the Somme and, 113–115; bombing campaign against England; 122, 129; creation of protection flights, 114; criticism of, 115, doctrinal boundaries, 83, 118; operational tempo, 118, 120, 207–209, 216; fliegerabteilung, 207, 249n62; forced into a defensive strategy, 114, 118–121; frontline strength of, 46, 216, 267n13; Gruppe Wytschaete, 216; headquarters strength, 47, 229n19; impact of operational wastage, 113, 213–217; innovative tactics, 82; interference with British artillery cooperation effort, 210–212; 247n40; limited success during Hundred days campaign, 117–118 'never defeated' claim, 120–21; 249n16; jagdstaffeln, 113, 118, 210, 213, 216, 239n33; low sortie generation, 77, 113; operational tempo, 118, 120, 207–209, 216; policy on command appointments, 228n4; reorganization of, 114; pilot shortages, 213–214, 266n5; post-war history of, 249n61; resources committed to homeland air defence, 175; technical superiority of, 110; use of fighters for escort duties, 117
Luftwaffe, 133

Mackay, Charles, 65, 235n9
Maclean, Veronica, 71
Macmillan, Norman, 55
Macready, Gordon, 230n37
Macready, Nevil, 154
Mais, Petre "S.P.B.", 193
Maitland, Edward, 191
Malaya, 184
Malcolm, Douglas, 62
Manchester Guardian, 155
Manchuria. *See* Russo-Japanese War
Mannheim, 127
Marconi scandal, 147, 256n54
Marne, First Battle of, 13, 42
Marne, Second Battle of, 79
Marsh, Edward "Eddy", 18, 58, 91, 195, 223n33
Marson, Thomas, 69, 88–89, 93, 95, 98, 150, 168, 180, 182, 187, 221n15
Maynard, "Sammy", 93
Membland, South Devon, 16
Messines, Battle of, 77, 93, 216
Metropolitan Police, commissioner of the, 183, 184
military aviation, 2–3, 8–9, 15, 39, 44, 46–47, 52, 55, 59, 65, 77, 82, 107, 110, 123–125, 127–128, 133, 134, 137, 192, 199
Milner, Alfred, 128, 129, 138, 152–153, 251n26
Mitchell, William "Billy", 252n40
Mons, Battle of, 42, 59
Montgomery, Bernard, 33–38, 226n41, 232n34, 241n22.
Moore-Brabazon, John, 56, 87, 90, 241n13
Morning Post, 17, 232n31
munitions production, fall in, 127, 172
Munitions, Ministry of, 75, 138, 147, 185, 233n40, 253n7
Murat, Michel, 43, 229n17

Netheravon, 39
Neuve Chapelle, Battle of, 76, 230n39

New South Wales, 184
New York Times, 149
New Zealand, 97, 258n4
Newall, Cyril, 167–168, 173, 178, 237n7
Nicod, Alfred, 54
Nigeria, 23, 87
Nivelle, Robert, 13
Norman, Henry: appointed to aerodromes committee, 148; challenges future development programme, 148; character of, 147; concerns about flying training, 144–146; influence over Rothermere, 138–139, 143, 147, 152; joins air council, 139; Marconi scandal and, 147, 256n54; support to Rothermere, 154, 156, 163, 258n1, 259n25; resignation from air council, 166; political connections of, 138; proposals for bombing Germany, 148; selects Harry Segrave as private secretary, 139; war office wireless committee, 253n7
Northcliffe, Lord. *See* Harmsworth, Alfred
Nouvelle revue, 170

offensive counter-air. *See* air operations
official histories: Canadian, 119; British (*War In The Air*), 139, 171, 180, 182; German, 175, 213, 216
Ohio, 29
Oberste Heeresleitung (OHL). *See* German Army
operational tempo. *See* Luftstreitkräfte; RFC
Orpen, William, 70, 226n29, 236n23
Oxford University, 15, 17–18, 58

Paine, Godfrey, 126–127, 129, 145–146, 152, 154, 157, 161, 151n14, 254n20, 258n10
Pall Mall Gazette, 138
parachutes, 182, 190. *See also* RFC
Paris, 17, 28, 62, 125, 138, 153, 166, 168, 170, 174, 183, 185, 260n8
Park, Keith, 101, 191
Patton, George S., 224n10, 226n10
Paul, Christopher, 183
Pearson, Weetman (Lord Cowdray), 250n11, 125, 128–129, 155

Pelham, Charles, 136
Pentagon, 37
PSO (personal staff officer). *See* generalship
Pétain, Philippe, 13, 78–79, 185, 247n34
Peter the Great, 200–201
Peuty, Paul du, 78, 111–112, 182, 237n33, 246n1. *See also* French Ar Service
Philippi, George, 137, 144, 150, 166, 186, 253n4, 257n67
Pickwick Cottage, Greenwich, 180
Pierrefeu, Jean de, 28
Pirie, George, 66, 235n9
Pope-Hennessy, Richard, 52, 73, 230n41, 230n4, 234n6
Preston, Raph, 183
Prince George (Duke of Cambridge), 132
Prince Joachim Murat. *See* Murat, Michel
Pringle, William, 159
Privy Council, 130, 253n7
Pyle, Ernie, 36

First Quartermaster General. *See* Ludendorff
Queen Mary, 60
Quickswood, Lord. *See* Cecil, Hugh

R.E.8, cooperation machine, 148, 257n57
R.F.C. H.Q. 1914–1918 (Baring), 12, 14–15, 40, 45, 151, 174–175, 180–182, 186, 231n15. *See also* Baring
Rabagliati, Euan, 137, 139, 144, 253n4
Raleigh, George, 47
Raleigh, Walter, 171, 183, 244n1, 261n25
Ravenscroft, Samuel, 166
Rawlins, John, 29–31, 37–38, 204, 225n18
Rawlinson, Henry, 31, 79–80, 239n23
Read, Willie, 105
reconnaissance. *See* air operations
Reichsarchiv, 113
"relentless and incessant offensive". *See* Henderson; RFC; Trenchard
Repington, Charles à Court, 85, 158, 168
reprisal raids. *See* strategic bombing
Revelstoke, 1st Baron. *See* Baring, Edward
Revelstoke, 2nd Baron. *See* Baring, John
Reynolds, Herbert "Alf", 52
Ritz, hotel, 132, 137, 140

Roberts, Arthur, 166, 254n20, 255n33, 260n6
Robertson, William, 4, 132, 151, 153–155, 178, 219n10
Robin Hood, 89, 95
Robinson, Geoffrey, 32–33, 131, 226n32
Rome, 17
Rose, Charles de, 82, 239–240n33
Rothermere, Lord. *See* Harmsworth, Harold
RAF (Royal Air Force): "air force spirit", nature of, 97, 194, 197; creation of, 122–129; post-war drawdown and reconstruction, 189, 190–197; as a meritocracy, 4; CAS (chief of the air staff), 6–7, 14, 90, 109, 131, 137, 154, 160, 264n8; SLT (senior leadership team) concept, 3; senior officers, differences in temperament and personality, 3–4; social cohesion within, 5; Trenchard's defence of, 15, 183, 193; post-war political support for, 159. *See also* RFC
RAF IF (Royal Air Force Independent Force), 13, 165–166, 168, 170–174, 184
Royal Aircraft Factory, 125, 232n30
Royal Australian Air Force, 3
Royal Field Artillery, 103
RFC (Royal Flying Corps): aircraft strength, 75; aircraft wastage, 77; approach to innovation 53, 82, 112, 192; arguments and tensions between senior leaders, 2–3; aviation logistics, 41, 44, 49, 52, 66, 72; class distinctions within, 98; collaborative approach to developing operational techniques, 65–66; command and control (in a time-sensitive environment), 76; comparative sortie generation, 77, 207–209, 216; constant (relentless and incessant) offensive, 76–77, 107–109, 111; creation of the headquarters brigade 75; employment of signals intelligence, 82; establishment of dedicated fighter units, 74; frontline strength of, 46, 50, 75, 148, 264; HQ RFC composition, 40–41, 68, 72; intelligence role, 80, 97, 119; management of personnel, 74; medical policy of, 101; operational tempo; 72, 76, 118, 173, 207–209; organizational model, 39, 76, 96, 199; parachutes, policy, 72, 237n37; selection of squadron commanders, 47; shortage of staff officers, 60; social behaviour of, 98; training division, 100, 144–145; training manual, 73, 110, 245n15
RFC brigades: third, 155; fifth, 100; eighth, 167–168; ninth, 100, 106; northern training, 144–145; southern training, 145
RFC squadrons: 2, 229n25; 4, 47, 103; 5, 253n4; 6, 66; 8, 66, 235n10; 9, 101, 207–209; 11, 103; 13, 235n17; 15, 97, 103; 16, 105, 106; 23, 105; 27, 242n37; 45, 55,105, 248n47; 46, 242n34; 55, 173; 56, 70, 88, 187, 206, 221n15, 261n25; 59, 66; 60, 54, 106, 235n14, 253n4; 64, 236n27; 84, 101; 99, 173; 104, 173; 207, 105
RFC wings: First, 44–45, 55; Second, 104; Third, 49, 100; Ninth Headquarters, 75, 78; Fifteenth, 65
royal household, 32, 60, 223n34
RNAS (Royal Naval Air Service), 2, 49, 55, 63, 74, 93, 102, 125, 130, 141, 158, 190–191
RNAS squadrons: 10, 243n26; 8, 55
Royal Navy: Admiralty, 72, 124, 129, 139, 146–147, 154, 179, 230n42; aircraft for coastal patrols, 146; alert bugle call of, 67; creation of own air service, 123; position vs army, 125; objections to Smuts' proposals, 133; senior leadership of, 2. *See also* RNAS
Royal Scots Fusiliers, 21, 42
Russell, Conrad, 11, 15, 18, 41, 220n3, 220–1n5, 228n6
Russia, 17, 89–90, 195, 222n24, 241n17
Russo-Japanese war, 17, 41, 228n11

Salmond, Geoffrey, 228n12, 264n8
Salmond, John "Jack", 75–76, 85, 104, 106, 109, 111, 120, 126, 131, 142–145, 166–167, 175, 179, 229n16, 237n8, 240n1, 253n2, 257n65, 264n8

San Stefano, hospital, 17
Sandhurst, military academy, 19, 223n39
Sassoon, Philip, 31–33, 37, 40, 156, 204, 226n28, 226n32, 228n9
School of Special Flying, 144. *See also* Gosport
schutzstaffeln, protection flights, 114. See also Luftstreitkräfte
SE5A, single-seat fighter, 55
Segrave, Henry "Harry", 137, 139, 150, 166, 186, 253n4, 254n13
Sha-Ho, 17. *See also* Russo-Japanese war
Sheffield, Gary, 203
Sheppard, Jack, 89
Simon, John: air ministry role, 136–137, 253n2; Baring and, 68; friendship with Hugh Cecil, 234n48; Game's jealousy of, 136; guest at Trenchard's wedding, 263n41; joins HQ RFC, 61–62; opinion of Trenchard, 62; parliamentary intervention on Trenchard's behalf, 156–157, 159, 259n21; post-war appointments 184, 234n45; returns to France, 166; Trenchard's ambitions for, 149
Singapore, 184
Slessor, John "Jack", 83
Smith-Barry, Robert, 137, 144–146, 150, 152, 158, 163, 166, 186, 253n4, 255n38, 256n40, 256n44, 257n67
Smith, Bedell "Beetle", 34, 37
Smith, Frederick, 135
Smuts, Jan: air reorganization (Smuts Report), 123, 125–127, 133, 141, 251n17; Alfred Milner and, 128; arrival in London, 122; authorship and committee membership, 125; establishment of Smuts committee, 123; Douglas Haig's reaction, 125–127, 134, 142; further committees created, 126–128; John French and, 123; London's air defences, 123; personal reputation of, 125; replacement of Trenchard, 153–154; Rothermere and, 129; selection of CAS, 131; speech on air reprisals, 127
Smyth, Ethel, 18, 201, 223n32

Smythies, Bernard, 69, 99, 104, 236n27
Somerset, 19, 224n44
Somme bridges. *See* Hundred Days campaign
Somme, Battle of the, 53, 76, 79, 100, 106, 108, 113-114, 116–117, 122, 188, 207, 235n14, 244n38, 244n3, 246n29, 247n41, 248n50
South African War, 22–23, 125. *See also* Trenchard
Southampton docks (mutiny at), 177
Soviet Union, 16
Spears, Edward, 42
spring offensive. *See* German Army
squadrons. *See* RFC
St-Andre (Saint-André-aux-Gouy) headquarters, 167–168, 229n18, 238n10
St-Marie-Cappel, 55
St-Mihiel, Battle of, 261n28
St-Omer (Saint-Omer), vii, 43, 45, 75–76, 81, 200, 229n18
Stanley, Edward (Lord Derby), 93, 130–131,142, 162, 242n29
Stewart, Oliver, 108, 119, 248n47
Stonehaven, Lord. *See* Baird, John
Storr, Lancelot, 125, 250n9
Strange Louis, 80
strategic bombing: British plans for, 9, 75, 119, 127, 130, 133, 139–140, 148, 165–166, 171, 173–175; control of, 142. French reservations, 169–171; *See also* RAF Independent Force
Strategic Council, 153, 163, 258n2,
Stuttgart, 127
suppression of enemy air defences. *See* air operations
Sykes, Frederick: appointment as CAS, 152–154, 230n42, 258n3; appointment as chief of staff, 41; appointment as director general civil aviation, 178, 183; creation of Strategic Council, 163; criticism of Trenchard, 108; defended by Lloyd George, 159; divisive influence of, 49; comments about Haig and aviation, 55; difficult relationship with Henderson, 41, 49, 228n13; influence on flying

training, 109; performance as CAS, 165, 260n2; 254n17; relationship with Rothermere, 161, 164, 178; relationship with Weir, 165; replacement by Trenchard as CAS, 177; reputation of, 42, 228n14, 230n14; rivalry with Trenchard, 41–42, 166; sent to Dardanelles, 49, 51; staff training of, 53; Trenchard and RAF IF, 171, 174; Trenchard's reaction to appointment of Sykes as Henderson's successor, 44–45; views on RFC expansion, 44

Tanks Corps, 81, 219n7
Tatler, 194
Taunton, 19, 21, 224n44
Taylor, Gordon, 93
Tedder, Arthur, 105, 191
Templewood, Samuel. *See* Hoare, Sam
"The Expressions". *See* Baring-Ponsonby private language
Times, 12, 17–18, 32, 88, 129, 131,160, 185, 201, 226n32, 252n29
Todd, George, 103
Tomlinson, Henry, 131
Tory. *See* Conservative Party
Trans-Atlantic flight (Alcock & Brown), 185
Trenchard, Henry (father), 19–20, 22, 70
Trenchard, Hugh; ability to cut to the heart of a problem, 56; accepts command of First Wing, 45; appointed GOC RFC, 51; appreciation for the Bow and Arrow Brigade, 7; attitude to homosexuality, 32, 196; awareness of personal weaknesses, 86, 199–200; Baring, relationship with, 10, 12, 14–15, 51–61, 57–58, 67, 71, 88–92, 99, 114, 116–117, 174–175, 177, 179–180, 200–204; contribution of senior leadership team, 51–54, 67, 136, 190–191, 199–200; character of, 10, 20, 23, 60, 85–87, 89, 93, 95, 109, 131–132, 199; de Castelnau, dealings with, 12–14; dominant figure in development of British airpower, 9, 64–65, 76–77, 83–84, 85, 107, 109–112, 119, 126, 132, 139, 180, 183; dyslexia diagnosis, 19; emotional immaturity and, 87, 194, 202; encourages innovation in RFC, 76, 81–82, 199; family and early life, 19; fights army for control of artillery cooperation squadrons, 79–80; frontline visits, 53–55; General Strike (1926) and, 33; Henderson, relationship with, 42, 45–46, 49, 64, 73, 115, 182, 199, 263n41; impact of father (Henry Trenchard)'s bankruptcy; 19–21, 90; inability to express thoughts clearly, 19, 56–57, 85; indivisibility of the air, 165, 197; influence over future senior RAF leaders, 74; Inter–Allied Aircraft Committee (IAAC) and, 160, 170, 260n8; Inter–Allied Bombing Force (IABF) and, 171; intolerance of physical weakness, 87; joins Royal Scots Fusiliers, 21; King George V's views on, 171; leadership style, 97, 99, 140, 190–191, 202–203; learns to fly and joins RFC, 23; medical policy and, 67; mistaken about fighter units, 74; management of subordinates, 80–81, 102–6; parachutes and, 72; personal values of, 20, 22; policy of sustaining existing rather than creating additional squadrons, 66, 217; post–war criticism of, 117; plans for post-war RAF ("permanent organization"), 190; poor health of, 23, 87, 179; posted to Central Flying School (CFS), 23, 252n33; reaction to casualties, 69–70; relations with family, 21; reorganization of RFC, 44; reprisal raids and, 132; relationship with Douglas Haig, 55–56; reputation with army commanders, 78; reputation within RFC, 55, 64–5, 92–94; retirement as CAS, 7; rivalry with Sykes, 41–42, 45, 49; RFC's offensive strategy and, 76–78, 107–108, 114, 111, 119; state honours, 23; service with West Africa Field Force, 23; social inadequacies, 21, 59; South African war and, 22–23; support for signals intelligence, 82; thinking about airpower, 76,

83–84; understanding of logistics, 77, 199; vulnerability as young man, 21

Trenchard, Kitty: comments on Trenchard's loneliness, 21; first meeting with Trenchard, 87; marriage of, 14, 186; nurses Trenchard, 179; rejects marriage proposal, 90

Trinity College, Cambridge, 16

Turkey, 105

U.S. Air Force, 37

USAS (U.S. Air Service), 63, 166, 172, 252n40

U.S. War Department, 77, 238n16

U.S., British Air Mission to, 166, 186

Upavon, 23

Uxbridge, 189

Vane-Tempest-Stewart, Charles, 160, 162

Verdun, Battle of, 13, 108, 112–114, 117, 239n33

Verney, Harry, 159

Vichy, regime, 185

Voisin, Andre, 65, 79, 235n8

Voss, Werner, 206

Vyell Vivian, Arthur, 140, 254n17

Walker, Henry, 103–104

War Office: 11, 39–40, 43–44, 47, 50, 61, 64, 72, 74, 115, 124, 128, 137–138, 177, 200

War Office Wireless Committee, 253n7

wastage. *See* aircraft

Wedgewood-Benn, William, 159

Weir, William, 127, 132, 146–148, 163, 165–167, 169, 175, 177–178, 184, 251n18, 260n1

Wells, Herbert (H.G.), 18, 60, 123, 223n34

West Africa, 23, 102, 177. *See also* Trenchard

West Point, 29

Western Front, 8–10, 14, 26, 41, 46, 59, 66, 73–74, 82, 96, 99–102, 116–117, 119, 124, 126, 131–132, 135, 136, 172, 175, 180, 184, 191, 194, 203, 216

Western Gazette, 19

Westminster Gazette, 155, 179

Wilkinson, Spenser, 58, 232n31, 247n32

Williams, George, 175

Wilson, Henry, 153, 258n3

Winter, Denis, 101

Woolwich, military academy, 19, 223n39

World War I: air force traditions forged in, 190–191; Armistice, 9, 63, 75, 120, 148, 158, 175, 183, 190, 192, 207, 210, 213; books about, 14; British declaration of war on Germany, 11; development of military aviation in, 199; example of generals, 35; German invasion of Belgium, 11; lessons learned during, 83; manpower losses in, 65; reputation of staff officers, 65. *See also* British airpower

World War II: campaign medal for Bomber Command ground crew, 193: combat aircraft development, 106; combined bomber offensive, 9, 174, 220n18; Pétain and Vichy regime, 185; RAF senior commanders, 191; shadow aircraft factories, 184

Wrench, Evelyn, 137, 140, 150, 166, 253n4

Wrest Park, 70

Wright, Robert, 2

Wynn, Humphrey, 183

Xenophon of Athens, 25

Ypres, Third Battle of, 76, 102, 117, 122, 207, 213, 247n41

Zeppelin, airship, 83, 123, 126

About the Author

Peter Dye is a graduate of Imperial College London and Birmingham University. He served in the Royal Air Force for more than thirty-five years and was awarded the Order of the British Empire for service during the first Gulf War. He retired as an air vice-marshal and served as director general of the Royal Air Force Museum from 2008 to 2014.

The Naval Institute Press is the book-publishing arm of the U.S. Naval Institute, a private, nonprofit, membership society for sea service professionals and others who share an interest in naval and maritime affairs. Established in 1873 at the U.S. Naval Academy in Annapolis, Maryland, where its offices remain today, the Naval Institute has members worldwide.

Members of the Naval Institute support the education programs of the society and receive the influential monthly magazine *Proceedings* or the colorful bimonthly magazine *Naval History* and discounts on fine nautical prints and on ship and aircraft photos. They also have access to the transcripts of the Institute's Oral History Program and get discounted admission to any of the Institute-sponsored seminars offered around the country.

The Naval Institute's book-publishing program, begun in 1898 with basic guides to naval practices, has broadened its scope to include books of more general interest. Now the Naval Institute Press publishes about seventy titles each year, ranging from how-to books on boating and navigation to battle histories, biographies, ship and aircraft guides, and novels. Institute members receive significant discounts on the Press' more than eight hundred books in print.

Full-time students are eligible for special half-price membership rates. Life memberships are also available.

For more information about Naval Institute Press books that are currently available, visit www.usni.org/press/books. To learn about joining the U.S. Naval Institute, please write to:

Member Services
U.S. Naval Institute
291 Wood Road
Annapolis, MD 21402-5034
Telephone: (800) 233-8764
Fax: (410) 571-1703
Web address: www.usni.org